Peter Perkins Pitchlynn, 1806-1881
of Folsom lineage and Choctaw interpreter.

Other Books and Series by Jeff Bowen

Compilation of History of the Cherokee Indians and Early History of the Cherokees by Emmet Starr with Combined Full Name Index
(Hardbound & Softbound)

1901-1907 Native American Census Seneca, Eastern Shawnee, Miami, Modoc, Ottawa, Peoria, Quapaw, and Wyandotte Indians (Under Seneca School, Indian Territory)

1932 Census of The Standing Rock Sioux Reservation with Births And Deaths 1924-1932

Kiowa, Comanche, Apache, Fort Sill Apache, Wichita, Caddo and Delaware Indians Birth and Death Rolls 1924-1932

Census of The Blackfeet, Montana, 1897- 1901 Expanded Edition

Eastern Cherokee by Blood, 1906-1910, Volumes I* thru *XIII

Choctaw of Mississippi Indian Census 1929-1932 with Births and Deaths 1924-1931 Volume I
Choctaw of Mississippi Indian Census 1933, 1934 & 1937, Supplemental Rolls to 1934 & 1935 with Births and Deaths 1932-1938, and Marriages 1936-1938 Volume II

Eastern Cherokee Census Cherokee, North Carolina 1930-1939
Census 1930-1931 with Births And Deaths 1924-1931 Taken By Agent L. W. Page Volume I
Eastern Cherokee Census Cherokee, North Carolina 1930-1939
Census 1932-1933 with Births And Deaths 1930-1932 Taken By Agent R. L. Spalsbury Volume II
Eastern Cherokee Census Cherokee, North Carolina 1930-1939
Census 1934-1937 with Births and Deaths 1925-1938 and Marriages 1936 & 1938 Taken by Agents R. L. Spalsbury And Harold W. Foght Volume III

Seminole of Florida Indian Census, 1930-1940 with Birth and Death Records, 1930-1938

Texas Cherokees 1820-1839 A Document For Litigation 1921

Starr Roll 1894 (Cherokee Payment Rolls) Districts: Canadian, Cooweescoowee, and Delaware Volume One
Starr Roll 1894 (Cherokee Payment Rolls) Districts: Flint, Going Snake, and Illinois Volume Two
Starr Roll 1894 (Cherokee Payment Rolls) Districts: Saline, Sequoyah, and Tahlequah; Including Orphan Roll Volume Three

Cherokee Intruder Cases Dockets of Hearings 1901-1909 Volumes I & II

Other Books and Series by Jeff Bowen

Indian Wills, 1911-1921 Records of the Bureau of Indian Affairs
Books One thru *Seven*
Native American Wills & Probate Records 1911-1921

Turtle Mountain Reservation Chippewa Indians 1932 Census with Births & Deaths, 1924-1932

Chickasaw By Blood Enrollment Cards 1898-1914 Volume I thru *V*

Cherokee Descendants East An Index to the Guion Miller Applications Volume I
Cherokee Descendants West An Index to the Guion Miller Applications Volume II (A-M)
Cherokee Descendants West An Index to the Guion Miller Applications Volume III (N-Z)

Applications for Enrollment of Seminole Newborn Freedmen, Act of 1905

Eastern Cherokee Census, Cherokee, North Carolina, 1915-1922, Taken by Agent James E. Henderson
Volume I (1915-1916)
Volume II (1917-1918)
Volume III (1919-1920)
Volume IV (1921-1922)

Complete Delaware Roll of 1898

Eastern Cherokee Census, Cherokee, North Carolina, 1923-1929, Taken by Agent James E. Henderson
Volume I (1923-1924)
Volume II (1925-1926)
Volume III (1927-1929)

Applications for Enrollment of Seminole Newborn Act of 1905 Volumes I & II

North Carolina Eastern Cherokee Indian Census 1898-1899, 1904, 1906, 1909-1912, 1914 Revised and Expanded Edition

1932 Hopi and Navajo Native American Census with Birth & Death Rolls (1925-1931) Volume 1 - Hopi
1932 Hopi and Navajo Native American Census with Birth & Death Rolls (1930-1932) Volume 2 - Navajo

Western Navajo Reservation Navajo, Hopi and Paiute 1933 Census with Birth & Death Rolls 1925-1933

Cherokee Citizenship Commission Dockets 1880-1884 and 1887-1889
Volumes I thru *V*

Applications for Enrollment of Chickasaw Newborn Act of 1905
Volumes I thru *VII*

Other Books and Series by Jeff Bowen

Cherokee Intermarried White 1906 Volume I thru *X*

Applications for Enrollment of Creek Newborn Act of 1905 Volumes I thru *XIV*

Applications for Enrollment of Choctaw Newborn Act of 1905 Volumes I thru *XX*

Choctaw By Blood Enrollment Cards 1898-1914 Volumes I thru *XX*

Oglala Sioux Indians Pine Ridge Reservation 1932 Census Book I
Oglala Sioux Indians Pine Ridge Reservation Birth and Death Rolls 1924-1932 Book II

Census of the Sioux and Cheyenne Indians of Pine Ridge Agency 1896 - 1897 Book I
Census of the Sioux and Cheyenne Indians of Pine Ridge Agency 1898 - 1899 Book II

Northern Cheyenne Tongue River, Montana 1904 - 1932 Census 1904-1916 Volume I
Northern Cheyenne Tongue River, Montana 1904 - 1932 Census 1917-1926 Volume II

Sac & Fox - Shawnee Estates 1885-1910 (Under Sac & Fox Agency) Volumes I-VIII
Sac & Fox - Shawnee Estates 1920-1924 (Under The Sac & Fox Agency, Oklahoma) & Wills 1889-1924 Volume IX
Sac & Fox - Shawnee Deaths, Cemetery, Births, & Marriage Cards (Under The Sac & Fox Agency, Oklahoma) 1853-1933 Volume X
Sac & Fox - Shawnee Marriages, Divorces, Estates Log Books Volumes 1 & 2, Log Book Births & Deaths (Under Sac & Fox Agency, Oklahoma)1846-1924 Volume XI
Sac & Fox - Shawnee Guardianships Part 1 (Under Sac & Fox Agency, Oklahoma) 1892-1909 Volume XII
Sac & Fox - Shawnee Guardianships, Part 2 (Under The Sac & Fox Agency, Oklahoma) 1902-1910 Volume XIII
Sac & Fox - Shawnee Guardianships, Part 3 (Under The Sac & Fox Agency, Oklahoma) 1906-1914 Volume XIV

Census of the Pima, Tohono O'odham (Papago), and Maricopa Indians of the Gila River, Ak Chin & Gila Bend Reservations 1932 with Birth and Death Rolls 1924-1932

Identified Mississippi Choctaw Enrollment Cards 1902-1909 Volumes I, II & III

Visit our website at **www.nativestudy.com** to learn more about these and other books and series by Jeff Bowen

IDENTIFIED MISSISSIPPI CHOCTAW ENROLLMENT CARDS' DAWES PACKETS 1902 - 1909 VOLUME IV

TRANSCRIBED BY

JEFF BOWEN

NATIVE STUDY
Gallipolis, Ohio
USA

Native Study LLC
Gallipolis, OH
www.nativestudy.com

Library of Congress Control Number: 2021924446

ISBN: 978-1-64968-163-8

Bookcover: Ha-Tchoo-Tuck-Nee (The Snapping Turtle) or
Colonel Peter Perkins Pytchlynn [Pitchlynn]

All images compliments of Smithsonian Institution.

Made in the United States of America.

This series is dedicated to the

Mississippi Choctaw,

and their ancestors who fought for what was theirs.

Table of Contents

"Brother: When you were young we were strong; we fought by your side; but our arms are now broken. You have grown large. My people have become small.

"Brother: My voice is weak; you can scarcely hear me; it is not the shout of a warrior but the wail of an infant. I have lost it in mourning over the misfortunes of my people. These are their graves, and in those aged pines you hear the ghosts of the departed.--Their ashes are here, and we have been left to protect them. Our warriors are nearly all gone to the far country west; but here are our dead. Shall we go too, and give their bones to the wolves?

. . . .

"Brother: Our hearts are full. Twelve winters ago our chiefs sold our country. Every warrior that you see here was opposed to the treaty. If the dead could have counted, it could never have been made, but alas! though they stood around, they could not be seen or heard. Their tears came in the raindrops, and their voices in the wailing wind, but the pale faces knew it not, and our land was taken away.

". . . .When you took our country, you promised us land. There is your promise in the book. Twelve times have the trees dropped their leaves, and yet we have received no land. Our houses have been taken from us. The white man's plough turns up the bones of our fathers. We dare not kindle our fires; and yet you said we might remain and you would give us land."

The distrust which they felt toward the proposals of the federal officials is shown by the reply of Chief Cobb to Capt. J. J. McRea, who had addressed them in Council in 1843, urging them to remove.

The above from *The Rise And Fall Of The Choctaw Republic*, page 70, by Angie Debo. 1934.

INTRODUCTION

Having finished three volumes of Identified Mississippi Choctaw Enrollment Cards 1902-1909 (922 Cards); the next books in the series will be covering a different phase of the work so to speak. You will find full transcriptions (or copies thereof) of the coinciding Dawes Packets for each individual card when provided by the original record keepers. **NOTE: Each Dawes Packet is identified by CARD NO - CHOC. MCR NUMBER and NAME OF APPLICANT, then separated with a large, bolded black line.**

The copious amount of information these people had to provide to the Commission to the Five Civilized Tribes is just incredible. You will have dates for births, deaths, marriages; correspondence between attorney and client; the ruling of the Commission handed down to the applicants; and so much more.

It's exciting to be able to share this material with those for the most part that normally wouldn't have access to such an overwhelming amount of family record as well as providing it to those that need it the most. This is one of the few times in over twenty years of record transcriptions that this author will be able to provide highly readable material so the family member now can actually learn through their ancestor's testimony and conversation who they were and what they went through.

It was felt that each packet needed to be fully transcribed so as not to leave any information unrecorded in case the records herein may possibly be important for someone's family history and research. The Dawes Packets were a wealth of information in many cases with great detail for getting the correct information when a card was difficult to read and completing the work rather than guessing what it might say.

So, if you or someone you know is researching their Choctaw heritage these books could be an important addition to yours or their research library. These cards and Dawes Packets could well mix with our original series *Choctaw By Blood Enrollment Cards 1898 - 1914* because of the relations of both those that moved to Indian Territory and those that stayed in Mississippi, thus connecting thousands of tribal members and bloodlines from both sides of the spectrum.

These *Identified Mississippi Choctaw Enrollment Cards* were found in the National Archive film records M-1186, Roll 57, under the heading of Enrollment Cards of the Five Civilized Tribes, 1898-1914. In the Dawes index they are listed as the Final Roll of Mississippi Choctaws September 25, 1902. "After the signing of the Treaty of Dancing Rabbit Creek in 1830, the U.S. government began the methodical removal of the Choctaw Indians from their native land in present-day Mississippi, uprooting about 20,000 of the estimated 25,000 tribesmen in the process. What became of the thousands of people who remained? A few hundred households stayed behind with government approval and were given individual parcels of land reservations as a treaty stipulation. Some other Choctaw--mixed-bloods who had already abandoned their ancestral ways and had chosen white culture as a life-style--simply merged with the incoming white settlers and stayed in the community as white people. Several thousand Indians, however, faded into the wilderness until they were forced out by an expanding white population."[1] As in this quote, it states that a few hundred households stayed behind with government approval to receive their own reservation of 640 acres but it wasn't to be in many cases. Even if they were supplying these surveys for the reservations they were laying out, the plats weren't being supplied so they could formally organize where the Choctaw families could settle. There wasn't going to be any cooperation. But even though they didn't get what was needed to claim their land the government managed to allow the whites to overrun their homes.

After the signing it wasn't that simple, as expected there was dissension almost immediately between the mixed-bloods and the full bloods. The full bloods not wanting to give up their land and the mixed-bloods seeing dollar signs. Andrew Jackson's Secretary of War John Eaton decided to threaten anyone not wanting to cooperate while deciding only to work with those who were willing to sign the treaty. After petrifying the people with a threat of arrest he managed to coax approximately 15,000 to immigrate to Indian Territory while just about 6,000 stayed to fight for their lands, though mostly full-bloods. What's amazing is that after being ratified by Congress President Andrew Jackson signed the Treaty of Dancing Rabbit Creek in February of 1831. Post treaty the Mississippi Choctaw were assigned an agent by the name of William Ward who would almost single handedly destroyed the chance of receiving any form of fair treatment in making their claims for the land promised. The Choctaw had six months to register their claims after ratification. They came from near and far seeking assistance. "Some full-bloods who spoke little if any English probably did not understand the specific procedures or requirements for registering. Even those who did, however, found themselves without effective power to protect their rights. Nevertheless, they refused to abandon their homeland. The majority of the 4,000 Choctaw living in Mississippi today have direct kinship ties to Indians who resisted removal in the 1830s.

The Choctaw who remained in Mississippi after 1833 were victims of one of the most flagrant cases of fraud, intimidation, and speculation in American history. Although the Senate took six months to ratify the treaty, squatters and speculators began moving in immediately after the negotiations. As whites inundated the Choctaw cession, the War Department made some efforts to evict the intruders in accordance with the terms of the treaty. The influx of Americans continued, however, and the actions of Agent Ward not only encouraged white squatters and speculators but also blatantly obstructed the treaty rights of the Choctaw."[2]

Even after the removal of 1831 to 1833 many of the Choctaw people continued to travel back and forth between Mississippi and Oklahoma never really feeling settled in at either place because of such pressure from not only the government but also those scheming to take their lands. The intruders were being assisted while the Choctaw were being defrauded daily. The treaty had been signed in 1830 yet massive deception would

---

[1] *After Removal The Choctaw in Mississippi*; Introduction Pg. vii Para 1.

[2] *After Removal The Choctaw in Mississippi*; Pg. 8 Para 2-3.

be applied for decades. The very cards within these pages show that approximately 70 years later the descendants of the original people forced off of their land were still being made to prove who they were. They not only had to prove their heritage but they had to be demeaned by people who could care less. As an example, in the front of this book, you can actually find the documentation of a full blood Mississippi Choctaw named Bob Thomas along with his wife showing what they had to go through on December 18, 1900, titled as "Examination by the Commission". Seventy years previous his ancestors had been forced off of their land and told we'll stand by our word and Article XIV guarantees we'll give you some of your land back. But in realty Bob was in a position where he had to take what they gave him and where. Sadly, his ancestors were never given the land that was promised and Bob was again sitting in front of a Commission being asked questions about whom he was and where he came from. They were once more working to push another Choctaw family out of their home and into Indian Territory. Bob could only guess what his future would be, hoping to receive land from a government that was only concerned with him leaving the very same ground they made his ancestors abandon unwillingly.

There are examples of two different documents (1. the Dawes Folder for Bob Thomas, approximately 35 pages; 2. The full Dawes Index, FINAL ROLL OF MISSISSIPPI CHOCTAWS Ages calculated to September 25, 1902) that can be seen inside the front matter of this book along with the full transcription of the Identified Mississippi Choctaw Cards. You will find full-bloods as well as mixed-bloods on the roll with an extreme amount of full bloods making you think the trouble they were having to go through was just a form of discouragement in hopes they'd give up asking for their home ground. The cards show the person's name, the names of their relations, their ages, blood quantum, parents' names and application numbers. On the cards the settlement addresses show as mostly being in Indian Territory but in the Dawes Folders which not all are complete it shows for many testimony being given in places such as Hattiesburg, Mississippi and as living in Mississippi their whole lives. These in most cases were full bloods asking for the documentation to be rightfully classified by the government as who they were, full-blood Choctaws from Mississippi. But the decision appears to be put off as you can see in letters from the packet to make sure they were going to go west and leave their homes even seventy years later. After all that time the bureaucrats were still concerned as to whether their ancestors had claimed their own land under a treaty and Article XIV in the year 1830 otherwise we won't let you claim your own racial status.

It seems that Article XIV of the treaty was of the greatest importance in that fight for those that planned to stay. Even though there was never any intention to help them get what was promised, or at least let them keep a part of what was originally theirs in the first place they would have to battle massive corruption and greed because the whites wanted their land to grow cotton and so did Andrew Jackson who saw the Choctaw as a nuisance to progress. The trouble for them was obvious but who would have thought their descendants who lived their whole lives through in Mississippi would inherit the very same circumstances from the very same but different scoundrels many years later. The term repeated for them over and over was, "The Commission has not, up to the present time, reached any opinion or decision relative to the right of the full blood Choctaws residing in Mississippi to be identified as Mississippi Choctaws, but is now considering their applications, and it is probable decisions will be rendered in the near future."

ARTICLE XIV. Each Choctaw head of family being desirous to remain and become a citizen of the States, shall be permitted to do so, by signifying his intention to the Agent within six months from the ratification of this Treaty, and he or she shall thereupon be entitled to a reservation of one section of six hundred and forty acres of land, to be bounded by sectional lines of survey; in like manner shall be entitled to one half that quantity for each unmarried child which is living with him over ten years of age; and a quarter section to, such child as be under 10 years of age, to adjoin the location of the parent. If they reside upon said lands intending to become citizens of the States for years after the ratification of this Treaty, in that case a grant in fee simple shall issue; said reservation shall include the present improvement of the head of the family, or a portion of it. Persons who claim under this article shall not lose the privilege of a Choctaw citizen, but if they ever remove are not to be entitled to any portion of the Choctaw annuity.

Even though Article XIV seems to be extremely clear when it would come time to make those claims the rules would soon be clear as mud for the true owners of the land. For those who planned on staying the deception they'd face from those in power would now prove out their real intentions. These very people the Choctaw of 1830 are the ancestors of those living in Mississippi today.

After reading Grant Foreman's description of the Choctaw removal between the careless timing and terrible treatment of it was nothing short of brutal and deadly. So this quote needs to be left with you so these people will never be forgotten....

"Here they disembarked before the middle of December to organize for their march westward through Washington to the Kiamichi river. Two weeks later, still in camp on the river, Harkins wrote: ". . .*We sent our horses and oxen by land, and about 250 head of horses have died on the road. We have had very bad weather. Since we landed at this place about twenty of Nail's party have died, and still they are continuing to die. Two of my party have died. We are about 200 miles from my country on Red river. It will be some time in February before we get to where we want to settle. There are 1,200 of us in company, and we are compelled to travel slow, as there are so many sick people. I am afraid a great many will die before we get home. Nail has 400 with him. He had been very sick but now is on the mend."*[3]

It is the hope that these cards and few records will help many and grant the Mississippi Choctaw people the respect they deserved then and their descendants today.

Jeff Bowen
Gallipolis, Ohio
Nativestudy.com

---

[3] *Indian Removal*; Pg. 59 Para 1.

Creator: Henry Bascom Collins, 1899-1987 (1925)

Jim family (Isaac?, Will, David D, Martha and Wilson) outside their cabin near Philadelphia, Mississippi.

Photo Lot 24 SPC Se Choctaw NAA 4974 01778000, National Anthropological Archives, Smithsonian Institution

Within the identified Mississippi Choctaw enrollment cards you will find members of the Jim family some with the same names as well as members of the same family mentioned within the pages of the Final Roll of Mississippi Choctaws in the front of this book.

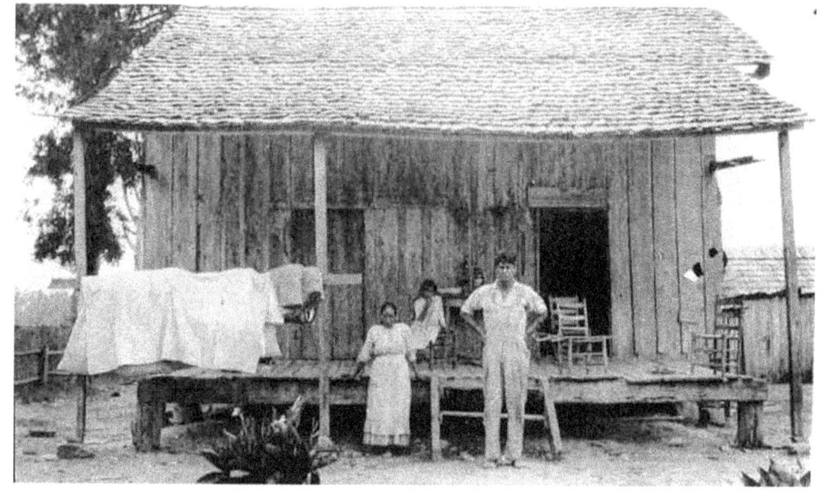

Creator: Henry Bascom Collins, 1899-1987 (1925)

Will and Louisa Jim, with unidentified girl outside their home near Philadelphia, Mississippi.

Photo Lot 24 SPC Se Choctaw NAA 4974 01773200, National Anthropological Archives, Smithsonian Institution

[Copy]

Treaty of Dancing Rabbit Creek

1830

~~1831~~

Treaty
with the
Choctaws

~~Sep. 15.~~ 27. 1830

And 28th Sepr 1830

Ratified Feby 24th 1831.

A treaty of perpetual friendship, cession and limits entered into by John H. Eaton and John Coffee for and in behalf of the Government of the United States and the Mingoes Chiefs Captains and Warriors of the Choctaw Nation begun and held at Dancing Rabbit Creek on the 15th of September in the year 1830.

Whereas the General Assembly of the State of Mississippi has extended the laws of said State to persons and property within the chartered limits of the same and the President of the United States has said that he cannot protect the Choctaw people from the operation of these laws; Now therefore that the Choctaw may live under thier own laws in peace with the United States and the State of Mississippi they have determined to sell thier lands east of the Mississippi & have accordingly agreed to the following articles of treaty —

Article 1st

Perpetual peace and friendship is pledged and agreed upon by and between the United States and the Mingoes, Chiefs, & Warriors of the Choctaw Nation of Red People; and that this may be considered the ~~[illegible]~~ treaty existing between the parties all other treaties heretofore existing & inconsistent with the provisions of this are hereby declared null and void. —

Article 2nd

The United States under a grant specially to be made by the President of the U.S. shall cause to be conveyed to the Choctaw Nation a tract of Country west of the Mississippi River, in fee simple to them & their descendants, to inure to them while they shall exist as a nation and live on it, beginning near Fort Smith where the Arkansas boundary crosses the Arkansas River, Running thence ~~[illegible]~~ to the source of the Canadian fork; ~~[illegible]~~ in the limits of the United States, or to those limits; thence due South to Red River, and down Red River to the West boundary of the Teratory of Arkansas; thence North along that line to the beginning, the boundary of the same to be agreeably to the treaty made and concluded at Washington City in the year 1825— The grant to be executed so soon as the present Treaty shall be ratified— Article 3rd

In consideration of the provisions contained in the several articles of this Treaty, the Choctaw Nation of Indians consent and hereby cede to the United States, the entire Country they own and possess, East of the Mississippi River; and they agree to remove beyond the Mississippi River, early as practicable, and will so arrange their removal that as many as possible of their people not exceeding one half of the whole number, shall depart during the falls of 1831 and 1832; the residue to follow during the succeeding fall of 1833; a better opportunity in this manner will be afforded the Government, to extend to them the facilities and comforts which it is desireable should be extended in conveying them to their new Homes.— Article 4th

The Government and people of the United States are hereby obliged to secure to the said Choctaw Nation of Red People the Jurisdiction and Government, of all the Persons & Property that may be within their limits West, so that no territory or State shall ever have a right to pass laws for the Government of the Choctaw Nation of Red People & their Descendants; and that no part of the land granted them shall ever be embraced in any territory or State; but the U.S. shall forever secure said Choctaw Nation from, & against, all laws except such as from time to time may be enacted in their own National Councils, not inconsistent with the Constitution, Treaties, and laws of the United States; & except such as may, & which have been enacted by Congress, to the extent that Congress under the Constitution are required to exercise a legislation over Indian affairs. But the Choctaws, should this treaty be ratified, express a wish that Congress may grant to the Choctaws the right of punishing by their own laws, any white man who shall come into their Nation, & infringe any of their National regulations.

Article 5th

The United States are obliged to protect the Choctaws from domestic strife & from foreign enemies on the same principles that the Citizens of the United States are protected, so that whatever would be a legal demand upon the U.S. for defence or for wrongs committed by an Enemy, on a Citizen of the U.S. shall be equally binding on ~~in favour~~ of the Choctaws, & in all cases where the Choctaws shall be called upon by a legally authorized Officer of the U.S. to fight an Enemy, such Choctaw shall receive the pay & other emoluments, which Citizens of the U.S. receive in such cases, provided, no war shall be undertaken or prosecuted by said Choctaw Nation but by declaration made in full Council, & to be approved by the U.S. unless it be in self defence against an open rebellion or against an enemy marching into their country, in which cases they shall defend, until the U.S. are advised thereof.

Article 6th

Should a Choctaw or any party of Choctaws commit acts of violence upon the person or property of a Citizen of the U.S., or join any war party against any neighbouring tribe of Indians, without the authority in the preceding article; & except to oppose an actual or threatened invasion or rebellion, such person so offending, shall be delivered up to an Officer of the U.S. if in the power of the Choctaw Nation, that such Offender may be punished as may be provided in such cases, by the laws of the U.S.; but if such Offender is not within the control of the Choctaw Nation, then said Choctaw Nation shall not be held responsible for the injury done by said Offender.

Article 7th

All acts of violence committed upon persons and property of the ~~Red~~ people of the Choctaw Nation either by Citizens of the U.S. or Neighbouring tribes of Red people, shall be reffered to some authorized agent by him to be reffered to the ~~U.S.~~ President of the U.S., Who shall examine into such cases and see that every possible degree of justice is done to said Indian party of the Choctaw Nation –

Article 8th

Offenders against the laws of the U.S. or any individual State shall be apprehended & delivered to any duly authorized person where such Offender may be found in the Choctaw Country, having fled from any part of U.S. but in all such cases application must be made to the Agent or Chiefs & the expense of his apprehension and delivery provided for & paid by the U.States

Article 9th

Any Citizen of the U.S. who may be Ordered from the Nation by the Agent & Constituted Authorities of the Nation and refusing to obey or return into the Nation without the Consent of the aforesaid persons, shall be subject to such pains and penalties as may be provided by the laws of the U.S. in such cases. Citizens of the U.S. travelling peaceably under the authority of the laws of the U.S. shall be under the care & protection of the Nation

Article 10th

No person shall expose goods or other article for sale as a trader, without a written permit from the Constituted Authorities of the Nation, or authority of the laws of the Congress of the U.S. under penalty of forfeiting the Articles, & the Constituted authorities of the Nation shall grant no license except to such persons as reside in the Nation and are answerable to the laws of the Nation. The U.S. shall be particularly obliged to assist to preventing ardent spirits from being introduced into the Nation

Article 11th.

Navigable streams shall be free to the Choctaws who shall pay no higher toll or duty than Citizens of the U.S. It is agreed further that the U.S. shall establish one or more Post Offices in said Nation, & may establish such military post roads, and posts, as they may consider necessary

Article 12th

All intruders shall be removed from the Choctaw Nation and kept without it. Private property to be always respected & on no occasion taken for public purposes without just compensation being made therefor to the rightfull owner. If an Indian unlawfully take or steal any property from a White Man a citizen of the U.S. the offender shall be punished. And if a white Man unlawfully take or steal any thing from an Indian, the property shall be restored & the offender punished. It is further agreed that when a Choctaw shall be given up to be tried for any offence against the laws of the U.S. if unable to employ Counsel to defend him, the U.S. will do it, that his trial may be fair and impartial

Article 13th.

It is consented that a qualified Agent shall be appointed for the Choctaws every Four Years, unless sooner removed by the President; and he shall be removed on petition of the Constituted Authorities of the Nation the President, being satisfied there is sufficient Cause shown. The Agent shall fix his residence convenient to the great body of the people; & in the selection of an Agent immediately after the ratification of this Treaty, the wishes of the Choctaw Nation on the subject shall be entitled to great respect

Article 14th.

Each Choctaw head of a family being desirous to remain & become a Citizen of the States, shall be permitted to do so, by signifying his intention to the Agent within six Months from the ratification of this Treaty, and he shall thereupon be entitled to a reservation of one Section of Six Hundred and forty Acres of Land, to be bounded by Sectional lines of Survey; in like Manner he shall be entitled to one half that quantity for each unmarried Child which is living with him over Ten Years of Age; & a quarter section to such child as may be under 10 years of age, to adjoin the location of the Parent. If they reside upon said lands intending to become Citizens of the States for five Years after the ratification of this Treaty in that Case a grant in fee simple shall issue; said reservation shall include the present improvements of the head of the family, or a portion of it. Persons who claim under this Article shall not loose the priviledge of a Choctaw Citizen, but if they ever remove are not to be entitled to any portion of the Choctaw Annuity;

Article 15th

To each of the chiefs in the Choctaw nation (to wit) Greenwood Laflore, Nutackachie, and Mushulatubbe there is granted a reservation of four Sections of land, two of which shall include and adjoin their present improvements & the other two located where they please but on unoccupied unimproved lands, such sections shall be bounded by sectional lines, & with the consent of the President they may sell the same. Also to the three principal Chiefs & to their successors in office there shall be paid Two Hundred and fifty Dollars

Annually, while they shall continue in thier respective Offices, except to Mushulatubbe who as he has an annuity of One Hundred & fifty Dollars for life under a former treaty, shall receive only the additional sum of One Hundred Dollars, while he shall continue in office as Chief; & if in addition to this the Nation shall think propper to elect an additional principal Chief of the whole to superintend and govern upon republican principles he shall receive annually for his services Five Hundred Dollars, which allowance to the chiefs and thier Successors in office, shall continue for Twenty Years. At any time when in Military service, & while in service by authority of the U.S. the district Chiefs under and by selection of the President shall be entitled to the pay of Majors; the other Chief under the same Circumstances shall have the pay of a Lieutenant-Colonel. The Speakers of the three districts, shall receive Twenty five Dollars a Year each for four Years each & the three Secretaries One to each of the Chiefs, fifty Dollars each for four years. Each Captain of the Nation, the number not to exceed Ninety nine, thirty three from each District shall be furnished upon removing to the West, with each a good suit of clothes & a broad Sword as an outfit, & for four Years commencing with the first of thier removal, shall each receive Fifty Dollars a Year, for ~~four years~~ the trouble of keeping thier people ~~at~~ order in settling; & whenever they shall be in military service by authority of the U.S. shall receive the pay of a captain

Article 16th

In waggons; & with Steam Boats as may be found necessary The U.S. agree to remove the Indians to thier new Homes at thier expense and under the care of discreet and carefull persons, who will be kind & brotherly to them. They agree to furnish them with ample corn and beef, or pork for themselves & families for Twelve Months after reaching thier new homes.

It is agreed further that the U.S. will take all thier cattle, at the valuation of some discreet person to be appointed by the President, & the same shall be paid for in Money after thier arrival at thier new homes; or in other cattle such as may be desired shall be furnished them, notice being given through thier Agent of thier wishes upon this subject before thier removal that time to supply the demand may be afforded.

Article 17th

The several Annuities and sums secured under former Treaties to the Choctaw Nation and People shall continue as tho. this Treaty had never been made. And it is further agreed that the U.S. in addition will pay the sum of Twenty thousand Dollars for Twenty Years, commencing after thier removal to the west, of which, in the first year after thier removal, ten thousand Dollars shall be divided and arranged to such as may not receive reservations under this Treaty.

Article 18th

The U.S. shall cause the lands hereby ceded to be surveyed, & surveyors may enter the Choctaw Country for that purpose, conducting themselves properly & disturbing or interrupting none of the Choctaw people. But no person is to be permitted to settle within the Nation, or the lands to be sold before the Choctaws shall remove. And for the payment of the several amounts secured in this Treaty, the lands hereby ceded are to remain a fund pledged to that purpose, until the debt shall be provided for and arranged. And further it is agreed, that in the construction of this Treaty wherever well founded doubt shall arise, it shall be construed most favourably towards the Choctaws.

Article 19th

The following reservations of land are hereby admitted. To Col. David Folsom Four Sections of which Two shall include his present improvements, & two may be located elsewhere, on unoccupied, unimproved land.

To I. Garland, Col. Robert Cole, Tuppanahomer, John Pytchlynn, Charles Juzan, Toho ke betubbe, Eaychahobia, Ofehoma two sections, each to include thier improvements, and to be bounded by sectional lines, & the same may be disposed of and sold with the consent of the President. And that others not provided for, may be provided for, there shall be reserved as follows.

First, One section to each head of a family not exceeding Forty in number, who during the present year, may have had in actual cultivation, with a dwelling House thereon Fifty Acres or more. Secondly three quarter sections after the manner aforesaid to each head of a family not exceeding Four Hundred and Sixty, as shall have cultivated Thirty Acres and less than Fifty, to be bounded by quarter section lines of survey, & to be contiguous & adjoining.

Third, One half section as aforesaid to those who shall have cultivated from Twenty to Thirty Acres the number not to exceed Four Hundred. Fourth, a quarter section as aforesaid to such as shall have cultivated from twelve to twenty Acres, the number not to exceed three hundred and fifty, and one half that quantity to such as shall have cultivated from two to twelve Acres, the number also not to exceed three hundred and fifty persons. Each of said class of cases shall be subject to the limitations contained in the first class, & shall be so located as to include that part of the improvement which contains the dwelling House. If a greater number shall be found to be entitled to reservations under the several classes of this article, than is stipulated for under the limitation prescribed, then & in that case the Chiefs separately or together shall determine the persons

who shall be excluded in the respective districts.
Fifth; Any Captain the number not to exceed Ninety
persons, who under the provisions of this article shall
receive less than a section, he shall be entitled, to an
additional quantity of half a section adjoining
to his other reservation. The several reservations
secured under this Article, may be sold with the
consent of the President of the U.S., but should any
prefer it, or omit to take a reservation for the quantity
he may be entitled to the U.S. will on his removing
pay fifty cents an acre, after reaching thier new
homes, provided that before the first of January next
they shall adduce to the Agent, or some other authorized
person to be appointed, proof of his claim & the quantity
of it. Sixth, likewise Children of the Choctaw Nation
residing in the Nation, who have neither Father nor Mother
a list of which, with satisfactory proof of Parentage
and Orphanage being filed with Agent in six months
to be forwarded to the War Department, shall be entitled
to a quarter section of Land, to be located under the direction
of the President, & with his consent the same may be sold
and the proceeds applied to some beneficial purpose for the
benefit of said Orphans —

Article 20th.

The U.S. agree & stipulate as follows, that for the benefit
and advantage of the Choctaw people, & to improve
thier condition, thier shall be educated under the
direction of the President & at the expense of the U.S.
forty Choctaw Youths for Twenty years. This number
shall be kept at school, & as they finish thier education
others to supply thier places shall be received for
the period stated. The U.S. agree also to erect a
Council House for the Nation at some convenient
central point, after thier people shall be settled, &
a House for each Chief, also a church for each
of the three Districts, to be used also as School

Houses, until the Nation may conclude to build others; & for these purposes Ten thousand Dollars shall be appropriated, also Fifty thousand Dollars (Viz) Twenty Fifty Hundred Dollars Annually shall be given for the Support of three Teachers of Schools for Twenty Years. Likewise there shall be furnished to the Nation, three Blacksmiths one for each District for Sixteen Years, & a qualified Mill wright for five years, Also there shall be furnished the following articles, Twenty One Hundred Blankets, To each warrior who emigrates a ~~twelve Hundred~~ rifles, Moulds, Wipers and ammunition. One thousand Axes, Ploughs, Hoes, Wheels and Cards each; and four Hundred looms. There shall also be furnished One Ton of Iron & two hundred weight of Steel annually to each District for Sixteen years.

Article 21st

A few Choctaw Warriors yet survive who marched and fought in the Army with General Wayne the whole number stated not to exceed Twenty. These it is agreed shall hereafter while they live receive Twenty five dollars a year; a list of them to be early as practicable, & within six months made out, and presented to the Agent to be forwarded to the War Department, —

Article 22d

The Chiefs of the Choctaws have suggested that their people are in a State of rapid advancement in education and refinement, and have expressed a solicitude that they might have the priveledge of a Delegate on the floor of the House of Representatives extended to them. The Commissioners do not feel, that they can under a treaty Stipulation accede to the request, but at their desire, present it in the Treaty, that Congress may consider of and decide the application.

Done and Signed and executed by the Commissioners of the United States and the Chiefs Captains and Head Men of the Choctaw Nation at Dancing Rabbit Creek this 27th day of September Eighteen Hundred and Thirty.

his mark

In Presence of
E. Breathitt Secty to the Commrs =
William Ward Agt for Choctaws.
John Pitchlyn US Int.
M Mackey US Intr.
Geo S Gaines of Alabama
R P Currin
Luke Howard
Sam S. Worcester
Jno N Byrn
John Bell
Jno Bond

Name	Seal	his mark
Jno H Eaton	(Seal)	
Jno Coffee	(Seal)	
Greenwood Leflore	(Seal)	
Musholatubbee	(Seal)	X
Nittucachee	(Seal)	X
Eyarhocuttubbee	(Seal)	X
Iyacherhopia	(Seal)	X
Offahoomah	(Seal)	X
Archalater	(Seal)	X
Onnahubbee	(Seal)	X
Holarterhoomah	(Seal)	X
Hopiaunchahubbee	(Seal)	X
Tishomingo	(Seal)	X
Captain thalko	(Seal)	X
James Shield	(Seal)	X
Pisinyubbee	(Seal)	X
Tobaharunchahubbee	(Seal)	X
Holubbee	(Seal)	X
Robert Cole	(Seal)	X
Mokelarcharhopin	(Seal)	X
Lewis Perry	(Seal)	X
Artonamarstubbee	(Seal)	X
Hopiatubbee	(Seal)	X
Hoshahoomah	(Seal)	X
Chuallahoomah	(Seal)	X
Joseph Kincaide	(Seal)	X
Artooklubbeetubbee	(Seal)	X
Metubbee	(Seal)	X
Arsarkatubbee	(Seal)	X
Issaterhoomah		X

Chohtahmatahah (seal) X
Tunnupashubbee (seal) X
Okechanyer (seal) X
Hoshhopier (seal) X
Warsharshahopia (seal) X
Maarshunchahubbee (seal) X
Mishaiyubbee (seal) X
Daniel McCurtain (seal) X
Tushkerharcho (seal) X
Hoktoontubbee (seal) X
Nuknacrahookmarhee (seal) X
Mingohoomah (seal) X
Pisinhocuttubbee (seal) X
Tullarhacher (seal) X
Little leader (seal) X
Maanhutter (seal) X
Cowehoomah (seal) X
Tillamoer (seal) X
Imnullacha (seal) X
Artopilachubbee (seal) X
Shupherunchahubbee (seal) X
Nitterhoomah (seal) X
Oaklaryubbee (seal) X
Pukumna (seal) X
Arpalar (seal) X
Holber (seal) X
Hoparmingo (seal) X
Isparhoomah (seal) X
Tieberhoomah (seal) X
Tishoholarter (seal) X
Mahayarchubbee (seal) X
Artlartar (seal) X
Nittahubbee (seal) X
Tishonouan (seal) X
Warsharshahoomah (seal) X

Isaac James X
Hopiaintushker X
Aryohkerma X
Shemotar X
Hopiaiskaterna X
Thomas Leflore X
Annokechatubbee X
Shokoperlukna X
Posherhoomah X
Robert Folsom X
Arharyotubbee X
Kushonolarter X
James Vaughan X
James Karnes X
Tishohakubbee X
Narfenalar X
Pennasha X
Inharyarker X
Motubbee X
Narharyubbee X
Ishmaryubbee X
James McKing
Lewis Wilson X
Istonarkerharcho X
Hoshimhamartar X
Kinsunnechubbee X
Eyarhuntubbee X
Saml. Garland
Thomas Wall
Saml. S. Worcester
Jacob Folsom
William Foster
Ontioerharcho X
Hugh A. Foster
Pierre Juzan

5-13

Jno. Pitchlynn Jr. (Seal)
David Folsom (Seal)
Sholohommastube (Seal) X
Tisho (Seal) X
Lauwechubee (Seal) X
Hoshehamma (Seal) X
Ofenowa (Seal) X
Ahekoche (Seal) X
Kaloshaube (Seal) X
Atoko (Seal) X
Ishtemeleche (Seal) X
Emthtohabe (Seal) X
Silas D. Fisher (Seal)
Isaac Folsom (Seal) X
Hekatube (Seal) X
Hakseche (Seal) X
Jerry Carney (Seal) X
John Washington (Seal) X
Phillip (Seal) X
Meshameye (Seal) X
Ishteheka (Seal) X
Heshohommo (Seal) X
John McKelbery (Seal) X
Benjm. James (Seal)
Tikbachahambe (Seal) X
Aholiktube (Seal) X
Walking Wolf (Seal) X
John Waide (Seal) X
Big Axe (Seal) X
Bob (Seal) X
Tushkochaubbe (Seal) X
Ittabe (Seal) X
Tishowakayo (Seal)

Holekomma (Seal) X
John Garland (Seal) X
Kushona (Seal) X
Ishteyohommbe (Seal) X
Oklanowa (Seal) X
Neto (Seal) X
James Fletcher (Seal) X
Silas D. Pitchlynn (Seal)
Wm. William Trahorn (Seal)
Tush ka hem mit ta (Seal) X
Te the ta yo (Seal) X
Emo la tha ho kie (Seal) X
Tisho imita (Seal) X
Thomas Fl... Foster (Seal)
Zadoc Brashears

	Seal	mark
Levi Perkins	Seal	X
Isaac Perry	Seal	X
Ishlonocka Hoomah	Seal	X
Hiram King	Seal	
Ogla Enlah	Seal	X
Nulthlahtubbee	Seal	X
Tuska Hollattuh	Seal	X
Panshastubbee	Seal	X
P P Pitchlynn	Seal	
Joel H Nail	Seal	
Hopaia Iskitini	Seal	+
Tishoomma	Seal	+
William Wade	Seal	+
Panshstickubbee	Seal	+
Holittankchahubbee	Seal	+
Kaahlanchahubbee	Seal	+
	Seal	
Eyarpulubbee	Seal	X
Okentahubbee	Seal	+
Living War Club	Seal	+
John Jones	Seal	+
Charles Jones	Seal	
Isaac Jones	Seal	x
Hocklucha	Seal	+
Muscogee	Seal	+
Eden Nelson	Seal	

In the Senate of the United States
February 21st: 1831.

Resolved, (two thirds of the Senators present concurring,) That the Senate do advise and consent to the ratification of the Treaty, between the United States of America and the Mingoes, Chiefs, Captains and Warriors of the Choctaw Nation, concluded at Dancing Rabbit Creek on the 15 th of September 1830, together with the supplement thereto, concluded at the same place the 28 th of September 1830; with the exception of the preamble.

Attest, Walter Lowrie

Andrew Jackson.
President of the United States of America,
To all and singular to whom these presents shall come,
Greeting:

Whereas a Treaty between the United States of America, and the Mingoes, Chiefs, Captains and Warriors of the Choctaw Nation was entered into at Dancing Rabbit Creek, on the twenty-seventh day of September in the Year of our Lord one thousand eight hundred and thirty, and of the Independence of the United States, the fifty-fifth, by John H. Eaton and John Coffee, Commissioners on the part of the United

States, and the Chiefs, Captains and Head-Men of the Choctaw Nation on the part of said Nation; — which Treaty, together with the Supplemental article thereto, is in the words following, To wit:

A Treaty

Various Choctaw persons have been presented by the chiefs of the Nation with a desire that they might be provided for, Being particularly deserving, an earnestness has been manifested that provision might be made for them, It is therefore by the undersigned Commissioners here assented to with the understanding that they are to have no interest in the reservations which are directed and provided for under the general Treaty to which this is a supplement.

As evidence of the liberal and kind feelings of the President and Government of the United States the Commissioners agree to the request as follows (to wit) Pierre Juzan, Peter Pitchlynn, G.W. Harkins, Jack Pitchlynn, Israel Fulsom, Louis Laflore, Benjamin James, Joel H. Nail, Hopoynjahubbee, Onorkubbee, Benjamin Laflore, Michael Laflore ^and Allen Yates & wife shall be entitled to a reservation of two sections of land each to include thier improvement where they at present reside, with the exception of the three first named persons ^& Benjn Laflore who are authorized to locate one of thier sections on any other unimproved and unoccupied land, within thier respective districts.

Article 2d

And to each of the following persons there is allowed a reservation of a section and a half of land, ^(to wit) James L. McDonald, Robert Jones, Noah Wall, James Campbell, G. Nelson, and Vaughn Brasheans, R. Harris, Little Leader, S. Foster, J. Vaughn, L. Durant, Samuel Long, T. Magagha, Thos. Everge, ~~[illegible]~~ Giles Thompson ~~[illegible]~~ Garland, John Bond, William Laflore, and Turner Brasheans; the two first named persons, may locate one section each, and one section jointly on any unimproved and unoccupied land, these not residing in the Nation; The others are to include thier present residence and improvement.

Also one section is allowed to the following persons (to wit) Middleton Mackey, ^Wesley Train – Choclehomo, Moses Foster, D.W. Wall, Charles Scott

Molly Nail, Susan Colbert, who was formerly Susan James, Saml. Garland, Silas Fisher, D. McCurtain, Oaklahoma, & Polly Fillecuthey, to be located in entire sections to include their present residence and improvement, with the exception of Molly Nail & Susan Colbert, who are authorized to locate theirs, on any unimproved unoccupied land.

John Pitchlynn has long and faithfully served the Nation in Character of U. States interpreter, he has acted as such for forty years, in Consideration it is agreed, in addition to what has been done for him there shall be granted to two of his Children, (to wit) Silas Pitchlynn, & Thomas Pitchlynn one Section of land each to adjoin the location of their father. likewise to James Madison and Peter Sons of Mushulatubbe One section of land each to include the Old House and improvement where their father formerly lived on the Old Military road, adjoining a large Prarie.

And to Henry Groves Son of the Chief — Natticache there is one Section of land given to adjoin his fathers land.

And to each of the following persons Half a Section of land is granted on any unoccupied and unimproved lands in the Districts where they respectively live (to wit) Willis Harkins, James D Hamilton, William Juzan, Tobias Laflin, Jo Doake, Jacob Fulsom, P. Hays, Saml. Worcester, Geo. Hunter, William Train and Robert Nail and Alexander McKee.

And there is given a quarter section of land each to Delila and her five fatherless Children, she being a Choctaw woman residing out of the Nation, also the same quantity to Peggy Trihan another Indian Woman residing out of the Nation & her two fatherless Children; & to the Widows of Pushmilaha, & Puckshenubbee, who were formerly distinguished Chiefs of the Nation and for their Children four quarter Sections of land, each in trust for themselves & their Children

All of said last mentioned reservations are to be located under and by direction of the President of the U States

Article 3

The Choctaw people now that they have Ceded thier lands are solicitous to get to thier new Homes early as possible & accordingly they wish that a party may be permitted to proceed this fall to ascertain where abouts will be most advantageous for thier people to be located.

It is therefore agreed that three or four persons (from each of the three districts) under the guidance of some discreet and well qualified person or persons may proceed during this fall to the West upon an examination of the Country.

For thier time and expenses the U. States agree to allow the said twelve persons Two Dollars a day each, not to exceed One Hundred days, which is deemed to be ample time to make an examination.

If necessary Pilots acquainted with the Country will be furnished when they arrive in the West.

Article 4th

John Donly of Alabama who has several Choctaw grand children, and who for twenty years has carried the mail through the Choctaw Nation, a desire by the Chiefs is expressed that he may have a section of land, it is accordingly granted, to be located in one entire section, on any unimproved & unoccupied land.

Allen Glover and George S. Gaines licensed Traders in the Choctaw Nation, have accounts amounting to upwards of Nine thousand Dollars against the Indians who are unable to pay thier said debts without distressing thier families; a desire is expressed by the Chiefs that two sections of land be set apart to be sold and the proceeds thereof to be applied toward the payment of the aforesaid debts. It is agreed that two sections of any unimproved and unoccupied land be granted to George S. Gaines who will sell the same for the best price he can obtain and apply the proceeds thereof to the credit of the Indians on their accounts due to the before mentioned Glover and Gaines; and shall make the application to the poorest Indian first

At the earnest and particular request of the Chief Greenwood Leflore there is granted to David Haley one half section of land to be located in a half section on any unoccupied and unimproved land as a compensation for a journey to Washington City with dispatches to the Government and returning others to the Choctaw Nation

The foregoing is entered into, as supplemental to the treaty concluded yesterday.

Done at Dancing Rabbit Creek the 28th day of September 1830

Jno H Eaton (seal)

In presence of
E. Breathitt Secty to Com.
W. Ward Agt for Choctaws
M. Mackey US Intr.
John Pitchlynn
US Intr.
R. P. Currin
[illegible]
Geo. S. Gaines

Jno Coffee (seal)
Greenwood Leflore
Nittucachee his x mark
Mushulatubbee his x mark
Ofahoomah his x mark
Eyarhocuttubbee his x mark
Iyacherhopia his x mark
Holubbee his x mark
Onarhubbee his x mark
Robert Cole his x mark
Hopiaunchahubbee his x mark
David Folsom
John Garland his x mark
Hopiahoomah his x mark
Captain Thalko his x mark
Pierre Juzan
Immarstarher his x mark
Hoshimhamartar his x mark

The following words in this supplement were interlined before being signed 1st Article "& Allen Yates & wife" also 8 Benj. Leflore ... Dr. Nesley, Travis ... Choolehoma ... "person or persons"

In presence of
E. Breathitt Secty to Com.

Now, therefore, be it known, that I, Andrew Jackson, President of the United States of America, having seen and considered said Treaty, do, in pursuance of the advice and consent of the Senate, as expressed by their Resolution of the twenty-first day of February, one thousand eight hundred and thirty-one, accept, ratify and confirm the same, and every clause and article thereof, with the exception of the Preamble.

In Testimony whereof, I have caused the seal of the United States to be hereunto affixed, having signed the same with my hand.

Done at the City of Washington, this twenty fourth day of February, in the Year of our Lord one thousand eight hundred and thirty-one, and of the Independence of the United States, the fifty-fifth.

Andrew Jackson

By the President,

M. Van Buren
Secty of State

[Transcription of Original]

Treaty of Dancing Rabbit Creek

1830

~~1831~~

Treaty

with the

Choctaws

Sep. ~~15~~ 27, 1830

And 28th Sepr 1930
Ratified Feb^{r} 24th 1831

A treaty of perpetual friendship, cession and limits entered into by John H. Eaton and John Coffee for and in behalf of the Government of the United States and the Mingoes Chiefs Captains and Warriors of the Choctaw Nation begun and held at Dancing Rabbit Creek on the 15th of September in the year 1830.

WHEREAS the General Assembly of the State of Mississippi has extended the laws of said State to persons and property within the chartered limits of the same and the President of the United States has said that he cannot protect the Choctaw people from the operation of these laws; Now therefore that the Choctaw may live under their own laws in peace with the United States and the State of Mississippi they have determined to sell their lands east of the Mississippi & have - accordingly agreed to the following articles of treaty ———

Article 1st

Perpetual peace and friendship is pledged and agreed on by and between United States and the Mingoes, Chiefs, & Warriors of the Choctaw Nation of Red People; and that this may be considered the ~~only~~ treaty existing between the parties all other treaties heretofore existing and inconsistent with the provisions of this are hereby declared null and void. ———

Article 2nd

The United States under a grant specially to be made by the President of the U. S. shall cause to be conveyed to the Choctaw Nation a tract of country west of the Mississippi River in fee simple to them & their descendants, to insure to them while they shall, exist as a nation and live on it beginning near Fort Smith where the

Arkansas boundary crosses the Arkansas River, Running thence ~~with~~ to the scource[sic] of the Canadian fork; if in the limits of the United States, or to those limits; thence due South to Red River, and down Red River to the West boundary of the Territory of Arkansas; thence North along that line to the beginning. The boundary of the same to be agreably[sic] to the treaty made and concluded at Washington City in the year 1825 The grant to be executed so soon as the present Treaty shall be ratified ——

Article 3^{d}

In consideration of the provisions contained in the several articles of this Treaty, the Choctaw Nation of Indians consent and hereby cede to the United States, the entire country they own and possess, East of the Mississippi River; and they agree to remove beyond the Mississippi River, early as practicable, and will so arrange their removal, that as many as possible of thier[sic] people not exceeding one half of the whole number, shall depart during the falls of 1831 and 1832; the residue to follow during the succeeding fall of 1833; a better opportunity in this manner will be afforded the Government, to extend to them the facilities and comforts which it is desirable should be extended in conveying them to thier new Homes.——

Article 4th

The Government and people of the United States are hereby obliged to secure to the said Choctaw Nation of Red People the Jurisdiction and Government of all the Persons and Property that may be within thier limits West, so that no territory or State shall ever have a right to pass laws for the Government of the Choctaw Nation of Red People and thier Descendants; and that no part of the land granted them shall ever be embraced in any territory or State; but the U. S. shall forever secure said Choctaw Nation from, & against, all laws except such as from time to time may be enacted in their own National Councils, not inconsistent with the Constitution, Treaties, and laws of the United States; & except such as may, & which have been enacted by Congress, to the extent that Congress under the Constitution are required to exerscise[sic] a legislation over Indian Affairs. But the Choctaws, should this treaty be ratified, express a wish that Congress may grant to the Choctaws the right of punishing by thier own laws, any white man who shall come into thier Nation, & infringe any of their National regulations.

Article 5th

The United States are obliged to protect the Choctaws from domestic strife & from foreign enemies on the same principles that the citizens of the United States are protected, so that whatever would be a legal demand upon the U. S. for defence[sic] or for wrongs committed by an Enemy, on a Citizen of the U. S, shall be equally binding in favour[sic] of the Choctaws, & in all cases where the Choctaws shall be called upon by a legally authorized officer of the U. S. to fight an Enemy, such Choctaw shall receive the pay & other emoluments, which citizens of the U. S. receive in such cases, provided, no war shall be undertaken or prosecuted by said Choctaw Nation but by declaration made in full Council, & to be approved by the U. S. unless it be in self defence against an open rebellion or against an enemy marching into thier country, in which cases they shall defend, until the U. S. are advised thereof.

Article 6th

Should a Choctaw or any party of Choctaws commit acts of violence upon the person or property of a citizen of the U. S, or join any war party against any neighbouring[sic] tribe of Indians, without the authority in the preceding article; & except to oppose an actual or threatened invasion or rebellion, such person so offending shall be delivered up to an Officer of the U. S. if in the power of the Choctaw Nation, that such offender may be punished as may be provided in such cases, by the laws of the U. S.; but if such Offender is not within the control of the Choctaw Nation, then said Choctaw Nation shall not be held responsible for the injury done by said offender.

Article 7th

All acts of violence committed upon persons and property of the ~~Cho~~ people of the Choctaw Nation either by Citizens of the U. S. or neighbouring[sic] tribes of Red people, shall be referred to some authorized agent by him to be referred to the ~~U.S.~~ President of the U. S, who shall examine into such cases and see that every possible degree of justice is done to said Indian party of the Choctaw Nation.

Article 8th

Offenders against the laws of the U. S. or any individual State shall be apprehended & delivered to any duly authorized person where such offender may be found in the Choctaw Country, having fled from any part of U. S. but in all such cases application must be made to the Agent or Chiefs & the expense of his apprehension and delivery provided for & paid by the U States.

Article 9th

Any citizen of the U. S. who may be ordered from the Nation by the Agent & constituted authorities of the Nation and refusing to obey or return into the Nation without the consent of the aforesaid persons, shall be subject to such pains and penalties as may provided by the laws of the U. S. in such cases. Citizens of the U. S.

travelling peaceably under the authority of the laws of the U. S. shall be under the care and protection of the Nation.

Article 10th

No person shall expose goods or other article for sale as a trader, without a written permit from the constituted authorities of the Nation, or authority of the laws of the Congress of the U. S. under penalty of forfeiting the articles, & the constituted authorities of the Nation shall grant no license except to such persons as reside in the Nation and are answerable to the laws of the Nation. The U. S. shall be particularly obliged to assist to prevent ardent spirits from being introduced into the Nation.

Article 11th

Navigable streams shall be free to the Choctaws who shall pay no higher toll or duty than Citizens of the U. S. It is agreed further that the U. S. shall establish one or more Post Offices in said Nation, & may establish such military post roads, and posts, as they may consider necessary.

Article 12th

All intruders shall be removed from the Choctaw Nation and kept without it. Private property to be always respected & on no occasion taken for public purposes without just compensation being made therefor to the rightful owner. If an Indian unlawfully take or steal any property from a white man a citizen of the U. S. the offender shall be punished. And if a white man unlawfully take or steal any thing from an Indian, the property shall be restored & the offender punished. It is further agreed that when a Choctaw shall be given up to be tried for any offence against the laws of the U. S. if unable to employ Counsel to defend him, the U. S. will do it, that his trial may be fair and impartial.

Article 13th

It is consented that a qualified Agent shall be appointed for the Choctaws every Four Years, unless sooner removed by the President; and he shall be removed on petition of the constituted authorities of the Nation the President being satisfied there is sufficient cause shown. The Agent shall fix his residence convenient to the great body of the people; & in the selection of an Agent immediately after the ratification of this Treaty, the wishes of the Choctaw Nation on the subject shall be entitled to great respect.

Article 14th

Each Choctaw head of a family being desirous to remain & become a Citizen of the States, shall be permitted to do so, by signifying his intention to the Agent within Six Months from the ratification of this Treaty & he or she shall thereupon be entitled to a reservation of one section of Six Hundred and forty Acres of Land, to be bounded by sectional lines of survey; in like manner shall be entitled to one half that quantity for each unmarried child which is living with him over Ten years of Age; & a quarter section to such child as be under 10 years of age, to adjoin the location of the Parent. If they reside upon said lands intending to become Citizens of the States for five Years after the ratification of this Treaty in that case a grant in fee simple shall issue; said reservation shall include the present improvement of the head of the family, or a portion of it. Persons who claim under this article shall not lose the privilege of a Choctaw Citizen, but if they ever remove are not to be entitled to any portion of the Choctaw Annuity;

Article 15th

To each of the Chiefs in the Choctaw Nation (to wit) Greenwood Laflore Nutackachie, and Mushulatubbe there is granted a reservation of four sections of land, two of which shall include and adjoin thier[sic] present improvement, and the other two located where they please but on unoccupied unimproved lands, such sections shall be bounded by sectional lines, & with the consent of the President they may sell the same. Also to the three principal Chiefs & to their successors in office there shall be paid Two Hundred and fifty Dollars annually while they shall continue in their respective offices, except to Mushulatubbe who as he has an annuity of One Hundred & fifty Dollars for life under a former treaty, shall receive only the additional sum of One Hundred Dollars, while he shall continue in office as Chief; & if in addition to this the Nation shall think propper[sic] to elect an additional principal Chief of the whole to superintend and govern upon republican principles he shall receive annually for his services Five Hundred Dollars, which allowance to the Chiefs and their successors in office, shall continue for Twenty Years. At any time when in Military Service, & while in service by authority of the U. S. the district Chiefs under and by selection of the President shall be entitled to the pay of Majors; the other Chief under the same circumstances shall have the pay of a Lieutenant-Colonel. The speakers of the three districts, shall receive Twenty five Dollars a year for four years ~~each~~ for four years each & the three secretaries one to each of the Chiefs, fifty dollars each for four years. Each Captain of the Nation, the number not to exceed ninety nine, thirty three from each District shall be furnished upon removing to the West, with each a good suit of clothes & a broad sword as an outfit, & for four years commencing with the first of thier removal, shall each receive Fifty Dollars a Year, for the trouble of keeping thier people at order in settling; & whenever they shall be in military service by authority of the U. S. shall receive the pay of a captain.

Article 16th

In wagons; & with steam boats as may be found necessary the U. S. agree to remove the Indians to thier new Homes at thier expense and under the care of discreet and carefull[sic] persons, who will be kind and brotherly to them. They agree to furnish them with ample corn and beef, or pork for themselves & families for Twelve months after reaching thier new homes.

It is agreed further that the U. S. will take all thier cattle, at the valuation of some discreet person to be appointed by the President, & the same shall be paid for in money after thier arrival at thier new homes; or in other cattle such as may be desired shall be furnished them, notice being given through thier Agent of thier wishes upon this subject before thier removal that time to supply the demand may be afforded.

Article 17th

The several annuities and sums secured under former Treaties to the Choctaw Nation and People shall continue as tho. this Treaty had never been made. And it is further agreed that the U. S. in addition will pay the sum of Twenty thousand Dollars for Twenty Years, commencing after thier removal to the west, of which, in the first year after thier removal, Ten thousand Dollars shall be divided and arranged to such as may not receive reservations under this Treaty.

Article 18th

The U. S. shall cause the lands hereby ceded to be surveyed; & surveyors may enter the Choctaw Country for that purpose, conducting themselves properly & disturbing or interrupting none of the Choctaw people. But no person is to be permitted to settle within the Nation, or the lands to be sold before the Choctaws shall remove. And for the payment of the several amounts secured in this Treaty, the lands hereby ceded are to remain a fund pledged to that purpose, until the debt shall be provided for and arranged. And further it is agreed, that in the construction of this Treaty wherever well founded doubt shall arise, it shall be construed most favorably towards the Choctaws.

Article 19th

The following reservations of land are hereby admitted. To Col David Fulsom Four Sections of which Two shall include his present improvement, & two may be located else where, on unoccupied, unimproved land.
To I. Garland, Col Robert Cole, Tuppanahomer, John Pytchlynn[sic], Charles Juzan, Johokebetubbe, Eaychahobia, Ofehoma two sections, each to be include thier improvements, and to be bounded by sectional lines, & the same may be disposed of and sold with the consent of the President. And that others not provided for, may be provided for, there shall be reserved as follows:
First; One section to each head of a family not exceeding Forty in number, who during the present year, may have had in actual cultivation, with a dwelling House thereon Fifty Acres or more. Secondly three quarter sections after the manner aforesaid to each head of a family not exceeding Four Hundred and Sixty, as shall have cultivated Thirty Acres and less than Fifty, to be bounded by quarter section lines of survey, & to be contiguous and adjoining.
Third; One half section as aforesaid to those who shall have cultivated from Twenty to Thirty acres the number not to exceed Four Hundred. Fourth; a quarter section as aforesaid to such as shall have cultivated from twelve to twenty acres, the number not to exceed three hundred and fifty, and one half that quantity to such as shall have cultivated from two to twelve acres, the number also not to exceed three hundred and fifty persons. Each of said class of cases shall be subject to the limitations contained in the first class, & shall be so located as to include that part of the improvement which contains the dwelling House. If a greater number shall be found to be entitled to reservations under the several classes of this article, than is stipulated for under the limitation prescribed, then & in that case the Chiefs separeately[sic] or together shall determine the persons who shall be excluded in the respective districts.
Fifth; Any Captain the number not exceeding ninety persons, who under the provisions of this article shall receive less than a section, he shall be entitled, to an additional quantity of half a section adjoining to his other reservation. The several reservations secured under this article, may be sold with the consent of the President of the U. S; but should any prefer it, or omit to take a reservation for the quantity he may be entitled to the U. S. will on his removing pay fifty cents an acre, after reaching thier new homes, provided that before the first of January next they shall adduce to the Agent; or some other authorized person to be appointed, proof of his claim & the quantity of it. Sixth; likewise children of the Choctaw Nation residing in the Nation, who have neither Father nor Mother a list of which, with satisfactory proof of Parentage and orphanage being filed with Agent in six months to be forwarded to the War Department, shall be entitled to a quarter section of Land, to be located under the direction of the President, & with his consent the same may be sold and the proceeds applied to some beneficial purpose for the benefit of said orphans

Article 20th

The U. S. agree & stipulate as follows, that for the benefit and advantage of the Choctaw people, & to improve thier condition, thier[sic] shall be educated under the direction of the President & at the expense of the U. S. forty Choctaw Youths for Twenty years. This number shall be kept at school, & as they finish thier education others to supply thier places shall be received for the period stated. The U. S. agree also to erect a Council House for the Nation at some convenient central point, after thier people shall be settled; & a House for each Chief, also a church for each of the three Districts, to be used also as school Houses, until the Nation may conclude to build others; & for these purposes Ten thousand Dollars shall be appropriated; also Fifty thousand Dollars (viz) Twenty Five Hundred Dollars annually shall be given for the support of three Teachers of schools for Twenty Years. Likewise there shall be furnished to the Nation, three Blacksmiths one for each District for sixteen years, & a qualified Mill Wright for five years; Also there shall be furnished the following articles, Twenty One Hundred Blankets, To each warrior who emigrates a rifle, moulds, wipers and ammunition. One thousand axes, Ploughs, Hoes, Wheels and Cards each; and four Hundred looms. There shall also be furnished one Ton of iron & two hundred weight of steel annually to each District for sixteen years.

Article 21st

A few Choctaw Warriors yet survive who marched and fought in the Army with General Wayne the whole number stated not to exceed Twenty.
These it is agreed shall hereafter while they live receive Twenty Five dollars a year; a list of them to be early as practicable, & within six months made out, and presented to the Agent to be forwarded to the War Department.—

Article 22d

The Chiefs of the Choctaws have suggested that thier people are in a state of rapid advancement in education and refinement; and have expressed a solicitude that they might have the privilege of a Delegate on the floor of the House of Representatives extended to them. The Commissioners do not feel, that they can under a treaty stipulation accede to the request, but at thier desire, present it in the Treaty, that Congress may consider of and decide the application.

Done and signed and executed by the Commissioners of the United States and the Chiefs Captains and Head Men of the Choctaw Nation, at Dancing Rabbit Creek this 27th day of September Eighteen Hundred and Thirty.

			His Mark
In presence of	Jn° H. Eaton	(Seal)	
E. Breathitt Secty	Jn°. Coffee	(Seal)	
to the Commss^{r} =	Greenwood Leflore	(Seal)	
William Ward Agt.	Musholatubbee	(Seal)	X
for Choctaws.	Nittucachee	(Seal)	X
John Pitchlynn	Eyarhocuttubbee	(Seal)	X
US Int^{r}	Iyacherhopia	(Seal)	X
M Mackey	Offahoomah	(Seal)	X
US Intr.	Archalater	(Seal)	X
Geo. S. Gaines	Onnahubbee	(Seal)	X
of Alabama	Holarterhoomah	(Seal)	X
RP Currin	Hopiaunchahubbee	(Seal)	X
Luke Howard	Zishomingo	(Seal)	X
Sam. L. Worchester	Captain thalke	(Seal)	X
Jn° W Byrn	James Shield	(Seal)	X
John Bell	Pistiyubbee	(Seal)	X
Jn° Bond	Yobalarunehahubbee	(Seal)	X
	Holubbee	(Seal)	X
	Robert Cole	(Seal)	X
	Mokelareharhopin	(Seal)	X
	Lewis Perry	(Seal)	X
	Artonamarstubbe	(Seal)	X
	Hopeatubbee	(Seal)	X
	Hoshahoomah	(Seal)	X
	Chuallahoomah	(Seal)	X
	Joseph Kincaide	(Seal)	X
	Artooklubbetushpar	(Seal)	X
	Metubbee	(Seal)	X
	Arsarkatubbee	(Seal)	X
	Issaterhoomah		X
	Chohtahmatahah	(Seal)	X
	Tunnuppashubbee	(Seal)	X
	Okocharyer	(Seal)	X
	Hoshhopia	(Seal)	X
	Warsharshahopia	(Seal)	X
	Maarshunchahubbee	(Seal)	X
	Misharyubbee	(Seal)	X
	Daniel McCurtain	(Seal)	X
	Tushkerharcho	(Seal)	X
	Hoktoontubbee	(Seal)	X
	Nuknacrahookmarhee	(Seal)	X
	Mingohoomah	(Seal)	X
	Pisinhocuttubbee	(Seal)	X
	Tullarhacher	(Seal)	X
	Little leader	(Seal)	X
	Maanhutter	(Seal)	X
	Cowehoomah	(Seal)	X

	Tillamoer	(Seal)	X
	Imnullacha	(Seal)	X
	Artopilachubbee	(Seal)	X
	Shupherunchahubbee	(Seal)	X
	Nitterhoomah	(Seal)	X
	Oaklaryubbee	(Seal)	X
	Pukumma	(Seal)	X
	Arpalar	(Seal)	X
	Holber	(Seal)	X
	Hoparmingo	(Seal)	X
	Isparhoomah	(Seal)	X
	Tieberhoomah	(Seal)	X
	Tishoholarter	(Seal)	X
	Mahayarchubbee	(Seal)	X
	Arlarter	(Seal)	X
	Nittahubbee	(Seal)	X
	Tishonouan	(Seal)	X
	Warsharchaboomah	(Seal)	X
	Isaac James	(Seal)	X
	Hopiaintushker	(Seal)	X
	Aryoshkermer		X
	Shemotar		X
	Hopiaisketina		X
	Thomas Leflore		X
	Arnokechatubbee		X
	Shokoperlukna		X
	Posherhoomah		X
	Robert Folsom		X
	Arharyotubbee		X
	Kushonolarter		X
	James Vaughan		X
	James Karnes		X
	Tishohakubbee		X
	Narlanalar		X
	Pennasha		X
	In har yar ker		X
	Motubbee		X
	Narharyubbee		X
	Ishmaryubbee		X
	James M King		
	Lewis Wilson		X
	Istonarkerharcho		X
	Hoshinshamartarher		X
	Kinsulachubbee		X
	Eyarhinstubbee		X
	Sam[l] Garlands		
	Thomas Wall		
	Sam. S. Worcester		

	Jacob Folsom		
	William Foster		
	Ontioerharcho		X
	Hugh A. Foster		
	Pierre Juzan		
	Jno. Pitchlynn Jr.	(Seal)	
	David Folsom	(Seal)	
	Sholohommastube	(Seal)	X
	Tesho	(Seal)	X
	Lauwechubee	(Seal)	X
	Hoshehammo	(Seal)	X
	Ofenowo	(Seal)	X
	Ahekoche	(Seal)	X
	Kaloshoube	(Seal)	X
	Atoko	(Seal)	X
	Ishtemeleche	(Seal)	X
	Emthtohabe	(Seal)	X
	Silas D. Fisher	(Seal)	
	Isaac Folsom	(Seal)	X
	Hekatube	(Seal)	X
	Hakseche	(Seal)	X
	Jerry Carney	(Seal)	X
	John Washington	(Seal)	X
	Phiplip	(Seal)	X
	Meshameye	(Seal)	X
	Ish te he ka	(Seal)	X
	Heshohomme	(Seal)	X
	John McKelbery	(Seal)	X
	Benj^{m}. James	(Seal)	
	Tik ba cha ham be	(Seal)	X
	Aholiktube	(Seal)	X
	Walking Wolf	(Seal)	X
	John Waide	(Seal)	X
	Big Axe	(Seal)	X
	Bob	(Seal)	X
	Tush ko cha u bbe	(Seal)	X
	It ta be	(Seal)	X
	Tish o wa ka you	(Seal)	
	Folehommo	(Seal)	X
	John Garland	(Seal)	X
	Koshona	(Seal)	X
	Ish le you ham ube	(Seal)	X
	Ok la no wa	(Seal)	X
	Neto	(Seal)	X
	James Fletcher	(Seal)	X
	Silus D Pitchlynn	(Seal)	
	William Trahorn	(Seal)	
	Tosh ka hem mit to	(Seal)	X

	Te the ta yo	(Seal)	X
	Emokloshahopie	(Seal)	X
	Tishoimita	(Seal)	X
	Thomas W Foster	(Seal)	
	Zadoc Brashears		
	Levi Perkins	(Seal)	X
	Isaac Perry	(Seal)	X
	Isblonocka Hoomah	(Seal)	X
	Hiram King	(Seal)	
	Ogla Enlah	(Seal)	X
	Nu1tlahtubbee	(Seal)	X
	Tuska Hollattuh	(Seal)	X
	Panshastubbee	(Seal)	X
	P. P. Pitchlynn	(Seal)	
	Joel H. Nail	(Seal)	
	Hopia Stonakey	(Seal)	X
	Kocohomma	(Seal)	X
	William Wade	(Seal)	X
	Pansh stick ubbee	(Seal)	X
	Ho lit tank chah ubbee	(Seal)	X
	Ko th^{o} ant chah ubbee	(Seal)	X
	Eyarpulubbee	(Seal)	X
	Oken tah ubbe	(Seal)	X
	Living War Club	(Seal)	X
	John Jones	(Seal)	X
	Charles Jones	(Seal)	
	Isaac Jones	(Seal)	X
	Hocklucha	(Seal)	X
	Muscogee	(Seal)	X
	Eden Nelson	(Seal)	

And 28th Sep^{t} 1830
Ratified Feby 24th 1831.

In the Senate of the United States
February 21st: 1831.

Resolved, (two thirds of the Senators present concurring) That the Senate do advise and consent to the ratification of the Treaty, between the United States of America and the Mingoes, Chiefs, Captains and Warriors of the Choctaw Nation, concluded at Dancing Rabbit Creek on the 15th of September 1830, together with the Supplement thereto, concluded at the same place the 28th of September 1830: with the exception of the preamble.

Attest, Walter Lowrie

Treaty of Dancing Rabbit Creek

Andrew Jackson,
President of the United States of America,
To all and singular to whom these presents shall come,

Greeting:

Whereas a Treaty between the United States of America, and the Mingoes, Chiefs, Captains and Warriors of the Choctaw Nation was entered into at Dancing Rabbit Creek, on the twenty-seventh day of September in the Year of our Lord one thousand eight hundred and thirty, and of the Independence of the United States, the fifty-fifth, by John H. Eaton and John Coffee, Commissioners on the part of the United States, and the Chiefs, Captains and Head-Men of the Choctaw Nation on the part of said Nation; - which Treaty, together with the supplemental article thereto, is in the words following,

To wit:

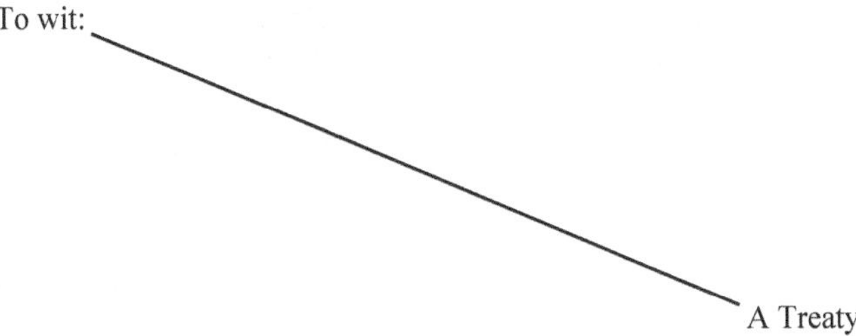

A Treaty

Various Choctaw persons have been presented by the chiefs of the Nation, with a desire that they might be provided for, Being particularly deserving, an earnestness has been manifested that provision might be made for them. It is therefore by the undersigned commissioners here assented to with the understanding that they are to have no interest in the reservations which are directed and provided for under the general Treaty to which this is a supplement.

As evidence of the liberal and kind feelings of the President and Government of the United States the Commissioners agree to the request as follows (to wit) Pierre Juzan, Peter Pitchlynn, G.W. Harkins, Jack Pitchlynn, Israel Fulsom, Louis Laflore, Benjamin James, Joel H. Nail, Hopoynjahubbee, Onorkubbee, Benjamin Laflore, Michael Laflore & Allen Yates & wife shall be entitled to a reservation of two sections of land each to include thier improvement where they at present reside, with the exception of the three first named persons & Benja. Laflore who are authorized to locate one of thier sections on any other unimproved and unoccupied land, within thier respective districts.

Article 2^{d}

And to each of the following persons there is allowed a reservation of a section and a half of land, (to wit) James L. McDonald, Robert Jones, Noah Wall, James Campbell, G. Nelson, ~~and~~ Vaughn Brashears, R. Harris, Little Leader, S. Foster, J.

Vaughn, L. Durand, Samuel Long, T. Magagha, Tho[s]. Everge, Giles Thompson, Thomas Garland, John Bond, William Laflore, and Turner Brashears; the two first named persons, may locate one section each, and one section jointly on any unimproved and unoccupied land, these not residing in the Nation; The others are to include thier present residence and improvement.

Also one section is allowed to the following persons (to wit) Middleton Mackey, Wesley Train, Choclehomo, Moses Foster, D. W. Wall, Charles Scott, Molly Nail, Susan Colbert, who was formerly Susan James, Samuel Garland, Silas Fisher, D. McCurtain, Oaklahoma, & Polly Fillecuthey, to be located in entire sections to include thier resent residence and improvement, with the exception of Molly Nail and Susan Colbert, who are authorized to locate thiers, on any unimproved unoccupied land.

John Pitchlynn has long and faithfully served the Nation in character of U. States interpreter, he has acted as such for forty years, in consideration it is agreed, in addition to what has been done for him there shall be granted to two of his children, (to wit) Silas Pitchlynn, & Thomas Pitchlynn one section of land each to adjoin the location of thier father likewise to James Madison and Peter sons of Mushulatubbee one section of land each to include the old house and improvement ~~of~~ where thier father formerly lived on the old military road adjoining a large Prerarie[sic].

And to Henry Groves son of the Chief Natticache there is one section of land given to adjoin his father's land.

And to each of the following persons half a section of land is granted on any unoccupied and unimproved lands in the Districts where they respectively live (to wit) Willis Harkins, James D. Hamilton, William Juzan, Tobias Laflore, Jo Do~~a~~ke, Jacob Fulsom, P. Hays, Sam[l] Worcester, Geo. Hunter, William Train ~~and~~ Robert Nail and Alexander McKee.

And there is given a quarter section of land each to Delila and her five fatherless children, she being a Choctaw woman residing out of the Nation; also the same quantity to Peggy Trihan, another Indian woman residing out of the Nation & her two fatherless children; & to the widows of Pushmilaha, & Puck she nubbee, who were formerly distinguished Chiefs of the Nation and for thier children four quarter sections of land, each in trust for themselves & thier children

All of said last mentioned reservations are to be located under and by direction of the President of the U States

Article 3

The Choctaw people now that they have ceded thier[sic] lands are solicitous to act to thier new homes early as possible & accordingly they wish that a party may be permitted to proceed this fall to ascertain where abouts will be most advantageous for thier people to be located.

It is therefore agreed that three or four persons (from each of the three districts) under the guidance of some discreet and well qualified person or persons ~~man~~ may proceed during this fall to the West upon an examination of the country.

For thier time and expenses the U. States agree to allow the said twelve persons Two Dollars a day each, not to exceed one hundred days, which is deemed to be ample time to make an examination.

If necessary Pilots acquainted with the country will be furnished when they arrive in the West.

Article 4th

John Donly of Alabama who has several Choctaw grand children, and who for Twenty years has carried the mail through the Choctaw Nation, a desire by the Chiefs is expressed that he may have a section of land, it is accordingly granted, to be located in one entire section, on any unimproved & unoccupied land.

Allen Glover and George S. Gaines licensed Traders in the Choctaw Nation, have accounts amounting to upwards of Nine thousand Dollars against the Indians who are unable to pay thier said debts without distressing thier families; a desire is expressed by the Chiefs that Two sections of land be set apart to be sold and the proceeds thereof to be applied toward the payment of the aforesaid debts. It is agreed that two sections of any unimproved and unoccupied land be granted to George S. Gaines who will sell the same for the best price he can obtain and apply the proceeds thereof to the credit of the Indians on thier accounts due to the before mentioned Glover and Gaines; & shall make the application to the poorest Indian first.

At the earnest and particular request of the Chief Greenwood Laflore there is granted to David Haley one half section of land to be located in a half section on any unoccupied and unimproved land as a compensation for a journey to Washington City with dispatches to the Government and returning others to the Choctaw Nation.

The foregoing is entered into, as supplemental to the treaty concluded yesterday.

Done at Dancing Rabbit creek the 28th day of September 1830.

In presence of	Jn° H Eaton Seal
E. Breathitt Secty to Com^{r}.	Jn°. Coffee Seal
W. Ward Agt. for Choctaws	Greenwood Leflore
M Mackey US Intr.	Nittucachee his x mark
John Pitchlynn	Musholatubbee his x mark
US Int^{r}	Ofahoomah his x mark
RP Currin	Eyarhoeuttubbee his x mark
Jn° W Byrn	Iyaeherhopia his x mark

Geo. S. Gaines	Holubbee his x mark
The following words in this supplement	Onarhubbee his x mark
were interlined before being signed	Robert Cole his x mark
1st Article "& Allen Yates & wife" also	Hopiaunchahubbee his x mark
& Benja Laflore	David Folsom
Do. Wesley Train - Choclehomo	John Garland his x mark
	Hopiahoomah his x mark
"person or persons"	Captain Thalko his x mark
	Pierre Juzan
In presence of	Immarstarher his x mark
E. Breathitt Secty to Comr.	Hoshimhamarter his x mark

Now, therefore, be it known, that I, Andrew Jackson, President of the United States of America, having seen and considered said Treaty, do in pursuance of the advice and consent of the Senate, as expressed by their Resolution of the twenty-first day of February, one thousand eight hundred and thirty-one, accept, ratify and confirm the same, and every clause and article thereof, with the exception of the Preamble.

In Testimony whereof, I have caused the seal of the United States to be hereunto affixed, having signed the same with my hand.

Done at the City of Washington, this twenty fourth day of February, in the Year of our Lord one thousand eight hundred and thirty-one, and of the Independence of the United States, the fifty-fifth.

Andrew Jackson

By the President,

M. VanBuren
Secty of State

Dawes Packet
of
Bob Thomas, et al.

In the matter of the application of Bob Thomas, et al., for identification as Mississippi Choctaws.

MISS.-CHOCTAW R-1136
ENROLLMENT

Bob Thomas ET AL

IDENTIFIED

Decision rendered Feb. 14, 1903.

Copy of decision forwarded
Attorneys for Choctaw and Feb 21, 1903.
Chickasaws

Copy of Decision forwarded applicant. Mar. 11,1903

R-1136

DEPARTMENT OF THE INTERIOR

COMMISSION TO THE FIVE CIVILIZED TRIBES

In the matter of the application of Bob Thomas, et al., for identification as Mississippi Choctaws---------------------------M.C.R. 1136

------ INDEX --------

.TI 1136

DEPARTMENT OF THE INTERIO R
COMMISSION TO THE FIVECIVILIZED TRIBES
Hattiesburg, Miss. Dec. 18, 1900.

In the matter of the application for identification as Mississippi Choctaws of Bob Thomas, his wife and five children. Bob Thomas being duly sworn by Acting Chairman Bixby, testified as follows:

Examination by the Commission.
Through Jeff D. Neal, Interpreter.

Q What is your name? A Bob Thomas.
Q What is your age? A About thirty seven.
Q What is your post-office? A Brown.
Q Mississippi? A Yes sir.
Q How long have you lived in Mississippi? A All my life. Born here.
Q Never lived any where else? A No sir.
Q What is your father's name? A Jake Thomas.
Q What is his Indian name? A Sakaubbee.
Q Is he living? A No sir.
Q What is your mothers name? A Martha.
Q Martha Thomas? A Yes sir.
Q Is she living? A No sir.
Q They were both full blood Indians? A Yes sir.
Q And you are a full blood are you? A Yes sir.
Q Is your name on any of the tribal rolls of the Choctaw Nation in the Indian Territory? A No sir.
Q Did you ever make application to the Choctaw authorities in the Indian Territory for citizenship? A No sir.
Q Did you make application to this Commission in 1896 under the act of June 10th, 1896, that is four years ago? A No sir.
Q Did you make application when the Commission was in Mississippi in 1899, in January and February, about two years ago. A No sir.
Q What is your wife's name? A Daley Thomas.
Q Is she a full blood? A Yes sir.
Q What is her father's name? A His name was Jim.
Q Did he have an Indian name? A Yes sir.
Q What was his Indian name? A Wahkiatubbee.
Q Is he dead? A Yes sir.
Q What is your wife's mother's name? A I don't know.
Q Was she a full blood Indian? A Yes sir.
Q How old is your wife? A Thirty three.
Q What are the names of your children? A Ransom.
Q Ransom Thomas? A Yes sir.
Q How old is Ransom? A Fifteen.
Q What is the next one? A Berry.
Q How old is Berry? A Thirteen.
Q The next one? A Emeline.
Q How old is Emeline? A Ten years old.
Q Any more? A Yes sir.
Q All right. A Sam.
Q How old is Sam? A Five years old.
Q You have another haven't you? A Yes sir.
Q What is the other one? A Samawail.
Q How old is that one? A Three years old.
Q Daley Thomas is the mother of all these children? A Yes sir
Q You are the fatherof all of them? A Yes sir.
Q These children have always lived in Mississippi? A Yes sir.

1

Bob Thomas 2

Q You are making application for the identification of yourself your wife and your children as Mississippi Choctaws? A Yes sir.

Q Did any of your ancestors or any of your wife's ancestors ever remove from Mississippi to the Indian Territory? A No sir .

Q Have always as far back as you can remember lived in Mississippi? A Yes sir, I don't remember.

Q You are making your claim under the fourteenth article of the treaty of 1830 are you? A Yes sir.

Q Did any of your ancestors or your wife's ancestors ever signify to the United States Indian Agent their intention to remain and become citizens of the United States in preference to removing to the Indian Territory? A I don't remember.

Q Do you know what your grand father's name was? A I don't remember.

Q Don't remember their Indian names? A Inokachintubbee.

Q Did he die in Mississippi? A Yes sir.

Q Never went to the Indian Territory? A Yes sir, he went and came back.

Q Did he go to the Indian Territory when the rest of the Indians were moved out there? A I remember hearing that he went there but don't know when it was.

Q Do you remember ever seeing your grand father? A I just can recollect.

Q That was your father's father? A Yes sir.

Q Do you remember your mother's parents? A No sir.

Q Did you ever hear their names? A No sir.

Q Do you know anything about them? A No sir.

Q Now as to your wife's people. Your wife has always lived in Mississippi, has she? A Yes sir.

Q Has she ever lived in the Indian Territory? A No sir.

Q Did her father and mother go to the Indian Territory? A I don't remember anything about it.

Q Did you ever hear of them going to the Indian Territory? A I heard some other people talking but I don't remember what it was.

Q Do you know what your wife's grand mother and grand father's names were? A No sir.

Q Did you or your wife ever receive any benefits from the Choctaw Nation in the Indian Territory? A No sir.

Q Ever draw any money from the Choctaw Nation in the Indian Territory? A No sir.

Q Did any of your wife's ancestors or your ancestors ever receive any land in Mississippi from the United States government under the fourteenth article of the treaty of 1830? A I don't remember anything about it.

Q In the event that the Commission is enabled to identify you and your wife and your children as Mississippi Choctaws entitled to allotment in the Choctaw lands in the Indian Territory, is it your intention to remove to the Indian Territory? A Yes sir.

Q Is there any other statement you want to make? A No sir.

Q Any written evidence that you desire to submit to the Commission?

> Here L. P. Hudson, attorney for the applicant asks leave to file written evidence in support of this ~~xix~~ claim in thirty days from this date.

The applicant is to all appearances a full blood Choctaw Indian. Is unable to speak the English language and understands but little that is said to him, the examination being conducted through an interpretor. It further appears that he and his wife and children have always been residents of the state of Mississippi and that none of them have ever derived any benefits from the Choctaw tribe in the Indian Territory.

2

Bob Thomas 3

The decision of the Commission as to your application and the application you make on behalf of your wife and five minor children for identification as Mississippi Choctaws will be mailed to you to your present post-office address.

Myra Young, having been first duly sworn upon her oath states that as stenographer to the Commission to the Five Civilized Tribes she reported in full all proceedings had in the above entitled cause on the 18th day of December, 1900, and that the above and foregoing is a full, true and correct transcript of her stenographic notes of said proceedings on said date.

Myra Young.

Subscribed and sworn to before me this 19th day of December, 1900.

Acting Chairman.

3

DEPARTMENT OF THE INTERIOR

COMMISSION TO THE FIVE CIVILIZED TRIBES

In the matter of the application of Bob Thomas, et al., for identification as Mississippi Choctaws---------------------------------M.C.R. 1136

----D E C I S I O N------

It appears from the record herein that application for identification as Mississippi Choctaws was made to this Commission on December 18, 1900, by Bob Thomas for himself, his wife Daley and his five minor children, Ransom, Berry, Emeline, Sam and Samawail Thomas, under the following provision of the Act of Congress approved June 28, 1898(30 Stats . 495):

> "Said Commission shall have authority to determine the identity of Choctaw Indians claiming rights in the Choctaw lands under article fourteen of the treaty between the United States and the Choctaw Nation, concluded September twenty-seventh, eighteen hundred and thirty, and to that end may administer oaths, examine witnesses and perform all other acts necessary thereto and make report to the Secretary of the Interior."

From the evidence submitted in support of said application it appears that all the applicants are full blood Mississippi Choctaw Indians.

4

-2-

Section forty-one of the Act of Congress entitled "An Act to ratify and confirm an agreement with the Choctaw and Chickasaw tribes of Indians, and for other purposes" approved July 1, 1902 (32 Stats. 641) and ratified by the Choctaw and Chickasaw Nations September 25, 1902, provides as follows:

> "The application of no person for identification as a Mississippi Choctaw shall be received by said Commission after six months subsequent to the date of the final ratification of this agreement and in the disposition of such applications all full blood Mississippi Choctaw Indians and the descendants of any Mississippi Choctaw Indians whether of full or mixed blood who received a patent to land under the said fourteenth article of the said treaty of eighteen hundred and thirty who had not moved to and made bona fide settlement in the Choctaw-Chickasaw country prior to June twenty-eighth, eighteen hundred and ninety-eight, shall be deemed to be Mississippi Choctaws, entitled to benefits under article fourteen of the said treaty of September twenty-seventh, eighteen hundred and thirty, and to identification as such by said Commission, but this direction or provision shall be deemed to be only a rule of evidence and shall not be invoked by or operate to the advantage of any applicant who is not a Mississippi Choctaw of the full blood, or who is not the descendant of a Mississippi Choctaw who received a patent to land under said treaty, or who is otherwise barred from the right of citizenship in the Choctaw Nation, all of said Mississippi Choctaws so enrolled by said Commission shall be upon a separate roll."

It is, therefore, the opinion of this Commission that Bob Thomas, Daley Thomas, Ransom Thomas, Berry Thomas, Emeline Thomas, Sam Thomas and Samawail Thomas should be identified as Mississippi Choctaws, and it is so ordered.

COMMISSION TO THE FIVE CIVILIZED TRIBES

Acting Chairman

Commissioner

C. R. Breckinridge
Commissioner

Muskogee, Indian Territory
FEB 14 1903

5

M.C.R. 1136

COPY.

Muskogee, Indian Territory, February 21, 1903.

Mansfield, McMurray & Cornish,
Attorneys for the Choctaw and Chickasaw Nations,
South McAlester, Indian Territory.

Gentlemen:

Enclosed herewith you will find a copy of the decision of the Commission rendered February 14, 1903, identifying Bob Thomas, his wife Daley Thomas, and minor children Ransom Thomas, Berry Thomas, Emeline Thomas, Sam Thomas and Samawail Thomas as Mississippi Choctaw Indians under the provisions of the forty-first section of the act of Congress approved July 1, 1902, (32 Stats., 641).

You are hereby advised that you will be allowed fifteen days from the date hereof, in which to file with this Commission such protest as you desire to make against the action of the Commission in identifying the said Bob Thomas, his wife and children as Mississippi Choctaws, and make satisfactory proof of service of said protest upon the applicants herein.

If you fail to file such protest within the time allowed, the names of the applicants herein will be placed upon the schedule of duly identified Mississippi Choctaws now being prepared by this Commission.

Respectfully,

(SIGNED)
Tams Bixby.

~~Acting~~ Chairman.

Registered.
Enc. H.M.V. 20

M.C.R. 1136.

Muskogee, Indian Territory, March 11, 1903.

Bob Thomas,

Hugo, Indian Territory.

Dear Sir:

Enclosed herewith you will find a copy of the decision of the Commission to the Five Civilized Tribes, rendered February 14, 1903, identifying yourself, your wife, Daley Thomas, and your five minor children, Ransom, Berry, Emeline, Sam and Samawail Thomas, as Mississippi Choctaw Indians under the provisions of Section 41 of the Act of Congress approved July 1, 1902, (32 Stats., 641).

If you remove to the Choctaw-Chickasaw country, Indian Territory, before August 14, 1903, you will have six months from that date, or until February 14, 1904, within which to make proof of such removal and settlement at the office of the Commission at Atoka, Choctaw Nation, or Tishomingo, Chickasaw Nation.

Respectfully,

Tams Bixby.

Chairman.

Registered.

Enc. 1136.

C O P Y .

DEPARTMENT OF THE INTERIOR
COMMISSION TO THE FIVE CIVILIZED TRIBES
CHOCTAW LAND OFFICE.
Atoka, Indian Territory, January 8, 1904.

In the matter of the proof of settlement within the Choctaw Chickasaw country of Bob Thomas, his wife, Daley Thomas, and their five minor children, Ransom, Berry, Emeline, Sam and Samawail Thomas, duly identified Mississippi Choctaws Card No. 31, approved roll Nos. 83 to 89 inclusive.

- - - - - - - - - - - - - - -

BOB THOMAS being first duly sworn testifies as follows:

EXAMINATION BY THE COMMISSION:

Q What is your name? A Bob Thomas.
Q What is your age? A Well, I believe that when I went before them down there I told them that I was about 37 and that would make me about 39 or 40 now.
Q What was the name of your father? A Jake Thomas.
Q What was the name of your mother? A Martha Thomas.
Q Are either of your parents living? A No sir.
Q Are you married? A Yes sir.
Q What is the name of your wife? A Daley.
Q What is the name of her father? A Wahkistubbee.
Q Is he living? A No sir, dead.
Q Do you know the name of your wife's mother? A No sir.
Q Is she living? A No sir.
Q How many children have you? A Five.
Q Name your children beginning with the oldest, will you? A Ransom, Berry, Emeline, Sam and Samawail Thomas.
Q Are these children all living now and are they living with you? A Yes sir.
Q Is your wife now living and is she living with you? A Yes sir.
Q Are you the identical Bob Thomas, and is your wife the identical Daley Thomas, and these five children you have named the identical persons who were by the Commission to the Five Civilized Tribes on February 14, 1903, identified as Mississippi Choctaws, entitled to allotments of the lands of the Choctaws and Chickasaws in Indian Territory? A Yes sir.
Q When did you remove from the State of Mississippi to the Indian Territory? A It was January 26, 1903.
Q Did your wife, Daley, accompany you from the state of Mississippi to the Choctaw Nation, Indian Territory? A Yes sir.
Q Did your five minor children whom you have named, accompany you from Mississippi to the Indian Territory? A Yes sir.
Q What is your present post office address in the Choctaw Nation? A Spencerville, Indian Territory.
Q Are you and your wife now living together as husband and wife? A Yes sir.
Q What, if any, of your property did you bring from Mississippi with you to the Indian Territory? A We just brought our bedding and quilts.
Q Have you, your wife, and these five minor children, resided continuously in the Choctaw-Chickasaw country since the 26th day of last January up to the present time? A Yes sir.

M C L 31

Q Is it the intention of yourself and family to accept lands in allotment in the Choctaw Chickasaw country and the make your permanent home in the Indian Territory? A Yes sir.
Q Who paid your expenses from the state of Mississippi to the Choctaw Nation, Indian Territory? A A white fellow.
Q What was his name? A Charley Bayless.
Q Who paid your expenses from Spencerville to Atoka today? A This white fellow here.
Q What is his name? A Tom Black.
Q Did Tom Black bring you here from your home for the purpose of having you file on certain land for yourself and family? A Yes sir; this fellow here lives at Hugo and he is a partner of this man Bayless and Bayless has gone back to Mississippi and this man brought me here.
Q What is the citizenship of Mr. Tom Black? A I do not think he is an Indian .

Witness excused:

Fred V. Kinkade being first duly sworn on oath states that above and foregoing is a true and correct translation of his stenographic notes as taken in said cause on date first above written.

(Signed) Fred V. Kinkade.

Sworn to before me this 26 day of January, 1904.

(-SEAL-) David Shelby, Notary Public.

- -

Lewis T. Martin, stenographer to the Commission to the Five Civilized Tribes, on oath sates that the above and foregoing is a true, full, and correct copy of the original transcript of the testimony of Bob Thomas filed in Mississippi Choctaw Jacket roll No. 83, at the Choctaw Land Office.

Lewis T. Martin

Sworn to before me this November 22, 1904.

David Shelby
Notary Public

COPY

DEPARTMENT OF THE INTERIOR
COMMISSION TO THE FIVE CIVILIZED TRIBES
CHICKASAW LAND OFFICE
Tishomingo, I. T. April 11, 1904.

In the matter of the selection of an allotment and designation of a homestead for Ransom Thomas, Mississippi Choctaw card 31, Mississippi Choctaw roll No. 85.

Thomas Ransom being first duly sworn testifies as follows

EXAMINATION BY THE COMMISSION:

Q What is your name? A Ransom Thomas.
Q What is your age? A Nineteen.
Q What is your post office address? A Spencerville.
Q What is the name of your father? A Bob Thomas.
Q What is the name of your mother? A Daley Thomas.
Q Are you a full blood Mississippi Choctaw? A Yes.
Q Are you married? A Yes.
Q What is the name of your wife? A Mamie.
Q Who is Mamie's father? A Frank Johnson.
Q Who is Mamie's mother? A I don't know.
Q Is Mamie a full blood Missisppippi Choctaw? A Yes.
Q What is Mamie's post office address in Mississippi? A Avera.

Wife of witness is identified as Mamie Johnson, Mississippi Choctaw card 411, Mississippi Choctaw roll No. 1195

Q Is your wife Mamie living with you now? A No.
Q When did you separate from her? A The 18th day of December.
Q 1903? A Yes.
Q Have either of you been divorced from the other? A No.
Q When were you married to Mamie? A 29th of August, 1901.
Q By whom were you married? A J. J. Courtney.
Q Was he a minister of the gospel? A Justice.

There is offered in evidence marked Exhibit "A" marriage certificate of Ranston B. Thomas and Mimie Johnson.

Q Are you the Ranston B. Thomas mentioned in this marriage certificate? A Yes.
Q Is the Mimie Johnson, the Mamie Johnson who was identified as a full blood Mississippi Choctaw on Fenruary 14, 1903? A Yes.
Q Whwn did you leave Mississippi to come to the Choctaw-Chickasaw country? A Last January a year ago.
Q Did you come directly to the Indian Territory? A Yes.
Q Did you bring your wife Mamie with you at that time? A Yes.
Q Did you brign your wife with you at that time? A Yes.
Q Did you come with your father, Bob Thomas? A Yes.

Reference is made to the testimony of Bob Thomas taken at Atoka, January 8, 1904, relative to the removal to and settlement within the Choctaw-Chickasaw country of himself, his wife and five minor children, Mississippi Choctaw card 31, Mississippi Choctaw roll Nos. 83 to 89 inclusive.

Q Why have you not appeared before this land office before in order to make proof of settlement within the Choctaw-Chickasaw country? A I had no way to get to the Land Office.

Q Did you not know that it was necessary that you appear before the Commission within a year of your identification to make proof of settlement? A Yes but I didn't have any way to get here.

Helen C. Miller being first duly sworn on oath states that as stenographer for the Commission to the Five Civilized Tribes she reported the above proceedings, and that same is a correct transcript of her stenographic notes.

(Signed) Helen C. Miller.

Subscribed and sworn to before me this 12th day of April, 1904.

(-SEAL-) (Signed) J. E. Williams,
Notary Public.

- -

Lewis T. Martin, stenographer to the Commission to the Five Civilized Tribes, on oath states that the above and foregoing is a full, true, and correct copy of a certified copy of the transcript of the testimony of Ransom Thomas, filed at this office in Mississippi Choctaw jacket, roll No. 85.

Lewis T. Martin

Sworn to before me this November 22, 1904.

Edwin Shelly
Notary Public.

DEPARTMENT OF THE INTERIOR,
COMMISSION TO THE FIVE CIVILIZED TRIBES,
CHOCTAW LAND OFFICE.

Atoka, Indian Territory, November 12, 1904.

MCI Card-411 Roll-1195

In the matter of the application of Mamie Johnson, Identified Mississippi Choctaw, card number 411, approved roll number 1195, for the selection of land in allotment.

- - - - - - - - - - - - - - - - - - - -

Mamie Johnson being duly sworn testifies as follows--through Jacob Homer, Official Interpreter.

EXAMINATION BY THE COMMISSION:

Q What is your name? A Mamie Pisachabe.
Q That is your married name, is it? A Yes sir.
Q What was your name before you married Pisachabe? A Mamie Thomas.
Q Were you married more than one time? A I have been married twice
Q What was your maiden name? A Mamie Johnson.
Q What was the name of your father? A Frank Johnson
Q What was the name of your mother? A Josephine Johnson.
Q Where did you live in Mississippi? A In Perry County.
Q Near what post office? A Brown.
Q Did you ever live near Avena? A I don't know.
Q Where was the Commission to the Five Civilized Tribes holding sessions when you went before it? A At Meridian, Mississippi.
Q Are you the identical Mamie Johnson who was on February 14, 1903, identified by the Commission to the Five Civilized Tribes as a Mississippi Choctaw, entitled to an allotment of lands of the Choctaws and Chickasaws? A Yes sir.
Q When did you remove from Mississippi to the Choctaw Nation? A About three years ago.
Q With whom did you come to the Choctaw Nation? A I came with Ransom Thomas and his father and mother and my father.
Q Is Ransom Thomas living now? A Yes sir.
Q Is he in the Choctaw Nation at this time? A Yes sir.
Q Is your father, Frank Johnson, living? A Yes sir, he is living in the Chickasaw Nation.
Q When Frank Johnson first came to the Indian Territory where did he locate? A At Kilgore.

Reference is made to Identified Mississippi Choctaw card No. 110 for the enrollment of Farnk Johnson, proof of settlement within the Choctaw-Chickasaw coubtry made May 18, 1903, Settlement address, Hugo, I. T.

Q Who was Ransom Thomas's father? A Bob Thomas.
Q What was his mother's name? A Daley Thomas.
Q Where is Ransom Thomas living at this time? A On the other side of Kiamitia.
Q What is his post office address? A Spencerville, I. T.

The name of Ransom Thomas appears as number 3 on Identified Mississippi Choctaw card number 31, approved roll number 85; proof of settlement within the Choctaw-Chickasaw country made January 8, 1904; settlement address, Spencerville, I. T.

MCI Card-411--------2:

Q What is the name of your husband that you are living with at this time? A Harrison Pisachabe.
Q How long have you been married to him? A About a year.
Q Are you married to him or just living with him? A Married to him.
Q Were you divorced from Ransom Thomas? A Yes sir.

The name of Harrison Pisachabe appears as No. 1 on Choctaw by blood card No. 3737, approved roll No. 10559.

Q Is this the first time you have appeared before the land offices of the Commission to the Five Civilized Tribes for the purpose of making proof of settlement within the Choctaw-Chickasaw country as a Mississippi Choctaw? A Yes sir, this is the first time.
Q Where are you now living in the Choctaw Nation? A In Kiamitia County.
Q What is your post office address? A Hugo, I. T.
Q Have you been living in the vicinity of Hugo, I. T. since your removal from Mississippi to the Choctaw Nation? A Yes sir.

Reference is made to the testimony of Ransom Thomas, former husband of the witness, taken at Tishomingo, Indian Territory, April 11, 1904, and to the testimony of his father, Bob Thomas, taken at the Choctaw Land Office, Atoka, Indian Territory, January 8, 1904, relative to the marriage of the witness to said Ransom Thomas; also as to the time of her removal to, and settlement within the Choctaw-Chickasaw country, copies of which are attached hereto.

Q How old are you? A Twenty years old.
Q Have you entered into any agreement or contract with any person looking to the sale or incumbrance of any part of the land which you may be permitted to select in allotmnt? A No sir.
Q Where were you living at the time you separated from Ransom Thomas? A On this side of Kiamitia in the Choctaw Nation.
Q And since you were divorced from him you married Harrison Pisachabe? A Yes sir.

Your testimony will be submitted to the Commission to the Five Civilized Tribes at the General Office at Muskogee, Indian Territory, who will pass upon your right to select lands in allotment at this time.

You were identified as a Mississippi Choctaw by the Commission to the Five Civilized Tribes on February 14, 1903, and the treaty of September 25, 1902 covering the allotment of lands to Mississippi Choctaws, requires that proof of residence within the Choctaw-Chickasaw country must be made by each Identified Mississippi Choctaw within one year from the date of such identification; your identification having been made February 14, 1903, more than one year has elapsed.

Witness excused.

- -

Lewis T. Martin, stenographer to the Commission to the Five Civilized Tribes, on oath states that the above and foregoing is a full, true and correct copy of his stenographic notes as taken in said cause November 18, 1904. Lewis T. Martin

Sworn to beforeme this November 22, 1904. [signature], Notary Public

Q Did you not know that it was necessary that you appear before the Commission within a year of your identification to make proof of settlement? A Yes but I didn't have any way to get here.

Helen C. Miller being first duly sworn on oath states that as stenographer for the Commission to the Five Civilized Tribes she reported the above proceedings, and that same is a correct transcript of her stenographic notes.

(Signed) Helen C. Miller.

Subscribed and sworn to before me this 12th day of April, 1904.

(-SEAL-) (Signed) J. E. Williams, Notary Public.

- -

Lewis T. Martin, stenographer to the Commission to the Five Civilized Tribes, on oath states that the above and foregoing is a full, true, and correct copy of a certified copy of the transcript of the testimony of Ransom Thomas, filed at this office in Mississippi Choctaw jacket, roll No. 85.

Lewis T. Martin

Sworn to before me this November 22, 1904.

Notary Public

Miss. Choctaw 1136
2007,2008,2010.

Muskogee, Indian Territory, November 15, 1902.

T. M. Black,

Woodville, Indian Territory,

Dear Sir:

Your letter of November 5, addressed to J. Blair Shoenfelt, Indian Agent, Muskogee, Indian Territory, has been referred to this Commission for reply. You ask therein to be advised if the names of five Mississippi Choctaws, Charley Thomas, Bob Thomas, Elijah Thomas, Frank Johnson and John Hogan, and their families, are on the tribal rolls.

In reply you are advised that it appears from our records that Frank Johnson, of Hickory, Mississippi, and Elijah Thomas, of Augusta, Mississippi, are applicants to this Commission for identification as Mississippi Choctaws; it further appears from the records of this office that Bob Thomas and Charlie Thomas, of Brown, Mississippi, are applicants for the identification of themselves, their wives and their minor children as Mississippi Choctaws. The records further show that all of the above applicants are full blood Choctaw Indians. The Commission has not yet passed upon the rights of these applicants to identification as Mississippi Choctaws, but it is probable that within the near future their applications for identification as full blood Mississippi Choctaws will be passed upon and they will be notified of the action of the Commission.

It does not appear from our records that John Hogan is an applicant for identification as a Mississippi Choctaw under the name of John Hogan. If application has been made by him as such Mississippi it would appear that the same was made under another name.

Respectfully,

Acting Chairman.

Miss. Choctaw
1136, 2007,
2008, 2010.

Muskogee, Indian Territory, November 18, 1902.

T. M. Black,

Woodville, Indian Territory,

Dear Sir:

Receipt is hereby acknowledged of your letter of November 14 asking the status of the following Mississippi Choctaws: Charley Thomas, Bob Thomas and Frank Johnson.

In reply your attention is invited to a letter of the Commission of November 15, 1902, which it is believed fully answers the questions contained in your letter of November 14, 1902.

Respectfully,

Commissioner in Charge.

M C R 1136
M C R 2010

Muskogee, Indian Territory, January 23, 1903.

T. M. Black,

Paris, Texas.

Dear Sir:

Receipt is hereby acknowledged of your letter of the 14th inst., to Mr. David Shelby and by him referred to this Commission for consideration and appropriate action: therein you ask to be advised if the [illegible] of Bob and Charley Thomas complied with the fourteenth article of the treaty of 1830.

In reply to your letter you are informed that it appears from the records of the Commission that Bob Thomas and Charley Thomas are applicants to this Commission for the identification of themselves and families as Mississippi Choctaws. The Commission has not, up to the present time, reached any opinion or decision relative to the rights of these persons to be identified as Mississippi Choctaws, but is now considering their applications and it is probable decisions will be rendered in the near future. The applicants will be duly notified of the action of the Commission and of the forwarding of the records to the Secretary of the Interior.

You are further advised that the Commission cannot take up and pass upon the sufficiency of evidence offered in support of applications for identification as Mississippi Choctaws until such cases are taken up for final consideration and determination.

Respectfully,

Acting Chairman.

M C R 1136
M C R 2010

Muskogee, Indian Territory, January 25, 1903.

T. M. Black,

Paris, Texas.

Dear Sir:

Receipt is hereby acknowledged of your letter of the 17th inst., in which you ask to be advised if Charley Thomas, his wife and five children, and Bob Thomas, his wife, and five children, and Mamie Johnson, who, you state, are full blood Mississippi Choctaws, are enrolled.

In reply to your letter you are advised that it appears from the records of the Commission that Charley Thomas is an applicant for the identification of himself, his wife and five minor children as Mississippi Choctaws, and that Bob Thomas is also an applicant for the identification of himself, his wife and five minor children as Mississippi Choctaws. The Commission has not, up to the present time, reached any opinion or decision relative to the right of the full blood Choctaws residing in Mississippi to be identified as Mississippi Choctaws, but is now considering their applications, and it is probable decisions will be rendered in the near future. Upon the rendition thereof, such applicants will be duly notified of the action of the Commission and of the

T. M. Black---2

forwarding of the records to the Secretary of the Interior.

It does not appear from the records of the Commission that any application has been made for the identification as a Mississippi Choctaw of Mamie Johnson, daughter of Bob Thomas: if she is an applicant, kindly advise the Commission when and where and under what name she made application and such other date as will enable the Commission to identifi her as an applicant, when your enquiry regarding her status as a Mississippi Choctaw will receive further consideration.

Respectfully,

Acting Chairman.

2748
M C R--- 2087
1136

Muskogee, Indian Territory, January 28, 1903.

Ed P. Scott,

Paris, Texas.

Dear Sir:

Receipt is hereby acknowledged of your letter of the 19th inst., from Mr. Homer Needles and by him referred to this Commission for consideration and appropriate action. Therein you ask to be advised if "Bob Thomas, Kit Reed and Tom Fortune, all full blood Mississippi Choctaws, have been enrolled."

In reply you are informed that it appears from the records in the possession of the Commission that Bob Thomas, Kit Reed and Tom Fortune are applicants to this Commission for the identification of themselves and families as Mississippi Choctaws. The Commission has not, up to the present time, reached any opinion or decision relative to the right of these persons to be identified as such Mississippi Choctaws but is now considering their applications and it is probable that decisions will be rendered in the near future. The several applicants will be duly notified of the action of the Commission and of the forwarding of the records to the Secretary of the Interior.

Respectfully,

Acting Chairman.

M C R 1136
M C R 3010

Muskogee, Indian Territory, February 9, 1903.

T. M. Black,

Woodville, Indian Territory.

Dear Sir:

Your letter of January 17, 1903, addressed to the Secretary of the Interior, has been by him referred to this Commission for consideration and appropriate action.

You ask therein if the ancestors of Bob and Charley Thomas, full blood Mississippi Choctaws, complied with article fourteen of the treaty of 1830. You state that you want to move these Choctaws to the Indian Territory if they are going to get a claim. You also ask for a copy of of the treaty of 1830 between the United States and the Choctaw Nation, and a copy of the treaty of Dancing Rabbit Creek.

In reply to your letter you are informed that it appears from our records that Bob and Charley Thomas are both full blood Mississippi Choctaws, and are applicants to this Commission for the identification of themselves and their families as Mississippi Choctaws, but the Commission has not yet passed upon their rights to identification as such full blood Mississippi Choctaws.

You are further advised that the treaty between the United States and the Choctaw Nation, concluded September 27, 1830,

T M Black------2

sometimes called the treaty of Dancing Rabbit Creek, may be found in volume 7 of the United States Statutes, page 333.

There is enclosed herewith a copy of the act of Congress of July 1, 1902, which was ratified by the Choctaw and Chickasaw Nations on September 25, 1902, and your attention is invited to sections forty-one, forty-two, forty-three, and forty-four thereof.

Respectfully,

Acting Chairman.

Enc.Choctaw-Chickasaw agreement.

M C R 1136

Muskogee, Indian Territory, April 30, 1903.

Ransom Thomas,

Miah, Indian Territory.

Dear Sir:

It appears from our records that on the 23rd day of March 1903, there was received at this office the affidavit of the mother, Mamie Thomas, and that of the midwife, Easter James, relative to the birth on the 8th day of June, 1902, of Anison Thomas, infant son of Ransom and Mamie Thomas.

It further appears from our records that on December 18, 1900, Bob Thomas appeared before the Commission at Hattiesburg, Mississippi, and made application for the identification of himself, his wife Daily Thomas, and minor children Ransom, Berry, Emeline, Sam and Samawail Thomas, as Mississippi Choctaws.

If you are the identical Ransom Thomas for whom application was made at that time, you are requested to inform the Commission when and where you were married to your wife Mamie and whether or not application has heretofore been made to this Commission for her identification as a Mississippi Choctaw. If application has heretofore been made for your wife Mamie Thomas, please state when and where and under what name such application was made and how much Choctaw blood your wife possesses.

R T 2

This matter should receive your immediate attention as no further steps can be taken in the matter of the application for the identification of your infant child as a Mississippi Choctaw until this information is furnished.

Respectfully,

Chairman.

M.C.R. 2008
" 1136
" 2007
" 2010

Muskogee, Indian Territory, February 13, 1903.

Bob Thomas,

Hugo, Indian Territory.

Dear Sir:

Receipt is hereby acknowledged of the joint letter of yourself, Charlie Thomas, Elijah Thomas and Frank Johnson, advising that Hugo, Indian Territory, is your present address.

The same has been made a matter of record with the Commission.

Respectfully,

Acting Chairman.

M.C.R. 1136

COPY.

Muskogee, Indian Territory, February 21, 1903.

Mansfield, McMurray & Cornish,
Attorneys for the Choctaw and Chickasaw Nations,
South McAlester, Indian Territory.

Gentlemen:

Enclosed herewith you will find a copy of the decision of the Commission rendered February 14, 1903, identifying Bob Thomas, his wife Daley Thomas, and minor children Ransom Thomas, Berry Thomas, Emeline Thomas, Sam Thomas and Samawail Thomas as Mississippi Choctaw Indians under the provisions of the forty-first section of the act of Congress approved July 1, 1902, (32 Stats., 641).

You are hereby advised that you will be allowed fifteen days from the date hereof, in which to file with this Commission such protest as you desire to make against the action of the Commission in identifying the said Bob Thomas, his wife and children as Mississippi Choctaws, and make satisfactory proof of service of said protest upon the applicants herein.

If you fail to file such protest within the time allowed, the names of the applicants herein will be placed upon the schedule of duly identified Mississippi Choctaws now being prepared by this Commission.

Respectfully,

(SIGNED)

Tams Bixby.

~~Acting~~ Chairman.

Registered.
Enc. H.M.V. 20

M.C.R. 1136.

COPY

Muskogee, Indian Territory, March 11, 1903.

Bob Thomas,

Hugo, Indian Territory.

Dear Sir:

Enclosed herewith you will find a copy of the decision of the Commission to the Five Civilized Tribes, rendered February 14, 1903, identifying yourself, your wife, Daley Thomas, and your five minor children, Ransom, Berry, Emeline, Sam and Samawail Thomas, as Mississippi Choctaw Indians under the provisions of Section 41 of the Act of Congress approved July 1, 1902,(32 Stats.,641).

If you remove to the Choctaw-Chickasaw country, Indian Territory, before August 14, 1903, you will have six months from that date, or until February 14, 1904, within which to make proof of such removal and settlement at the office of the Commission at Atoka, Choctaw Nation, or Tishomingo, Chickasaw Nation.

Respectfully,

SIGNED: Tams Bixby

Chairman.

Registered.

Enc. 1136.

M C R 1136

Muskogee, Indian Territory, March 31, 1903.

Bob Thomas,

Hugo, Indian Territory.

Dear Sir:

Receipt is hereby acknowledged of the affidavit of the mother, Mamie Thomas, and that of the midwife, Easter James, relative to the birth of your infant son, Anison Thomas, June 8, 1902. The same have been filed with the record in your case.

Respectfully,

Chairman.

M C R 1136

Muskogee, Indian Territory, July 10, 1903.

Ransom Thomas,

Spencerville, Indian Territory.

Dear Sir:

Receipt is hereby acknowledged of your letter of June 29, 1903, inclosing marriage license and certificate between Ransom Thomas and Mamie Johnson, offered in support of the Mississippi Choctaw case of Ransom Thomas, et al. The same has been filed with the record in said case.

Respectfully,

Commissioner in Charge.

No. 1136

For Identification as a Mississippi Choctaw.

Date DEC 18 1900

Name Bob Thomas.

Age 37. Blood full.

Post Office, Brown, Miss

Father: Jake Thomas - dead.

Mother: Martha Thomas - dead

Claims through both

WIFE:

Daily Thomas. - 33.

FATHER: Unkkiatubbee. - dead

MOTHER: ~~~~~~ - dead

Children:

Ransom Thomas 15.

Berry " " 13.

Emeline " " 10.

Sam " " 5.

Samawait " " 3.

Stenographer.

Myra Young.

FINAL ROLL

OF

MISSISSIPPI CHOCTAWS

Ages calculated to September 25, 1902.

[Dawes]

FINAL ROLL OF MISSISSIPPI CHOCTAWS

Ages calculated to September 25, 1902.

Roll No.	Name	Age	Sex	Blood
1	Hussey, William Hancock	8	M	1-16
2	Hussey, Alvin McDowell	3	M	1-16
3	Roe, J. Folsom	44	M	1-4
4	Roe, Jeannette C.	17	F	1-8
5	Hancock, Jubal A.	26	M	1-8
6	Gibson, Alex	24	M	Full
7	Johnson, Frank	32	M	Full
8	Johnson, Allen	9	M	Full
9	Johnson, Lela	7	F	Full
10	Baptiste, Joseph, Jr.	26	M	Full
11	Taylor, Baptiste	26	M	Full
12	Taylor, Elizabeth	28	F	Full
13	Taylor, Lem	10	M	Full
14	Taylor, Stanley	5	M	Full
15	Taylor, Louisa	3	F	Full
16	Tom, Lina	80	F	Full
17	Tom, Amos	11	M	Full
18	Tom, Leona	3	F	Full
19	Bansby, Jacob	29	M	Full
20	Billey, Cornelius	15	M	Full
21	Billey, Eliza	33	F	Full
22	Bob, Jim	10	M	Full
23	Billey, Wicks	8	M	Full
24	Cottie, Annie	12	F	Full
25	Wallace, Tom	21	M	Full
26	Isom, John	47	M	Full
27	Isom, Mary	41	F	Full
28	Isom, Rosie	6	F	Full
29	Isom, John, Jr.	5	M	Full
30	Philip, Nasey	14	F	Full
31	Davis, Tom	47	M	Full
32	Davis, Rena	47	F	Full
33	Davis, Walton	19	M	Full
34	Davis, Alice	17	F	Full
35	Davis, Emma	15	F	Full
36	Davis, Oscar	10	M	Full
37	Davis, John	6	M	Full
38	Ellis, Habett	19	M	Full
39	Gibson, Walter	20	F	Full
40	In-pun-nobbee, Mingo	69	M	Full
41	Chubbee, Cully	15	M	Full
42	Kelly, Joe	24	M	Full
43	Kelly, Lizzie	23	F	Full
44	Willis, Mary	52	F	Full
45	Willis, Silly	19	F	Full
46	Willis, Mandy	15	F	Full
47	Willis, Anna	5	F	Full
48	Willis, Abel	4	M	Full
49	Thomas, Bob	57	M	Full
50	Thomas, Daley	33	F	Full
51	Thomas, Ransom	15	M	Full
52	Thomas, Berry	13	F	Full
53	Thomas, Emeline	10	F	Full
54	Thomas, Sam	6	M	Full
55	Thomas, Samawell	3	M	Full
56	Cooper, Jacob	41	M	Full
57	Cooper, Julia	36	F	Full
58	Cooper, Foster	13	M	Full
59	Cooper, Janie	8	F	Full
60	Cooper, Susie	3	F	Full
61	Cooper, Georgie	1	M	Full
62	Davis, Alex	22	M	Full
63	Joshua, Levisa	12	F	Full
64	Toby, William	27	M	Full
65	Jackson, Melvina	45	F	Full
66	Jackson, Marcelene	15	F	Full
67	Solomon, Winnie	68	F	Full
68	Jackson, Henry	23	M	Full
69	Jackson, Sealy	21	F	Full
70	Tom, Ablean	50	F	Full
71	Tom, John	34	M	Full
72	Tom, Sallie	3	F	Full
73	Sampson, Johnson	42	M	Full
74	Sampson, Sallie	41	F	Full
75	Sampson, Senie	16	F	Full
76	Sampson, Jim	14	M	Full
77	Sampson, George	12	M	Full
78	Sampson, Sealy Ann	50	F	Full
79	Sampson, Pauline	8	F	Full
80	Sampson, Gus	6	M	Full
81	Sampson, Bennie	4	M	Full
82	Sampson, Mary Ann	2	F	Full
83	Golden, Abe	28	M	Full
84	Golden, Louisa	27	F	Full
85	Golden, Mollie	3	F	Full
86	Byrnes, Cricket	23	F	Full
87	Sweeney, Robert	26	M	Full
88	Sweeney, Ara Ann	23	F	Full
89	Sweeney, Joseph	2	M	Full
90	Sweeney, Frank	1	M	Full
91	Smith, Seborn	38	M	Full
92	Smith, Emma	40	F	Full
93	Amos, Dan	12	M	Full
94	Sam, Huddleston	21	M	Full
95	Willis, John (Tom-ola-tubbee)	53	M	Full
96	Willis, Susie Ann (or Susie Ann)	42	F	Full
97	Willis, Lee	14	M	Full
98	Willis, Adolphus	8	M	Full
99	Willis, Will	6	M	Full
100	Willis, Walter	5	M	Full
101	Willis, Mary	1	F	Full
102	Hawkins, Billy	48	M	Full
103	Hawkins, Jerden	12	M	Full
104	York, Dixon	42	M	Full
105	York, Josephine	38	F	Full
106	York, Sydney	19	M	Full
107	York, Bettie	14	F	Full
108	York, Sallie	11	F	Full
109	York, Lee	9	M	Full
110	York, Alice	4	F	Full
111	York, Lola	1	F	Full
112	Wallace, Jim	27	M	Full
113	Wallace, Mary	22	F	Full
114	Toby, Lewis	50	M	Full
115	Toby, Ellen	60	F	Full
116	Wallace, Jim	26	M	Full
117	Wallace, Lizzie	20	F	Full
118	Wallace, Walter	11	M	Full
119	Wallace, David	5	M	Full
120	Wallace, Mary	1	F	Full
121	Jasper, John	42	M	Full
122	Isaac, Lucy	36	F	Full
123	Isaac, Clinton	18	M	Full
124	Isaac, Tennis	15	M	Full
125	Isaac, Haimond	12	M	Full
126	Isaac, Hollis	8	M	Full
127	Isaac, Nabors	4	M	Full
128	Isaac, Tommie	3	M	Full
129	Isaac, Mandy	2	F	Full
130	Foley, Davis	21	M	Full
131	Jim, Lucy (Lo-mah)	21	F	Full
132	Phillip, Wesley	29	M	Full
133	Phillip, Maggie	4	F	Full
134	Wilkerson, Sam (or John)	52	M	Full
135	Wilkerson, Annie	27	F	Full
136	Wilkerson, Mollie	9	F	Full
137	Wilkerson, Lemie	8	F	Full
138	Wilkerson, Ietralen	3	F	Full
139	Wilkerson, Mary	1	F	Full
140	Wilkerson, Cora	1	F	Full
141	Postoak, Jack	27	M	Full
142	Postoak, Fee Kelly	6	M	Full
143	Postoak, Sam	2	M	Full
144	Willis, Mack	53	M	Full
145	Dixon, John	38	M	Full
146	Dixon, Feely	18	F	Full
147	Guss, Nancy	20	F	Full
148	Guss, Sina	16	F	Full
149	Guss, Rafe	12	M	Full
150	Guss, Alice	8	F	Full
151	Shoemake, Jackson (La-we-tubbee)	48	M	Full
152	Shoemake, Jennie	36	F	Full
153	Shoemake, Watson	7	M	Full

Roll No.	Name	Age	Sex	Blood
154	Shoemake, Ernest	5	M	Full
155	Shoemake, Manzi	3	F	Full
156	Shoemake, Ada	1	M	Full
157	Shoemake, Rhoda	1	F	Full
158	Phillip, Sock	33	M	Full
159	Phillip, Pica Tinsey	20	M	Full
160	Phillip, Bettie	18	F	Full
161	Phillip, Lewis	10	M	Full
162	Phillip, Celia Ann	3	F	Full
163	Sockey, Will	22	M	Full
164	Willis, John	58	M	Full
165	Willis, Hickman	19	M	Full
166	Willis, Margaret	17	F	Full
167	Willis, Lillie	8	F	Full
168	Willis, Fannie	7	F	Full
169	Willis, Elma	3	F	Full
170	Willis, Sam Houston	1	M	Full
171	Wilson, Billy	38	M	Full
172	Wilson, Maggie	33	F	Full
173	Wilson, Sampson	12	M	Full
174	Wilson, Sammie	8	M	Full
175	Wilson, Jimmie	7	M	Full
176	Wilson, Freeman	4	M	Full
177	Wilson, Dick Russell	1	M	Full
178	Toby, John	22	M	Full
179	Sampson, John	37	M	Full
180	Sampson, Louisiana	36	F	Full
181	Sampson, Emeline	16	F	Full
182	Sampson, Steve	14	M	Full
183	Sampson, Oscar	11	M	Full
184	Sampson, Arlone	9	F	Full
185	Sampson, Spencer	7	M	Full
186	Sampson, Artis	6	M	Full
187	Sampson, Cenie	3	F	Full
188	Billey, Ben	40	M	Full
189	Bull, John (On-ta-tubbee)	80	M	Full
190	Willie, Billy	39	M	Full
191	Simmons, Leona	18	F	Full
192	Simmons, Robert	9	M	Full
193	Simmons, Maggie	8	F	Full
194	Simmons, King	5	M	Full
195	Simmons, Pigfoot	2	M	Full
196	Simmons, Mamie	1	F	Full
197	Johnson, Louis	20	M	Full
198	Johnson, Mattie	18	F	Full
199	Wallace, John	53	M	Full
200	Wallace, Leona	30	F	Full
201	Wallace, William	15	M	Full
202	Baptiste, Joseph	46	M	Full
203	Baptiste, Felice	40	F	Full
204	Baptiste, Louise	14	F	Full
205	Baptiste, Madlina	12	F	Full
206	Baptiste, Sammy	10	M	Full
207	Baptiste, Johnnie	6	M	Full
208	Lewis, Smith	28	M	Full
209	Lewis, Chuly	25	F	Full
210	Lewis, Jacob	4	M	Full
211	Charley, Emil	18	M	Full
212	Postoak, Sarah	68	F	Full
213	Chubbee, Leanna	53	F	Full
214	Wallace, Comby	17	M	Full
215	John, Sidney	23	M	Full
216	John, Bettie	28	F	Full
217	John, Eva	3	F	Full
218	John, Elis	2	F	Full
219	Jackeway, Cora	12	F	Full
220	Johnson, Henry	23	M	Full
221	Johnson, Rosey	23	F	Full
222	Johnson, Amos	1	M	Full
223	Johnson, Thomas	1	M	Full
224	Johnson, Will	24	M	Full
225	Johnson, Frank	60	M	Full
226	Johnson, John	73	M	Full
227	Johnson, Margaret	68	F	Full
228	Johnson, Fayette	26	M	Full
229	Johnson, Isby	27	F	Full
230	Johnson, Oscar	5	F	Full
231	Johnson, Jimmie	4	M	Full
232	Johnson, Lona	2	F	Full
233	A-me-ah-tubbee, Lewis	52	M	Full
234	A-me-ah-tubbee, Henry	18	M	Full
235	A-me-ah-tubbee, Sidney	12	M	Full
236	Pistemah, Nancy	78	F	Full
237	Gibson, Ona	17	F	Full
238	York, Scott	43	M	Full
239	York, John	19	M	Full
240	York, Taylor	17	M	Full
241	York, Evan	15	M	Full
242	Bob, Winnie	60	F	Full
243	Lewis, Young	10	M	Full
244	Jim, Ellen	46	F	Full
245	Austin, Stewart	21	M	Full
246	Austin, Alice	12	F	Full
247	Phillips, Meeks	22	M	Full
248	Wickson, Sim	24	M	Full
249	Wickson, David	2	M	Full
250	Bob, Morris	45	M	Full
251	Johnson, Andy	24	M	Full
252	Allen, John (or Dixey John) (A-chok-mat-ek-tubbee)	45	M	Full
253	Polk, Jim	54	M	Full
254	Polk, Melissie	33	F	Full
255	Morris, Clemmans	16	M	Full
256	Morris, Frank	14	M	Full
257	Morris, Tracy	12	M	Full
258	Davis, Jeff	55	M	Full
259	Primus, Ben	22	M	Full
260	Eliz, Davis	32	M	Full
261	Ned, Annie (Mehiolimah)	33	F	Full
262	Ned, John	15	M	Full
263	Ned, Francis	12	M	Full
264	Ned, Frank	8	M	Full
265	Ned, Ernest	5	M	Full
266	Ned, Reuben	1	M	Full
267	Simpson, Jefferson	47	M	Full
268	Simpson, Sallie	36	F	Full
269	Simpson, Marcelline	9	F	Full
270	Simpson, Backus	7	M	Full
271	Simpson, Barnett	5	M	Full
272	Simpson, Mary Corria	1	F	Full
273	Billey, William	38	M	Full
274	Billey, Fannie	30	F	Full
275	Billey, Oma	12	F	Full
276	Billey, Wilson	6	M	Full
277	Billey, Katie	3	F	Full
278	Billey, Enoch	1	M	Full
279	Boston, Lizzie	30	F	Full
280	Boston, Bennie	10	M	Full
281	Boston, Dora	8	F	Full
282	Betsey, Wilson	27	M	Full
283	Betsey, Nannie	23	F	Full
284	Betsey, Preston	6	M	Full
285	Betsey, Eva	4	F	Full
286	Betsey, Cornelius	1	M	Full
287	Tomby, Franklin	30	M	Full
288	Tomby, Fannie	23	F	Full
289	Tomby, Sibera	6	F	Full
290	Tomby, Limmer	1	F	Full
291	Morris, Watkins	25	M	Full
292	Jackson, Becky	60	F	Full
293	Thomas, Smith	22	M	Full
294	Barcus, Bob	22	M	Full
295	Old Hannah	75	F	Full
296	Tookolo, Sealy	50	F	Full
297	Tookolo, Leo Jim	2	M	Full
298	Williamson, Ben (Ni-nee-a-tubbee)	41	M	Full
299	Williamson, Amie	41	F	Full
300	Williamson, Joe	19	M	Full
301	Williamson, Pres	11	M	Full
302	Williamson, Rosie	5	F	Full
303	Neal, Jeff D.	28	M	Full
304	Neal, Dora	38	F	Full
305	Neal, Cora	3	F	Full
306	Neal, Earnest	1	M	Full
307	Lewis, David	31	M	Full
308	Lewis, Emily	2	F	Full
309	Simpson, Becky	24	F	Full
310	Simpson, Leslie	2	F	Full
311	Billey, Alice	36	F	Full
312	Billey, Nannie	8	F	Full
313	Billey, Clay	4	M	Full
314	Meely, Leanna	45	F	Full
315	Meely, Kelley	16	M	Full
316	Meely, Botman	14	M	Full
317	Meely, Eunice	8	F	Full
318	Meely, Sallie	6	F	Full
319	Willis, Riley	26	M	Full
320	Willis, Lena	24	F	Full
321	Arkansas, Susan	67	F	Full
322	Reese, Salina	21	F	Full

Roll No.	Name	Age	Sex	Blood
323	Reese, Manuel	3	M	Full
324	Johnson, John	65	M	Full
325	Johnson, Nancy	50	F	Full
326	Johnson, Hickman	18	M	Full
327	Johnson, Albert	3	M	Full
328	Smith, Mollie	35	F	Full
329	Smith, Amon	11	M	Full
330	Smith, Sibbie	6	F	Full
331	Smith, Martin	3	M	Full
332	Postoak, William	30	M	Full
333	Davis, Frank	20	M	Full
334	Neal, John (Me-ah-ta-kubbee)	52	M	Full
335	Lewis, Sina	18	F	Full
336	Bob, Sallie	2	F	Full
337	Billey, Frank	24	M	Full
338	Billey, Lilly	23	F	Full
339	Bertis, Bill	51	M	Full
340	Bertis, Niah	50	F	Full
341	Bertis, Sam	15	M	Full
342	Bertis, Dixie	8	F	Full
343	Brokeshoulder, Morris	28	M	Full
344	Brokeshoulder, Martha	25	F	Full
345	Brokeshoulder, Obediah W.	4	M	Full
346	Brokeshoulder, Severa M.	2	F	Full
347	Jim, Stephen	65	M	Full
348	Jim, Betsy	60	F	Full
349	Billey, Rena	30	F	Full
350	Billey, Charles B.	10	M	Full
351	Billey, Dawson	7	M	Full
352	Billey, Ormand	2	M	Full
353	James, Mollie	24	F	Full
354	James, Jeff	1	M	Full
355	Johnson, Wallace	57	M	Full
356	Johnson, Mary	56	F	Full
357	Johnson, Effie	4	F	Full
358	Tuffamah, Ishaman	53	M	Full
359	Tuffamah, Suella	21	F	Full
360	Tuffamah, Moses	3	M	Full
361	Tuffamah, Emma	1	F	Full
362	Jackson, Jim	30	M	Full
363	Reese, Fannie	15	F	Full
364	Willis, Robison	30	M	Full
365	Willis, Lizzie	24	F	Full
366	Willis, Davis	7	M	Full
367	Willis, Ballison	4	M	Full
368	Thompson, Isaac	39	M	Full
369	Thompson, Betsy	41	F	Full
370	Thompson, Jannie	15	M	Full
371	Thompson, Sarah	14	F	Full
372	Thompson, Arthur	11	M	Full
373	Thompson, Leonie	8	F	Full
374	Johnson, Jim	54	M	Full
375	Johnson, Amie	52	F	Full
376	Johnson, Lottie	8	F	Full
377	Smith, Jeff	22	M	Full
378	Smith, Mary Jane	20	F	Full
379	Smith, Williamson	4	M	Full
380	Smith, Emma	1	F	Full
381	Smith, Isabel		F	Full
382	Smith, Richardson	27	M	Full
383	Smith, Bettie	25	F	Full
384	Smith, Doyle	6	M	Full
385	Smith, Louina	2	F	Full
386	Williamson, Joe	45	M	Full
387	Williamson, Deanna	42	F	Full
388	Williamson, Steve Smith	16	M	Full
389	Williamson, Malissa	6	F	Full
390	Hickman, John	33	M	Full
391	Hickman, Dennis	22	M	Full
392	Hickman, Ben	11	M	Full
393	Williams, Rainy	23	F	Full
394	Williams, Bessie	7	F	Full
395	Williams, Maggie	5	F	Full
396	Williams, Cathlena	3	F	Full
397	Williams, Micheal	1	M	Full
398	Jamison, Hattie	20	F	Full
399	Alex, Polly	65	F	Full
400	Lewis, Jim	56	M	Full
401	Lewis, Moseley	13	M	Full
402	Lewis, Mary	7	F	Full
403	Lewis, Sarah	14	F	Full
404	Shoemaker, Billy	77	M	Full
405	Shoemaker, Eliza	56	F	Full
406	Scott, Emil	13	M	Full

Roll No.	Name	Age	Sex	Blood
407	Neal, Nancy	50	F	Full
408	Lemons, Sallie	80	F	Full
409	John, Lewis	28	M	Full
410	John, Simpson	4	M	Full
411	Wilson, Sam	38	M	Full
412	Stephen, Jim Polk	22	M	Full
413	Stephen, Agnes	18	F	Full
414	Rasha, Mary	37	F	Full
415	Rasha, Jim	13	M	Full
416	Rasha, John	12	M	Full
417	Williams, Jack	25	M	Full
418	Williams, Emaline	23	F	Full
419	Williams, Mamie	7	F	Full
420	Williams, Smith	4	M	Full
421	Stricken from roll.			
422	Johnnie, Lucy	30	F	Full
423	Johnnie, Hickman	14	M	Full
424	Johnnie, Sutt	11	M	Full
425	Johnnie, Criset	9	F	Full
426	Johnnie, George G.	5	M	Full
427	Johnnie, Freeney	1	F	Full
428	Johnson, Willie	24	M	Full
429	Jackson, Elder	70	M	Full
430	Willis, Jim	13	M	Full
431	Jeff, Elian	21	F	Full
432	Primus, Seaby	21	F	Full
433	Willis, Wallace	37	M	Full
434	Willis, Nancy	27	F	Full
435	Willis, Fannie	14	F	Full
436	Willis, Charlie	8	M	Full
437	Willis, Eddie	5	M	Full
438	Willis, Moses	1	M	Full
439	Frazer, Jacoway	40	M	Full
440	Frazer, Frank	7	M	Full
441	Frazer, John	5	M	Full
442	Frazer, Sadie	4	F	Full
443	Frazer, Henry	2	M	Full
444	Baptiste, Emily (Chumpa-honah)	76	F	Full
445	Umber, Ida	28	F	Full
446	Umber, Joe	7	M	Full
447	Umber, Minnie	3	F	Full
448	Horton, Bob	11	M	Full
449	York, Pauline	30	F	Full
450	York, William	2	M	Full
451	Pis-tubbee, Horace	40	M	Full
452	Pis-tubbee, Lena	32	F	Full
453	Pis-tubbee, Mattie	7	F	Full
454	Pis-tubbee, Selsah	4	F	Full
455	Pis-tubbee, Maggie	1	F	Full
456	Philip, Nancy	18	F	Full
457	Williamson, Flemus	21	M	Full
458	Williams, Smith	45	M	Full
459	Jim, Austin	22	M	Full
460	Jim, Ott	23	F	Full
461	Jim, Martha	10	F	Full
462	Jim, Bessie	4	F	Full
463	Shoemaker, Willie	38	M	Full
464	Shoemaker, Lucy	35	F	Full
465	Shoemaker, Joe	12	M	Full
466	Shoemaker, Amie	9	F	Full
467	Shoemaker, Dock	7	M	Full
468	Shoemaker, Fannie	5	F	Full
469	Shoemaker, Dan	2	M	Full
470	Philip, Thomas	24	M	Full
471	Philip, Louisa	22	F	Full
472	Philip, John Lumpkin	1	M	Full
473	Tom, Thomas	15	M	Full
474	Johnson, Isaac	65	M	Full
475	Johnson, Susie (Ah-ho-ho-ka)	45	F	Full
476	Johnson, Sallie	13	F	Full
477	Johnson, Painey	8	F	Full
478	Johnson, Mattie	3	F	Full
479	Peter, Emaly	35	F	Full
480	Peter, Nathan	6	M	Full
481	Thompson, Simmons	22	M	Full
482	Thompson, Callie	24	F	Full
483	Billy, George	32	M	Full
484	Billy, Minerva	30	F	Full
485	Billy, Lee	1	M	Full
486	Tubbee, Columbus	43	M	Full
487	Tubbee, Willis	48	M	Full
488	Tubbee, Martha	42	F	Full
489	Tubbee, Lucy	12	F	Full
490	Tubbee, Ada	7	F	Full

Roll No.	Name	Age	Sex	Blood
491	Cunnatomby, Thompson	54	M	Full
492	Cunnatomby, Sealy	53	F	Full
493	Robinson, Dilese	40	F	Full
494	Robinson, Annie	1	F	Full
495	Simpson, Jennie	21	F	Full
496	Simpson, Lewis	51	M	Full
497	Simpson, Adaline	20	F	Full
498	Simpson, George	20	M	Full
499	Simpson, Simms	12	M	Full
500	Simpson, Johnnie	10	M	Full
501	Simpson, Celia	7	F	Full
502	Simpson, Leta	2	F	Full
503	Simpson, Cinda	1	F	Full
504	Bull, Robert E.	22	M	Full
505	York, Pickens	20	M	Full
506	York, Nannie	10	F	Full
507	Tookolo, William O.	52	M	Full
508	Tookolo, Lillie	18	F	Full
509	Bob, Willis	57	M	Full
510	Bob, Betsie	42	F	Full
511	Sam, Tilwa	14	M	Full
512	Bob, Johnnie	1	M	Full
513	Ah-no-sa-chubbee	83	M	Full
514	Lewis, John	51	M	Full
515	Taylor, Lawrence	21	M	Full
516	Post-Oak, Malissa	41	F	Full
517	Wickson, Mike	22	M	Full
518	Wickson, Amie	28	F	Full
519	Wickson, Cleo	7	F	Full
520	Wickson, Leotie	6	F	Full
521	Wickson, Nancy	3	F	Full
522	Wickson, Holiston	1	M	Full
523	Stemons, Eliza	48	F	Full
524	Foley, Betsie	45	F	Full
525	Foley, Oscar	18	M	Full
526	Foley, Stella	6	F	Full
527	Chubbee, Susie	49	F	Full
528	Chubbee, Rosanna	24	F	Full
529	Chubbee, Julia	22	F	Full
530	Chubbee, Lucy	19	F	Full
531	Chubbee, Agnes	17	F	Full
532	Chubbee, Anna	5	F	Full
533	Chubbee, Janie	7	F	Full
534	Chubbee, Willie	8	M	Full
535	Chubbee, Pink	2	F	Full
536	Washington, Billy	41	M	Full
537	Washington, Liza	19	F	Full
538	Washington, Hannah	17	F	Full
539	Washington, Martha	14	F	Full
540	York, Solomon (Tuck-a-lum-bee)	56	M	Full
541	Walter, Martha	26	F	Full
542	Walter, Robert	5	M	Full
543	Sampson, Lillie	21	F	Full
544	Sampson, Salonie	6	M	Full
545	Simpson, Gill	22	M	Full
546	Simpson, Mertine	8	F	Full
547	York, Rufus	53	M	Full
548	York, Malissa	46	F	Full
549	York, Ida	18	F	Full
550	York, Jamison	12	M	Full
551	York, Jesse	7	M	Full
552	York, Annie	4	F	Full
553	John, Sam	66	M	Full
554	John, Nancy	62	F	Full
555	West, John	28	M	Full
556	Carter, Nettie Frances	21	F	1-8
557	Lewis, Jim	40	M	Full
558	Thompson, Ben	36	M	Full
559	Thompson, Martha	35	F	Full
560	Thompson, Leona	15	F	Full
561	Thompson, Thomas	11	M	Full
562	Thompson, Maggie	8	F	Full
563	Morris, L. P.	22	M	Full
564	Morris, Bessie	18	F	Full
565	Billey, Young	56	M	Full
566	Billey, Sallie	40	F	Full
567	Billey, Fabie	17	M	Full
568	Billey, Alan	12	M	Full
569	Billey, Betty	8	F	Full
570	Billey, Ina	4	F	Full
571	Billey, Charley	2	M	Full
572	Willis, John (Il-le-ah-Tubbee)	69	M	Full
573	Williams, Tom	26	M	Full
574	Williams, Mary		F	Full
575	Williams, Chloris	17	F	Full
576	Williams, Sam	18	M	Full
577	Williams, Harvey	6	M	Full
578	Williams, Susan	4	F	Full
579	Wickson, John (Con-ne-ma-tubbee)	60	M	Full
580	Bull, Pink	25	M	Full
581	Bull, Emma	17	F	Full
582	Willis, Charley	34	M	Full
583	Billey, Sam	24	M	Full
584	Alderman, Christian	25	M	Full
585	Johnson, Taylor	66	M	Full
586	Johnson, Jennie	70	F	Full
587	Cooper, James	32	M	Full
588	Cooper, Annie	20	F	Full
589	Cooper, Lonnie	5	M	Full
590	Cooper, Nancy	2	F	Full
591	Cooper, Mary	1	F	Full
592	Simon, Albert	26	M	Full
593	Simon, Mary Jane	26	F	Full
594	Simon, Amos	8	M	Full
595	Mose, John	49	M	Full
596	Mose, Lula	32	F	Full
597	Mose, Steen	20	M	Full
598	Mose, Frank	8	M	Full
599	Mose, William Davis	3	M	Full
600	Mose, Lark Davis	1	M	Full
601	John, Big (Ondocha-tubbee)	74	M	Full
602	John, Sally	68	F	Full
603	John, Charley	21	M	Full
604	John, Lena	9	F	Full
605	John, Julia	7	F	Full
606	Jack, Jim	24	M	Full
607	Dansby, Lewis	52	M	Full
608	Jack, Billy	53	M	Full
609	Jack, Leanna	52	F	Full
610	Jack, Minnie	17	F	Full
611	Jack, Nettie	16	F	Full
612	Jack, Camille	7	F	Full
613	Sturdevant, Charley	60	M	Full
614	Johnson, John P.	29	M	Full
615	Dixon, Julia	22	F	Full
616	Dixon, Columbus	40	M	Full
617	Dixon, Sallie	58	F	Full
618	Martin, Bettie	18	F	Full
619	Philip, Mack	25	M	Full
620	Philip, Sallie	22	F	Full
621	Philip, Arlena	4	F	Full
622	Philip, Mary	1	F	Full
623	Philip, Winston	25	M	Full
624	Philip, Tom	21	M	Full
625	Dansby, Isom	52	M	Full
626	Dixon, John	30	M	Full
627	Dixon, Mary	39	F	Full
628	Dixon, Leanna	8	F	Full
629	Dixon, Sarah Jane	6	F	Full
630	Dixon, Lena	4	F	Full
631	Dixon, Beauty	1	F	Full
632	Billey, Richmond	27	M	Full
633	Billey, Martha	23	F	Full
634	Billey, Lizzie	3	F	Full
635	Billey, Harrison	8	M	Full
636	Billey, Sallie	80	F	Full
637	Sam, Dennis	18	M	Full
638	Sam, Acy	16	F	Full
639	Bull, Houston	20	M	Full
640	Sam, Thomas	68	M	Full
641	Sam, Minnie	32	F	Full
642	Sam, Amos	18	M	Full
643	Sam, Joe	15	M	Full
644	Sam, George	13	M	Full
645	Sam, Delia	11	F	Full
646	Sam, Nancy	8	F	Full
647	Sam, Sis	4	F	Full
648	Parker, Logan	34	M	Full
649	Parker, Sidney	9	M	Full
650	Parker, Jim	6	M	Full
651	James, Wash	26	M	Full
652	James, Easter	27	F	Full
653	James, Harbar	2	M	Full
654	Ellis, Jim	20	M	Full
655	Ellis, Nancy	38	F	Full
656	Ellis, Mary	1	F	Full
657	Ellis, Leroy	3	M	Full
658	Dixon, Doctor	38	M	Full

Roll No.	Name	Age	Sex	Blood
659	Dixon, Nancy	65	F	Full
660	Jackson, Cornelia	9	F	Full
661	Lee, Lizzie	3	F	Full
662	Billy, Moss	23	M	Full
663	Billy, Ada	18	F	Full
664	Billy, Hullison	1	M	Full
665	Bob, Johnnie	26	M	Full
666	Bob, Martha	20	F	Full
667	Adam, Toney	33	M	Full
668	Thomas, Elijah	52	M	Full
669	Stephen, Frank	23	M	Full
670	Stephen, Lizzie	27	F	Full
671	Stephen, Allie	5	F	Full
672	Stephen, Eliza	2	F	Full
673	Sockey, Solomon	60	M	Full
674	Sockey, Phoebe	58	F	Full
675	Sockey, Mary	18	F	Full
676	John, Simon	30	M	Full
677	John, Georgia	22	F	Full
678	John, Johnnie	4	M	Full
679	John, Minnie	6	F	Full
680	John, Alex	1	M	Full
681	Jack, Allen	27	M	Full
682	Simpson, Sookie	30	F	Full
683	Ok-chi-tubbee, Josephene	40	F	Full
684	Jim, Filicah	15	F	Full
685	Jim, Rosie	13	F	Full
686	Jim, Thomas	10	M	Full
687	Jim, Selena	7	F	Full
688	Billey, Jim	48	M	Full
689	Billey, Bud	11	M	Full
690	Lewis, Leanna	28	F	Full
691	Lewis, William	12	M	Full
692	Lewis, Thomas	10	M	Full
693	Lewis, Nelson	8	M	Full
694	Lewis, Mary	6	F	Full
695	Lewis, Annie	4	F	Full
696	Lewis, Easter	2	F	Full
697	Ha-cubbee, Mollie	40	F	Full
698	Thomas, John B.	25	M	Full
699	Thomas, Emma	35	F	Full
700	Thomas, Ada	7	F	Full
701	Thomas, Henry	1	M	Full
702	John, Jack	28	M	Full
703	John, Olevia	6	F	Full
704	Bob, Mollie	52	F	Full
705	Onah-fal-a-ma-tubbee	82	F	Full
706	Jacob, Charley	24	M	Full
707	Jacob, Louisa	21	F	Full
708	Jacob, Ebbie	1	F	Full
709	James, Ore	1	F	Full
710	Jim, Simpson	50	M	Full
711	Jim, Eliza	45	F	Full
712	Jim, Robert	15	M	Full
713	Jim, Egburt	13	M	Full
714	Jim, Tessie	10	F	Full
715	Jim, Clemmon	7	M	Full
716	Jim, Evan	5	M	Full
717	Moses, Ike	28	M	Full
718	Moses, Ann	27	F	Full
719	Moses, Nicey	14	F	Full
720	Moses, Lottie	10	F	Full
721	Moses, Edna	5	F	Full
722	Moses, Elsie	1	F	Full
723	Porter, Isaac	45	M	Full
724	Porter, Betsey	40	F	Full
725	Porter, Jenkins	18	M	Full
726	Porter, Thornton	9	M	Full
727	Lewis, Mollie	24	F	Full
728	Lewis, Martha	2	F	Full
729	Robison, Mary Jane	40	F	Full
730	Robison, Alice	7	F	Full
731	Robison, Eula	5	F	Full
732	Lewis, Caroline	48	F	Full
733	Lewis, Ollie	10	F	Full
734	Lewis, Martha	8	F	Full
735	Lewis, Charles (Kon-ni-ah-tubbee)	63	M	Full
736	Lewis, Lila	60	F	Full
737	Davis, Edna	27	F	Full
738	Davis, Linnie	6	F	Full
739	Davis, Leuella	4	F	Full
740	Lewis, Sim	30	M	Full
741	Lewis, Minnie	19	F	Full
742	Lewis, Louis	1	F	Full
743	Lewis, Jesse	33	M	Full
744	Lewis, John	33	M	Full
745	Johnson, Cook	28	M	Full
746	Johnson, Eliza	20	F	Full
747	Meely, Jim	24	M	Full
748	Meely, Lula	28	F	Full
749	Meely, Amos	3	M	Full
750	Meely, Fannie	1	F	Full
751	Martin, Sallie	63	F	Full
752	Martin, Jacob	19	M	Full
753	Isaac, King	31	M	Full
754	Isaac, Eliza	30	F	Full
755	Isaac, Sias	9	F	Full
756	Cotton, Willie	5	M	Full
757	Jack, Tom	37	M	Full
758	Jack, Eliza	36	F	Full
759	Jack, Ethel	7	F	Full
760	Jack, Sliman	1	M	Full
761	Jack, Evaline	4	F	Full
762	Gibson, Ben	47	M	Full
763	Gibson, Sallie	48	F	Full
764	Gibson, Mullen	19	M	Full
765	Gibson, Lena	17	F	Full
766	Gibson, Lulu	14	F	Full
767	Gibson, Sammon	11	M	Full
768	Isaac, George	53	M	Full
769	Isaac, Mary	67	F	Full
770	Martin, Sam B.	29	M	Full
771	Martin, Winnie	28	F	Full
772	Meely, Clark	21	M	Full
773	Meely, Mary	20	F	Full
774	Jackson, Annie	19	F	Full
775	Isaac, Wilson	54	M	Full
776	Isaac, Siney	29	F	Full
777	Isaac, Gift	12	M	Full
778	Isaac, Ellen	7	F	Full
779	Isaac, Jim	5	M	Full
780	Isaac, Lela	2	F	Full
781	Simpson, Sam	55	M	Full
782	Amos, Wes	52	M	Full
783	Amos, Liza	55	F	Full
784	Amos, Jasper	30	M	Full
785	Amos, Dora	19	F	Full
786	Amos, Cleveland	17	M	Full
787	Amos, Bennett	14	M	Full
788	Amos, Willie	8	M	Full
789	Lewis, Noble	10	M	Full
790	Lewis, Webb	20	M	Full
791	Anderson, Lucy	40	F	Full
792	Anderson, Artie	3	M	Full
793	Anderson, John Harrison	6	M	Full
794	Anderson, John Amos	2	M	Full
795	Anderson, Lola	1	F	Full
796	Toonubbee, Allen	62	M	Full
797	Toonubbee, Sias	16	F	Full
798	Toonubbee, Bissie	6	F	Full
799	Gilmore, Nettie Bessie	21	F	Full
800	Gilmore, Ramond	4	M	Full
801	Gilmore, Emma	2	F	Full
802	Gilmore, Mabell	1	F	Full
803	Gibson, Leona	15	F	Full
804	Gibson, Billie	35	M	Full
805	Gibson, Christiana	30	F	Full
806	Gibson, Ethan S.	4	M	Full
807	Gibson, Mattie	2	F	Full
808	Gibson, Emmie	40	F	Full
809	Gibson, Sallie	5	F	Full
810	Gibson, Willie	20	M	Full
811	Gibson, Mollie	24	F	Full
812	Gibson, Mike	1	M	Full
813	Shoemaker, Ben	41	M	Full
814	Shoemaker, Mary (Sti-ymah)	36	F	Full
815	Shoemaker, Sister	17	F	Full
816	Shoemaker, Coleman	14	M	Full
817	Shoemaker, Henry	10	M	Full
818	Shoemaker, Selest	8	F	Full
819	Shoemaker, Will	4	M	Full
820	Shoemaker, Sally	1	F	Full
821	Phillips, Caroline	36	F	Full
822	Phillips, Lena	15	F	Full
823	Phillips, Seulis	13	F	Full
824	Phillips, Germain	9	F	Full
825	Phillips, Custer	1	M	Full
826	Philip, Sallie	67	F	Full
827	Arkansas, Jim	68	M	Full

Roll No.	Name	Age	Sex	Blood
828	Arkansas, Catherine (Tiah-ah-yah-honah)	27	F	Full
829	Arkansas, Marsalina	3	F	Full
830	Arkansas, Fannie	6	F	Full
831	Arkansas, Missie	3	F	Full
832	Arkansas, Linnie	1	F	Full
833	Jacoway, Charlie	52	M	Full
834	Jacoway, Mandy	34	F	Full
835	Jacoway, Martin	6	M	Full
836	Jacoway, Oma	4	F	Full
837	Jacoway, Elsie	3	F	Full
838	Jacoway, Onus	1	M	Full
839	Johnson, Big Wiley	56	M	Full
840	Johnson, Patsie	42	F	Full
841	Gilmore, Allen	9	M	Full
842	Farmer, Solomon	41	M	Full
843	Farmer, Louisa	38	F	Full
844	Fillihemah, Nancy	60	F	Full
845	Gibson, Ben	60	M	Full
846	Gibson, Sealy	56	F	Full
847	Jackson, Billie	36	M	Full
848	Jackson, Jennie	26	F	Full
849	Jackson, Leroy	6	M	Full
850	Jackson, Mary	1	F	Full
851	Stoliby, Folsom	15	M	Full
852	Thompson, Allison	40	M	Full
853	Thompson, Martha	55	F	Full
854	Austin, Hortense Thompson	18	F	Full
855	Thompson, Lena	14	F	Full
856	Gibson, Jeff	28	M	Full
857	Gibson, Lucy	29	F	Full
858	Gibson, William	6	M	Full
859	Gibson, Ellis	4	M	Full
860	Gibson, Snowdon	2	M	Full
861	Gibson, Amy	1	F	Full
862	Davis, Julia	44	F	Full
863	Davis, Mary	15	F	Full
864	Stallaby, Anderson	45	M	Full
865	Scott, Chubby	23	M	Full
866	Bob, Nancy Jane	42	F	Full
867	Houston, Willie	20	M	Full
868	Bob, Woodward	8	M	Full
869	Bob, Lena	7	F	Full
870	Thomas, Charlie	38	M	Full
871	Thomas, Mary	28	F	Full
872	Thomas, Peter Foster	14	M	Full
873	Thomas, Esau	12	M	Full
874	Thomas, Fisher	8	M	Full
875	Thomas, Enoch	3	M	Full
876	Thomas, Nicholas	1	M	Full
877	Ned, Willie	25	M	Full
878	Ned, Lona	24	F	Full
879	Ned, Marvin	2	M	Full
880	Ned, Russell	2	M	Full
881	Wilson, Willie	30	M	Full
882	Wilson, Janie	26	F	Full
883	Wilson, John	2	M	Full
884	Wilson, Donald	1	M	Full
885	Shook, Bettie	10	F	Full
886	Bob, Boyd	44	M	Full
887	Bob, Lisby	38	F	Full
888	Bob, Preston	13	M	Full
889	Bob, Rainey	8	F	Full
890	Bob, Lewis	2	M	Full
891	Billey, Nolie	50	F	Full
892	Billey, Charley Columbus	16	M	Full
893	Billey, Paulina	4	F	Full
894	Billey, Frank Bishop	15	M	Full
895	Billy, Purwood	28	M	Full
896	Billy, Fannie	23	F	Full
897	Billy, John	1	M	Full
898	Wilkinson, Harrison	77	M	Full
899	Gilmore, Tom	33	M	Full
900	Gilmore, Martha	28	F	Full
901	Gilmore, Johnnie	9	M	Full
902	Gilmore, Mamie	1	F	Full
903	Gilmore, Ludie	1	F	Full
904	Gilmore, Benjamin	37	M	Full
905	Gilmore, Jane	24	F	Full
906	Ha-cubbee, Amie (Il-le-mah-ho-ki)	78	F	Full
907	Pistubbee, Tinsley	35	M	Full
908	Pistubbee, Archie	17	M	Full
909	Henry, John	56	M	Full
910	Henry, Sarah	8	F	Full
911	Henry, Dennis	7	M	Full
912	Lewis, Mary	15	F	Full
913	Lewis, Jim	10	M	Full
914	Lewis, Jessie	9	M	Full
915	Himonubbe, Shook	50	M	Full
916	Himonubbe, Bobbie	19	F	Full
917	Himonubbe, Laben	12	M	Full
918	Tom, Nicholas	35	M	Full
919	Tom, Watson	15	M	Full
920	Tom, Moses	13	M	Full
921	Tom, Sicily	6	F	Full
922	Johnston, Isham	43	M	Full
923	Johnston, Lemma	11	F	Full
924	Johnston, Jesse	18	M	Full
925	Johnston, Lena	50	F	Full
926	Johnston, Malissie	1	F	Full
927	Tom, Willie	35	M	Full
928	Taylor, Willie	28	M	Full
929	Taylor, Jennie	26	F	Full
930	Taylor, Elizabeth	3	F	Full
931	Taylor, Johnson	2	M	Full
932	Jeff, Allie	11	F	Full
933	Brokeshoulder, Adam (Oklah-nah-nubbee)	79	M	Full
934	Jackson, Charlie	49	M	Full
935	Jackson, Frances	48	F	Full
936	Jackson, Ben	9	M	Full
937	Jackson, Stephen	3	M	Full
938	Jacoway, Davis	50	M	Full
939	Jacoway, Sealy	38	F	Full
940	Jacoway, Rose	1	F	Full
941	Jamus, Lula	12	F	Full
942	Lick, John (Hintubbee)	75	M	Full
943	Morris, Elizabeth	38	F	Full
944	Philip, George	23	M	Full
945	Philip, Bettie	18	F	Full
946	Philip, Sissy	1	F	Full
947	Hochernah, Mary	67	F	Full
948	Jack, Martha	75	F	Full
949	Him-o-nubbe, Davis	52	M	Full
950	Him-o-nubbe, Emmon	90	M	Full
951	Him-o-nubbe, Ella	18	F	Full
952	Him-o-nubbe, Carson	18	F	Full
953	Him-o-nubbe, Larbin	14	M	Full
954	Jack, Lena	18	F	Full
955	Jack, Sarah Jane	1	F	Full
956	Jack, Willie	22	M	Full
957	Jack, Nancy	21	F	Full
958	Jack, Ellen	12	F	Full
959	Jack, Lillie	3	F	Full
960	Jack, Robert	1	M	Full
961	Jackson, Tecumseh	37	M	Full
962	Jackson, Sophia	34	F	Full
963	Jackson, Walter	11	M	Full
964	Jackson, McElroy	5	M	Full
965	Jackson, Salina	4	F	Full
966	Jackson, Winnie	2	F	Full
967	Lewis, Sam	30	M	Full
968	Lewis, Pollie	27	F	Full
969	Lewis, Jim	11	M	Full
970	Lewis, Dorano	7	M	Full
971	Lewis, Ump	5	M	Full
972	Lewis, Claire	1	F	Full
973	Lewis, Charlie	45	M	Full
974	Lewis, Sallie	35	F	Full
975	Lewis, Larnie	10	M	Full
976	Lewis, Minnie	8	F	Full
977	Lewis, Bud	3	M	Full
978	Lewis, Body	1	F	Full
979	Shoemaker, Wiggin	30	M	Full
980	Shoemaker, Margaret (Iah-te-mah)	30	F	Full
981	Shoemaker, Emerson	1	M	Full
982	Lewis, Betty	1	F	Full
983	Johnson, Jesse Porter	1	M	Full
984	Reese, Lelie	1	F	Full
985	Williams, Telan	1	F	Full
986	Simpson, William	33	M	Full
987	Simpson, Caroline	26	F	Full
988	Simpson, Ben	7	M	Full
989	Simpson, Fannie	5	F	Full
990	Simpson, Ira	3	M	Full
991	Simpson, Mabel	1	F	Full
992	Smith, Mack	10	M	Full
993	York, Amos	23	M	Full
994	York, Bettie Lee	2	F	Full

c

Roll No.	Name	Age	Sex	Blood
995	Bob, Sallie	23	F	Full
996	Bob, Emma	5	F	Full
997	Johnson, Wiley	21	M	Full
998	Johnson, Stella	16	F	Full
999	Jackson, Willis	50	M	Full
1000	Jackson, Jameson	15	M	Full
1001	Jackson, Ida	18	F	Full
1002	Jackson, Albert	7	M	Full
1003	Jackson, Nixie	4	F	Full
1004	Philip, Williamson	55	M	Full
1005	Philip, Jinnie	55	F	Full
1006	Philip, Leanna	20	F	Full
1007	Philip, Sina	14	F	Full
1008	Philip, Albert	16	M	Full
1009	Philip, Dibin	9	M	Full
1010	Philip, Bob	5	M	Full
1011	Williamson, Tom	18	M	Full
1012	Williamson, Mary	19	F	Full
1013	Williamson, Davis	1	M	Full
1014	Tom, Willie	18	M	Full
1015	Emi-yah-tubbe, Wallace	55	M	Full
1016	Emi-yah-tubbe, Nancy	54	F	Full
1017	Emi-yah-tubbe, Martha	15	F	Full
1018	Emi-yah-tubbe, Minnie	16	F	Full
1019	Emi-yah-tubbe, Flemmon	14	M	Full
1020	Emi-yah-tubbe, Johnnie	11	M	Full
1021	Billey, Lem	21	M	Full
1022	Sam, Wallace	21	M	Full
1023	Thompson, Lem	21	M	Full
1024	Thompson, Susie	18	F	Full
1025	Thompson, Lonie	16	F	Full
1026	Thompson, Sydney	14	M	Full
1027	Thompson, Leona	12	F	Full
1028	Thompson, Marsaline	10	F	Full
1029	Wallace, Wesley	27	M	Full
1030	Wallace, Letitia	23	F	Full
1031	Jackson, Tom	18	M	Full
1032	Wallace, Lemmie	3	F	Full
1033	Wallace, Bailey	1	M	Full
1034	Jackson, Nancy	65	F	Full
1035	Jackson, Bessie	6	F	Full
1036	Jackson, Patsey	9	F	Full
1037	Reed, Kit	27	M	Full
1038	Reed, Victoria	26	F	Full
1039	Hawkins, Sillie	4	F	Full
1040	Tom, Sealy Ann	15	F	Full
1041	Solomon, Fannie	10	F	Full
1042	Dixey, Jim	7	M	Full
1043	Wallace, John R.	22	M	Full
1044	Wallace, Lillie	26	F	Full
1045	Wallace, Arna	3	F	Full
1046	Wallace, Ora	1	F	Full
1047	Gibson, Sarah	27	F	Full
1048	Gibson, Robison	4	M	Full
1049	Gibson, Mary Jane	2	F	Full
1050	Frenchman, Lotie	12	F	Full
1051	Frenchman, Mollie	5	F	Full
1052	Billey, Jesse	46	M	Full
1053	Billey, John Almon	18	M	Full
1054	Billey, Lewis	13	M	Full
1055	Parker, John	48	M	Full
1056	Parker, Mary	38	F	Full
1057	Parker, Joseph	17	M	Full
1058	Parker, Frances	9	F	Full
1059	Parker, Winnie	6	F	Full
1060	Parker, Sasteline	4	F	Full
1061	Jeff, George	22	M	Full
1062	Jeff, Lula	19	F	Full
1063	Willis, Tishomingo	54	M	Full
1064	Henderson, Ben	21	M	Full
1065	Henry, Frank	30	M	Full
1066	Jimmerson, Joe	52	M	Full
1067	Jimmerson, Martha	56	F	Full
1068	Jack, Marsaline	10	F	Full
1069	Jack, Joe	9	M	Full
1070	Jack, Tom	5	M	Full
1071	Jack, Jane	3	F	Full
1072	Henry, Wallace	28	M	Full
1073	Henry, Lillie	[illegible]	F	Full
1074	Henry, Isaac	2	M	Full
1075	Taylor, Frank	21	M	Full
1076	Taylor, Lulie	19	F	Full
1077	Johnson, Sealy	60	F	Full
1078	Johnson, Maggie	17	F	Full
1079	Johnson, Sam	19	M	Full
1080	Johnson, Tarum	7	M	Full
1081	Phillip, Lucie	45	F	Full
1082	Phillip, Lena	13	F	Full
1083	Blue-eye, Amos	44	M	Full
1084	Blue-eye, Adolphe	6	M	Full
1085	Blue-eye, Ida	3	F	Full
1086	Womack, Maggie	28	F	Full
1087	Henry, John	57	M	Full
1088	Kelly, Fannie	45	F	Full
1089	Sam, Jim	46	M	Full
1090	Taylor, Madeline	45	F	Full
1091	Taylor, Nettie	12	F	Full
1092	Taylor, Mary	10	F	Full
1093	Peter, Thompson	33	M	Full
1094	Peter, Richardson	3	M	Full
1095	Jimmerson, Lucy	60	F	Full
1096	Arkansas, Louisa	38	F	Full
1097	Arkansas, Freeman	14	M	Full
1098	Arkansas, Lawyer	12	M	Full
1099	Arkansas, Lawson	8	M	Full
1100	Arkansas, Irene	6	F	Full
1101	Henry, George	3	M	Full
1102	Lewis, John	60	M	Full
1103	Lewis, Lucy	8	F	Full
1104	Lewis, Dan	7	M	Full
1105	Lewis, Jim	5	M	Full
1106	Thomas, Anison	2	M	Full
1107	Williamson, Edmund	2	M	Full
1108	Sockey, Rafe	24	M	Full
1109	Billey, Oscar	25	M	Full
1110	Billey, Beauty	27	F	Full
1111	Stricken from roll.			
1112	Stricken from roll.			
1113	Stricken from roll.			
1114	Billey, Louisa	3	F	Full
1115	Billey, Sallie Dora	2	F	Full
1116	Billey, Emerson	1	M	Full
1117	Post-oak, Johnson	38	M	Full
1118	Post-oak, Susie	40	F	Full
1119	Post-oak, Eli	10	M	Full
1120	Post-oak, Sweeney	6	M	Full
1121	Thomas, Silmey	10	F	Full
1122	Thomas, Beckey	8	F	Full
1123	Burton, Susan S.	73	F	1-8
1124	Burton, Henry D.	39	M	1-8
1125	Burton, Austin G.	11	M	1-16
1126	Burton, Susan G.	9	F	1-16
1127	Burton, Florence A.	7	F	1-16
1128	Burton, Jewel A.	5	F	1-16
1129	Marshall, Susan Cornelia	32	F	1-8
1130	Marshall, Valentine	5	F	1-16
1131	Marshall, John H.	3	M	1-16
1132	Lafontain, Victoria	22	F	Full
1133	Taylor, Henry	22	M	Full
1134	Faure, Marie	27	F	Full
1135	Stribling, Frank	28	M	Full
1136	Tonubbee, Jackson	45	M	Full
1137	Hawkins, Rollis	5	M	Full
1138	Dixon, John	30	M	Full
1139	Dixon, Manie	20	F	Full
1140	Dixon, Ennie	1	F	Full
1141	Marshall, Charles Harold	1	M	1-16
1142	Boston, Jim T.	2	M	Full
1143	Willis, Solomon	33	M	Full
1144	Brokeshoulder, Minnie	19	F	Full
1145	McCormick, Sarah Jane	37	F	Full
1146	Lewis, Lewis	16	M	Full
1147	Jefferson, Thomas	46	M	Full
1148	Lewis, Dan	23	M	Full
1149	McDonald, Susanna	26	F	Full
1150	McDonald, Lucy	27	F	Full
1151	Stout, Sis	66	F	Full
1152	Stout, Terese Annie	11	F	Full
1153	John, Emil	28	M	Full
1154	Mingo, Samuel Alexander	33	M	Full
1155	Jamison, Lula	31	F	Full
1156	Jamison, Finis	13	M	Full
1157	Jamison, Mike	11	M	Full
1158	Jamison, Reuben	10	M	Full
1159	Boaka, Jack	70	M	Full
1160	Morris, Betsy	26	F	Full
1161	Farve, Amelia	28	F	Full
1162	Jackson, Joe	33	M	Full
1163	Cooper, Spencer	21	M	Full
1164	Post-oak, Jim	42	M	Full
1165	Post-oak, Mary	32	F	Full
1166	Post-oak, Jim Brown	3	M	Full

Roll No.	Name	Age	Sex	Blood
1167	Clover, Matilda	70	F	1-2
1168	Clover, Josiah M.	44	M	1-4
1169	Clover, Nettie Lee	11	F	1-8
1170	Clover, Robert Arthur	9	M	1-8
1171	Clover, Leander Louis	1	M	1-8
1172	McClosky, Charlie	3	M	1-16
1173	Tucker, George	24	M	1-8
1174	Wilson, Katie	22	F	1-8
1175	Wilson, William C.	2	M	1-16
1176	Karr, Nancy F.	50	F	1-4
1177	Karr, Lon	18	M	1-8
1178	Franklin, Lou	25	F	1-8
1179	Franklin, Alfus R.	6	M	1-16
1180	Franklin, Homer Lee	3	M	1-16
1181	Franklin, Quinon Hubert	1	M	1-16
1182	Draper, Rosie	22	F	1-8
1183	Draper, Maggie	3	F	1-16
1184	Pebworth, William	42	M	1-4
1185	Pebworth, William H.	19	M	1-8
1186	Pebworth, Lillie May	16	F	1-8
1187	Pebworth, Pearl	13	F	1-8
1188	Pebworth, Zelma	7	M	1-8
1189	Pebworth, Maggie	6	F	1-8
1190	Pebworth, Josie	3	F	1-8
1191	Pebworth, David	38	M	1-4
1192	Pebworth, Artie	14	M	1-8
1193	Pebworth, Charley	11	M	1-8
1194	Pebworth, Lee	8	M	1-8
1195	Pebworth, Clarence	3	M	1-8
1196	Pebworth, Joe	29	M	1-4
1197	Pebworth, Josie Viola	1	F	1-8
1198	Clover, Earnest G.	17	M	1-16
1199	Clover, Thomas E.	14	M	1-16
1200	Clover, Eugie B.	6	F	1-16
1201	Hunter, Joewillie	23	F	1-8
1202	Hunter, Mary	2	F	1-16
1203	Hunter, Pearl	1	F	1-16
1204	Clover, Mary	70	F	1-2
1205	Clover, William Marshall	54	M	1-4
1206	Barr, Mary Ann	55	F	1-4
1207	Guice, Benjamin J.	33	M	1-8
1208	Lehuw, Willie Ann	23	F	1-8
1209	Lehuw, Floyd	3	M	1-16
1210	Lehuw, Ophelia	1	F	1-16
1211	Ricketts, Freddie C.	17	M	1-8
1212	Ricketts, Dassie	12	F	1-8
1213	Jordan, William G.	42	M	1-4
1214	Patterson, Dennis A.	9	F	1-8
1215	Patterson, Shelby A.	6	M	1-8
1216	Patterson, Howell M.	3	M	1-8
1217	Pebworth, Vassie V.	13	F	1-8
1218	Pebworth, Void Breston	7	M	1-8
1219	Pebworth, Roscoe W.	16	M	1-8
1220	Pebworth, Jepthar A.	12	M	1-8
1221	Pebworth, Marshal H.	10	M	1-8
1222	Roe, Harry F.	15	M	
1223	Roe, Tannie T.	11	M	
1224	Merly, John G.	1	M	Full
1225	Sockey, John	25	M	Full
1226	Frenchman, Sally	23	F	Full
1227	Thompson, Chatman	46	M	Full
1228	Bull, Asa Elmon	28	M	Full
1229	Lewis, Little Tom	60	M	Full
1230	Lewis, Lanie	50	F	Full
1231	Lewis, William	4	M	Full
1232	Lewis, Rufus	3	M	Full
1233	Thomas, Sincom	35	M	Full
1234	Thomas, Martha	4	F	Full
1235	Johnson, Jimmie	23	M	Full
1236	Johnson, Amy	23	F	Full
1237	Johnson, Freeman	10	M	Full
1238	Shoemaker, Susie	1	F	Full
1239	Scott, Liza	21	F	Full
1240	Scott, Aline	5	F	Full
1241	Marris, Minerva	26	F	Full
1242	Yearby, Thomas	17	M	Full
1243	Yearby, Christie	14	M	Full
1244	Byars, Luisa	22	F	Full
1245	Tucker, Henry	29	M	1-8
1246	Clover, Henry H.	11	M	1-16
1247	Clover, Josie	7	F	1-16
1248	Philip, Elijah	50	M	Full
1249	Philip, Edmond (or Fashur)	4	M	Full
1250	McMillan, Louie	20	F	Full
1251	Willis, Hugh	18	M	Full
1252	Seals, Annie	19	F	1-4
1253	Folsom, Andy	50	M	Full
1254	Plummer, Frank E.	43	M	1-8
1255	Plummer, Frank S.	6	M	1-16
1256	Plummer, Raymond S.	3	M	1-16
1257	Plummer, Joseph R.	1	M	1-16
1258	Marris, Jim	28	M	5-8
1259	Marris, Arch	1	M	13-16
1260	Marris, Annie	2	F	13-16
1261	Marris, Dibbin	60	M	1-2
1262	Marris, Wench	19	M	3-4
1263	Marris, Steve	17	M	3-4
1264	Marris, Nancy	17	F	3-4
1265	Marris, Missy	11	F	3-4
1266	Marris, Mat	10	F	3-4
1267	Marris, Liss	6	M	3-4
1268	McDonald, Indian	62	M	1-2
1269	McDonald, Lee	27	M	3-4
1270	McDonald, Lee Poe	2	M	7-8
1271	McDonald, William	25	M	3-4
1272	McDonald, Mack	1	M	7-8
1273	McDonald, Vinny	8	F	7-8
1274	McDonald, Hugh	31	M	3-4
1275	McDonald, Sealy	20	F	3-4
1276	McDonald, John Patty	4	M	3-4
1277	McDonald, Mollie	1	F	3-4
1278	McDonald, Jane	20	F	3-4
1279	Jack, Bicey	14	F	7-8
1280	Davis, Bissie	7	F	7-8
1281	Davis, Fronie	4	F	7-8
1282	Tonubbee, Sissie	43	F	3-4
1283	Tonubbee, Lewis	17	M	7-8
1284	Tonubbee, Robert	14	M	7-8
1285	Tonubbee, Murphy	10	M	7-8
1286	Tonubbee, Lottie	4	F	7-8
1287	Marris, Tom H.	27	M	3-4
1288	Marris, Christian	4	M	7-8
1289	Marris, Winner	1	F	7-8
1290	Marris, Coleman	40	M	3-4
1291	Marris, Nannie	19	F	7-8
1292	Marris, Jane	8	F	7-8
1293	Marris, Lillie	7	F	7-8
1294	Marris, Tennis	4	M	7-8
1295	Kelley, Sealy	35	F	3-4
1296	Kelley, Presies	12	F	5-8
1297	Kelley, Lloyd	10	M	5-8
1298	Kelley, Eula	8	F	5-8
1299	Marris, Bobe	26	M	3-4
1300	Marris, Otis	2	M	7-8
1301	Marris, Sanderson	26	M	3-4
1302	Marris, Lula	9	F	7-8
1303	Bull, Susan	26	F	3-4
1304	Marris, Marris	30	M	5-8
1305	Sockey, Bettie	22	F	5-8
1306	Sockey, Maggie	6	F	13-16
1307	Sockey, Rufe	5	M	13-16
1308	Sockey, Ned	4	M	13-16
1309	Marris, Sam	11	M	3-4
1310	Marris, George	25	M	5-8
1311	Bell, Jane	50	F	3-4
1312	Bell, Rufus	18	M	7-8
1313	Bell, Callie	21	F	7-8
1314	Thompson, Austin	13	M	Full
1315	Barcus, Sanders	25	M	Full
1316	Moore, Ellen	46	F	1-2
1317	Moore, John N.	28	M	1-4
1318	Moore, Lizzie B.	24	F	1-4
1319	Moore, Callie H.	22	F	1-4
1320	Moore, Elisha N.	20	M	1-4
1321	Moore, Mattie J.	16	F	1-4
1322	Moore, Maggie M.	14	F	1-4
1323	Moore, Ruthe E.	10	F	1-4
1324	Moore, Willie N.	8	M	1-4
1325	Moore, L[illegible] A.	5	F	1-4
1326	Farmer, Wilsam	20	M	Full
1327	Gift, Jim	78	M	1-4
1328	Gift, Movella	17	F	1-4
1329	Gift, Sarah	16	F	1-4
1330	Gift, Johnson	22	M	1-4
1331	Gift, Effie	1	F	1-8
1332	Gift, Donnie	21	F	1-4
1333	Mosely, Maggie	24	F	1-4
1334	Seals, Emma	36	F	1-4
1335	Seals, James	24	M	1-4
1336	Seals, Ora	12	F	1-4
1337	Seals, Kernell	11	M	1-8

Roll No.	Name	Age	Sex	Blood
1338	Seals, Ada	5	F	1-8
1339	Seals, Talmadge	4	M	1-8
1340	Jones, Annie C.	38	F	1-16
1341	Jones, Maud	19	F	1-32
1342	Jones, May	16	F	1-32
1343	Jones, Leonard H.	3	M	1-32
1344	Wampler, Amanda L.	42	F	1-8
1345	Lenechan, Campbell	19	M	1-16
1346	Wampler, George W.	12	M	1-16
1347	Wampler, John	9	M	1-16
1348	Wampler, Daniel Edgar	5	M	1-16
1349	Smith, Victoria	22	F	1-16
1350	Stafford, Tinnie	5	F	1-32
1351	Snider, Sarah Pearl	17	F	1-16
1352	Snider, Esther D.	15	F	1-16
1353	Snider, Beulah Lee	12	F	1-16
1354	Jackson, Bob	29	M	3-4
1355	Jackson, Birdie	5	F	7-8
1356	Jackson, Maseline	1	F	7-8
1357	Gus, Leanna	42	F	Full
1358	Lewis, Jennie	77	F	Full
1359	Shoemaker, Jim	8	M	Full
1360	Lewis, Frank	12	M	Full
1361	Reese, John	23	M	Full
1362	Jamison, Arden	23	M	Full
1363	Chubbee, John	54	M	Full
1364	Golden, Margaret Ann	1	F	Full
1365	Tookolo, John Henry	1	M	Full
1366	Reed, Linnie	1	F	Full
1367	Bob, Alex	57	M	Full
1368	Bob, Edna	47	F	Full
1369	Chubbee, Sallie	13	F	Full
1370	Phillip, Sis	15	F	Full
1371	Hawkins, William	38	M	Full
1372	Hawkins, Jane	31	F	Full
1373	Wallace, Aben	22	M	Full
1374	Wallace, Sota	16	F	Full
1375	Yearby, Jesse	30	M	Full
1376	Huff, Zeno	46	M	Full
1377	Johnson, Mamie	16	F	Full
1378	Johnson, Nochie	21	F	Full
1379	Marris, Sealy	26	F	Full
1380	Thompson, Arba Lavenia	1	F	Full
1381	Beck, Frances	42	F	Full
1382	Brokeshoulder, James	53	M	7-8
1383	Brokeshoulder, John	16	M	3-4
1384	Brokeshoulder, Adam, Jr.	12	M	3-4
1385	Brokeshoulder, Cammack	8	M	3-4
1386	Morrison, George W.	37	M	1-16
1387	Morrison, Emma Z.	10	F	1-32
1388	Morrison, Amma May	8	F	1-32
1389	Morrison, Henry B.	5	M	1-32
1390	McPhail, Laura K.	48	F	1-16
1391	McPhail, Frank	26	M	1-32
1392	McPhail, Myra	23	F	1-32
1393	McPhail, Fannie	21	F	1-32
1394	McPhail, Grace	19	F	1-32
1395	McPhail, Gates	17	M	1-32
1396	McPhail, Preston	15	M	1-32
1397	McPhail, Virgil	10	M	1-32
1398	McPhail, Homer	8	M	1-32
1399	Dees, Mary E.	47	F	1-16
1400	Dees, Henry H.	27	M	1-32
1401	Wood, Mary E.	25	F	1-32
1402	Dees, George A.	23	M	1-32
1403	Dees, Edgar R.	15	M	1-32
1404	Dees, Oscar E.	12	M	1-32
1405	Dees, Fannie E.	9	F	1-32
1406	Dees, Katiebelle	6	F	1-32
1407	Fountain, Lillie M.	38	F	1-16
1408	Wiltshire, Fannie E.	51	F	1-16
1409	Marx, Sallie V.	31	F	1-16
1410	Marx, Moses	9	M	1-32
1411	Marx, Miriam	8	M	1-32
1412	Marx, Philip Aaron	5	M	1-32
1413	Willis, William	30	M	Full
1414	Moncrief, Joseph	49	M	1-8
1415	Amos, Jeff	14	M	Full
1416	Amos, Lucinda	2	F	Full
1417	Amos, Roselle	1	F	Full
1418	Wallace, Bill	11	M	Full
1419	Jefferson, Mary Jane	35	F	Full
1420	Jefferson, Ike	14	M	Full
1421	Jefferson, Velma	10	F	Full
1422	Jefferson, Susie	8	F	Full
1423	Jefferson, Abney	5	M	Full
1424	Postoak, Bessie	20	F	Full
1425	Yearby, Nancy	75	F	Full
1426	Isaac, Rogers	13	M	Full
1427	Washington, Sallie	60	F	Full
1428	Lewis, Mary	6	F	Full
1429	Peter, Socky	22	F	Full
1430	Arkansas, Reuben	17	M	Full
1431	Lewis, Lonie	13	F	Full
1432	Stout, Usan	60	M	Full
1433	Tubbee, Robert	30	M	Full
1434	Yearby, Joseph	19	M	Full
1435	Jackson, Lizzie	22	F	Full
1436	Bell, Sallie	50	F	Full
1437	Willis, Nannie	2	F	Full
1438	Sampson, Sella	3	F	Full
1439	Bonaham, Ed	21	M	3-4
1440	Taylor, Mollie	32	F	Full
1441	Brokeshoulder, Lee	19	M	3-4
1442	Patterson, Emma	26	F	1-4
1443	Brewer, Frank	60	M	Full
1444	Wilmond, Raymond	14	F	Full
1445	Dees, Walter T.	38	M	1-32

MISSISSIPPI CHOCTAW ROLL, CITIZENS BY BLOOD

(Enrolled under provisions of the Act of Congress Approved August 1, 1914. Public No. 160)

No.	Name	Age	Sex	Blood	Census Card No.
1446	Farve, Clemeens	17	F	Full	915
1447	Farve, Elizabeth	21	F	Full	916
1448	Adams, Mitchell C.	58	M	Full	916
1449	Adams, Lillie M	28	F	1-2	916
1450	Adams, Nova M.	21	F	1-2	916
1451	Nickey, Maggie now John	27	F	Full	917
1452	Nickey, Billy	29	M	Full	917
1453	Nickey, Sam	26	M	Full	917
1454	Nickey, Bettie Russell (Nickey, Bettie)	24	F	Full	917
1455	Nickey, Mollie Mass	22	F	Full	917
1456	Davis, Mond Amos	20	M	Full	918
1457	McDaniel, Houston	26	M	Full	919
1458	McDaniel, Joe	15	M	Full	919
1459	Taylor, Joseph	9	M	Full	920
1460	Charles, Sallie	62	F	3-4	921
1461	Charles, Minnie	32	F	7-8	921
1462	Charles, Bettie	26	F	7-8	921
1463	Charles, Louisa	16	F	7-8	921
1464	Charles, James	13	M	7-8	921
1465	John, Lillie Jackson	24	F	Full	922
1466	Adams, William C. (born May 29, 1902) (Age as shown hereon is computed to May 29, 1914. Approved November 16, 1914)	12	M	1-2	916

Memo:

Ages appearing on this schedule are shown as of August 1, 1914, except those of persons who died prior to said date in which cases the ages are shown as of date of death. See notations hereon.

FINAL ROLL OF NEW BORN MISSISSIPPI CHOCTAWS.

Enrolled under Act of March 3, 1905 (33 Stat. L., 1048).

Ages calculated to March 4, 1905.

No.	Name	Age	Sex	Blood	Census Card No
1	Meely, Lillian	1	F	Full	7
2	Jacob, Caroline	1	F	Full	8
3	Meely, Green	1	M	Full	33
4	John, Johnson	3	M	Full	47
5	Isaac, Lennie	3	F	Full	49
6	Smith, Susie Ann	3	F	Full	58
7	Wilson, Arvin Velma	1	M	1-16	74
8	Thomas, Bennie	2	M	Full	78
9	Ned, Colbert	1	M	Full	86
10	Henry, Lony	3	M	Full	117
11	Pehworth, David Clifford	2	M	1-8	88

FINAL ROLL OF MINOR MISSISSIPPI CHOCTAWS.

Enrolled under Act of April 26, 1906 (34 Stat. L., 137).

Ages calculated to March 4, 1906.

No.	Name	Age	Sex	Blood	Census Card No
1	Johnson, Effie	3	F	Full	3
2	Phillip, Joe	3	M	Full	10
3	Phillip, Nannie	1	F	Full	11
4	Shoemaker, Arlie	3	M	Full	20
5	Billey, Charley	1	M	Full	24
6	Sam, Abel	2	M	Full	28
7	Johnson, Lola	3	F	Full	36
8	Brokeshoulder, Arthur Mellen	3	M	Full	38
9	Bob, Gertrude	4	F	Full	42
10	Bob, Bicey	4	F	Full	43
11	Bob, Leana	2	F	Full	44

No.	Name	Age	Sex	Blood	Census Card No.
12	Philip, Asie	3	F	Full	46
13	Wilson, Lelia	3	F	Full	81
14	Scott, Luciel	2	F	7-8	58
15	Lafontain, Cecilia May	1	F	7-8	66
16	Lafontain, Sidney	12	M	7-8	67
17	Lafontain, Oscar	3	M	7-8	69
18	Lafontain, Victoria J.	4	F	7-8	70
19	Marris, Sam	1	M	13-16	86
20	Byars, Amiel	7	M	3-4	93
21	Thompson, Ida Jewell	1	F	1-8	106
22	Kelley, Annie	3	F	3-8	112
23	Philip, Sid	3	M	Full	116
24	Wickson, Winnie	4	F	Full	118
25	Wickson, James	2	M	Full	119
26	Wallace, Ida	1	F	Full	120
27	Billey, Leona	3	F	Full	124
28	Tonubbee, Lizzie	4	F	7-8	125
29	Jack, Billy	3	M	Full	126
30	Billy, Fannie	3	F	Full	129
31	Neal, Willie	1	M	Full	131
32	Jackson, Clark	3	M	Full	136
33	Jackson, LeFlore	1	M	Full	137
34	Henry, Bonnie	1	F	Full	139
35	Jackson, Emmett	1	M	Full	140
36	Johnson, Lester	4	M	Full	141
37	Johnson, Charley	2	M	Full	142
38	Isaac, Emily	1	F	Full	143
39	Lehuw, Mary M.	1	F	1-16	144
40	Taylor, Mamie Annie	1	F	Full	145
41	Lewis, Annie	1	F	Full	146
42	Morris, Nela	2	F	Full	149
43	Risher, None	1	F	1-2	150
44	Isaac, Sadie	1	F	Full	151
45	Marshall, Paul	1	M	1-16	153
46	Philip, Eli	1	M	Full	154
47	Williams, Jamen	2	M	Full	156
48	Post-oak, May Jane	1	F	Full	158
49	Draper, Effie Ethel May	1	F	1-16	159
50	Austin, Jimerson	3	M	Full	160
51	Thompson, Will	6	M	Full	161
52	Willis, Willis	2	M	Full	1
53	Lewis, Hattie	1	F	Full	2
54	Sweeney, Minna	1	F	Full	6
55	Golden, Allie Mamie	1	F	Full	13
56	Willis, Mary	3	F	Full	15
57	Simpson, Easton	1	M	Full	16
58	Lewis, Cother	2	M	Full	17
59	Betsey, Alice	1	F	Full	21
60	Jacoway, Sammie	3	F	Full	22
61	Betsey, Jessie	4	M	Full	23
62	Neal, Isa A.	3	F	Full	27
63	Jack, Ida	1	F	Full	28
64	Gibson, Jimmie	1	M	Full	29
65	Arkansas, Emer	3	F	Full	30
66	Dixon, Mian	1	F	Full	32
67	Smith, Martha Jane	1	F	Full	34
68	Smith, William B.	3	M	Full	35
69	Billy, Dewet	3	M	Full	37
70	York, Annice	2	F	Full	41
71	Lewis, Venie	2	F	Full	50
72	Wilkerson, Lonnie	1	M	Full	52
73	Wallace, Neeley	5	F	Full	53
74	Wallace, Annie	1	F	Full	54
75	Marshall, William H.	3	M	1-16	56
76	Gillard, John Lollie	1	M	1-2	59
77	Hunter, Bruce	2	M	1-16	60
78	Billey, Hampton	2	M	Full	61
79	Franklin, Aubie Lois	3	F	1-16	62
80	Lafontain, Salena	10	F	7-8	68
81	Wilson, Marvin Alma	1	M	1-16	75
82	Postoak, James	7	M	Full	15
83	Davis, Emmett	1	M	Full	26
84	Lewis, Bob	3	M	Full	40
85	Simpson, Barnard	2	M	Full	46
86	John, George	1	M	Full	48
87	Seale, Willie	3	M	1-2	92
88	McDonald, Philintah-honah	1	F	7-8	172
89	Isaac, Mitchell	3	M	Full	220
90	Stephen, Wade	2	M	Full	272
91	Hughes, Ovillar	3	F	1-8	101
92	Marris, Ida	4	F	7-8	109
93	Clover, Joe Cole	2	M	1-8	110
94	Seale, Anna	1	F	1-8	128
95	Draper, Evie Minnie May	1	F	1-16	152
96	Thompson, Sallie	1	F	Full	162
97	Phillip, Minnie	1	F	Full	164
98	Sam, Rhody	1	F	Full	166
99	Philip, Adam	1	M	Full	170
100	Johnson, Tony	1	F	Full	171
101	McDonald, Cola	1	F	7-8	173
102	Karr, Nina Virgul Lee	1	F	1-8	174
103	Hughes, Carrie	1	F	3-8	175
104	Lewis, Mack D.	3	M	Full	176
105	Marris, Mart	1	M	7-8	177
106	Billey, Lonie	4	F	Full	180
107	Williamson, Tom Frank	1	M	Full	182
108	Henry, Norman	1	M	Full	183
109	Arkansas, Nora	1	F	Full	187
110	Jordan, Linnie M.	1	F	1-8	189
111	Morris, Annie	1	F	Full	191
112	Shoemake, Labon	1	M	Full	228
113	Frenchman, Clarence	1	M	7-8	198
114	Frenchman, Atlas	3	M	7-8	199
115	Frenchman, Agnes	2	F	7-8	200
116	Billey, Sidney	1	M	Full	202
117	Bull, Foreman	2	M	Full	227
118	James, Johnie	1	M	Full	208
119	Thompson, Jim	1	M	Full	209
120	Marris, Gilbert	1	M	7-8	210
121	Jamus, Jodie	1	M	1-2	225
122	Franklin, General D.	1	M	1-16	226
123	Parker, Sam	4	M	Full	4
124	Parker, Elizabeth	1	F	Full	5
125	Tookolo, Ida Rena	2	F	Full	12
126	Jacoway, Rhoda	3	F	Full	19
127	Post-oak, Sam	1	M	Full	31
128	Cooper, Mandy	2	F	Full	39
129	McDonald, Bettie	3	F	7-8	57
130	Tucker, Docia May	1	F	1-16	73
131	Gift, E. F.	4	M	1-8	99
132	Gift, Johnson, Jr.	2	M	1-8	100
133	Phillips, Joseph	4	M	Full	122
134	Mose, Margaret	10	F	Full	178
135	Lewis, Mettie	1	F	Full	186
136	York, Wm. Baston	2	M	Full	196
137	Johnson, Ed	1	M	Full	204
138	John, Ida	2	F	Full	322
139	Gibson, Mita Mullen	2	F	Full	9
140	John, Becca	1	F	Full	14
141	Sockey, Robert	1	M	1-2	44
142	McCormick, Hettie	9	F	3-4	65
143	McCormick, Lizzie	11	F	3-4	77
144	Taylor, Emily F.	5	F	7-8	78
145	Taylor, Ritchard	4	M	7-8	79
146	Taylor, Dewey W.	2	M	7-8	80
147	James, Cora	4	F	Full	81
148	Hickman, Gaston	1	M	7-8	83
149	McDonald, Ollie	1	F	3-4	87
150	McDonald, Lavada	3	F	3-4	88
151	Plummer, Charles W., Jr.	1	M	1-16	90
152	Marris, Hale	3	M	7-8	91
153	Pis-tubbee, Stinnes	3	M	Full	106
154	Mingo, Douglas	18	M	1-8	107
155	Wallace, Newt	3	M	Full	119
156	Wallace, Lee	1	M	Full	121
157	Bob, Mary	4	F	Full	138
158	Gibson, Rosa	4	F	Full	163
159	Stribling, Jimmie Jefferson	9	M	5-8	186
160	Willis, Nellie	1	F	Full	218
161	Tubbee, Lena	1	F	Full	231
162	Post-oak, Lena	6	F	Full	253
163	Post-oak, Oscar	9	M	Full	254
164	Willis, Willie	11	M	5-8	315
165	Willis, Sarah Jane	9	F	5-8	316
166	Willis, Henney Lee	7	M	5-8	317
167	Davis, Malissa Wadlington	1	F	Full	355
168	Morrison, Frank L.	2	M	1-32	361
169	Morrison, Fannie H.	1	F	1-32	361
170	Dees, Willie W.	5	M	1-32	362
171	Dees, Tommie W.	3	M	1-32	362
172	Dees, Herbert	2	M	1-32	362
173	Wood, Sammie D.	2	M	1-32	365
174	Marx, Susan Burton	4	F	1-32	363
175	Marx, Ruby	1	F	1-32	363

No.	Name	Age	Sex	Blood	Census Card No.
176	Wallace, Jennie	1	F	Full	130
177	Farve, Forrest	14	M	3-4	71
178	Farve, Elvener	9	F	3-4	72
179	Simpson, Jennie	3	F	Full	366
180	Taylor, Celestine	1	F	Full	370
181	Patterson, Joseph Allen	3	M	1-8	380
182	Tubbee, Effie	17	F	5-8	371
183	Tubbee, Rachel	15	F	5-8	371
184	Tubbee, Annie	14	F	5-8	371
185	Tubbee, Maisie (or Bessie)	11	F	5-8	371
186	Tubbee, Betsey	8	F	5-8	371
187	Patterson, Ruby Elnora	1	F	1-8	380

FINAL ROLL OF CHICKASAWS BY BLOOD.

Ages calculated to September 25, 1902.

No.	Name	Age	Sex	Blood	Census Card No.
1	Walker, Tandy C.	65	M	1-8	1
2	Walker, J. T.	28	M	1-16	1
3	Walker, J. C.	30	M	1-16	1
4	Byrd, Ida	26	F	1-16	1
5	Walker, G. C.	17	M	1-16	1
6	Walker, Minnie	15	F	1-16	1
7	Byrd, Eugene	6	M	1-32	1
8	Byrd, Chester Temple	1	M	1-32	1
9	Walker, Mary Cornelia	1	F	1-32	1
10	Walker, Robert T.	21	M	1-16	2
11	Mayer, Cornelia	22	F	1-16	3
12	Mayer, Myrtle J.	3	F	1-32	3
13	Colbert, Humphrey	64	M	3-4	4
14	Colbert, Salina	48	F	3-4	4
15	Colbert, Jackson R.	40	M	Full	7
16	Colbert, Mary Wolfe	32	F	Full	7
17	Cuberry, Davis	22	M	Full	7
18	Colbert, Lucy	2	F	Full	7
19	Colbert, Amanda	1	F	Full	7
20	Loving, Isabelle	64	F	3-4	8
21	Ayakatubby, Thompson	48	M	Full	9
22	Ayakatubby, Mina	44	F	Full	9
23	Ayakatubby, Agnes	22	F	Full	9
24	Ayakatubby, Mary	16	F	Full	9
25	Ayakatubby, Dixson	8	M	Full	9
26	Ayakatubby, Durena	7	F	Full	9
27	Ayakatubby, Minnie	18	F	Full	9
28	Davis, Martha	31	F	1-2	10
29	Davis, Maggie P.	10	F	1-4	10
30	Benton, Peter	68	M	Full	11
31	Benton, Ellen	22	F	Full	11
32	Yancey, Minnie	26	F	1-16	12
33	Yancey, Lillian	7	F	1-32	12
34	Yancey, Clara	5	F	1-32	12
35	Stricken from roll.				
36	Yancey, Enid Anaker	1	M	1-32	12
37	Apala, Kizzie	29	F	Full	14
38	Apala, Henrietta	10	F	Full	14
39	Apala, Ophelia	6	F	Full	14
40	Apala, Lemuel	4	M	Full	14
41	Apala, Mutbert	1	M	Full	14
42	Underwood, George	49	M	Full	15
43	Stricken from roll.				
44	Folsom, Charlie	19	M	Full	15
45	Harris, Walton	11	M	1-2	15
46	Brown, Levi	34	M	Full	16
47	Brown, Elizabeth	35	F	Full	16
48	Beans, Rosa	5	F	Full	16
49	Brown, Scott	6	M	Full	16
50	Brown, Andy	2	M	Full	16
51	Holloway, Kitsie	71	F	1-2	17
52	Alberson, Cornelia	24	F	3-4	17
53	Chapman, Harriet E. G.	41	F	1-8	18
54	Chapman, Charles J.	21	M	1-16	18
55	Chapman, James W.	17	M	1-16	18
56	Chapman, Virginia C.	16	F	1-16	18
57	Chapman, Claud C.	8	M	1-16	18
58	Chapman, Richard F.	3	M	1-16	18
59	Lewis, Galloway	23	M	Full	19
60	Lewis, Jackson	12	M	Full	19
61	Lewis, Wilson	1	M	Full	19
62	Lewis, Nancy	26	F	Full	19
63	Trentham, Henderson	31	M	1-16	20
64	Trentham, Lena	9	F	1-32	20
65	Trentham, Mary	3	F	1-32	20
66	Colbert, Walton	35	M	3-4	21
67	Colbert, Louisa	34	F	Full	21
68	Colbert, Amanda	16	F	7-8	21
69	Colbert, Minnie	13	F	7-8	21
70	Colbert, Frank	12	M	7-8	21
71	Colbert, Berena	10	F	7-8	21
72	Colbert, Nora	8	F	7-8	21
73	Colbert, Mack	5	M	7-8	21
74	Stricken from roll.				
75	Perry, Albert	61	M	1-2	22
76	Perry, Charles Guy	11	M	3-4	22
77	Perry, Ella	8	F	3-4	22
78	Perry, Billie	6	M	3-4	22
79	Perry, Eliza	50	F	1-2	23
80	Perry, James	18	M	5-8	23
81	Perry, Lee	16	M	5-8	23
82	Perry, Lena	12	F	5-8	23
83	Perry, Wilson	9	M	5-8	23
84	Sealy, Eli	34	M	Full	24
85	Sealy, Annie	29	F	Full	24
86	Sealy, Josephine	9	F	Full	24
87	Stricken from roll.				
88	Sealy, Sampson	3	M	Full	24
89	Hawkins, Morris H.	22	M	Full	25
90	Hawkins, Charlie	1	M	1-2	25
91	Phillips, Sallie Walker	41	F	1-8	26
92	Phillips, Ada	17	F	1-16	26
93	Phillips, Louisa	15	F	1-16	26
94	Phillips, Lucy	14	F	1-16	26
95	Phillips, Hill, Jr.	11	M	1-16	26
96	Phillips, Elmer	8	M	1-16	26
97	Phillips, Robert B.	6	M	1-16	26
98	Phillips, Winona	2	F	1-16	26
99	Walker, David	23	M	1-16	27
100	Brown, Margaret	9	F	Full	29
101	Collins, Odus Lynn	28	M	Full	30
102	Collins, Wm. B.	12	M	1-8	33
103	Collins, S. C.	11	M	1-8	33
104	Collins, George R., Jr.	9	M	1-8	33
105	Stricken from roll.				
106	Nelson, Ward	26	M	1-2	35
107	Alberson, Nicholas	48	M	Full	36
108	Alberson, Fannie	51	F	Full	36
109	Johnson, Napoleon B.	44	M	1-2	37
110	Johnson, Leewellyn	9	M	1-4	37
111	Johnson, Gertrude	4	F	1-4	37
112	Truax, Mary	28	F	1-2	38
113	Truax, Pearl E.	11	F	1-4	38
114	Truax, Ruby G.	7	F	1-4	38
115	Truax, William B.	5	M	1-4	38
116	Truax, Jewel	1	F	1-4	38
117	Underwood, Gabriel	47	M	Full	39
118	Underwood, Nancy	45	F	Full	39
119	Underwood, Wesley	19	M	Full	39
120	Underwood, Alice	18	F	Full	39
121	Underwood, Bina	16	F	Full	39
122	Underwood, Hagen	14	M	Full	39
123	Underwood, Louis	12	M	Full	39
124	Gully, Jim	14	M	1-2	39
125	Sealy, Sallie	20	F	Full	39
126	Dyer, Dawes	4	M	Full	39
127	Underwood, Phoebe	4	F	Full	39
128	Crosby, Annie	22	F	1-2	[illegible]
129	King, Wall	33	M	Full	40
130	King, Cellan	28	F	Full	40
131	King, Patsey	10	F	Full	40
132	Grayson, Gibson T.	59	M	Full	41
133	Grayson, Emy	37	F	Full	41
134	Grayson, Felix	25	M	Full	41
135	Grayson, James J.	21	M	Full	41
136	Grayson, Annie	19	F	Full	41
137	Stricken from roll.				

IDENTIFIED MISSISSIPPI CHOCTAWS 1900 - 1909
DAWES PACKETS Volume IV

CARD NO. 1 - Choc. MCR 1620 - Josephine Hussey
See MCR 1114, 1619, 1712

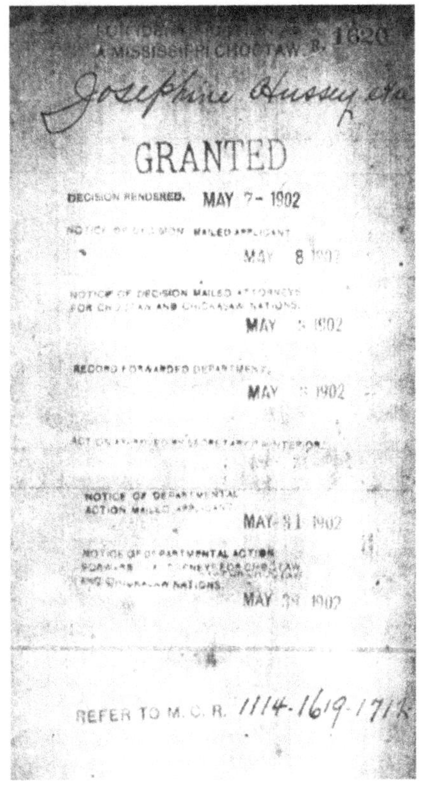
A MISSISSIPPI CHOCTAW. R. 1620

Josephine Hussey et al

GRANTED

DECISION RENDERED. MAY 7 - 1902

NOTICE OF DECISION MAILED APPLICANT
MAY 8 1902

NOTICE OF DECISION MAILED ATTORNEYS FOR CHOCTAW AND CHICKASAW NATIONS.
MAY 8 1902

RECORD FORWARDED DEPARTMENT.
MAY 8 1902

ACTION APPROVED BY SECRETARY OF INTERIOR.

NOTICE OF DEPARTMENTAL ACTION MAILED APPLICANT
MAY 31 1902

NOTICE OF DEPARTMENTAL ACTION FORWARDED ATTORNEYS FOR CHOCTAW AND CHICKASAW NATIONS.
MAY 31 1902

REFER TO M. C. R. 1114-1619-1712

Department of the Interior
Commission to the Five Civilized Tribes,
Meridian, Mississippi, April 3, 1901.

In the matter of the application of Josephine Hussey for the identification of herself and her two minor children as Mississippi Choctaws: Josephine Hussey being first duly sworn, testified as follows:

Examination by the Commission.

Q What is your name? A Josephine Hussey.
Q What is your age? A 37.
Q What is your post-office address? A 607 Carondalet Street, New Orleans, Louisiana.

Q You live in Louisiana? A Yes sir since I have been married.

Q Where did you live before that? A I Mississippi, in Meridian.

Q How long did you live in Meridian? A All my life. I was born in Quitmas[sic], Clark County, Mississippi.

Q And lived in Mississippi uo[sic] until the time of your removal to New Orleans? A Yes sir, until my marriage in 1892.

Q What is your father's name? A William Mitchell Hancock.

Q Is your father living? A No, my father's dead.

Q What is your mother's name? A Josephine Lilly.

Q Is your mother living? A My mother is dead.

Q Were your parents both possessed of Choctaw blood.[sic] [sic] No. My great grand mother was a full blooded squaw and my grand mother was half.

Q You claim your Choctaw blood through which one of your parents? A My father.

Q How much Choctaw blood do you claim? A I claim one eighth. My father was one quarter and my grand mother was one half.

Q Is your name on any of the tribal rolls of the Choctaw Nation in the Indian Territory? A Not that I know of.

Q Have you ever made application to the Choctaw tribal authorities in the Indian Territory for citizenship in that tribe? A No sir.

Q In 1896 the Commission to the Five Civilized Tribes was empowered to determine original applications for citizenship in the Choctaw Nation under the act of June 10th, 1896. Did you make an application at that time? A No sir.

Q Have you ever been admitted to citizenship in the Choctaw Nation by the Choctaw tribal authorities, the Commission to the Five Civilized Tribes or the United States Court in the Indian Territory? A No, I have never.

Q Have you ever prior to this time made any application to either the tribal authorities of the Choctaw Nation or to the duly constituted authorities of the United States for either citizenship or enrollment as a Choctaw Indian? A No sir.

Q This is the first application of any description that you have ever made? A Yes sir.

Q You are now making application for identification as a Mississippi Choctaw? A Yes sir.

Q You claim as a descendant of a Mississippi Choctaw who was a resident of this state in 1830 and as a beneficiary under the 14th article of the treaty of 1830? A Yes sir.

Q Do you know the name of your ancestor or ancestors who were residents of the state of Mississippi in 1830 at the time the treaty was entered into between the United States and the Choctaw Indians? A I suppose my grand mother was living here then, Sophia Mitchell.

Q Did you ever see her or do you remember her? A I never saw her nor my great grand mother.

Q If your grand mother was living do you know about how old she would be at this time? A No sir.

Q Do you know what your great grand mother's name was? A Mollie. She married a full blooded white man by the name of Samuel Mitchell.

Q Did you ever know her Indian name? A No sir, I only knew her name as Mollie. Her daughter Sophia Mitchell was my grand mother.

Q Did any of your ancestors ever claim or receive any land in Mississippi from the United States government as beneficiaries under this 14th article of the treaty of 1830? A No sir.

Q Were your ancestors recognized members of the Choctaw Tribe of Indians in Mississippi in 1830? A Yes sir.

Q Have you any evidence of the fact of such recognition? A No, I haven't. The records of my grand father's marriage - he was married in White County, Tennessee, the court house was burned and of course I cant[sic] get a record. But I can get affidavits. He was married in 1817 and my father was born in 1818 in Sparta Tennessee.

Q Did your father live in Tennessee? A He moved to Mississippi. He was judge for about twenty years for Lauderdale county[sic]. I suppose lots of these Indians knew him. He spoke the Choctaw language.

Q Do you speak the Choctaw language? A No sir.

Q Did you ever hear whether any of your ancestors ever removed from Mississippi to the Indian Territory at the time of the removal? A No, my grand mother Sophia remained here in Mississippi but after that she went to the Territory and she died there.

Q Was she recognized as a member of the Choctaw tribe of Indians in the Indian Territory? A Yes sir.

Q And participated in all the rights of citizenship? A Yes sir.

Q When did she die? A I really don't know. She died when I was a child. I have heard my father say but I don't remember. I have cousins in the Indian Territory. The Spains of White bead. I correspond with my cousin Dave Spain. He is my father's sister's child. My first cousin.

Q He derives his Choctaw blood from the same ancestors you so? A Yes sir. They are brothers and sisters children.

Q Has he always lived in the Indian Territory.[sic] A He has lived there because my father's sister, Mary went to the Indian Territory and she married a Mr. Spain there. She is dead now but her children live there.

Q You are making your claim at this time solely as a beneficiary under the fourteenth article of the treaty of 1830? A Yes sir.

Q Are you married? A Yes sir, here is my certificaye[sic], I was married November 15th, 1892.

Q What is your husband's name? A Samuel McCron Hussey.

Q He is a white man is he? A Yes sir, a full blooded white man.

Q You don't make any claim for him? A No sir, just for myself and my two children.

Q What are you children's names? A William Hancoch Hussey aged seven.

Q The other one? A Alvin McDowell Hussey aged two years.

Q You are the mother of both of these children? A I am the mother of them.

Q Samuel McCron Hussey, is the father of both of them? A Yes sir.

Q These children live with you at your home? A Yes sir. They are here with me now with my mother.

Q Their claim is identical with yours? A Yes sir.

Q Is there any additional statement that you desire to make in support of your application? A No.

Q Have you any documentary evidence, any affidavits you wish to file? A No, only my mother's marriage certificate, I will have that probably tomorrow and I have my own and I will get an affidavit if that is needed from White County, Tennessee stating the marriage of my grand father and grant[sic] mother.

Q Have you any evidence of any description showing that your ancestors at the time of this treaty of 1830 were recognized Choctaws by the members of the tribe here or by the United States Indian Agent.[sic] A No sir, only I know that they lived here and were recognized citizens of the Mississippi Choctaw tribe.

Q And never removed from here to the Indian Territory? A No they staid here a number of years and my grand mother went back to the Indian Territory and she died there.

Permission is granted the applicant to file documentary evidence in support of this claim provided the same is offered for filing with the Commission within thirty days from the date hereof.

Q In the event that the Commission should be enabled to identify you and your two children as Mississippi Choctaws entitled to rights in the Choctaw lands under the provisions of the 14th article of the treaty of 1830, is it your intention to remove with your children to the Indian Territory to establish your permenent[sic] home? A Yes sir. That is my intention. My cousins have been wanting me and my husband to come out there but my husband could not arrange to leave his business, he is with the Times-Democrat, and I am going out in June myself on a visit to them. They wanted me to come last year.

The decision of the Commission as to your application and the application you make on behalf of your two minor children for identification as Mississippi Choctaws will be mailed to you some time in the future to your present post-office address.

Myra Young having been first duly sworn upon her oath states that as stenographer to the Commission to the Five Civilized Tribes she reported in full all proceedings had in the above entitled cause on the 3rd day of April, 1901, and that the above and foregoing is a full, true and correct transcript of her stenographic notes of said proceedings on said date.

Myra Young

Subscribed and sworn to before me at Meridian, Mississippi, this the 4th day of April, 1901.

J P McKee Jr
Notary Public.

C.M.W.
A.B.
C.v.W.
WmOB.

DEPARTMENT OF THE INTERIOR.

COMMISSION TO THE FIVE CIVILIZED TRIBES.

ooOoo

In the matter of the application of Josephine Hussey, et al., for identification as Mississippi Choctaws, consolidating the applications of

Josephine Hussey, et al.,	M.C.R. 1620
J. Folsom Roe, et al.,	M.C.R. 1114
Jubal A. Hancock,	M.C.R. 1619
Charles Rushing Hancock,	M.C.R. 1712

--:: D E C I S I O N. ::--

The record in the above consolidated case shows that there were, originally, four applications, made separately by the parties named, at the times and places herein set forth, to-wit:

In the matter of the application of Josephine Hussey for the identification of herself and her two minor children, William Hancock Hussey and Alvin McDowell Hussey, as Mississippi Choctaws, taken at Meridian, Mississippi, April 3, 1901.

In the matter of the application of J. Folsom Roe for the identification of himself and his minor child, Jeannette C. Roe, taken at Hattiesburg, Mississippi, December 17, 1900.

In the matter of the application of Jubal A. Hancock for identification as a Mississippi Choctaw, taken at Meridian, Mississippi, April 3, 1901.

In the matter of the application of Charles Rushing Hancock for identification as a Mississippi Choctaw, taken at Meridian, Mississippi, April 8, 1901.

While these several applications have been consolidated and are to be considered together as a whole, yet, in view of the varied proceedings had in each, it will be necessary to consider them in a measure separately.

Taking them in the order above named, we find from the record in the case of Josephine Hussey, et al., that on April 3, 1901, the said Josephine Hussey appeared before the Commission at Meridian, Mississippi, and there made personal application for the identification of herself and her two minor children, William Hancock Hussey and Alvin McDowell Hussey, as Mississippi Choctaws, claiming to be descendants of Choctaw Indians who resided in the state of Mississippi in 1830, and took advantage of the provisions of article fourteen of the treaty between the United States and the Choctaw Nation concluded September 27, 1830, and known as the treaty of Dancing Rabbit Creek. The principal applicant claims descent from Sophia Mitchell, an alleged one half blood Choctaw woman, who married Jubal B. Hancock, a white man; said Jubal B. Hancock and Sophia Hancock, nee Mitchell, were the parents of William Mitchell Hancock, who married a white woman named Josephine Lilly, and said William Mitchell Hancock and Josephine Hancock nee Lilly, are the parents of this applicant.

The record in this case further shows that the principal applicant, Josephine Hussey, and her two minor children for whom application is made, have never been enrolled by the tribal authorities of the Choctaw Nation as citizens of that tribe, nor are their names found upon any of the tribal rolls of the Choctaw Nation in the possession of the Commission, nor have they ever been admitted to Choctaw citizenship by a duly constituted court or committee of the Choctaw Nation, or by the Commission to the Five Civilized Tribes, or by a decree of the United States Court in Indian Territory under the provisions of the act of Congress of June 10, 1896, (29 Stats., 321).

It appears from an examination of the records in the possession of the Commission that in 1896 an application for citizenship in the Choctaw Nation was made to this Commission, under the act of Congress of June 10, 1896, on behalf of William Hancock Hussey, a minor, by his mother, Josephine Willie Blanche Hussey, the principal applicant herein, as next friend' that the Commission denied the application for citizenship in the Choctaw Nation on behalf of the said William

Hancock Hussey, in Choctaw citizenship case Number 1343, and no appeal was taken from the decision of the Commission denying said application, to the United States Court in Indian Territory, within the time prescribed by the Act of Congress of June 10, 1896, above referred to.

It does not appear from an examination of the records in the possession of the Commission that Josephine Hussey made application to this Commission in her own behalf, for citizenship in the Choctaw Nation, in 1896, under the act of Congress of June 10, 1896, (29 States., 321).

The evidence offered in support of this application, aside from the oral statement of the principal applicant, embraces the ex parte affidavit of J. F. Smith, a certified copy of the marriage license and certificate between Mr. Samuel McCarn[sic] Hussey and Miss W. B. J. Hancock; certified copy of the marriage certificate between Hon. Wm. M. Hancock and Miss Josephine Lilly, and copy of a certified copy of the marriage license and certificate between Juble[sic] B. Hancock and Miss Sophia W. Mitchell, to which is attached the affidavit of the principal applicant that the same is a true and correct copy of a certified copy of said marriage license and certificate, and that the original license and certificate have been lost or destroyed.

By the oral statement of the principal applicant, it is attempted to be shown that she was born in the state of Mississippi about the year 1864, and lived there up to the time of her marriage to Samuel McCron Hussey, in 1892; that since that time she has been and is now a resident of the state of Louisiana and claims to be an one eighth blood Choctaw. She traces her Choctaw blood from her great grandmother, Mollie, a full blood Choctaw woman who married Samuel Mitchell, a white man, and from their daughter, Sophia Mitchell, an one half blood Choctaw woman who was the mother of her father, William Mitchell Hancock; and she alleges that her said grandmother, Sophia Mitchell, was a recognized member of the Choctaw tribe of Indians in Mississippi, and some time after the removal of the Choctaws from Mississippi, the exact period not given, she removed to the Indian Territory, where she contined[sic] to reside until her death; the principal applicant alleges that her cousins, the Spains, are citizens of the Choctaw Nation, and enrolled as such.

By the ex parte affidavit of J. F. Smith, it is attempted to be shown that Josephine Hussey, the principal applicant herein, is the daughter of William M.

Hancock, and the grand daughter of Jubal B. Hancock, both of whom resided in the State of Mississippi for many years prior to their death, and with both of whom the affiant was well acquainted for many years. By the certified copy of the marriage certificate between Wm. M. Hancock and Josephine Lilly, it is evidenced that the said William M. Hancock, the father of the principal applicant herein, was legally married to Josephine Lilly, the mother of the said applicant, and that the applicant, Josephine Hussey is the legitimate issue of said marriage. By the certified copy of the marriage license and certificate of Juble[sic] B. Hancock and Sophia W. Mitchell to which is attached the affidavit of Mrs. S. M. Hussey to the correctness of the copy, is attempted to be shown the marriage of Jubal B. Hancock and Sophia W. Mitchell, the father and mother of William M. Hancock, and that said William M. Hancock is the legitimate issue of said marriage.

There is filed herewith a written statement of the applicant, but the same is not made under oath, and cannot be considered in evidence. It is a repetition of the statements made by the applicant in her oral testimony. The certified copy of the marriage license and certificate between Samuel McCarn[sic] Hussey and Miss. W. B. J. Hancock is evidence of the marriage of the principal applicant and of the legitimacy of the issue of said marriage, the children for whom application is made herein.

The next in order of the above applications is that of J. Folsom Roe, et al., and the record therein - Yshows that on December 17, 1900 the said J. Folsom Roe appeared before the Commission at Hattiesburg, Mississippi, and there made personal application for the identification of himself and his minor child, Jeannette C. Roe, as Mississippi Choctaws, claiming to be descendants of Choctaw Indians who resided in the State of Mississippi in 1830, and took advantage of the provisions of article fourteen of the treaty between the United States government and the Choctaw tribe of Indians, concluded September 27, 1830, and known as the Treaty of Dancing Rabbit Creek. The principal applicant claims descent from Mollie Mitchell, an alleged full blood Choctaw woman, who, he states, is his grand mother.

The record in this case further shows that the principal applicant, J. Folsom Roe, and his minor child for whom application is made have never been enrolled by the tribal authorities of the Choctaw Nation, as citizens of that tribe, nor are their names found upon any of the tribal rolls of the Choctaw Nation in the possession of the Commission, nor have they ever been admitted to Choctaw citizenship by a duly constituted court or committee of the Choctaw Nation, nor by the Commission to the Five Civilized Tribes, nor by a decree of the United States Court in Indian Territory under the provisions of the act of Congress of June 10, 1896, (29 Stats., 321).

It appears from an examination of the records in the possession of the Commission that John Folsom Roe, the principal applicant herein made application to this Commission in 1896 for citizenship in the Choctaw Nation, under the act of Congress of June 10, 1896, above referred to, and that the Commission to the Five Civilized Tribes denied his application for citizenship in the Choctaw Nation in Choctaw citizenship case Number 450, and no appeal was taken from said decision of the Commission, to the United States Court in Indian Territory within the time prescribed by the act of Congress of June 10, 1896 above referred to.

It does not appear that an application for citizenship in the Choctaw Nation was made to this Commission in 1896 for Jeannette G. Roe, under the act of Congress of June 10, 1896, (29 Stats., 321).

The evidence offered in support of this application, aside from the oral statement of the principal applicant is a certified copy of the marriage license and certificate of John F. Roe and Onie Gressett. By the oral statement of the principal applicant, it is attempted to be shown that he was born in Indian Territory and lived there until he was five years old; that he then removed to Mississippi, and has since been a resident of that state, and claims to be an[sic] one quarter blood Choctaw. He attempts to trace his Choctaw descent from Mollie Mitchell an alleged full blood Choctaw Indian who he claims was his grandmother, but it is apparent from the evidence of other members of the family that the Mollie Mitchell through whom the principal applicant claims his Choctaw blood was the mother of Sophia W. Mitchell who married Jubal B. Hancock, and the said Jubal B. Hancock and Sophia W. Hancock, nee Mitchell, were the grand parents of this applicant. It is alleged in the oral testimony of the principal applicant that Jubal B. Hancock was the father of Callie D. Hancock who was married to John F. Roe and that said John F. Roe and Callie D. Roe, nee Hancock, are the father and mother of the principal applicant.

It is alleged in the oral testimony of the principal applicant that his mother, Callie D. Roe, removed from Mississippi to the Choctaw Nation, Indian Territory, in

1858 and was recognized as a Choctaw Indian; that she remained in said Choctaw Nation, Indian Territory, until the principal applicant herein was about five years old and that, her husband having died, she then returned to Mississippi; that a sister of his mother remained in the Choctaw Nation, Indian Territory and married a man named Thomas Spain, and that her descendants, the cousins of the principal applicant, are recognized and enrolled as citizens of the Choctaw Nation.

The certified copy of the marriage license and certificate filed herewith is simply evidence of the marriage between the principal applicant and his wife Onia E. Roe and of the legitimacy of the issue of said marriage.

The next in order of the above applications is that of Jubal A. Hancock and the record herein shows that on April 3, 1901, the said Jubal A. Hancock appeared before the Commission at Meridian, Mississippi and made personal application for identification as a Mississippi Choctaw, claiming to be a descendant of Choctaw Indians, who resided in the state of Mississippi in 1830 and took advantage of the provisions of article fourteen of the treaty between the United States government and the Choctaw tribe of Indians concluded September 27, 1830, and known as the Treaty of Dancing Rabbit Creek.

The principal applicant claims descent from Sophia Mitchell an alleged one half blood Choctaw woman, who was the mother of William M. Hancock who married Mary Jane West, and said William M. Hancock and Mary Jane Hancock, nee West, are the parents of this applicant.

The record in this case further shows that the principal applicant, Jubal A. Hancock has never been enrolled by the tribal authorities of the Choctaw Nation as a citizen of that tribe, nor is his name found upon any of the tribal rolls of the Choctaw Nation in the possession of the Commission, nor has he ever been admitted to Choctaw citizenship by a duly constituted court or committee of the Choctaw Nation or by the Commission to the Five Civilized Tribes or by a decree of the United States Court in Indian Territory under the provisions of the act of Congress of June 10, 1896, (29 Stats. 321).

It appears from an examination of the records in the possession of the Commission that in 1896 Jubal Avera Hancock, the applicant herein, made application to this Commission for citizenship in the Choctaw Nation under the act of Congress of

June 10, 1896, above referred to; that the Commission denied the application for citizenship in the Choctaw Nation of the said Jubal Avera Hancock in Choctaw citizenship case Number 1367, and no appeal was taken from the decision of the Commission denying said application, to the United States Court in Indian Territory, within the time prescribed by the act of Congress of June 10, 1896, above referred to.

The evidence offered in support of this application, aside from the oral statement of the principal applicant, embraces the ex parte affidavit of J. F. Smith, a certified copy of the marriage license and certificate between Wm. M. Hancock and Mary Jane West, and copy of a certified copy of the marriage license and certificate between Juble[sic] B. Hancock and Sophia W. Mitchell, to which is attached the affidavit of Mrs. S. M. Hussey that it is a true copy of a certified copy of said marriage license and certificate and that the original certificate has been lost or destroyed.

By the oral statement of the applicant, it is attempted to be shown that he was born and raised in Mississippi and is now a resident of that state and claims to be an[sic] one eighth blood Choctaw. He traces his Choctaw descent from Sophia Mitchell, an alleged one half blood Choctaw woman who had a son, William Mitchell Hancock, an alleged one quarter blood Choctaw who is the father of this applicant. He alleges that his father, William Mitchell Hancock and his grandmother Sophia Mitchell were living in Mississippi in 1830, and recognized members of the Choctaw tribe of Indians; that some time after the conclusion of the treaty of 1830, the exact period not given, Sophia Mitchell, the grandmother of the applicant removed to the Choctaw Nation, Indian Territory where she was a recognized and enrolled member of the Choctaw tribe of Indians and where she remained until her death.

By the ex parte affidavit of J. F. Smith, it is attempted to be shown that Jubal A. Hancock, the applicant herein, is the son of W. M. Hancock, and the grandson of Jubal B. Hancock, both of whom resided in the state of Mississippi for many years prior to their death, and with both of whom the affiant was well acquainted for many years. The certified copy of the marriage license and certificate between Wm. M. Hancock and Mary Jane West, is evidence that William M. Hancock was legally married to Mary Jane West, and that the applicant, Jubal A. Hancock, is the legitimate issue of said marriage.

By the copy of the certified copy of the marriage license and certificate of Juble[sic] B. Hancock and Sophia W. Mitchell to which is attached the affidavit of Mrs. S. M. Hussey to the correctness of the copy, is attempted to be shown the marriage of Jubal B. Hancock and Sophia W. Mitchell, the father and mother of William M. Hancock, and that said William M. Hancock is the legitimate issue of said marriage.

There is filed herewith a written statement of the applicant but the same is not made under oath, and cannot be considered in evidence. It is a repetition of the statements made by the applicant in his oral testimony.

The last in order of the above applications is that of Charles Rushing Hancock, and the record therein shows that on April 8, 1901, the said Charles Rushing Hancock appeared before this Commission at Meridian, Mississippi and there made personal application for identification as a Mississippi Choctaw claiming to be a descendant of Choctaw Indians who resided in the state of Mississippi in 1830 and took advantage of the provisions of article fourteen of the treaty between the United States government and the Choctaw tribe of Indians, concluded September 27, 1830 and known as the treaty of Dancing Rabbit Creek.

The applicant claims descent from Sophia Mitchell, an alleged one half blood Choctaw, who was the mother of William M. Hancock, who married Mary Jane West, and said William M. Hancock and Mary Jane Hancock, nee West, are the parents of this applicant.

The record in this case shows that the applicant, Charles Rushing Hancock has never been enrolled by the tribal authorities of the Choctaw Nation as a citizen of that tribe nor is his name found upon any of the tribal rolls of the Choctaw Nation in the possession of this Commission nor has he ever been admitted to Choctaw citizenship by a duly constituted court or committee of the Choctaw Nation, by the Commission to the Five Civilized Tribes or by a decree of the United States Court in Indian Territory under the provisions of the act of Congress of June 10, 1896. (29 Stats. 321).

It appears from an examination of the records in the possession of the Commission that in 1896 Charles Rushing Hancock, the applicant herein, applied to this Commission for citizenship in the Choctaw Nation under the act of Congress of June 10, 1896, above referred to, and that the Commission denied his application for citizenship in the Choctaw Nation, in Choctaw citizenship case Number 1374 and no appeal was taken from the decision of the Commission denying said application, to the United States Court in Indian Territory within the time prescribed by the act of Congress of June 10, 1896, above referred to. The evidence offered in support of this application aside from the oral statement of the applicant, embraces the ex parte affidavit of J. F. Smith, a certified copy of the marriage license and certificate between Wm. M. Hancock and Mary Jane West, and a copy of a certified copy of the marriage license and certificate between Juble[sic] B. Hancock and Sophia W. Mitchell, to which is attached the affidavit of Mrs. S. M. Hussey that it is a true copy of a certified copy of said marriage license and certificate and that the original certificate has been lost or destroyed.

By the oral statement of the applicant, it is attempted to be shown that the applicant was born in the state of Mississippi and has been a resident of that state all his life, and claims to be an one eighth blood Choctaw. He traced his Choctaw descent from Sophia Mitchell and her son William M. Hancock, who is a one quarter blood Choctaw, and is the father of this applicant.

The applicant alleges that his father William M. Hancock was recognized as a member of the Choctaw tribe of Indians in Mississippi by the Choctaw tribe, but he knows of no compliance on the part of his ancestors with the provisions of the fourteenth article of the treaty of 1830. By the ex parte affidavit of J. F. Smith, it is attempted to be shown that Charles Rushing Hancock, the applicant herein, is the son of W. M. Hancock and the grandson of Jubal B. Hancock, both of whom resided in the state of Mississippi and with both of whom the affiant was well acquainted for many years. The certified copy of the marriage license and certificate between Wm. M. Hancock and Mary Jane West is evidence that the said Wm. M. Hancock was legally married to Mary Jane West, and that Charles Rushing Hancock, the applicant herein, is the legitimate issue of said marriage. By the copy of the certified copy of the marriage license and certificate of Juble[sic] B. Hancock and Sophia W. Mitchell, to which is attached the affidavit of Mrs. S. M. Hussey to the correctness of the copy, is attempted to be shown the marriage of Jubal B. Hancock and Sophia W. Mitchell, the father and mother of William M. Hancock, and that said William M. Hancock is the legitimate issue of said marriage.

There is filed herewith a written statement of the applicant but the same is not made under oath and cannot be considered in evidence. It is sa repetition of the statements made by him in his oral testimony.

In accordance with the instructions of the Commission of Indian Affairs of July 25, 1901, the above names cases have been consolidated, the applicants all claiming descent from Sophia Mitchell, an alleged one half blood Choctaw woman who married a white man named Jubal B. Hancock. The record in this consolidated case shows that Jubal B. Hancock and Sophia Hancock, nee Mitchell, had three children, William M. Hancock, who resided in the state of Mississippi until his death, and who is the father of all the principal applicants except J. Folsom Ro, M. C. R. 1114; Callie D. Hancock, who is the mother of J. Folsom Roe; and another daughter, whose name is not given, who removed to the Indian Territory some time after the removal of the Choctaws from Mississippi to the present Choctaw Nation, and who married a man named Thomas Spain, who descendants are the cousins of the applicants herein.

It appears from an examination of the records of the Choctaw Nation, in the possession of the Commission, that Fidy Leewright, nee Spain, Thomas G. Spain, David M. Spain and S. Beauregard Spain, children of Thomas Spain and Mary Spain, are recognized citizens of the Choctaw Nation, their names appearing upon the 1896 census roll of the Choctaw Nation as Choctaws residing in the Chickasaw Nation. They have also been listed for enrollment as citizens of the Choctaw Nation by the Commission to the Five Civilized Tribes, having been identified from the tribal rolls of the Choctaw Nation in the possession of the Commission.

On page 557, Volume VIII, American State Papers, Public Lands, Class VIII, appears a report "On a Claim to a Choctaw Reservation Under the Fourteenth Article of the Treaty of Dancing Rabbit Creek", which was communicated to the House of Representatives, March 21, 1836, by Mr. Everett from the Committee on Indian Affairs, to whom was committed the petition of Jubal B. Hancock, as follows:

> "The petitioner claims two and a quarter sections of land, under the 14th section of the treaty of Dancing Rabbit Creek, made with the Choctaw nation[sic] on the 27th September, 1830, and ratified 24th February, 1831.
>
> That article is as follows: 'Article xiv. Each Choctaw head of a family, being desirous to remain and become a citizen of the State, shall be permitted

to do so, by signifying his intention to the agent within six months from the ratification of this treaty, and he or she shall thereupon be entitled to a reservation of 640 acres of land, to be bounded by sectional lines of survey; in like manner shall be entitled to one half the quantity for each unmarried child which is living with him, over ten years of age, and a quarter section to such child as may be under ten years of age, to adjoin the location of the parent. If they reside upon said lands, intending to become citizens of the State, for five years after the ratifications of this treaty, in that case a grant in fee simple shall issue; said reservation shall include the present improvement of the head of the family, or a portion of it. Persons who claim under this article shall not lose the privilege of a Choctaw citizen, but if they ever remove, are not to be entitled to any portion of the Choctaw annuity.'

The petitioner claims, as a 'Choctaw head of a family; one section for himself, two half-sections for his two unmarried children over ten years of age, then living with him, and a quarter-section for a child under ten years of age.

The rights of the children depend on that of the father, and his right depends on the questions, 1, whether he was, at the date of the treaty, a Choctaw head of a family; and 2, whether, within six months from the date of the treaty, he gave notice to the agent of his intention to remain and become a citizen of the State. In relation to these questions the petitioner and the United States are the only parties whose rights can be taken into consideration; other questions may arise in the case in which the rights of the petitioner may conflict with those of third persons.

In relation to the first question, it appears from the testimony that the petitioner is a white native-born citizen of the United States, and before becoming a member of the Choctaw nation[sic], was a resident of the State of Tennesee[sic], when he married a woman of Choctaw descent, by whom he had children; that long before the treaty of 1830, he removed to and became a member of the Choctaw nation, and at the date of the treaty was the head of a Choctaw family.

The question is, then, reduced to this: whether the head of a Choctaw family, on the facts stated, is a Choctaw head of a family, within the fair construction of the treaty. It would be unworthy of the justice of the United States to avail itself of the technical sense of the word, or of its position in the construction of a sentence, contrary to the manifest intention of the other party to a treaty, and especially in a treaty with a nation with whom it treats on unequal terms. With the Indian nations, treaties are made in our language. They are, however, assented to through the medium of interpreters, of our own interpreters; and without imputing any intention of error, it would have been difficult to have explained to their understanding the difference, if any can be supposed to exist, between a Choctaw head of a family, and a head of a Choctaw family. They had no reason to make a distinction between members of their nation, whether members by blood or by adoption, nor between members by adoption, whether previously citizens of the United States, aliens, or members of other tribes. Nor is there, in the opinion of the committee, any reason why the United States should make any such distinction.

The treaty was made with the Choctaw nation, and as a consequence with every member of that nation. It was competent for that nation to determine who should be entitled to the privileges, who should be members of the nation; and every person who, at the date of the treaty, was, in good faith, a member of the Choctaw nation, was a Choctaw within the meaning of the 14th article; and if the head of a family, was a Choctaw head of a family. Nor is it material whether the head, or the family, or both, were Choctaws by blood or by adoption. In either case, as members of the nation, they were entitled to remove west or remain, and such as chose to remove were entitled to a share of the annuities, and such as remained, being heads of families, to reservations.

The absurdity of a distinction will be obvious from its consequences. It is well know that there were, among the Choctaws, as in other tribes, many intermarriages between white persons and native Indians, and the consequent half-breeds; if none are Choctaws but those who are so by blood, then it would follow that the wife and children must remove because they were Choctaws, and the husband remain. The wife would not be entitled to a reservation because she is not the head of a family, nor the husband because he is not a Choctaw by blood.

The abstract question of natural allegiance and its consequences cannot be supposed to have been either thought of or understood by the Indians when they concluded the treaty. They well know who in fact were members of their nation, and that all, without distinction, were subject to their laws, and entitled to equal protection and to equal privileges; and that all, whether adopted native-born citizens of the United States, foreigners, or Indians of other tribes, were equally, with the native Choctaws, subject or not, to the laws of the State in which the nation was located.

While members of the Indian nation, they were not regarded as citizens of the State. To entitle them to reservations, each head of a family was to signify his intention "to remain", (the words which follow are but the consequence,) "and become a citizen of the State".

Were there, however, doubts as to the construction of this article, the committee might refer to the provision in the eighteenth article, viz.: 'and further, it is agreed that in the construction of this treaty, wherever well founded doubts shall arise, it shall be construed most favorably toward the Choctaws.'

The committee are then of the opinion that the petitioner was entitled, under the treaty, to claim a section of land in his own right, as a Choctaw head of a family.

In relation to the petitioner in right to his children, the words of the treaty are 'in like manner' (such head of a family) ' shall be entitled to one half that quantity for each unmarried child which is living with him, over ten years of age; and a quarter-section to such child as may be under ten years of age'. It appears from the testimony that at the date of the treaty the petitioner had two children over ten years of age, and one under that age; that the eldest resided in his house, and the two younger elsewhere, but that they were under his care and control. He had at that time separated from his wife, who had returned to Tennesee[sic]. It does not appear that the younger children resided with her, or where they resided, or under what circumstances they were under the care and control of the petitioner.

All the relations between a parent and child are presumed to continue until the contrary is shown, and the children, wherever actually residing, will be considered as a part of the family of the parent so long as they are under his care and control; and in this sense the term 'residing with him' is used in the treaty. His reservations are given to him as a head of a family, and also in right of the members of his family, who, it was to be expected, would remain if he remained. The committee are therefore of opinion that the petitioner was entitled to claim two and a quarter sections in right of his children.

The committee do not consider the right affected by the fact proved, that the petitioner did not live with his wife at the date of the treaty, or that he has since married another woman. It was not necessary to constitute him the head of a family that he should have had a wife then living, or that his children should even have been legitimate: much less would his subsequent misconduct have impaired any right vested in him by the treaty.

In relation to the second question, whether the petitioner, within six months after the ratification of the treaty, (24th February, 1831,) signified to the agent his intention to remain and become a citizen of the States. All that was necessary to entitle him to the reservation was, that he should signify such intention to the agent: that being done, the right vested in him could not be divested by any neglect of the agent. The treaty having provided that the notice should be given to the agent, the government looked to the agent for the evidence of the fact, and by a regulation directed him to return a register of all such notices.

It appears by the testimony, that the petitioner did, within six months, (viz., on the 12th August, 1831,) signify to the agent his intention to remain and become a citizen of the States, and claimed, and has ever since claimed, his right under the treaty; and that his name was entered by the agent, or the register, but by accident or mistake, was not returned to the War Department. He had thus perfected his right to the two and a quarter sections of land.

It further appears, that on the 1st of January, 1832, the petitioner applied to the Secretary of War for a location of his reservations under the treaty; to which an answer was given, that 'the name of J. B. Hancock is not upon the list of Choctaws entitled to reservations returned by the agent'. The petitioner then furnished evidence to the department of his having clearly given the notice required by the treaty, and of his being a Choctaw head of a family &c.; and in consequence of this, on the 3d February, 1834, the following instructions were given to the locating agent, and of which notice on the same day was given to the petitioner.

DEPARTMENT OF WAR, Office of Indian Affairs, February 3, 1834.

Sir: Juba[sic] B. Hancock has transmitted to this office papers to establish his claim to reservations for himself and two children, under the 14th article of the treaty of September 27, 1830. He states, that he is a white man, married to a Choctaw woman, the mother of these children; that his son, William Mitchell, was twelve years old on the 1st day of September, 1830, and his daughter, Mary Melinda, was ten years old on the 14th of February, 1830; that his name and theirs were registered by Col. Ward in August, 1831, but the leaf on which they were registered was lost. This statement is supported by the affidavit of Giles Thompson; and David Folsom and P. P. Pitchlynn certify that the claimant was for many years prior to the treaty, a citizen, and entitled to all the privileges of a citizen.

You are requested to inquire of Col. Ward whether these circumstances are truly stated; and if they are, you will locate a section for the father, and a half section for each of the children, and apprise the department of the result.

Very respectfully, &c.

ELBERT HERRING.

Col. George W. Martin, Columbus, Mississippi.

P. S.--- There is a third child, Caroline Delia, who is now about ten years of age, and, of course, entitled to a quarter-section.

On the 29th September, 1834, the petitioner applied to the locating agent to located his reservations on No. 13, 12, and remainder in No. 11, who answered that he had 'not see Colonel Ward, nor received any satisfactory evidence of the fact of Hancock's registration from him, and that he did not feel himself authorized by his instructions to receive proof of the fact from any source except from Colonel Ward, the witness to whom he was referred in his instructions, and declined to make or authorize the location applied for without further instructions.'

On the 16th October, 1834, Colonel Ward gave a deposition giving the facts required by the instructions of the 3d February, which was forwarded immediately to the War Department.

The department having thus recognized the right of the petitioner as a head of a Choctaw family, in his own right and in right of his children, and being furnished with the proof it required of his having duly signified his intention to remain under the fourteenth section, there appears then no reason why the location should not have been made by order of the department, and according to the provisions of the treaty; on what lands other than on such as should include his improvement or a portion of it, was subject to the discretion of the Department, with the restriction of boundaries by sectional lines of survey.

During the time thus spent in procuring testimony, other Indian reservations were located which conflicted with the claim of the petitioner. His improvement was on the southeast quarter-section of No. 13, township 19, range 3 west. Jerry Fulson, an Indian reservee, whose improvement was on the southwest quarter-section of said No. 13, located his reservation on said southeast quarter-section of No. 13, covering the whole of the petitioner's improvement, and on the west half of the northeast quarter-section of said No. 13, and on the west half of the southeast quarter-section of said No. 13, and the residue on No. 11 and 14. Israel Fulson, whose improvement was on No. 18, township 19, range 2 west, and adjoining the improvement of the petitioner, located his improvement on No. 18 and 7, and on southeast half and the southeast quarter-section one, on the south quarter of the northeast quarter section of said No. 12, and another Indian (whether a reservee or not does not appear) had an improvement on the west half of the northeast quarter of section No. 13, so that by these two locations all lands adjoining the improvement of the petitioner and his improvement itself were covered; and on portions of Nos. 12 and 36, in township 19, floats and pre-emption rights were claimed. In some cases the land was entered by the pre-emption claimants, the purchase money paid, and pre-emption certificates issued by the register of the land office.

Thus circumstanced, the petitioner, on the 21st October, 1834, procured the locating agent to locate and mark on the map his reservations on No.1, and on the east half of the southeast quarter of the southwest quarter of section No.2, and on the west half and northeast quarter of the northeast quarter of Section No. 12, township 19, range 3 west; and on the south half of section No. 36, in township 20, range 3 west; and in consequence of this location the lands have been secured from sale. It appears by a certificate of the register, that the locating agent had, before that time, made a location, in some parts differing from the one above mentioned, not, however, including any part of his improvement, but when, or by whose directions it was made, does not appear.

None of the Indian locations of reservations, or pre-emption or float claims have been confirmed, and until confirmed, the executive is at liberty to direct a relocation of the reservations of the Fulsons and of the petitioner, to be made in such manner as will give each his right according to the provisions of the treaty, and their locations might be so made as to give to each a portion of his improvement, and might be laid to each in an entire tract, unless the pre-emption claimants have, in the meantime, acquired-rights superior to those of the reservees.

The rights of the reservees originated from the treaty, and accrued to them when they gave notice to remain and become citizens. His right to have his reservation located conformably to the treaty, became perfect, and Congress could pass no law that could impair this right, nor have they passed a law of that character.

The act of the 19th June, 1834, revives the act of 1830, and extends its benefits to settlers of 1833, &c. The act of 1830 contains a proviso, that no entry or sale of any lands shall be made under the provisions of that act, which shall have been reserved for the use of the United States. By the treaty of 1830, the lands necessary to satisfy the reservation were reserved to the United States, to be by them appropriated for that purpose. They remained in the United States subject to this use; when the Choctaw head of a family gave notice of his intention to remain, the use becomes instantly vested to, at least as much of his improvements as would be contained in the least tract that could be bounded by sectional lines, and to the right to have the remainder located; when his location was made and approved, he was entitled to occupy it as long as he should choose; and when he should have resided on it five years, he was entitled to a grant in fee simple.

The right of the reservees is, therefore, prior and paramount to any claim or right that could be acquired under the act of 1834, no right is vested in the pre-emption claimants that entitles them to interpose between the United States and the petitioner, on the question of location.

The petitioner asks a confirmation of his last location, on the ground that he supposes it to be wholly invalid, because it did not include his improvement, and that location cannot now be made that will include his improvement.

The committee are not satisfied of the correctness of either of the positions taken. The locations after made by the locating agent are subject to the determination of the executive, when affirmed, and then only are they irrevocably made. Until confirmed, they may be altered, in whole or in part, and it is yet competent for the President to direct a new location, so as to include, the improvement of the petitioner, and to confirm so much of his several locations, as shall make up the whole quantity to which he is entitled.

The treaty guarantees a section of land, to include his improvements; by the term section is not meant an entire section, but a quantity equal to that contained in a section, or 640 acres, which is to be bounded by sectional lines, and sectional lines are not descriptive only of those lines which bound entire sections, but also of those which divide sections, and those divisions are into halves, quarters, eights, and sixteenths. It follows, then, that it is not necessary that the location should be in one entire tract; wherever practicable, it would be laid in one entire tract. But this may be impossible. Such may be the situation of adjoining improvements, that the reservation of every reservee could not be located in one tract, without taking the whole of the improvements of others; so if prior locations should surround a quarter-section on which was the improvement of a reservee, he could take only that quarter-section, unless permitted to locate the residue elsewhere.

In the case of the petitioner, his improvement was on the southeast quarter of section 13. To this he is entitled of right. The question as to where the residue shall be located, is open between him and the Executive, and without disturbing the locations of either of the Fulsons or other reservees, further than depriving Israel Fulson of the southeast quarter-section of 13, and for which he would be entitled to an equal quantity elsewhere, the Executive may locate the residue of the petitioner's reservation on any other sections not before located, in an entire or separate tract, as convenience may require. This construction is necessary to the execution of the treaty, and it is not perceived that any injustice can flow from it.

As between the United States and the reservee, the whole question of location is open. The provision that the reservation shall include the improvement is, in this treaty, solely for the benefit of the reservee. No provision is made that the United States should pay for improvements abandoned. It is competent, then, for the reservee, with the consent of the

United States, to relinquish this privilege, and to take other lands in exchange and it may be competent for Congress to give such assent. The committee, however, do not recommend a confirmation of his location, but that a relocation should be made, on the ground that it should be so made as to interfere with the claims of others as little as possible.

The five years having expired, the petitioner, if now entitled to a relocation, is also entitled to a grant in fee. To this an objection is made, on the ground that he did not reside on the reservation during the whole of the five years.

It appears, by the testimony, that his improvement was claimed by an Indian reservee under a location; that in January, 1835, he attempted to erect a house on a part of his localities, but was driven off by force by some of the pre-emption claimants and others; that in February or March, 1835, having resided on his improvement until that time, he left it, and has since resided at Livingston, about five miles distant, without any intention to abandon his claim or citizenship.

The issue of abandonment is between the petitioner and the United States. The petitioner gave notice to the agent according to the treaty; he has done everything on his part to prove a location of his reservation; and that it was not done in due time and manner is wholly the fault of the agents of the United States. The embarrassments into which the petitioner has been thrown are consequences of that default, and of which the United States cannot, in justice, take any advantage. His leaving his improvement, in 1835, was the effect of a supposed necessity; his improvement being taken by a prior location, and when he attempted to settle on his location he was driven off by force.

On a view, then, of the whole case, the committee are of the opinion that the petitioner is entitled to his reservation, notwithstanding the agent neglected to return his name to the War Department; and now to a grant in fee, notwithstanding that, under the circumstances stated, he removed from his improvement before the expiration of the five years, and report a bill accordingly for his relief. With a view to avoid, if possible, a conflict with existing claims, they have provided that on his relinquishment of his right to a location, according to the treaty, he may locate on any lands required by the treaty, not subject to prior locations or pre-emption claims."

On August 11, 1842, Congress passed an act entitled "An Act for the Relief of Jubal B. Hancock," which is as follows:

"Be It Enacted, &c., That Jubal B. Hancock be, and he is hereby authorized, on or before the first day of January, one thousand eight hundred and forty-four to enter at the proper land office in legal subdivisions, fourteen hundred and forty acres of any of the public lands of the United States, within the State of Mississippi, in lieu of a like quantity of land to which he and his three children, William M. Hancock, Mary M. Hancock, and Caroline D. Hancock, became entitled under the fourteenth article of the treaty of Dancing

> Rabbit creek[sic], concluded with the Choctaw Nation of Indians, on the twenty-seventh day of September, one thousand eight hundred and thirty, which was improperly located for them by George W. Martin, the locating agent of the United States, and of which they have been deprived, by the decision of the Secretary of War.
>
> Sec. 2. And be it further enacted, That it shall be the duty of the Commissioner of the General Land Office, on receiving certificates of said entry, to cause patents to be issued to Jubal B. Hancock, for six hundred and forty acres; to William M. Hancock, for three hundred and twenty acres; to Mary M. Hancock, for three hundred and twenty acres; and to Caroline D. Hancock, for one hundred and sixty acres; in conformity with the provisions of said treaty.-----Approved August 11, 1842." (6 Stat. 856).

On March 3, 1847 Congress passed an act entitled "An Act for the Relief of the Heirs of Hyacinth Lasselle," Section 2 of which is a follows:

> "And be it further enacted, That the act entitled 'An Act for the Relief of Jubal B. Hancock' be so amended that the time allowed for the location of the land therein specified be extended to thirtieth day of December, eighteen hundred and forty-seven.
>
> APPROVED, March 3, 1847" (9 Stats. 706).

It is the opinion of the Commission that the applicants in this consolidated case have clearly established their descent from Jubal B. Hancock named in the above Report of the Committee on Indian Affairs, and in the acts of Congress of August 11, 1842, (6 Stats., 856), and March 3, 1847, (9 Stats., 706), and that the William M. Hancock named therein is the father of the applicants, Josephine Hussey, Jubal A. Hancock, and Charles Rushing Hancock; and that the Caroline D. Hancock named therein, is the Callie D. Roe, nee Hancock, who is the mother of the applicant, J. Folsom Roe.

The Commission is of the opinion that its denial of the applications for citizenship in the Choctaw Nation of William Hancock Hussey, J. Folsom Roe, Jubal A. Hancock and Charles Rushing Hancock under the act of Congress of June 10, 1896, (29 Stats., 321), is not prejudicial to the rights which the applicants acquire under the twenty first section of the act of Congress of June 28, 1898, (30 Stats., 495), authorizing the Commission to determine the identity of persons claiming rights in the Choctaw lands under the provisions of the fourteenth article of the treaty between the United States and the Choctaw Nation concluded September 27, 1830.

The authority vested in the Commission by the twenty first section of the act of Congress of June 28, 1898 (30 Stats. 495), is as follows:

> "Said commission shall have authority to determine the identity of Choctaw Indians claiming rights in the Choctaw lands under article fourteen of the treaty between the United States and the Choctaw Nation concluded September twenty seventh, eighteen hundred and thirty and to that end may administer oaths, examine witnesses, and perform all other acts necessary thereto and make report to the Secretary of the Interior."

It is the opinion of the Commission that the evidence in this case is sufficient to determine the identity of Josephine Hussey, William Hancock Hussey, Alvin McDowell Hussey, J. Folsom Roe, Jeannette C. Roe, Jubal A. Hancock and Charles Rushing Hancock, as Choctaw Indians entitled to rights in the Choctaw lands under the provision of law above quoted, and that the application for their identification as such should be granted, and it is so ordered.

THE COMMISSION TO THE FIVE CIVILIZED TRIBES.

Tams Bixby
Acting Chairman.

T.B. Needles
Commissioner.

C. R. Breckinridge
Commissioner.

Dated at
Muskogee, Indian Territory,
this MAY - 7 1902

DEPARTMENT OF THE INTERIOR.

COMMISSION TO THE FIVE CIVILIZED TRIBES.

In the matter of the application of Josephine Hussey, et al., for identification as Mississippi Choctaws, consolidating the applications of

Josephine Hussey, et al.,	M.C.R. 1620
J. Folsom Roe, et al.,	M.C.R. 1114
Jubal A. Hancock,	M.C.R. 1619
Charles Rushing Hancock,	M.C.R. 1712

IDENTIFIED MISSISSIPPI CHOCTAWS 1900 - 1909
DAWES PACKETS Volume IV

List of papers forwarded the Secretary of the Interior with the record in the above case, together with page occupied by each in said record.

STATE OF LOUISIANA :
:
PARISH OF ORLEANS :
City of New Orleans

BEFORE ME, a Notary Public, in and for said Parish and State, personally appeared H. L. Sexton, M. D., a practicing physician in the City of New Orleans, La., and to me well known, and who, being by me duly sworn, doth say:

THAT he is and has been the regular family physician of Samuel Mc C. Hussey (who ~~is~~ was the husband of Mrs. Josephine (Hancock) Hussey) for the past eight years; and that he was the attending physician during the late illness of the said Mrs. Josephine (Hancock) Hussey, the wife of the said Samuel Mc C. Hussey, and that she died on the First day of September, 1902, of phthisis pulmonalis; and that about six weeks before her said death she gave birth to a male child, which said child is still living; and, further, that he verily believes, from having seen documents and other evidence~~s~~ long before and since her death, that the said Mrs. Josephine (Hancock) Hussey is the same identical person who was recognized by the Dawes Commission as a legal Choctaw claimant to allotment in the Indian Territory, and whose recognition as such was lately approved by the Honorable Secretary of the Interior.

L Sexton M. D.

SWORN TO AND SUBSCRIBED BEFORE ME this 12th day

[Beginning of document missing]

day of *September* A. D. 1902, in the City of New Orleans, La.

And I further certify that I am acquainted with Samuel Mc C. Hussey and his late wife, Mrs. Josephine (Hancock) Hussey, and I know that his said wife is the same person whose affidavits I have heretofore taken relative to the Choctaw claim as mentioned in above affidavit.

Chas. B. Stetson
Notary Public for the Parish of Orleans.
State of Louisiana

State of Louisiana
Parish of Orleans
City of New Orleans

Personally came and appeared before me the undersigned authority S. Mc C. Hussey who after having been duly sworn according to law did depose and say that the infant child mentioned in the above declaration died on the evening of Sept 12th 1902

Sworn to and subscribed before me this 15th day of Sept 1902

S. Mc C. Hussey

Chas. B. Stetson
Not Pub

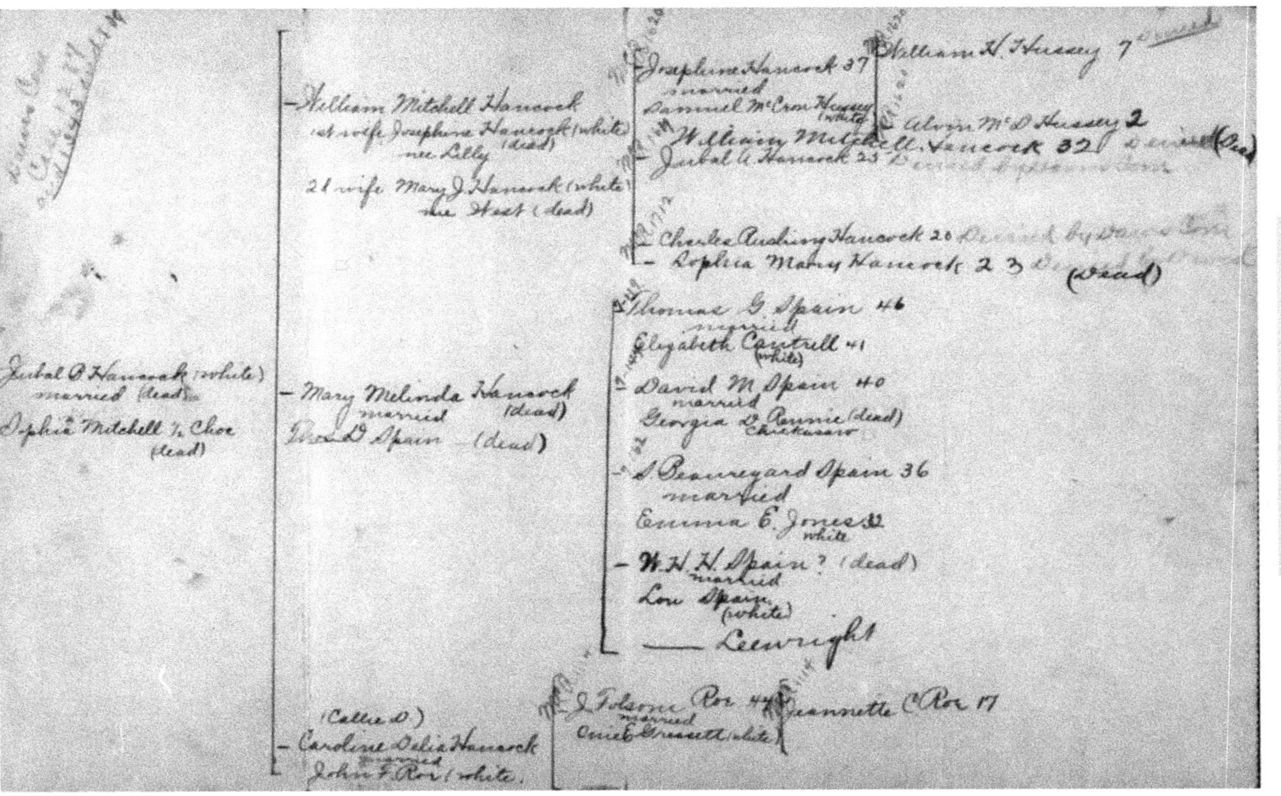

Jubal B Hancock (white)
married (dead)
Sophia Mitchell ½ Choc
(dead)

- William Mitchell Hancock
1st wife Josephine Hancock (white)
nee Lilly (dead)
2d wife Mary J. Hancock (white)
nee Hart (dead)

- Josephine Hancock 37
married
Samuel McCron Hussey (white)
- William H. Hussey 7
- Alvin McD Hussey 2

- William Mitchell Hancock 32
- Jubal A Hancock 25
- Charles Audrey Hancock 20
- Sophia Mary Hancock 23 (dead)

- Mary Melinda Hancock (dead)
married
Thos D Spain (dead)

- Thomas G. Spain 46
married
Elizabeth Cantrell 41 (white)
- David M Spain 40
married
Georgia L Rennie (dead) Chickasaw
- J Beauregard Spain 36
married
Emma E. Jones 32 white
- W.H.H. Spain? (dead)
married
Lou Spain (white)
— Leewright

(Callie D.)
- Caroline Delia Hancock
married
John F. Roe (white.

- J. Folsom Roe 44
married
Annie Bassett (white)
- Jeannette C Roe 17

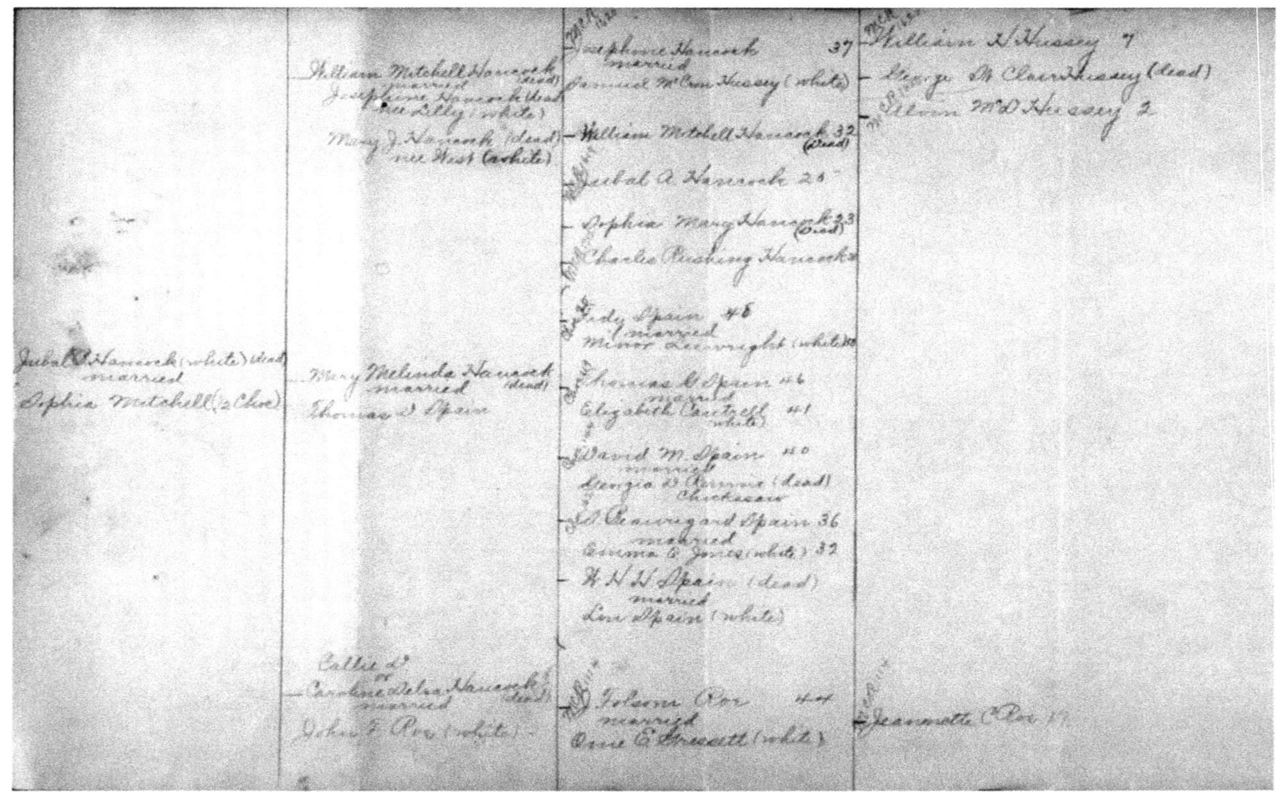

Jubal A. Hancock (white) dead
married
Sophia Mitchell (½ Choc)

William Mitchell Hancock (dead)
married
Josephine Hancock (dead) nee Lilly (white)
Mary J. Hancock (dead) nee West (white)

Josephine Hancock 37
married
Samuel McCra Hussey (white)

William Mitchell Hancock 32 (dead)

Jubal A. Hancock 25

Sophia Mary Hancock 23 (dead)

Charles Rushing Hancock

William D. Hussey 7

George St Clair Hussey (dead)

Alvin McD Hussey 2

Mary Melinda Hancock (dead)
married
Thomas J. Spain

Fedy Spain 48
married
Minor Wainright (white)

Thomas C. Spain 46
married
Elizabeth Cantrell 41 (white)

David M. Spain 40
married
Georgia D. Cannon (dead) Chickasaw

G. Beauregard Spain 36
married
Emma E. Jones (white) 32

H H S Spain (dead)
married
Lou Spain (white)

Callie L. or Caroline Leha Hancock (dead)
married
John F. Rox (white)

J. Folsom Rox 44
married
Ona E. Prescott (white)

Jeannette C. Rox 17

Muskogee, Indian Territory, September 13, 1901.

Mrs. Josephine Hancock Hussey,
#1607 Carondelet Street,
New Orleans, Louisiana.

Dear Madame:-

Receipt is hereby acknowledged of your letter of August 24th, in which you state that you appeared before the Commission in April, at Meridian, Mississippi, and applies for identification as a Mississippi Choctaw, and that up to this time yo have received no information in regard to this case.

In reply to your letter you are advised that it appears from our records that on April 3rd, 1901, Josephine Hussey appeared before the Commission at Meridian, Mississippi, and applied for the identification of herself and her minor children as Mississippi Choctaws. No action has yet been taken by the Commission in regard to this application, or any opinion rendered. When a decision is rendered, copy of the same, stating fully therein the reasons for any action taken by the Commission, will be mailed to you at your present Post Office address.

Yours truly,

M.C. 1620.

Muskogee, Indian Territory, December 6, 1901.

Josephine Hancock Hussey,
1607 Carondelet Street,
New Orleans, Louisiana.

Dear Madam:

Receipt is hereby acknowledged of your letter of December 2, in which you ask if it will be necessary for either you or your children to appear before the Commission again in January 1902, for the purpose of applying for identification as a Mississippi Choctaw.

In reply to your letter you are advised that it appears from our records that you appeared before the Commission at Meridian, Mississippi, April 3, 1901, and applied for identification for yourself and two minor children as Mississippi Choctaws. No decision has yet been reached or opinion rendered in regard to this application. When a decision is reached, you will be notified of the action taken by the Commission. If you wish to offer any further evidence in support of your application the Commission will hear the testimony of such witnesses as may present themselves at its office at Meridian, Mississippi, between January 15 and February 15, 1902. This appointment, however, is merely a continuation of the appointments made by the Commission in Mississippi in 1901, for the hearing of applications for identification as Mississippi Choctaws.

Yours truly,

Commissioner in Charge.

MC 1620.

M C-1620

Muskogee, Indian Territory, February 6, 1902.

Mrs. Josephine Hancock Hussey,
607[sic] Carondelet Street,
New Orleans, Louisiana.

Dear Madam:

Please advise the Commission whether your brother, William Mitchell Hancock, and your sister, Sophia Mary Hancock, are now living.

There is inclosed you herewith an envelope for reply which requires no postage.

Your early attention to this matter is requested.

Yours truly,

Commissioner in Charge.

(Copy)

New Orleans La. February 11, 1902.

To the Commissioners of the Five Civilized Tribes,

Muskogee, Ind. Ter.

My dear sir.

Your letter of inquiry dated February 6 received this morning, in reply will say that my brother William Mitchell Hancock died at his home in Meridian, Miss. of Consumption, December 15, 1896 and my sister, Sophia Mary Hancock died November 11, 1896 of Pneumonia. Dr. D. M. Spain and Mrs. F. O. L. Leewright of White Bead, Ind. Ter. are my first cousins.

Very Respect,

Mrs. Josephine Hancock Hussey

1607 Carondelet St.

N. O. La.

Muskogee, Indian Territory, March 11, 1902.

Mrs. Josephine Hussey,

1607 Carondelet Street,

New Orleans, La.

Dear Madam:

Receipt is hereby acknowledged of your letter of the 2nd instant, in which you state that you in April last appeared before the Commission to the Five Civilized Tribes at Meridian, Mississippi, as an applicant for identification as a Mississippi Choctaw and were then and there advised that you would in a short time be advised as to the decision of the Commission upon your claim.

You now desire to be informed what rights if any, you would have by removing to the Indian Territory and also as to when your application will be taken up for final action.

You are advised that the Commission now has under consideration the rights of the descendants of Jubal B. Hancock to be identified as Mississippi Choctaws under the provisions of the fourteenth article of the treaty of 1830 and it is probable that some decision will be rendered in the very near future, of which action you will be duly advised.

Relative to your right to now remove to and make settlement in the Choctaw Nation, your attention is invited to the following provision of the act of Congress of May 31, 1900:

""That any Mississippi Choctaw duly identified as such by the United States Commission to the Five Civilized Tribes shall have the right, at any time prior to the approval of the final rolls of the Choctaws and Chickasaws by the Secretary of the Interior, to make settlement within the Choctaw-Chickasaw country, and on proof of the fact of bona fide settlement may be enrolled by the said United States Commission, and by the Secretary of the Interior as Choctaws entitled to allotment: Provided, further, That all contracts or agreements looking to the sale or incumbrance in any way of the lands to be allotted to said Mississippi Choctaws, shall be null and void."

It is not believed that this legislation gives any person, an applicant for identification as a Mississippi Choctaw, any right to make settlement upon the public domain of the Choctaw or Chickasaw Nations in the Indian Territory until their rights as such Mississippi Choctaws have finally be adjudicated by this Commission.

Yours truly,

Commissioner in Charge.

Muskogee, Indian Territory, March 24, 1902.

The Commission to the

Five Civilized Tribes.

Gentlemen-

There is submitted herewith for your consideration, original and three carbon copies of a decision identifying Josephine Hussey[,] William Hancock Hussey, Alvin McDowell Hussey, J. Folsom Roe, Jeannette C. Roe, Jubal A. Hancock and Charles Rushing Hancock as Mississippi Choctaws under the provisions of the twenty-first section of the Act of Congress of June 28, 1898, (30 Stats., 495), as the descendants of a "Choctaw head of a family" whose right to receive benefits under the fourteenth article of the treaty of 1830 between the United States and the Choctaw Nation was adjudicated favorably to the claimant. The persons named herein are the direct lineal descendants of Jubal B. Hancock, a white man, and Sophia Mitchell Hancock, an one half blood Choctaw woman. The direct lineal descent of these applicants from Jubal B. Hancock and Sophia Mitchell Hancock is conclusively established by reliable testimony and evidence of marriage of the antecedents of the applicants.

While neither the name of Jubal B. Hancock or Sophia Mitchell Hancock is found upon the "Register" made by Colonel Wm. Ward of those Choctaws who within six months after the ratification of the treaty of 1830 signified their intention to remain and become citizens of the states under the provisions of the fourteenth article of the treaty of 1830, yet the records of the Government in the Possession of the Commission show that claim of Jubal B. Hancock, a "Choctaw head of a family", to one section for himself, two half-sections for two children over ten years of age, and one quarter section for a child under ten years of age, was established by an Act of Congress of August 11, 1842, entitled "An Act for the relief of Jubal B. Hancock", and that act of Congress is based upon the favorable report of the House of Representatives Committee on Indian Affairs, of March 21, 1836, the copy of said report and of the act of August 11, 1842, being included in and made a part of the decision.

Four of the applicants who are by this decision identified as Mississippi Choctaws, viz: William Hancock Hussey, J. Folsom Roe, Jubal A. Hancock and Charles Rushing Hancock, submitted original applications for citizenship in the Choctaw Nation under the Act of Congress of June 10, 1896, (29 Stats., 321), all of which applications were denied and there was no appeal prosecuted or perfected from such decision within the time prescribed by said Act. After a thorough investigation and a careful consideration of this matter, I am firmly of the opinion that the debial[sic] of "citizenship" in the Choctaw Nation to these persons under the Act of Congress of June 10, 1896 (29 Stats., 321), is not prejudicial to any rights that they might have as "Mississippi Choctaws" acquired under the provisions of the twenty-first section of the Act of Congress of June 28, 1898, (30 Stats., 495).

The authority vested in the Commission and the tribal authorities of the Choctaw Nation by the provisions of the Act of June 10, 1896 (29 Stats., 321), merely gave to such tribunals authority to determine whether or not an applicant under that Act was entitled to "citizenship" in the Choctaw Nation, and the jurisdiction conferred was to admit or reject, without limitations or conditions, and to determine conclusively the right of any applicant to citizenship in the Choctaw Nation in Indian Territory. The Act of June 10, 1896, was with a view of determining the right to citizenship of persons in the five tribes in Indian Territory, and provided that in so doing

"Said Commission shall respect all laws of the several nations or tribes not inconsistent with the laws of the United States, and all treaties with either of said nations or tribes, and shall give due force and effect to the rolls, usages and customs of each of said Nations or tribes."

The rights of these applicants were denied by the Commission under the authority vested by the Act of June 10, 1896, and as far as the acquisition of citizenship under the provisions of that act, their rights were finally determined. After the expiration of the time within which petitions filed under the act of June 10, 1896, could be received and determined, the act of June 28, 1898, empowered the Commission to determine the identity of Choctaw Indians claiming rights under the provisions of the fourteenth article of the treaty of 1830. This legislation is without limitation, and as those applicants have conclusively established the fact that they are descendants of a "Choctaw head of a family" who was a beneficiary under the provisions of the fourteenth article of the treaty of 1830, it is apparently obligatory upon the Commission, under the authority vested by the act of June 28, 1898, to identify, and, upon proof of bona fide settlement, enroll them as "Mississippi Choctaws", notwithstanding the denial of their right to "Choctaw citizenship" under the authority vested by the act of June 10, 1896.

I am of the opinion, after a thorough investigation of the rights of all the parties applicant herein, that they are entitled to and should be identified by the Commission as Mississippi Choctaws under the provisions of the Act of Congress of June 28, 1898.

Very respectfully,

Clerk in Charge
Choctaw-Chickasaw Enrollment
Division.

M C R 1620

COPY.

Muskogee, Indian Territory, May 8, 1902.

Josephine Hussey,

1607 Carondalet Street,

New Orleans, Louisiana.

Dear Madam:

You are hereby advised that on May 7, 1902, the Commission to the Five Civilized Tribes rendered a decision in the consolidated case of Josephine Hussey, et al., embracing the following applications for identification as Mississippi Choctaws.

Josephine Hussey, et al.,
J. Folsom Roe, et al.,
Jubal A. Hancock,
Charles Rushing Hancock.

Said decision after a review of the evidence submitted, concludes as follows:

"The authority vested in the Commission by the twenty first section of the act of Congress of June 28, 1898, (30 Stats., 495), is as follows;

> 'Said commission shall have authority to determine the identity of Choctaw Indians claiming rights in the Choctaw lands under article fourteen of the treaty between the United States and the Choctaw Nation concluded September twenty seventh, eighteen hundred and thirty and to that end may administer oaths, examine witnesses, and perform all other acts necessary thereto and make report to the Secretary of the Interior.'

It is the opinion of the Commission that the evidence in this case is sufficient to determine the identity of Josephine Hussey, William Hancock Hussey, Alvin McDowell Hussey, J. Folsom Roe, Jeannette C. Roe, Jubal A. Hancock and Charles Rushing Hancock, as Choctaw Indians entitled to rights in the Choctaw lands under the provision of law above quoted, and that the application for their identification as such be granted, and it is so ordered."

You are further advised that the Commission has on this date forwarded the record in this case to the Secretary of the Interior for review and you will be informed in due time of such action as may be taken by him.

Yours truly,

(SIGNED). *T. B. Needles.*

Commissioner in Charge.

Register.

M.C.R. 1620

COPY.

Muskogee, Indian Territory, May 8, 1902.

Messrs Mansfield, McMurray & Cornish,

Attorneys for the Choctaw and Chickasaw Nations,

South McAlester, Indian Territory.

Gentlemen:

You are hereby advised that on May 7, 1902, the Commission to the Five Civilized Tribes rendered a decision in the consolidated case of Josephine Hussey, et al., embracing the following applications for identification as Mississippi Choctaws.

Josephine Hussey, et al.,
J. Folsom Roe, et al.,
Jubal A. Hancock,
Charles Rushing Hancock.

Said decision after a review of the evidence submitted, concludes as follows:

"The authority vested in the Commission by the twenty first section of the act of Congress of June 28, 1898, (30 Stats., 495), is as follows;

'Said commission shall have authority to determine the identity of Choctaw Indians claiming rights in the Choctaw lands under article fourteen of the treaty between the United States and the Choctaw Nation concluded

September twenty seventh, eighteen hundred and thirty and to that end may administer oaths, examine witnesses, and perform all other acts necessary thereto and make report to the Secretary of the Interior.'

It is the opinion of the Commission that the evidence in this case is sufficient to determine the identity of Josephine Hussey, William Hancock Hussey, Alvin McDowell Hussey, J. Folsom Roe, Jeannette C. Roe, Jubal A. Hancock and Charles Rushing Hancock, as Choctaw Indians entitled to rights in the Choctaw lands under the provision of law above quoted, and that the application for their identification as such be granted, and it is so ordered."

You are further advised that the Commission has on this date forwarded the record in this case to the Secretary of the Interior for review and you will be informed in due time of such action as may be taken by him.

Yours truly,

(SIGNED). *T. B. Needles.*

Commissioner in Charge.

Register.

M.C.R. 1620

COPY.

Muskogee, Indian Territory, May 8, 1902.

The Honorable,

The Secretary of the Interior.

Sir:

There is transmitted herewith the record in the consolidated case of Josephine Hussey, et al., applicants to the Commission for identification as Mississippi Choctaws, including the decision of the Commission of May 7, 1902.

The above consolidated case embraces the following original applications for identification as Mississippi Choctaws heard by the Commission:

Josephine Hussey, et al.,	M.C.R. 1620
J. Folsom Roe, et al.,	M.C.R. 1114
Jubal A. Hancock,	M.C.R. 1619
Charles Rushing Hancock,	M.C.R. 1712

The Commission has the honor to report that the principal applicants in the several separate applications and the attorneys for the Choctaw and Chickasaw Nations have been duly advised by registered letter of the action of the Commission, copies of said letters being attached to the record.

Respectfully,

Through the Commissioner
of Indian Affairs. (SIGNED). T. B. Needles.

1 inclosure. Commissioner in Charge.

COPY.

30382

D. C. No. 8589.

Refer in reply to
the following
Land-28269-1902

DEPARTMENT OF THE INTERIOR.

Office of Indian Affairs,

Washington, May 15, 1902.

The Honorable,

The Secretary of the Interior.

Sir:

The office transmits herewith the papers in the consolidated case of Josephine Hussey et al., applicants for identification as Mississippi Choctaws and recommends that the decision of the Commission, holding that the applications should be granted, be affirmed.

The record evidence shows conclusively that the applicants are descendants of Mississippi Choctaw ancestors, who were recognized as such, enrolled and granted land under the fourteenth article of the treaty between the United States and the Choctaw Nation concluded on the 27th day of September, 1830, by Act of Congress entitled "An Act for the relief of Jubal B. Hancock, passed August 11th, 1842, all of which is verified by the records in this office.

It is further shows by the record that in 1896, William Hancock Hussey, a minor, by his mother as next friend, J. Folsom Roe, Jubal A. Hancock and Charles Rushing Hancock made application for citizenship in the Choctaw Nation under the Act of Congress of June 10th, 1896, and that their said applications were denied by the Commission and no appeal taken from the adverse decision.

This is no bar to filing an application for identification as a Mississippi Choctaw under the Act of Congress of June 28th, 1898 (30 Stats., 495) and having their rights under that Act adjudicated by the proper tribunal.

Section 21 of that Act expressly provides that "Said commission shall have authority to determine the identity of Choctaw Indians claiming rights in the Choctaw lands under article fourteen of the treaty between the United States and the Choctaw Nation concluded September twenty seventh, eighteen hundred and thirty and to that end may administer oaths, examine witnesses, and perform all other acts necessary thereto and make report to the Secretary of the Interior."

It is under this provision the applications herein are made, and no previous adjudication of their status can be construed as an estoppel that will exclude claimants from the benefits conferred by the Act when the facts support their claim to the rights intended to be established thereby.

Very respectfully,

Your obedient servant,

Acting Commissioner.

W.C.B.(Cg.)

COPY.

30382.

I.T.D.3142-1902.
L.R.S.

DEPARTMENT OF THE INTERIOR.

Washington, May 21, 1902.

Commission to the Five Civilized Tribes,

Muskogee, I. T.

Gentlemen:

The Department has considered the Mississippi Choctaw case 1620, embracing the applications of Josephine Hussey, William Hancock Hussey, Alvin McDowell Hussey, J. Folsom Roe, Jeanette C. Roe, Jubal A. Hancock and Charles Rushing Hancock, transmitted with your letter of May 8, 1902.

You found that the evidence was sufficient to establish the descent of the claimants from Jubal B. Hancock who took advantage of the 14th article of the treaty of 1830, and to determine the identity of the applicants as Choctaw Indians entitled to rights in the Choctaw Nation, in which opinion the Acting Commissioner of Indian Affairs in letter of May 15, 1902, concurs.

He states that it is shown that the applicants are descendants of Mississippi Choctaw ancestors who were recognized as such, enrolled and granted lands under the 14th article of the treaty of 1830, by an Act of Congress entitled "An Ace for the relief of Jubal B. Hancock," passed August 11, 1842; that, while it is shown that in 1896 William Hancock Hussey, J. Folsom Roe, Jubal A. Hancock and Charles Rushing Hancock made application for citizenship in the Choctaw Nation under the Act of June 10, 1896, and that their applications were denied by your Commission and no appeal taken, that is no bar to the consideration of an application for identification as a Mississippi Choctaw under the 21st section of the Act of June 28, 1898 (30 Stats., 495).

The Department has carefully considered the matter and finds no reason to disturb your decision, and it is accordingly affirmed. A copy of the Acting Commissioner's letter is enclosed.

You will advise the claimants, residents of Mississippi, hereof, and that to be entitled to enrollment in the Choctaw Nation, and to an allotment, it will be necessary for them to remove in good faith to the Choctaw-Chickasaw country, Indian Territory; also to that portion of the Choctaw-Chickasaw agreement pending in Congress, in regard to Mississippi Choctaws.

Respectfully,

Thos. Ryan,

Acting Secretary.

1 enclosure. E.M.D.

Miss. Choctaw 1620.

Muskogee, Indian Territory, May 31, 1902.

Mansfield, McMurray & Cornish,

Attorneys for the Choctaw and Chickasaw Nations,

South McAlester, Indian Territory.

Gentlemen:

You are hereby notified that on May 21, 1902, the Secretary of the Interior affirmed the decision of the Commission in the consolidated case of Josephine Hussey, et al., applicants for identification as Mississippi Choctaws.

Yours truly,

Acting Chairman.

Miss. Choctaw 1620

Muskogee, Indian Territory, May 31, 1902.

Josephine Hussey,

1607 Carondelet Street,

New Orleans, Louisiana,

Dear Madam:

You are hereby advised that on the twenty first day of May, 1902, the Secretary of the Interior affirmed the decision of the Commission to the Five Civilized Tribes granting the application made by you for the identification of yourself and your two minor children, William H. and Alvin McDowell Hussey, as Mississippi Choctaws, entitled to rights in the Choctaw lands in Indian Territory as beneficiaries under the provisions of article fourteen of the treaty between the United States and the Choctaw Nation, concluded September 27, 1830.

You are now advised, that, in order for you and your minor children to be enrolled as citizens of the Choctaw Nation entitled to allotment, it is necessary that you remove to and make settlement within the Choctaw-Chickasaw country, as provided by the act of Congress of May 31, 1900, (31 Stats., 221):

"That any Mississippi Choctaw duly identified as such by the United States Commission to the Five Civilized Tribes shall have the right, at any time prior to the approval of the final rolls of the Choctaws and Chickasaws by the Secretary of the Interior, to make settlement within the Choctaw-Chickasaw country, and on proof of the fact of bona fide settlement may be enrolled by the said United States Commission, and by the Secretary of the Interior as Choctaws entitled to allotment: Provided further, That all contracts or agreements looking to the sale or incumbrance in any way of the lands to be allotted to said Mississippi Choctaws, shall be null and void."

Your attention is further invited to the following sections of an agreement entered into at Washington, D.C. March 21, 1901, between Commissioners on the part of the United States and the Choctaw and Chickasaw Nations, and now pending before the Congress of the United States for ratification:

"41. All persons duly identified by the Commission to the Five Civilized Tribes under the provisions of section 21 of the act of Congress approved June 28, 1898 (30 Stats., 495), as Mississippi Choctaws entitled to benefits under article 14 of the treaty between the United States and the Choctaw Nation concluded September 27, 1830, may, at any time within six months after the date of the final ratification of this agreement, make bona fide settlement within the Choctaw-Chickasaw country, and upon proof of such settlement to such Commission within one year after the date of the final ratification of this agreement may be enrolled by such Commission as Mississippi Choctaws entitled to allotment as herein provided for citizens of the tribes, subject to the special provisions herein provided as to Mississippi Choctaws, and said enrollment shall be final when approved by the Secretary of the Interior. The application of no person for identification as a Mississippi Choctaw shall be received by said Commission after the date of the final ratification of this agreement.

42. When any such Mississippi Choctaw shall have continuously resided upon the lands of the Choctaw and Chickasaw Nations for a period of three years, including his residence thereon before and after such enrollment, he shall, upon due proof of such continuous residence, made in such manner and before such officer as may be designated by the Secretary of the Interior, receive a patent for his

allotment, as provided in the Atoka agreement, and he shall hold the lands allotted to him as provided in this agreement for citizens of the Choctaw and Chickasaw nations.

43. Applications for enrollment as Mississippi Choctaws, and applications to have land set apart to them as such, must be made personally before the Commission to the Five Civilized Tribes. Fathers may apply for their minor children; and if the father be dead, the mother may apply; husbands may apply for wifes. Applications for orphans, insane persons, and persons of unsound mind may be made by duly appointed guardian or curator, and for aged and infirm persons and prisoners by agents duly authorized thereunto by power of attorney, in the discretion of said Commission.

44. If within four years after such enrollment any such Mississippi Choctaw, or his heirs or representatives if he be dead, fails to make proof of such continuous bona fide residence for the period so prescribed, or up to the time of the death of such Mississippi Choctaw, in case of his death after enrollment, he, and his heirs and representatives if he be dead, shall be deemed to have acquired no interest in the lands set apart to him, and the same shall be sold at public auction for cash, under rules and regulations prescribed by the Secretary of the Interior, and the proceeds paid into the Treasury of the United States to the credit of the Choctaw and Chickasaw tribes, and distributed per capita with other funds of the tribes. Such lands shall not be sold for less than their appraised value. Upon payment of the full purchase price patent shall issue to the purchaser."

Yours truly,

Acting Chairman.

Miss. Choc. 1

Muskogee, Indian Territory, July 12, 1902.

Samuel McC. Hussey,

1607 Carondelet Street,

New Orleans, Louisiana.

Dear Sir:

Receipt is hereby acknowledged of your letter of June 17, 1902, written in behalf of your wife, Josephine Hussey and in which you desire to be informed as to the latest date on which it is necessary for your wife and her minor children to remove to the Indian Territory to be enrolled as Mississippi Choctaws.

It is presumed your letter is written in reply to our communication of May 31, 1902, addressed to your wife, wherein she was advised that on the 21st day of May, 1902, the Secretary of the Interior affirmed the decision of the Commission of May 7, 1902, identifying your wife and her two minor children, William H. and Alvin McD. Hussey as Choctaw Indians entitled to allotment under the provisions of the act of Congress of June 28, 1898.

Relative to the removal of your wife to the Choctaw-Chickasaw country and the making of a bona fide residence, you are advised that the only provision of law now effective regarding the bona fide settlement of Mississippi Choctaws in the Choctaw-Chickasaw country, is contained in the following [illegible...]

"Any Mississippi Choctaw duly identified as such by the United States Commission to the Five Civilized Tribes shall have the right, at any time prior to the approval of the final rolls of the Choctaws and Chickasaws by the Secretary of the Interior, to make settlement within the Choctaw-Chickasaw country, and on proof of the fact of bona fide settlement may be enrolled by the said United States Commission, and by the Secretary of the Interior as Choctaws entitled to allotment: Provided, further, That all contracts or agreements looking to the sale or incumbrance in any way of the lands to be allotted to said Mississippi Choctaws, shall be null and void."

This legislation would grant to your wife and her two minor children the right to at any time prior to the approval of the final rolls of the Choctaws and Chickasaws by the Secretary of the Interior, to remove to the Choctaw-Chickasaw country, Indian Territory and make settlement.

This legislation is, however, slightly amended by an agreement recently entered into between representatives of the Choctaw and Chickasaw Nations and the Commission to the Five Civilized Tribes and ratified by an act of Congress approved July 1, 1902, and which provides as follows:

"All persons duly identified by the Commission to the Five Civilized Tribes under the provisions of section 21 of the act of Congress approved June 28, 1898 (30 Stats., 495), as Mississippi Choctaws entitled to benefits under article 14 of the treaty between the United States and the Choctaw Nation concluded September 27, 1830, may, at any time within six months after the date of the final ratification of this agreement, make bona fide settlement within the Choctaw-Chickasaw country, and upon proof of such settlement to such Commission within one year after the date of their said identification as Mississippi Choctaws shall be enrolled by such Commission as Mississippi Choctaws entitled to allotment as herein provided for citizens of the tribes, subject to the sprcial[sic] provisions herein provided as to Mississippi Choctaws:"

This agreement is not effective at this time but is subject to ratification by a majority vote of the legal voters of the Choctaw and Chickasaw Tribes and is to be submitted to the Tribes for ratification at a special election to be called by the chief executives of these two Tribes within one hundred and twenty days after July 1, 1902.

It is suggested that if your wife and her two minor children anticipate taking advantage of the privileges accorded them by their identification by this Commission and the Secretary of the Interior that they as early as practicable remove to and make settlement within the Choctaw-Chickasaw country and when such settlement is made that your wife personally appear before this Commission at its office at Muskogee, Indian Territory for the purpose of making her proof of such bona fide settlement.

Yours truly,

Acting Chairman.

Miss. Choctaw I 1.

Muskogee, Indian Territory, October 3, 1902.

S. McC. Hussey,

Care M. Leewright,

McGee, Indian Territory.

Dear Sir:

Receipt is hereby acknowledged of your letter of September 27, 1902, asking relative to obtaining land for allotments for your two children who have been identified as Mississippi Choctaws, and stating that all the good land is under fence and thousands of acres are held by a few persons who claim to be citizens.

In reply to your letter your attention is invited to the following provision of the agreement recently entered into between the United States and the Choctaw and Chickasaw Nations, which was ratified September 25, 1902:

"It shall be unlawful after ninety days after the date of the final ratification of this agreement for any member of the Choctaw or Chickasaw tribes to enclose or hold possession of in any manner, by himself or through another, directly or indirectly, more lands in value than that of three hundred and twenty acres of average allottable lands of the Choctaw and Chickasaw nations, as provided by the terms of this agreement, either for himself or for his wife, or for each of his minor children if members of said tribes; and any member of said tribes found in such possession of lands, or having the same in any manner enclosed after the expiration of ninety days after the date of the final ratification of this agreement, shall be deemed guilty of a misdemeanor."

Respectfully,

Acting Chairman.

C O P Y

Land

DEPARTMENT OF THE INTERIOR

17977- 1903

OFFICE OF INDIAN AFFAIRS,

Washington, March 23, 1903.

The Honorable,

The Secretary of the Interior

Sir:

Referring to Department letter of May 21, 1902, (ITD 3142) there is enclosed herewith report from the Commission to the Five Civilized Tribes, dated March 10, 1903, forwarding partial roll of Mississippi Choctaw applicants found entitled to identification. The names of all of the persons who appear on said roll, except No. 1013, Nettie Frances Carter, were identified by the Commission in its decision of May 7, 1902, which was duly approved by the Department in letter above referred to.

Nettie Frances Carter was identified by the Commission December 4, 1902, which decision was affirmed by the Department February 24, 1903 (ITD 1176). May 21, 1902, it was found by the Department that Josephine Hussey, William Hancock Hussey, Alvin McDowell Hussey, J. Folsom Roe, Jeanette C. Roe, Jubal A. Hancock, and Charles Rushing Hancock were entitled to identification as Mississippi Choctaws. All of said persons' names appear on the partial roll now transmitted, except that of Josephine Hussey. The Commission states in its report that the persons whose names now appear on the partial roll were living on September 25, 1902.

The approval of the roll is recommended, and it is suggested that the Commission be instructed to advise the Department why the name of Josephine Hussey was not included in said partial roll.

Very respectfully,

(Signed) A. C. Tonner

Acting Commissioner

CAW -O

M C R 1620

Muskogee, Indian Territory, July 6, 1903.

Mansfield, McMurray & Cornish,

Attorneys for the Choctaw and Chickasaw Nations,

South McAlester, Indian Territory.

Gentlemen:

Receipt is hereby acknowledged of your letter of June 18, 1903, in which you ask for a copy of the record in the Mississippi Choctaw case of Josephine Hussey, et al.

In compliance with your request there is herewith enclosed you copy of testimony of Josephine Hussey, Samuel Mc. Hussey, Samuel McCron Hussey, and a copy of the decision of the Commission in the consolidated Mississippi Choctaw case of Josephine Hussey, et al.

Respectfully,

Commissioner in Charge.

McM 12

No.

For Identification as a Mississippi Choctaw.

Date APR 3 1901

Name Josephine Hussey.

Age 37 Blood 1/8

Post Office. 1607 Carondolet street, New Orleans, La.

Father: William M. Hancock - dead.

Mother: Josephine Lilly - dead.

Claims through father.

HUSBAND:

Saml. Mc Crow Hussey.

(no claim for husband).

Children:

William H. Hussey. 7.

Alvin Mc. D. " 2.

Claims for herself and two children.

Stenographer

Myro Young.

CARD NO. 2 - Choc. MCR 1114 - J. Folsom Roe
See MCR 1620

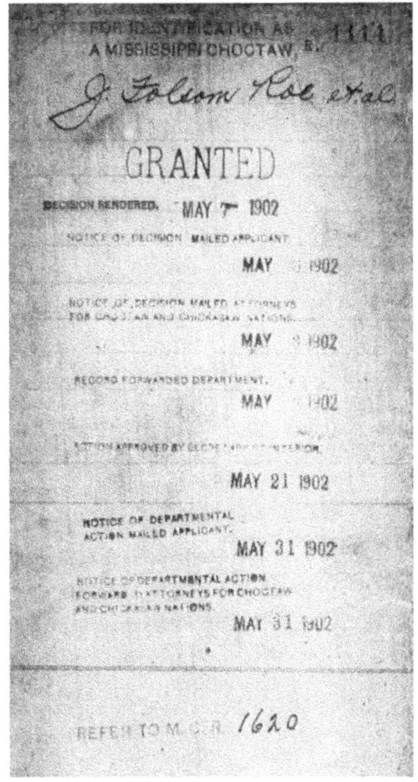

FOR IDENTIFICATION AS A MISSISSIPPI CHOCTAW, 1114

J. Folsom Roe et al

GRANTED

DECISION RENDERED. MAY 7 1902

NOTICE OF DECISION MAILED APPLICANT
MAY 1902

NOTICE OF DECISION MAILED ATTORNEYS FOR CHOCTAW AND CHICKASAW NATIONS
MAY 1902

RECORD FORWARDED DEPARTMENT.
MAY 1902

ACTION APPROVED BY SECRETARY OF INTERIOR.
MAY 21 1902

NOTICE OF DEPARTMENTAL ACTION MAILED APPLICANT.
MAY 31 1902

NOTICE OF DEPARTMENTAL ACTION FORWARD ATTORNEYS FOR CHOCTAW AND CHICKASAW NATIONS
MAY 31 1902

REFER TO M.C.R. 1620

Department of the Interior,
Commission to the Five Civilized Tribes.

I, Thomas B. Needles, member of the Commission to the Five Civilized Tribes, do hereby certify that J. Folsom Roe was duly identified by the Commission to the Five Civilized Tribes as a Mississippi Choctaw entitled to allotment under the provisions of the twenty-first section of the act of Congress of June 28, 1898 (30 Stat. 495), May 7, 1902, which identification was approved by the Secretary of the Interior on May 21, 1902.

T B Needles
Commissioner.

Muskogee, Indian Territory,

July 2, 1902.

DEPARTMENT OF THE INTERIOR.
COMMISSION TO THE FIVE CIVILIZED TRIBES.
HATTIESBURG, MISSISSIPPI, DECEMBER 17, 1900.

In the matter of the application of J. Folsom Roe for the identification of himself and his minor child a Mississippi Choctaws

J. Folsom Roe, having been first duly sworn by Acting Chairman Tams Bixby, testifies as follows:

Examination by the Commission.

Q What is your name? A J. Folsom Roe.
Q What is your age? A My age is forty four.
Q What is your post office address? A Meridian, Mississippi.
Q Are you a resident of the state of Mississippi? A Yes sir.
Q How long have you been living here? A I have been living here I suppose about thirty nine years. I came back from the Territory, I believe, when I was about five years old.
Q Were you born in Indian Territory? A Yes sir.
Q Where, Doaksville,
Q Choctaw Nation? A Yes sir.
Q What county? A I believe it is Blue; I won't be positive; you see I was quite young; all my parents died when I was small. I believe though, it is Blue County.
Q What was your father's name? A John F. Roe.
Q Is he living? A No sir, he is dead.
Q What is your mother's name? A Her name was Callie D. Roe.
Q Is your mother living? A No sir, she is dead.
Q Through which one of your parents do you claim your Choctaw blood?
A My mother's mother.
Q Through your mother's side? A Well, my grandmother.
Q Your mother's side? A Yes sir.
Q How much Choctaw? A She was a full blood, my mother's mother.
Q You are a quarter? A I suppose I would be at that rate.
Q Is your name on any of the tribal roll of the Choctaw Nation in Indian Territory?
A No sir, we moved away when I was young. I have got a whole lot of cousins out there, the Spains, White Bead Hill, they begged us to, we neglected it like everything else. After my my[sic] mother died. I heard about the Dawes Commission and thought I would go to see them to apply for citizenship.
Q Did you ever make application to the Choctaw tribal authorities in Indian Territory for citizenship in the Choctaw Nation? A No sir

Q Did you make application to the Dawes Commission in 1896, under the act of Congress of June 10, 1896, for citizenship in the Choctaw Nation? A No sir.
Q Ever been admitted to citizenship in the Choctaw Nation by judgment of the United States Court in Indian Territory? A No sir.
Q Did you ever, prior to this time, make any application either to the Choctaw tribal authorities or the authorities of the United States for either citizenship or enrollment in the Choctaw Nation? A Well, about a year ago up at Decatur there, I had an application, but I could not get it in. They seemed to be so busy; I had a lawyer there and he fooled around till I got disgusted and went away.
Q You didn't make any application? A No sir.
Q That was about two years ago? A I don't remember, it was something like that; it was up at Decatur. I had a lawyer there, a little young fellow who didn't know anything of course I depended on him.
Q It is now your purpose to make application for identification as a Mississippi Choctaw? A Sir.
Q It is now your purpose to make application for identification as a Mississippi Choctaw? A Yes sir.
Q Are you making your claim as a beneficiary under the fourteenth article of the treaty of 1830? A Yes sir.
Q Are you familiar with the provisions of that treaty? A No sir.
Q Have you a general idea of what it is? A Well, I have an idea that gives you a citizenship or a right or whatever you are entitled to.
Q The treaty of 1830 was entered into between the United States and the Choctaw Indians in Mississippi providing for the removal of the Indians from this country to the present Choctaw Nation. The fourteenth article of that treaty, however, allows those Choctaws who wanted to remain in Mississippi the privilege to stay here and become citizens of the United States, but he must have signified his intention to remain to the United States Indian Agent of the Choctaw Indians in Mississippi and have remained here five years. What is the name of your ancestor who was a recognized member of the Choctaw tribe of Indians in Mississippi at that time? A I suppose that was my father and mother at that time.
Q Well, would they have been of age in 1830? A When my mother died she was sixty nine and she died about five years ago.
Q Now your mother would have been under age; what was your mother's mother's name? A Before she married?
Q Yes. A Before she married her name was Callie D. Hancock, and she married Roe.
Q That was your mother's name? A Yessir[sic].
Q What was your mother's mothers' name? A Mollie Mitchell.
Q Was she a Choctaw Indian? A She was a full blood.
Q Your mother's maiden name you say was Hancock? A Yes sir, Callie D. Hancock.
Q What was her father's name? A Jubal B. Hancock.
Q Did any of your ancestors ever signify to the United States Indian Agent to the Choctaw Indians in Mississippi their intention to remain and become citizens of the United States within six months after the ratification of the treaty of 1830/
A To the best of my knowledge, I don't think they did; at least if they had, my mother would have told me.

Q Did your mother's people after the conclusion of the treaty of 1830 remove with the Choctaws from Mississippi to the present Indian Territory? A My mother went out there I think in '54. I think I have a list here that she made when she started to go. I believe it states the date she started. She left July the 15th, '58.
Q She went from here to the-- A She went from Meridian Mississippi to the Choctaw Nation. She went from Meridian to the Tombigby[sic] River and from Tombibbee[sic] River to Galveston and from Galveston by stage to the Indian Territory. There was no railroads there then.
Q That was in 1854? A '54, yes sr.
Q And your mother remained there-- A My mother remained there, I don't know how long, but I know shen[sic] she left I was two months old, I don't remember when she left or how long she stated[sic]. I never did - I suppose I have heard her say too.
Q Was she ever recognized by the Choctaw tribal authorities in Indian Territory during the time she stayed there? A No sir, she left there, she had a sister there now ~~if~~ she is not dead; they stayed and were recognized but after her husband died she came back to Mississippi.
Q What are the names of her brothers that are now in Indian Territory[sic]
A Thomas Sapin no~~w~~ he is dead now; he is her brother in law; she has no brother there; there is a lot of boys there now.
Q Your cousins? A Yes sir.
Q What are some of their names? A Let me see, I have a list of some of the names; I correspond with them. I have got a cousin out there named F. O. L. Leewright; her post office is White Bead Hill, Choctaw Nation, Indian Territory. I have got a cousin out there by the name of D. M. Spain whose post office is White Bead Hill. I have got a cousin out there by the name of S. B. Spain whose post office is Fleetwood. I have got a lot of others but I don't remember them unless I would look over my letters.
Q Were these people who went over there at the time your mother did adopted by the Choctaws as Mississippi Choctaws.[sic] A Well, I could not say they are I was not there.
Q They have always been recognized as citizens of the Choctaw Nation? A No sir, they moved out there way ahead of them and we followed them after my father died my mother moved back, and I don't know how long; they were all enrolled, I think by this Dawes Commission.
Q Did any of your ancestors ever claim or received any lands in Mississippi under the fourteenth article of the treaty of 1830? A Not as I know of; of course you know I was young then and I would not know.
Q Are you married? A Yes sir.
Q What is your wife's name? A Her name is Onia E. Roe.
Q Is she a white woman? A Yes sir.
Q Are you making any claim for her? A No sir.
Q How many children have you? A I have one.
Q What is the name? A Jeannette C. Roe.
Q How old? A She is seventeen years old.
Q This is a child of you and Onia E. Roe? A Yes sir.

It will be necessary for the Commission to be supplied with evidence of your marriage to your wife Onia E. Roe, in the matter if the application you make for identification of your daughter.

Applicant: I will have to mail that to you, I live in Meridian. If you will give me your address I can mail it to you any time you want it.

The decision of the Commission as to your application and the application you make on behalf of your daughter for identification as Mississippi Choctaws will be mailed to you in writing to your present post office address, Meridian, Mississippi.

Anna Bell, having been first duly sworn, on her oath states that as stenographer to the Commission to the Five Civilized Tribes she reported in full the proceedings in the above entitled cause on the 17th day of December, 1900, and that the above and foregoing is a full, true and correct transcript of her stenographic notes in said cause on said date.

Anna Bell

Subscribed and sworn to before me this 19" day of December, 1900.

Tams Bixby
Acting Chairman.

Department of the Interior.
Commission to the Five Civilized Tribes.
Muskogee, Indian Territory, July 2, 1902.

In the matter of the application of J. Folsom Roe to be enrolled as a Choctaw entitled to allotment under the provisions of the act of Congress of May 31, 1900, having been identified as a Mississippi Choctaw by the Commission to the Five Civilized Tribes, May 7, 1902, which identification was approved by the Secretary of the Interior May 21, 1902.

J. Folsom Roe being first duly sworn testified as follows:

Examinat ion[sic] by the Commission.

Q What is your name? J. Folsom Roe.
Q How old are you? A Will be forty-four years old the 4th of this coming November; born November 4, 1859.
Q You are the identical J. Folsom Roe who is an applicant to this Commission for identification as a Mississippi Choctaw? A Yes sir.

J. Folsom Roe is the identical person identified by the Commission to the Five Civilized Tribes as entitled to rights in the Choctaw lands under the provision of the fourteenth article of the treaty of 1830, by the decision of the Commission to the Five Civilized Tribes in the case of Josephine Hussey, et al., which identification was approved by the Secretary of the Interior May 21, 1902.

Q Your purpose in now appearing before the Commission is to conform to that provision of the act of Congress of May 31, 1900 relative to your removal to and settlement in good faith in the Choctaw Chickasaw Country? A Yes sir; that's what I came for; I came a year ago and my wife got dissatisfied and we went back to New York and then to Chicago and this time I come to stay.
Q Have you now since your identification as a Mississippi Choctaw by this Commission May 21, 1902, removed to the Choctaw Chickasaw Country for the purpose of making your bona fide residence there? A Yes sir; that's my intention.
Q What is your post office address at this time? A McGee. Yes sir; I have two or three cousins living there and come in close to them.
Q How much of a residence have you made there? A I haven't made any yet; I've just been there about two weeks.
Q Have you any personal property; any household belongings? A No sir; none at all.
Q You are a married man? A Yes sir.
Q Is your wife a white woman? A Yes sir.
Q Where is she? A In Meridian Mississippi.
Q Has she any personal belongings? A No sir; we sold out everything we had a year ago when we started out here.
Q Where is your daughter Jeanetta[sic]? A She's with her mother.
Q It will be necessary that she also make settlement in the Choctaw Chickasaw Country in order to be enrolled as a Choctaw entitled to enrollment.
A Yes sir; she's coming with her mother.
Q How much of a residence have you made in the Chickasaw Nation? A You mean in the way of improvements?
Q Yes sir. A I haven't did anything at all; just went to my cousin's and thought I would come down here when I got rested up which I did, and find out what I could do; a man cant[sic] locate if he wanted to - there's so many people there[sic]
Q It is your purpose now to remain in the Choctaw Chickasaw country is it?
A Yes sir.

The act of Congress of May 31, 1900, provides that:

"Any Mississippi Choctaw, duly identified as such by the United States Commission to the Five Civilized Tribes shall have the right at any time prior to the approval of the final rolls of the Choctaws and Chickasaws by the Secretary of the Interior, to make settlement within the Choctaw-Chickasaw country, and on proof of the fact of bona fide settlement may be enrolled by the said United States Commission and by the Secretary of the Interior as Choctaws entitled to allotment. Provided further, That all contracts or agreements looking to the sale or incumbrance in any way of the lands to be allotted to said Mississippi Choctaws shall be null and void."

The bona fide settlement referred to in the above legislation is further defined in an agreement entered into at Washington, D.C. on May 21, 1902, between Commissioners on the part of the United States and the Choctaw and Chickasaw Nations, and which provides:

"All persons duly identified by the Commission to the Five Civilized Tribes under the provisions of section 21 of the act of Congress approved June 28, 1898 (30 Stats., 495), as Mississippi Choctaws entitled to benefits under article 14 of the treaty between the United States and the Choctaw Nation concluded September 27, 1830, may, at any time within six months after the date of the final ratification of this agreement, make bona fide settlement within the Choctaw-Chickasaw country, and upon proof of such settlement to such Commission within one year after the date of the final ratification of this agreement may be enrolled by such Commission as Mississippi Choctaws entitled to allotment as herein provided for citizens of the tribes, subject to the special provisions herein provided as to Mississippi Choctaws, and said enrollment shall be final when approved by the Secretary of the Interior. The application of no person for identification as a Mississippi Choctaw shall be received by said Commission after the date of the final ratification of this agreement.

When any such Mississippi Choctaw shall have continously[sic] resided upon the lands of the Choctaw and Chickasaw nations[sic] for a period of three years, including his residence thereon before and after such enrollment, he shall, upon due proof of such continous[sic] residence, made in such manner and before such officer as may be designated by the Secretary of the Interior, receive a patent for his allotment, as provided in the Atoka agreement, and he shall hold the lands allotted to him as provided in this agreement for citizens of the Choctaw and Chickasaw nations.

Applications for enrollment as Mississippi Choctaws and applications to have land set apart to them as such, must be made personally before the Commission to the Five Civilized Tribes. Fathers may apply for their minor children; and if the father be dead, the mother may apply; husbands may apply for wifes[sic]. Applications for orphans, insane persons and persons of unsound mind may be made by duly appointed guardians or curator, and for aged and infirm persons and prisoners by agents duly authorized thereunto by power of attorney, in the discretion of said Commission.

If within four years after such enrollment any such Mississippi Choctaw, or his heirs or representatives if he be dead, fails to make proof of such continous[sic] bona fide residence for the period so prescribed, or up to the time of the death of such Mississippi Choctaw, in case of his death after enrollment, he, and his heirs and representatives if he be dead, shall be deemed to have acquired no interest in the lands set apart to him, and the same shall be sold at public auction for cash, under rules and regulations prescribed by the Secretary of the Interior, and the proceeds paid into the Treasury of the United States to the credit of the Choctaw and Chickasaw tribes, and distributed per capita with other funds of the tribes. Such lands shall not be sold for less than their appraised value. Upon payment of the full purchase price patent shall issue to the purchaser."

---O---

Clara Mitchell Wood being first duly sworn upon her oath states that as stenographer for the Commission to the Five Civilized Tribes she reported in full all proceedings had in the above entitled cause on the 2nd day of July 1902 and that the above and foregoing is a full true and correct transcript of her stenographic notes of said proceedings on said date.

Clara Mitchell Wood

Subscribed and sworn to before me this 2nd day of July 1902.

T B Needles
Commissioner.

Miss. Choc. 1114. 2
Miss. Choc. Ident'f'd. ~~72~~.

Department of the Interior
Commission to the Five Civilized Tribes
Muskogee, Indian Territory, February 19, 1903.

In the matter of the application of Jeannette C. Roe to be enrolled as a Choctaw entitled to allotment under the provisions of the act of Congress of May 31, 1900, as ratified by the citizens of the Choctaw and Chickasaw Nations, September 25, 1902, having been identified as a Mississippi Choctaw, entitled to allotment, by the Commission to the Five Civilized Tribes, May 7, 1902, which identification was approved by the Secretary of the Interior, May 21, 1902.

Jeannette C. Roe, the applicant, being duly sworn, testified as follows:

Examination by the Commission:

Q What is your name? A Jeannette C. Roe.
Q How old are you? A I'm going on nineteen years old.
Q What is the name of your father? A J. F. Roe.
Q Is he living? A Yes, sir.
Q What is the name of your mother? A Onie E. Roe.
Q Is she living? A Yes, sir.
Q Are you the identical Jeannette C. Roe for whom application was made by your father J. Folsom Roe, for identification as a Mississippi Choctaw? A Yes, sir.
Q And are you the identical Jeannette C. Roe identified by the Commission to the Five Civilized Tribes as entitled to rights in the Choctaw lands under the provisions of the fourteenth article of the treaty of 1830, by the decision of the Commission to the Five Civilized Tribes in the case of J. Folsom Roe et al., which identification was approved by the Secretary of the Interior, May 21, 1902?
A Yes, sir.

Q Your purpose in now appearing before the Commission is to conform to the provisions of the act of Congress of May 31, 1900, under which you are identified as a Mississippi Choctaw entitled to allotment, and the subsequent act of Congress of July 1, 1902, which was ratified by the citizens of the Choctaw and Chickasaw Nations September 25, 1902, relative to your removal to and make settlement in good faith in the Choctaw-Chickasaw country; that is your purpose is it?
A Yes, sir.
Q Are you at this time a bona fide resident of the Choctaw Chickasaw country?
A Yes, sir.
Q What is your post office address in the Choctaw Nation or Chickasaw Nation?
A Bartley.
Q Is it your intention to become a bona fide resident of the Choctaw-Chickasaw country? A Yes, sir.
Q Are you living at the home of your father? A Yes, sir.
Q He is a bona fide resident of the Choctaw-Chickasaw country? A Yes, sir.

---O---

Clara Mitchell Wood, being first duly sworn, upon her oath states, that as stenographer for the Commission to the Five Civilized Tribes she reported in full all proceedings had in the above entitled cause on the 19th day of February, 1903, and that the foregoing is a full true and correct transcript of her stenographic notes of said proceedings on said date.

Clara Mitchell Wood

Subscribed and sworn to before me this 21st day of February 1903.

Charles [?] *Sawyer*
Notary Public.

Muskogee, Indian Territory, April 10, 1901.

Mr. John F. Roe,

Meridian, Mississippi,

Dear Sir:

The Commission is in receipt of your letter of April 2 inquiring whether or not the marriage license forwarded by you on December 19, 1900, had been received by the Commission.

In reply to your letter you are advised that our records show that the marriage license and certificate between John F. Roe and Onie Gressett is on file, and has been made a part of the record in the matter of your application for the identification of yourself and child as Mississippi Choctaws.

Yours truly,

Acting Chairman.

MC 1114

Muskogee, Indian Territory, April 13, 1901.

Mr. John Folsom Roe,

Meridian, Mississippi,

Dear Sir:-

Receipt is hereby acknowledged of your letter of the 9th inst., in which it is stated that you wrote a letter some time ago inquiring if it would be necessary for you to go before the Commission at Meridian, as you had appeared before the Commission at Hattiesburg, Mississippi., December 17, 1900, and you ask to be advised inr elation thereto.

You are informed that if you have additional evidence to offer in support of your application for identification as a Mississippi Choctaw, it would be advisable for you to submit the same to the Commission at its office in Meridian, Mississippi. If you have no further testimony to offer, there appears to be no reason why you should again appear before the Commission.

Yours truly,

Acting Chairman.

M.C.R. 1114

[Handwritten letter and typed as given.]

Oklahoma City O.T.
May 18-1901
The Dawes Commission
Gentlemen, My post office address & Jeannette Roe - is now the above address, as we moved from Meridian Mississippi a week ago - please advise me if you receive this letter.

Respt
Jno. Folsom Roe

My Cousins F.O.L. Leewright of McGee I.T. S B Spain of White Bead Hill wrote me today that they & all their childrin had been enroled & had drew anuity one time- I gave them with my application as witness-

Yours &c
Jno Folsom Roe

[Back of handwritten letter]

7453

DEPARTMENT OF THE INTERIOR,
COMMISSION TO THE FIVE CIVILIZED TRIBES.
FILED
MAY 27 1901
ACTING CHAIRMAN

Muskogee, Indian Territory, May 27, 1901.

Mr. John Folsom Roe,

Oklahoma City, Oklahoma,

Dear Sir:

The Commission is in receipt of your letter of May 18, in which you give your present post office address as Oklahoma City, and state that you have removed from Meridian, the post office address heretofore given by you. You are advised that this information has been made a matter of record.

Yours truly,

MC 1114

Acting Chairman.

Wm OB.

COMMISSIONERS:

HENRY L. DAWES,
TAMS BIXBY,
THOMAS B. NEEDLES,
C. R. BRECKINRIDGE.

ALLISON L. AYLESWORTH,
SECRETARY.

ADDRESS ONLY THE
COMMISSION TO THE FIVE CIVILIZED TRIBES.

DEPARTMENT OF THE INTERIOR,

COMMISSION TO THE FIVE CIVILIZED TRIBES.

Muskogee, Indian Territory, July 24, 1901.

Mr. John Folsom Roe,

Oklahoma City, Oklahoma,

Dear Sir:

Receipt is hereby acknowledged of your letter which bears no date, written from McGee, Indian Territory, relative to the introduction of additional testimony in support of your application for identification of yourself and your daughter, Jeannetta[sic] C. Roe as Mississippi Choctaws.

You are informed that the Commission will hear the testimony of any witnesses in person which you may desire to present in support of your application for the identification of yourself and your daughter. Such witnesses should present themselves in person at the Commission's office at Atoka, Choctaw Nation, Indian Territory.

Yours truly,

TB Needles
Commissioner in Charge.

MC 1114

W^m OB.

COMMISSIONERS:

HENRY L. DAWES,
TAMS BIXBY,
THOMAS B. NEEDLES,
C. R. BRECKINRIDGE.

ALLISON L. AYLESWORTH,
SECRETARY.

ADDRESS ONLY THE
COMMISSION TO THE FIVE CIVILIZED TRIBES.

DEPARTMENT OF THE INTERIOR,

COMMISSION TO THE FIVE CIVILIZED TRIBES.

Muskogee, Indian Territory, July 26, 1901.

Mr. John Folsom Roe,

Oklahoma City, Oklahoma Territory.

Dear Sir:

Receipt is hereby acknowledged of your letter of the 12th of June, addressed to the Honorable Secretary of the Interior and by him referred to this Commission for consideration and appropriate action.

In your letter you state that you and your daughter Jeanetta[sic] are Choctaw Indians who have appeared before this Commission and that you are the cousins of certain Choctaw Indians who have already been enrolled by this Commission. You desire information as to whether you and your daughter will share in the payments of any of the annuities of the Choctaw Nation, also if you will be permitted to take your allotments in the Chickasaw Nation instead of the Choctaw Nation, and when the Commission to the Five Civilized Tribes will make an allotment of land in the Choctaw and Chickasaw Nation[sic].

You are informed that it appears from our records that the status of yourself and daughter is that of applicants for identification as Mississippi Choctaws. Your testimony was taken at the time of your personal appearance before the Commission at Hattiesburg, Mississippi, December 17th, 1900 and states that you claim your rights as beneficiaries under the provisions of the fourteenth article of the treaty of eighteen hundred and thirty. That article provides that persons who claim thereunder "are not entitled to any portion of the Choctaw annuities."

As to the allotment of land in the Choctaw and Chickasaw Nations, you are informed that such allotment will presumably be made under the agreement of April 23rd, 1897, between the United States and the Choctaw and Chickasaw Tribes of Indians. This agreement provides:

"That all lands within the Indian Territory belonging to the Choctaw and Chickasaw Indians shall be allotted to the members of said tribes so as to give to each member of these tribes so far as possible a fair and equal share thereof, considering the character and fertility of the soil and the location and value of the lands."

As there is no distinction made between the Choctaw and Chickasaw lands in this agreement it is probable that the citizens of these two Nations will be allowed to make their selections and file upon their allotments in either of the two Nations. We cannot inform you at this time as to the time of making such allotments to the citizens of the Choctaw and Chickasaw Nations for the reason that there has not yet been any roll of the citizens of these two Nations approved nor has the appraisement or the classification of the lands been completed. When such allotment is made by this Commission ample public notice will be given.

Yours truly,

TB Needles

MC-1114

Commissioner in charge.

Muskogee, Indian Territory, September 12, 1901.

Mr. W. S. Miller,

Secretary, Bush & Gerts Piano Company,

Chicago, Illinois.

Dear Sir:-

Receipt is hereby acknowledged of your letter of August 18th, in which you ask to be advised if one John F. Roe, of Meridian, Mississippi, has proven up his claims in the Indian lands, and back payments due him from the Government. You state that these lands are located in the Chickasaw Nation, and Mr. Roe is the son of one Mollie Mitchell.

In reply to your letter you are advised that on December 17th, 1900, J. Folsom Roe, of Meridian, Mississippi, the son of John F. and Callie D. Roe, appeared before the Commission at Hattiesburg, *Miss.* and applied for identification of himself and his minor child, as Mississippi Choctaws. No action has yet been taken in regard to this application, or any decision rendered. When such decision is rendered a copy of the same will be mailed to the applicant.

Yours truly,

M.C. 1114.

COMMISSIONERS:

HENRY L. DAWES,
TAMS BIXBY,
THOMAS B. NEEDLES,
C. R. BRECKINRIDGE.

ALLISON L. AYLESWORTH,
SECRETARY.

ADDRESS ONLY THE
COMMISSION TO THE FIVE CIVILIZED TRIBES.

DEPARTMENT OF THE INTERIOR,
COMMISSION TO THE FIVE CIVILIZED TRIBES.

Muskogee, Indian Territory, September 30, 1901.

Mr. John F. Roe,
McGee,
Indian Territory.

Dear Sir:-

Receipt is hereby acknowledged of your letter of September 13th, in which you state that your Post Office address is now McGee, Indian Territory. This change in address has been made a matter of record.

There are enclosed you herewith two letters which were addressed to you at Oklahoma City and returned uncalled for. These letters were written in response to communications from you.

Yours truly,

Tams Bixby

A.B. 2-30. Acting Chairman

Muskogee, Indian Territory, December 3, 1901.

J. Folsom Roe,

General Delivery,

New Orleans, Louisiana,

Dear Sir:

Receipt is hereby acknowledged of your letter of November 29, in which you state that you are now located at New Orleans. You also ask to be advised when allotment of the Choctaw lands will take place.

In reply to your letter, you are advised that it is impossible to say, at this time, when an allotment office will be opened in the Choctaw and Chickasaw Nations from the purpose of allowing the citizens of those two tribes to take their allotments. It appears from our records that you are an applicant for the identification of yourself and your minor child as Mississippi Choctaws, and that no opinion has yet been rendered or decision reached in regard to your claim.

When the allotment of the lands of the Choctaw and Chickasaw Nations is made it will be to those citizens of the Choctaw and Chickasaw tribes, whose names appear on the final roll of citizens of those two tribes, as approved by the Secretary of the Interior.

Your status is merely that of an applicant for identification as a Mississippi Choctaw, claiming rights in the Choctaw lands under the fourteenth article of the treaty of 1830, whose application has been passed upon in any manner by the Commission.

The change in your post office address has been made a matter of record.

Yours truly,

MC 1114 Commissioner in Charge.

Miss. Choctaw 1114
Miss. Choctaw 1929

Muskogee, Indian Territory, April 26, 1902.

J. Folsom Roe,

Mobile, Alabama,

Dear Sir:

Receipt is hereby acknowledged of your letter of April 21, asking with reference to your application for identification as a Mississippi Choctaw, and whether the allotment of the lands of the Choctaw-Chickasaw country has been begun by the Commission, and what length of time the Commission has in which to close matters up with the Choctaws. You also inquire if Nettie Carter had appeared before the Commission and state that she is your niece.

In reply to your letter you are informed that no decision has yet been reached nor opinion rendered relative to your rights as a Mississippi Choctaw. As soon as a decision is reached you will be notified of the action taken by the Commission.

You are further advised that the Commission has not yet commenced the work of allotment of the lands of the Choctaw-Chickasaw country, but when such allotment is made it will be to those citizens and freedmen of the Choctaw and Chickasaw Nations whose names appear upon the final rolls of those two nations as approved by the Secretary of the Interior. Relative to your removal to the Indian Territory your attention is invited to the following provision of the act of Congress of May 31, 1900:

"That any Mississippi Choctaw duly identified as such by the United Stated Commission to the Five Civilized Tribes shall have the right, at any time prior to the approval of the final rolls of the Choctaws and Chickasaws by the Secretary of the Interior, to make settlement within the Choctaw-Chickasaw country, and on proof of the fact of bona fide settlement may be enrolled by the said United States Commission and by the Secretary of the Interior as Choctaws entitled to allotment."

Your status is that of an applicant for identification as a Mississippi Choctaw whose rights have not yet been passed upon, and it is not believed that the benefits of the above legislation would accrue to applicants until they had been identified by this Commission as Choctaw Indians entitled to rights in the Choctaw lands under the fourteenth article of the treaty of 1830.

No date is now effective for the closing of the rolls of the Choctaw and Chickasaw Nations.

You are advised that is appears from our records that Nettie Frances Carter, daughter of Jubal Braxton Carter and Laura Bell Goldthorpe, applied to the Commission for identification as a Mississippi Choctaw, including the decision of the Commission of Mississippi Choctaw, at Meridian, Mississippi, April 24, 1901, and on March 7, 1902, a letter was addressed to her attorney, Fred W. Bacho, at Mobile, Alabama, advising him that there was not sufficient testimony in her case to establish the relationship of Nettie Frances Carter to the other applicants claiming descent from Sophia Mitchell who married Jubal B. Hancock, and that if she desired to introduce such testimony, the Commission would hear witnesses in her behalf, at its office at Meridian, Mississippi, between April 14 and April 30, 1902, inclusive. It does not appear from our records that any such testimony has been offered by her, up to this date.

Yours truly,

Commissioner in Charge.

COPY.

M.C.R. 1114

Muskogee, Indian Territory, May 8, 1902.

J. Folsom Roe,

Mobile, Alabama.

Dear Sir:

You are hereby advised that on May 7, 1902, the Commission to the Five Civilized Tribes rendered a decision in the consolidated case of Josephine Hussey, et al., embracing the following applications for identification as Mississippi Choctaws:

Josephine Hussey, et al.
J. Folsom Roe, et al.,
Jubal A. Hancock,
Charles Rushing Hancock.

Said decision after a review of the evidence submitted, concludes as follows:

"The authority vested in the Commission by the twenty first section of the act of Congress of June 28, 1898 (30 Stats. 495), is as follows:

'Said commission shall have authority to determine the identity of Choctaw Indians claiming rights in the Choctaw lands under article fourteen of the treaty between the United States and the Choctaw Nation concluded September twenty seventh, eighteen hundred and thirty and to that end may administer oaths, examine witnesses, and perform all other acts necessary thereto and make report to the Secretary of the Interior.'

It is the opinion of the Commission that the evidence in this case is sufficient to determine the identity of Josephine Hussey, William Hancock Hussey, Alvin McDowell Hussey, J. Folsom Roe, Jeannette C. Roe, Jubal A. Hancock and Charles Rushing Hancock, as Choctaw Indians entitled to rights in the Choctaw lands under the provision of law above quoted, and that the application for their identification as such should be granted, and it is so ordered.

You are further advised that the Commission has on this date forwarded the record in this case to the Secretary of the Interior for review and you will be informed in due time of such action as may be taken by him.

Yours truly,

(SIGNED). *T. B. Needles.*

Register. Commissioner in Charge.

C O P Y .

30382

D. C. No. 8589

Refer in reply to
the following:
Land-28269-1902.

DEPARTMENT OF THE INTERIOR.

Office of Indian Affairs,

Washington, May 15, 1902.

The Honorable

The Secretary of the Interior.

Sir:

The office transmits herewith the papers in the consolidated case of Josephine Hussey et al., applicants for identification as Mississippi Choctaws and recommends that the decision of the Commission, holding that the applications should be granted, be affirmed.

The record evidence shows conclusively that the applicants are descendants of Mississippi Choctaw ancestors, who were recognized as such, enrolled and granted land under the fourteenth article of the treaty between the United States and the Choctaw Nation concluded on the 27th day of September, 1830, by Act of Congress entitled "An Act for the relief of Jubal B. Hancock, passed August 11th, 1842, all of which is verified by the records in this office.

It is further shown by the record that in 1896, William Hancock Hussey, a minor, by his mother as next friend, J. Folsom Roe, Jubal A. Hancock and Charles Rushing Hancock made application for citizenship in the Choctaw Nation under the Act of Congress of June 10th, 1896, and that their said applications were denied by the Commission and no appeal was taken from the adverse decision.

This is no bar to filing an application for identification as a Mississippi Choctaw under the Act of Congress of June 28th, 1898 (30 Stats., 495) and having their rights under that Act adjudicated by the proper tribunal.

Section 21 of that Act expressly provides that "Said Commission shall have authority to determine the identity of Choctaw Indians claiming rights in the Choctaw lands under article fourteen of the treaty between the United States and the Choctaw Nation, concluded September twenty-seventh, eighteen hundred and thirty, and to that end may administer oaths, examine witnesses, and perform all other acts necessary thereto and make report to the Secretary of the Interior."

It is under this provision the applications here in are made, and as previous adjudication of their status can be construed as an estoppel that will exclude claimants from the benefits conferred by the Act when the facts support their claim to the rights intended to be established thereby.

Very respectfully,

Your obedient servant,

Acting Commissioner.

W.C.B. (Cg.)

C O P Y .

30382.

J.P.
F.

DEPARTMENT OF THE INTERIOR.

I.T.D. 3142-1902. Washington, May 21, 1902.

L.R.S.

Commission to the Five Civilized Tribes,

Muskogee, I. T.

Gentlemen:

The Department had[sic] considered the Mississippi Choctaw case 1620, embracing the applications of Josephine Hussey, William Hancock Hussey, Alvin McDowell Hussey, J. Folsom Roe, Jeannette C. Roe, Jubal A. Hancock and Charles Rushing Hancock, transmitted with your letter of May 8, 1902.

You found that the evidence was sufficient to establish the descent of the claimants from Jubal B. Hancock who took advantage of the 14th article of the treaty of 1830, and to determine the identity of the applicants as Choctaw Indians entitled to rights in the Choctaw lands, in which opinion the Acting Commissioner of Indian Affairs is letter of May 15, 1902, concurs.

He states that it is shown that the applicants are descendants of Mississippi Choctaws ancestors who were recognized as such, enrolled and granted lands under the 14th article of the treaty of 1830, by an Act of Congress entitled "An Act for the relief of Jubal B. Hancock," passed August 11, 1842; that, while it is shown that in 1896 William Hancock Hussey, J. Folsom Roe, Jubal A. Hancock and Charles Rushing Hancock made application for citizenship in the Choctaw Nation under the Act of June 10, 1896, and that their applications were denied by your Commission and no appeal taken, that is no bar to the consideration of an application for identification as Mississippi Choctaws under the 21st section of the Act of June 28, 1898 (30 Stats. 495).

The Department has carefully considered the matter and finds no reason to disturb you decision, and it is accordingly affirmed. A copy of the Acting Commissioner's letter is enclosed.

You will advise the claimants, residents of Mississippi, hereof, and that to be entitled to enrollment in the Choctaw Nation, and to an allotment, it will be necessary for them to remove in good faith to the Choctaw-Chickasaw country, Indian Territory; also to that portion of the Choctaw-Chickasaw agreement pending in Congress, regard to Mississippi Choctaws.

Respectfully,

Thos. Ryan,

Acting Secretary,

E.M.D.

1 enclosure.

Miss. Choctaw 1114

Muskogee, Indian Territory, May 23, 1902.

J. Folsom Roe,

General Delivery,

Montgomery, Alabama.

Dear Sir:

Receipt is hereby acknowledged of your letter of May 15, in which you ask if any allotments of land have been made to the Mississippi Choctaws, and if not, when such allotment will be begun.

In reply to your letter you are advised that on May 8, 1902, the Commission addressed a letter to you at Mobile, Alabama, advising you that you and other applicants claiming descent from Jubal B. Hancock and Sophia Mitchell had been identified as Mississippi Choctaws, and that the record in the case had been transmitted to the Secretary of the Interior for review and you would be advised at a later date of the action taken by him.

You are further advised that the allotment of the lands of the Choctaw-Chickasaw country has not yet been begun, and it is impossible at this time to say when an allotment office will be opened in the Choctaw-Chickasaw country for the purpose of allowing the citizens of those two nations to make selection of and file upon their prospective allotments, but due public notice will be given of the establishment of such office.

Relative to the lands to be allotted to the Mississippi Choctaws, your attention is invited to the following provision of the act of Congress of May 31, 1900:

"That any Mississippi Choctaw, duly identified as such by the United States Commission to the Five Civilized Tribes, shall have the right, at any time prior to the approval of the final rolls of the Choctaws and Chickasaws by the Secretary of the Interior, to make settlement within the Choctaw-Chickasaw country, and on proof of the fact of bona fide settlement may be enrolled by the said United States Commission and by the Secretary of the Interior as Choctaws entitled to allotment."

Yours truly,

Acting Chairman.

Miss. Choctaw 1114

Muskogee, Indian Territory, May 31, 1902.

J. Folsom Roe,

General Delivery, Montgomery, Alabama,

Dear Sir:

You are hereby advised that on the twenty first day of May, 1902, the Secretary of the Interior affirmed the decision of the Commission to the Five Civilized Tribes granting the application made by you for the identification of yourself and your daughter, Jeannette C. Roe, as Mississippi Choctaws entitled to rights in the Choctaw lands in Indian Territory as a beneficiary under the provisions of article fourteen of the treaty between the United States and the Choctaw Nation, concluded September twenty seventh, eighteen hundred and thirty.

You are now advised that, in order for you to be enrolled as a citizen of the Choctaw Nation entitled to allotment, it is necessary that you remove to and make settlement within the Choctaw-Chickasaw country, as provided by the act of Congress of May 31, 1900, (31 Stats., 221):

"That any Mississippi Choctaw duly identified as such by the United States Commission to the Five Civilized Tribes shall have the right, at any time prior to the approval of the final rolls of the Choctaws and Chickasaws by the Secretary of the Interior, to make settlement within the Choctaw-Chickasaw country, and on proof of the fact of bona fide settlement may be enrolled by the said United States Commission and by the Secretary of the Interior as Choctaws entitled to allotment: Provided further, That all contracts or agreements looking to the sale or incumbrance in any way of the lands to be allotted to said Mississippi Choctaws shall be null and void."

Your attention is further invited to the following sections of an agreement entered into at Washington, D.C., March 21, 1902, between Commissioners on the part of the United States and the Choctaw and Chickasaw Nations, and now pending before the Congress of the United States for ratification:

"41. All persons duly identified by the Commission to the Five Civilized Tribes under the provisions of section 21 of the act of Congress approved June 28, 1898 (30 Stats., 495), as Mississippi Choctaws entitled to benefits under article 14 of the treaty between the United States and the Choctaw Nation concluded September 27, 1830, may, at any time within six months after the date of the final ratification of this agreement, make bona fide settlement within the Choctaw-Chickasaw country, and upon proof of such settlement to such Commission within one year after the date of the final ratification of this agreement may be enrolled by such Commission as Mississippi Choctaws entitled to allotment as herein provided for citizens of the tribes, subject to the special provisions herein provided as to Mississippi Choctaws, and said enrollment shall be final when approved by the Secretary of the Interior. The application of no person for identification as a Mississippi Choctaw shall be received by said Commission after the date of the final ratification of this agreement.

42. When any such Mississippi Choctaw shall have continuously resided upon the lands of the Choctaw and Chickasaw Nations for a period of three years, including his residence thereon before and after such enrollment, he shall, upon due proof of such continuous residence, made in such manner and before such officer as may be designated by the Secretary of the Interior, receive a patent for his allotment, as provided in the Atoka agreement, and he shall hold the lands allotted to him as provided in this agreement for citizens of the Choctaw and Chickasaw nations.

43. Applications for enrollment as Mississippi Choctaws, and applications to have land set apart to them as such, must be made personally before the Commission to the Five Civilized Tribes. Fathers may apply for their minor children; and if the father be dead, the mother may apply; husbands may apply for wifes. Applications for orphans, insane persons, and persons of unsound mind may be made by duly appointed guardian or curator, and for aged and infirm persons and prisoners by agents duly authorized thereunto by power of attorney, in the discretion of said Commission.

44. If within four years after such enrollment any such Mississippi Choctaw, or his heirs or representatives if he be dead, fails to make proof of such continuous bona fide residence for the period so prescribed, or up to the time of the death of such Mississippi Choctaw, in case of his death after enrollment, he, and his heirs and representatives if he be dead, shall be deemed to have acquired no interest in the lands set apart to him, and the same shall be sold at public auction for cash, under rules and regulations prescribed by the Secretary of the Interior, and the proceeds paid into the Treasury of the United States to the credit of the Choctaw and Chickasaw tribes, and distributed per capita with other funds of the tribes. Such lands shall not be sold for less than their appraised value. Upon payment of the full purchase price patent shall issue to the purchaser."

Yours truly,

Acting Chairman.

Miss. Choctaw R1114
Miss. Choctaw 2

Muskogee, Indian Territory, June 11, 1902.

J. Folsom Roe,

Montgomery, Alabama,

Dear Sir:

Receipt is hereby acknowledged of your letter of June 6, in which you state that you have been advised that the Secretary of the Interior had affirmed the decision of the Commission identifying you and your daughter, Jeannette C. Roe, as entitled to share in the Choctaw lands in Indian Territory, and you now wish to be advised what procedure is necessary in order to be enrolled, as you state you want to remove to the Choctaw-Chickasaw country at once.

In reply to your letter you are advised that it will be necessary that you remove to the Choctaw-Chickasaw country, and there establish a bona fide residence; you should then appear before the Commission to the Five Civilized Tribes at its office at Muskogee, Indian Territory, and make proof of the establishment of such bona fide residence, and make application for the enrollment of yourself and your daughter as Choctaws entitled to allotment of lands, in the Choctaw-Chickasaw country.

The provisions of law governing such removal and enrollment were recited to you in our letter of May 31, 1902.

Yours truly,

Commissioner in Charge.

[The above letter given again.]

Miss. Choctaw I 2

Muskogee, Indian Territory, October 16, 1902.

Mrs. O. E. Roe,

General Delivery,

St. Louis, Missouri,

Dear Madam:

Receipt is hereby acknowledged of your letter of October 12, asking how soon it will be necessary for you to bring your daughter, Jeannette C. Roe to the

Indian Territory. You state that her father, John Folsom Roe is now settled in the Chickasaw Nation. You also ask what disposition has been made of the application of Nettie Carter for identification as a Mississippi Choctaw.

In reply to your letter you are advised that the agreement recently entered into between the United States and the Choctaw and Chickasaw Nations, which was ratified September 25, 1902, provides as follows:

"All persons duly identified by the Commission to the Five Civilized Tribes under the provisions of section 21 of the act of Congress approved June 28, 1898 (30 Stats., 495), as Mississippi Choctaws entitled to benefits under article 14 of the treaty between the United States and the Choctaw Nation concluded September 27, 1830, may, at any time within six months after the date of the final ratification of this agreement, make bona fide settlement within the Choctaw-Chickasaw country, and upon proof of such settlement to such Commission within one year after the date of the final ratification of this agreement may be enrolled by such Commission as Mississippi Choctaws entitled to allotment as herein provided for citizens of the tribes, subject to the special provisions herein provided as to Mississippi Choctaws, and said enrollment shall be final when approved by the Secretary of the Interior."

You are hereby advised that on May 7, 1902, Jeannette C. Roe was identified by this Commission as a Choctaw Indian entitled to lands in the Choctaw Nation under article fourteen of the treaty of 1830, and you will understand from the provision of the agreement above quoted that Jeannette C. Roe will have six months from the date of her identification by this Commission as a Mississippi Choctaw within which to make bona fide settlement within the Choctaw-Chickasaw country.

You are further advised that no decision nor opinion has yet been rendered by the Commission relative to the application of Nettie Frances Carter for identification as a Mississippi Choctaw.

Respectfully,

Acting Chairman.

M.C.R. 1114.
Identified 2

Muskogee, Indian Territory, December 4, 1902.

Gregory L. & H.T. Smith,

Attorneys at Law,

Mobile, Alabama.

Gentlemen:

Receipt is hereby acknowledged of your letter of the 15th ultimo, received this date, in which you state that Jeannette C. Roe, who at present resides in Mobile, Alabama, has received a number of mutilated letters from the Commission "addresses and other parts being cut out touching her heirship to Mollie Mitchell." You further state that she does not know to whom they were addressed nor by whom sent, and has requested your firm to ask the present status of her case.

In reply, you are informed that it appears from the records of the Commission that J. Folsom Roe made application for the identification of himself and his minor child, Jeannette C. Roe, as Mississippi Choctaws.

The Commission on May 7, 1902, rendered its decision identifying the applicants as such Mississippi Choctaws, and on May 8, 1902, advised the applicants of the action of the Commission and of the forwarding of the record to the Secretary of the Interior for review.

On May 21, 1902, the Secretary of the Interior approved the decision of the Commission identifying the applicants in this case as Mississippi Choctaws, and on May 31, 1902, the principal applicant, J. Folsom Roe, was duly notified of such departmental action.

Relative to the present status of the applicants in this case, your attention is invited to sections 41, 42, 43 and 44 of the act of Congress approved July 2, 1902, and ratified by the citizens of the Choctaw and Chickasaw Nations September 25, 1902, a copy of which is enclosed you herewith.

Respectfully,

Acting Chairman.

Enc. Sup. Agreement.

M C R 1114
M C I 2

Muskogee, Indian Territory, February 18, 1903.

J. Folsom Roe,

Bartley, Indian Territory.

Dear Sir:

Receipt is hereby acknowledged of your letter of the 7th instant, in which you state that your daughter Jeanette C. Roe has recently arrived in Mississippi. You ask when it will be necessary for her to appear before the Commission to make proof of bona fide settlement in the Choctaw-Chickasaw country.

In reply to your letter your attention is invited to the following provision of the act of Congress approved July 1, 1902, which was ratified by the citizens of the Choctaw and Chickasaw Nations September 25, 1902:

"All persons duly identified by the Commission to the Five Civilized Tribes under the provisions of section 21 of the act of Congress approved June 28, 1898 (30 Stats., 495), as Mississippi Choctaws entitled to benefits under article 14 of the treaty between the United States and the Choctaw Nation concluded September 27, 1830, may, at any time within six months after the date of the final ratification of this agreement, make bona fide settlement within the Choctaw-Chickasaw country, and upon proof of such settlement to such Commission within one year after the date of the final ratification of this agreement may be enrolled by such Commission as Mississippi Choctaws entitled to allotment as herein provided for citizens of the tribes, subject to the special provisions herein provided as to Mississippi Choctaws, and said enrollment shall be final when approved by the Secretary of the Interior."

Under the above quotation of law it will be necessary for your daughter Jeanette C. Roe to make personal appearance before this Commission some time prior to March 25, 1903, in order to make proof of such settlement.

Respectfully,

Acting Chairman.

M. C. R. 1114

Muskogee, Indian Territory, August 24, 1903.

Alvin F. Pyeatt,

Attorney at Law,

Pauls Valley, Indian Territory,

Dear Sir:

Receipt is hereby acknowledged of your letter of August 19, asking whether J. Folsom Roe and Jennette[sic] Roe or either of them are listed for enrollment as Choctaws or Mississippi Choctaws.

In reply to your letter you are informed that on May 8, 1903, the Commission rendered its decision identifying J. Folsom Roe and his daughter, Jeannette C. Roe, as Mississippi Choctaws entitled to rights in the Choctaw lands under the fourteenth article of the treaty of eighteen hundred and thirty, and on May 21, 1902, the decision of the Commission was affirmed by the Secretary of the Interior.

Respectfully,

Commissioner in Charge.

M C Roll #4

Muskogee, Indian Territory, December 17, 1904.

Mrs. Onie E. Roe,

Hannibal, Missouri.

Dear Madam:

Receipt is hereby acknowledged of your letter dated November 3, 1904, by reference from the Secretary of the Interior. Therein you ask to be advised relative to making selection of allotment in the name of Jeannette C. Roe, your deceased daughter.

In reply you are informed our records show that several communications have been addressed you in regard to this matter, and the Commission cannot render you any further advice than that contained in its letter to you under date of December 3, 1904.

Respectfully,

Chairman.

MCR 1114

Muskogee, Indian Territory, December 27, 1905.

J. Folsom Roe,

Byars, Indian Territory.

Dear Sir:

Receipt is hereby acknowledged of your letter of the 19th instant, requesting to be advised of the necessary steps to take in order to have your wife enrolled as an intermarried citizen.

In reply you are informed that this office knows of no law guaranteeing rights to persons by reason of their marriage to a Mississippi Choctaw.

Respectfully,

Commissioner.

G. 3 & 4.

Muskogee, Indian Territory, March 9, 1907.

Carr & Rogers,

Attorneys at Law,

Pauls Valley, Indian Territory.

Gentlemen:

Replying to your letter of February 18, 1907, you are advised that it does not appear from the records of this Office that any testimony has been submitted relative to the continuous residence in the Choctaw-Chickasaw country, Indian Territory, of J.

Folsom Roe and Jeanette C. Roe as identified Mississippi Choctaws up to the times of their deaths.

Respectfully,

Commissioner.

No. 1114

For Identification as a Mississippi Choctaw.

Date DEC 17 1900

Name J. Folsom Roe.

Age 44. Blood 1/4

Post Office, Meridian, Miss

Father: John F. Roe - dead.

Mother: Callie D. Roe - dead.

Claims through mother.

WIFE: Onie E. Roe.

(no claim for wife).

Children:

Jeanette C. Roe 17

Stenographer.

Anna Bell.

FOR IDENTIFICATION AS
A MISSISSIPPI CHOCTAW. R# 1114

REFUSED.

J. Folsom Roe et al.

JUDGMENT WRITTEN MARCH 28 1901 H.C.R.

3/27/1901
Latest address Oklahoma City. O.T. a.B.

9/28/1901
Latest address: McGee. I.T.

12/3/1901 Latest address New Orleans
La. Gen. Delivery.

REFER TO M.C.R. 1620

4/26/1902 Latest address
Mobile Ala

5/24/1902 P.O. Montgomery Ala.

M. C. R 1114 J. Folsom Roe. et al.

J. Folsom Roe, 44 years old, of Meridian, Mississippi, on December 17, 1900, appeared before the Commission at Hattiesburg, and applied for identification of himself and daughter Jeannette C. Roe as Mississippi Choctaws. No judgment has been rendered in this case.

Atoka, January 4, 1901.

AB

The testimony in this case has not been filed, although I wrote it up before I left Mississippi.

A.B.

CARD NO. 3 - Choc. MCR 1619 - Jubal A Hancock
See MCR 1620

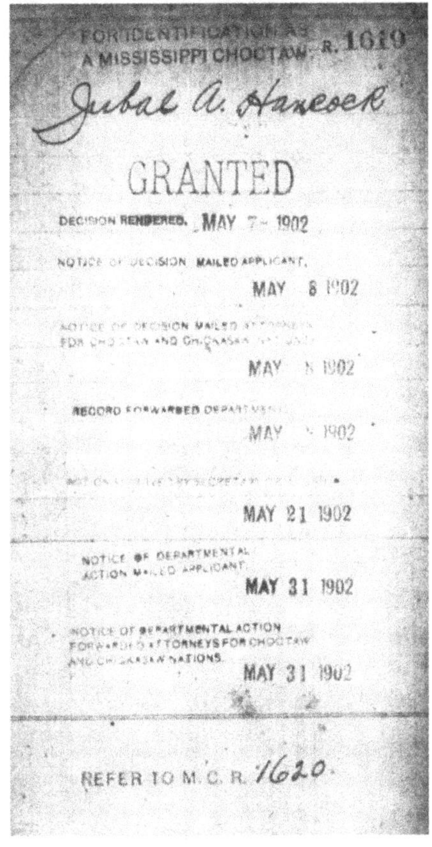
FOR IDENTIFICATION AS A MISSISSIPPI CHOCTAW. R. 1619

Jubal A. Hancock

GRANTED

DECISION RENDERED. MAY 7 - 1902

NOTICE OF DECISION MAILED APPLICANT. MAY 8 1902

NOTICE OF DECISION MAILED ATTORNEYS FOR CHOCTAW AND CHICKASAW NATIONS. MAY 8 1902

RECORD FORWARDED DEPARTMENT. MAY 9 1902

MAY 21 1902

NOTICE OF DEPARTMENTAL ACTION MAILED APPLICANT. MAY 31 1902

NOTICE OF DEPARTMENTAL ACTION FORWARDED ATTORNEYS FOR CHOCTAW AND CHICKASAW NATIONS. MAY 31 1902

REFER TO M. C. R. 1620.

Department of the Interior
Commission to the Five Civilized Tribes,
Meridian, Mississippi, April 3, 1901.

In the matter of the application of Jubal A. Hancock for identification as a Mississippi Choctaw. Jubal A. Hancock being first duly sworn testified as follows:

Examination by the Commission.

Q What is your name? A Jubal A. Hancock.
Q How old are you? A 25 years old.
Q What is your post-office address? A Gulfport, box 83.
Q Louisiana? A Mississippi.

Q How long have you resided in Mississippi? A All my life, 25 years.
Q Always lived here? A Yes sir.
Q Have you ever maintained a residence in the Indian Territory? A No sir.
Q What is your father's name? A William Mitchell Hancock.
Q Is your father living? A No sir.
Q What is your mother's name? A Mary Jane Hancock.
Q Is your mother living? A Yes sir.
Q Through which one of your parents do you derive your Choctaw blood?
A My father.
Q How much Choctaw blood do you claim? A I claim one eighth.
Q Is your name on any of the tribal rolls of the Choctaw Nation in the Indian Territory? A No sir.
Q Have you ever made application to the Choctaw tribal authorities in the Indian Territory for citizenship in the Choctaw Nation? A No sir.
Q In 1896, under the act of Congress of June 10th, 1896 did you make application to the Commission to the Five Civilized Tribes for citizenship in the Choctaw Nation? A No sir.
Q Have you ever been admitted to citizenship in the Choctaw Nation by the Choctaw tribal authorities, the Commission to the Five Civilized Tribes or the United States Court in the Indian Territory? A No sir.
Q Have you ever prior to this time made application to either the Choctaw authorities or the legally constituted authorities of the United States foe[sic] either citizenship or enrollment as a Choctaw Indian? A No sir.
Q This is the first application you have ever made of any description, is it?
A Yes sir.
Q You are now making application for identification as a Mississippi Choctaw?
A Yes sir.
Q Are you basing your claim as a beneficiary under the 14th article of the treaty of 1830? A Yes sir.
Q What was the name or names of your ancestors who were residents of the state of Mississippi and in the old Choctaw Nation here at the time the treaty of Sepetember[sic] 27th, 1830 was entered into between the United States and the Choctaw Tribe of Indians? A My father and grand mother.
Q Was your father living here at that time? A Yes sir.
Q Was he recognized and enrolled member of the Choctaw tribe of Indians here at that time? A Yes sir.
Q How old was your father? A When he died he was 73.
Q How long has he been dead? A He died in March, 1894.
Q What was his mother's name? A Sophia Mitchell.
Q She was a Choctaw Indian was she? A Yes sir.
Q Have you any evidence showing that she was ever recognized by the Choctaw Indians here or by the United States Indian Agent of the Choctaw Indians in Mississippi? A No sir, I can secure affidavits to that effect.
Q Did any of your ancestors ever remove from the state of Mississippi to the Indian Territory after the conclusion of the treaty of 1830 when the Choctaw Indians were removed to the western territory? A My grand mother went afterwards.
Q She went to the Choctaw Nation in the Indian Territory? A Yes sir.

Q Was she there recognized as a member of the Choctaw tribe and enrolled as such? A I think so.

Q Did you ever hear that she drew any annuity out there? A No sir.

Q Did you ever hear that she ever participated in any of their money? A No sir.

Q When did she die? A In the year '69 of '70.

Q Where did she live in the Choctaw Nation? A I don't know what place.

Q Have any of your ancestors ever claimed or received any land in Mississippi as beneficiaries under this fourteenth article of the treaty of 1830? A No sir.

Q You are making your claim solely as a beneficiary under that article of that treaty are you? A Yes sir.

Q Are you married? A Yes sir.

Q What is your wife's name? A Gertie Ella Hancock.

Q Are you making any claim for her? A No sir.

Q She is a white woman? A Yes sir.

Q Has no admixture of Indian blood? A No sir.

Q Have you any children? A No sir.

Q Just making this application for yourself alone? A Yes sir.

Q Is there any additional statement you desire to make in support of your application? A No, I don't know that there is.

> Permission is granted the applicant to file documentary evidence in support of this application provided the same is offered for filing with the Commission within thirty days from the date hereof.

The decision of the Commission as to your application for identification as a Mississippi Choctaw will be mailed to you in the future to your present post-office address.

Myra Young having been first duly sworn, upon her oath states that as stenographer to the Commission to the Five Civilized Tribes she reported in full all proceedings had in the above entitled cause on the 3rd day of April, 1901, and that the above and foregoing is a full, true and correct transcript of her stenographic notes of said proceedings on said date.

Myra Young

Subscribed and sworn to before me at Meridian, Mississippi, this 4th day of April, 1901.

J P McKee Jr
Notary Public.

M. C. Identified 3.

M.C.R. 1619.

Department of the Interior.
Commission to the Five Civilized Tribes.
Muskogee, Indian Territory, September 23, 1902.

In the matter of the application of Jubal A. Hancock to be enrolled as a Choctaw entitled to allotment under the provisions of the Act of Congress of May 31, 1900, having been identified as a Mississippi Choctaw by the Commission to the Five Civilized Tribes, May 7, 1902, which identification was approved by the Secretary of the Interior, May 21, 1902.

Jubal A. Hancock being first duly sworn testified as follows:

Examination by the Commission.

Q What is your name? A Jubal A. Hancock.
Q How old are you? A Twenty-seven years old.
Q You are the identical Jubal A. Hancock who is an applicant to this Commission for identification as a Mississippi Choctaw? A Yes sir.

Jubal A. Hancock is the identical person identified by the Commission to the Five Civilized Tribes as entitled to rights in the Choctaw lands under the provisions of the fourteenth article of the treaty of 1830 by the decision of the Commission to the Five Civilized Tribes in the case of Josephine Hussey et al., which identification was approved by the Secretary of the Interior, May 21, 1902.

Q Your purpose in appearing before the Commission at this time is to conform to a provision of the Act of Congress of May 31, 1900 relative to removal to and settlement in good faith in the Choctaw-Chickasaw Country, is it? A Yes sir.
Q Have you since your identification as a Mississippi Choctaw by this Commission, May 21, 1902, removed to the Choctaw Chickasaw Country for the purpose of making a bona fide residence there? A Yes sir.
Q How much of a residence have you make? A Well I haven't located at all yet.
Q Is it your intention to now locate in the Choctaw-Chickasaw country? A Yes sir.
Q At what place have you located or is it your intention to locate? A Around McGee there.
Q What will be your post office address? A McGee.
Q That's in the Chickasaw Nation is it? A Chickasaw Nation, yes sir.
Q Have you moved any of your belongings into the Indian Territory? A No sir; I've sold everything I had in Mississippi, and on account of the illness of my wife, have been unable to move her out to the Territory, but I do propose to settle in the vicinity of McGee, Chickasaw Nation, Indian Territory.
Q Have you any children born to you since you made application? A No sir.
Q You are the only person then interested in the application? A Yes sir.

Q Have you purchased or located on any improvements in the Choctaw Chickasaw country? A No sir.
Q You are before the Commission now, then, to give testimony as to your intention to locate within the next few days? A Yes sir as soon as I can.
Q Is it your purpose now to remain in the Choctaw-Chickasaw Country to make it your permanent home? A Yes sir.

---O---

Clara Mitchell Wood being first duly sworn upon her oath states that as stenographer for the Commission to the Five Civilized Tribes she reported in full all proceedings had in the above entitled cause on the 23rd day of September, 1902 and that the above and foregoing is a full, true and correct transcript of her stenographic notes of said proceedings on said date.

Clara Mitchell Wood

Subscribed and sworn to before me this 24th day of September 1902.

B.C. Jones

Notary Public.

M. C. R. 1619

COPY.

Muskogee, Indian Territory, May 8, 1902.

Jubal A. Hancock,

Gulfport, Mississippi. Post office Box 83,

Dear Sir:

You are hereby advised that on May 7, 1902, the Commission to the Five Civilized Tribes rendered a decision in the consolidated case of Josephine Hussey, et al., embracing the following applications for identification as Mississippi Choctaws:

Josephine Hussey, et al.,
J. Folsom Roe, et al.,
Jubal A. Hancock,
Charles Rushing Hancock.

Said decision after a review of the evidence submitted, concludes as follows:

"The authority vested in the Commission by the twenty first section of the act of Congress of June 28, 1898, (30 Stats., 495), is as follows;

> 'Said commission shall have authority to determine the identity of Choctaw Indians claiming rights in the Choctaw lands under article fourteen of the treaty between the United States and the Choctaw Nation concluded September twenty seventh, eighteen hundred and thirty and to that end may administer oaths, examine witnesses, and perform all other acts necessary thereto and make report to the Secretary of the Interior.'

It is the opinion of the Commission that the evidence in this case is sufficient to determine the identity of Josephine Hussey, William Hancock Hussey, Alvin McDowell Hussey, J. Folsom Roe, Jeannette C. Roe, Jubal A. Hancock and Charles Rushing Hancock, as Choctaw Indians entitled to rights in the Choctaw lands under the provision of law above quoted, and that the application for their identification as such be granted, and it is so ordered."

You are further advised that the Commission has on this date forwarded the record in this case to the Secretary of the Interior for review and you will be informed in due time of such action as may be taken by him.

Yours truly,

(SIGNED). T. B. Needles.

Commissioner in Charge.

Register.

COPY.

30382

D. C. No. 8589.

Refer in reply to
the following
Land-28269-1902

DEPARTMENT OF THE INTERIOR.

Office of Indian Affairs,

Washington, May 15, 1902.

The Honorable,

The Secretary of the Interior.

Sir:

The office transmits herewith the papers in the consolidated case of Josephine Hussey et al., applicants for identification as Mississippi Choctaws and recommends that the decision of the Commission, holding that the applications should be granted, be affirmed.

The record evidence shows conclusively that the applicants are descendants of Mississippi Choctaw ancestors, who were recognized as such, enrolled and granted land under the fourteenth article of the treaty between the United States and the Choctaw Nation concluded on the 27th day of September, 1830, by Act of Congress entitled "An Act for the relief of Jubal B. Hancock, passed August 11th, 1842, all of which is verified by the records in this office.

It is further shows by the record that in 1896, William Hancock Hussey, a minor, by his mother as next friend, J. Folsom Roe, Jubal A. Hancock and Charles Rushing Hancock made application for citizenship in the Choctaw Nation under the Act of Congress of June 10th, 1896, and that their said applications were denied by the Commission and no appeal taken from the adverse decision.

This is no bar to filing an application for identification as a Mississippi Choctaw under the Act of Congress of June 28th, 1898 (30 Stats., 495) and having their rights under that Act adjudicated by the proper tribunal.

Section 21 of that Act expressly provides that "Said commission shall have authority to determine the identity of Choctaw Indians claiming rights in the Choctaw lands under article fourteen of the treaty between the United States and the Choctaw Nation concluded September twenty seventh, eighteen hundred and thirty and to that end may administer oaths, examine witnesses, and perform all other acts necessary thereto and make report to the Secretary of the Interior."

It is under this provision the applications herein are made, and no previous adjudication of their status can be construed as an estoppel that will exclude claimants from the benefits conferred by the Act when the facts support their claim to the rights intended to be established thereby.

Very respectfully,

Your obedient servant,

W.C.B.(Cg.)

Acting Commissioner.

C O P Y .

30382. J.P.

I.T.D. 3142-1902. F.

L.R.S. DEPARTMENT OF THE INTERIOR.

Washington, May 21, 1902.

Commission to the Five Civilized Tribes,

Muskogee, I. T.

Gentlemen:

The Department has considered the Mississippi Choctaw case 1620, embracing the applications of Josephine Hussey, William Hancock Hussey, Alvin McDowell Hussey, J. Folsom Roe, Jeannette C. Roe, Jubal A. Hancock and Charles Rushing Hancock, transmitted with your letter of May 8, 1902.

You found that the evidence was sufficient to establish the descent of the claimants from Jubal B. Hancock who took advantage of the 14th article of the treaty of 1830, and to determine the identity of the applicants as Choctaw Indians entitled to rights in the Choctaw lands, in which opinion the Acting Commissioner of Indian Affairs is letter of May 15, 1902, concurs.

He states that it is shown that the applicants are descendants of Mississippi Choctaws ancestors who were recognized as such, enrolled and granted lands under the 14th article of the treaty of 1830, by an Act of Congress entitled "An Act for the relief of Jubal B. Hancock," passed August 11, 1842; that, while it is shown that in 1896 William Hancock Hussey, J. Folsom Roe, Jubal A. Hancock and Charles Rushing Hancock made application for citizenship in the Choctaw Nation under the Act of June 10, 1896, and that their applications were denied by your Commission and no appeal taken, that is no bar to the consideration of an application for identification as Mississippi Choctaws under the 21st section of the Act of June 28, 1898 (30 Stats. 495).

The Department has carefully considered the matter and finds no reason to disturb you decision, and it is accordingly affirmed. A copy of the Acting Commissioner's letter is enclosed.

You will advise the claimants, residents of Mississippi, hereof, and that to be entitled to enrollment in the Choctaw Nation, and to an allotment, it will be necessary for them to remove in good faith to the Choctaw-Chickasaw country, Indian Territory; also to that portion of the Choctaw-Chickasaw agreement pending in Congress, regard to Mississippi Choctaws.

Respectfully,

Thos. Ryan,

Acting Secretary,

1 enclosure. E.M.D.

Miss. Choctaw 1619

Muskogee, Indian Territory, May 31, 1902.

Jubal A. Hancock,

Box 83, Gulfport, Mississippi,

Dear Sir:

You are hereby advised that on the twenty first day of May, 1902, the Secretary of the Interior affirmed the decision of the Commission to the Five Civilized Tribes granting the application made by you for identification as a Mississippi Choctaw entitled to rights in the Choctaw lands in Indian Territory as a beneficiary under the provisions of article fourteen of the treaty between the United States and the Choctaw Nation, concluded September twenty seventh, eighteen hundred and thirty.

You are now advised, that, in order for you to be enrolled as a citizen of the Choctaw Nation entitled to allotment, it is necessary that you remove to and make settlement within the Choctaw-Chickasaw country, as provided by the act of Congress of May 31, 1900, (31 Stats., 221):

"That any Mississippi Choctaw duly identified as such by the United States Commission to the Five Civilized Tribes shall have the right, at any time prior to the approval of the final rolls of the Choctaws and Chickasaws by the Secretary of the Interior, to make settlement within the Choctaw-Chickasaw country, and on proof of the fact of bona fide settlement may be enrolled by the said United States Commission, and by the Secretary of the Interior as Choctaws entitled to allotment: Provided further, That all contracts or agreements looking to the sale or incumbrance in any way of the lands to be allotted to said Mississippi Choctaws, shall be null and void."

Your attention is further invited to the following sections of an agreement entered into at Washington, D.C. March 21, 1901, between Commissioners on the part of the United States and the Choctaw and Chickasaw Nations, and now pending before the Congress of the United States for ratification:

"41. All persons duly identified by the Commission to the Five Civilized Tribes under the provisions of section 21 of the act of Congress approved June 28, 1898 (30 Stats., 495), as Mississippi Choctaws entitled to benefits under article 14 of the treaty between the United States and the Choctaw Nation concluded September 27, 1830, may, at any time within six months after the date of the final ratification of this agreement, make bona fide settlement within the Choctaw-Chickasaw country, and upon proof of such settlement to such Commission within one year after the date of the final ratification of this agreement may be enrolled by such Commission as Mississippi Choctaws entitled to allotment as herein provided for citizens of the tribes, subject to the special provisions herein provided as to Mississippi Choctaws, and said enrollment shall be final when approved by the Secretary of the Interior. The application of no person for identification as a Mississippi Choctaw shall be received by said Commission after the date of the final ratification of this agreement.

42. When any such Mississippi Choctaw shall have continuously resided upon the lands of the Choctaw and Chickasaw Nations for a period of three years, including his residence thereon before and after such enrollment, he shall, upon due proof of such continuous residence, made in such manner and before such officer as may be designated by the Secretary of the Interior, receive a patent for his allotment, as provided in the Atoka agreement, and he shall hold the lands allotted to him as provided in this agreement for citizens of the Choctaw and Chickasaw nations.

43. Applications for enrollment as Mississippi Choctaws, and applications to have land set apart to them as such, must be made personally before the Commission to the Five Civilized Tribes. Fathers may apply for their minor children; and if the father be dead, the mother may apply; husbands may apply for wifes. Applications for orphans, insane persons, and persons of unsound mind may be made by duly appointed guardian or curator, and for aged and infirm persons and prisoners by agents duly authorized thereunto by power of attorney, in the discretion of said Commission.

44. If within four years after such enrollment any such Mississippi Choctaw, or his heirs or representatives if he be dead, fails to make proof of such continuous bona fide residence for the period so prescribed, or up to the time of the death of such Mississippi Choctaw, in case of his death after enrollment, he, and his heirs and representatives if he be dead, shall be deemed to have acquired no interest in the lands set apart to him, and the same shall be sold at public auction for cash, under rules and regulations prescribed by the Secretary of the Interior, and the proceeds paid into the Treasury of the United States to the credit of the Choctaw and Chickasaw tribes, and distributed per capita with other funds of the tribes. Such lands shall not be

sold for less than their appraised value. Upon payment of the full purchase price patent shall issue to the purchaser."

Yours truly,

Acting Chairman.

Miss. Choc. 3

Muskogee, Indian Territory, July 12, 1902.

Jubal A. Hancock,

Gulfport, Mississippi.

Dear Sir:

Receipt is hereby acknowledged of your letter of June 22, 1902, referring to our communication of May 31, advising you of the affirmation by the Secretary of the Interior of the decision of the Commission granting your application for identification as a Mississippi Choctaw.

You now desire to be informed if you can at this time remove to the Indian Territory and select a tract of land and homestead the same or if it will be necessary for you to wait until an allotment is made of the lands of the Choctaw and Chickasaw Nations.

You also desire to be advised if you can engage in any kind of business in the Indian Territory and further, what steps if any it will be necessary for you to take in order to establish your settlement in the Indian Territory and the amount of land you will receive in allotment.

Replying to your letter you are advised that the only legislation nor operative regarding the settlement of duly identified Mississippi Choctaw Indians in the Choctaw-Chickasaw country is contained in a provision of the act of Congress of May 31, 1900. This legislation defines the limit of time within which duly identified Mississippi Choctaws may remove to the Choctaw-Chickasaw country and make settlement as any time prior to the approval of the final rolls of citizenship of the Choctaw and Chickasaw Nations by the Secretary of the Interior. This limit is more clearly defined in an agreement entered into by the Unite States and the Choctaw and

Chickasaw Nations and which was ratified by the Congress of the United States, July 1, 1902, as follows:

"All persons duly identified by the Commission to the Five Civilized Tribes under the provisions of section 21 of the act of Congress approved June 28, 1898 (30 Stats., 495), as Mississippi Choctaws entitled to benefits under article 14 of the treaty between the United States and the Choctaw Nation concluded September 27, 1830, may, at any time within six months after the date of the final ratification of this agreement, make bona fide settlement within the Choctaw-Chickasaw country, and upon proof of such settlement to such Commission within one year after the date of the final ratification of this agreement may be enrolled by such Commission as Mississippi Choctaws entitled to allotment as herein provided for citizens of the tribes, subject to the special provisions herein provided as to Mississippi ChoctawsL[sic]"

This agreement has not at this time been ratified by the tribes and before becoming effective must be so confirmed and for this purpose will be submitted to a vote of the citizens of the Choctaw and Chickasaw Nations at a special election to be called by the chief executives of these two tribes within one hundred and twenty days after July 1, 1902.

In the event of the adoption of this agreement by the Choctaw and Chickasaw Tribes, you would have six months from May 7, 1902, the date on which you were identified by this Commission as a Mississippi Choctaw, to remove to and make settlement within the Choctaw-Chickasaw country, Indian Territory.

You are further advised that no allotment has up to this time been made of the lands of these two tribes and the only legislation or agreement now existing governing such allotment is the one made between the Choctaw and Chickasaw Nations and the United States, April 23, 1897 and which provides as follows:

"That all the lands within the Indian Territory belonging to the Choctaw and Chickasaw Indians shall be allotted to the members of said tribes so as to give to each member of these tribes so far as possible a fair and equal share thereof, considering the character and fertility of the soil and the location and value of the lands."

The recent agreement as confirmed by the act of Congress approved July 1, 1902, provides relative to the allotment of the lands of these two tribes, as follows:

"There shall be allotted to each member of the Choctaw and Chickasaw tribes, as soon as practicable after the approval by the Secretary of the Interior of his enrollment as herein provided, land equal in value to three hundred and twenty acres of the average allotable[sic] land of the Choctaw and Chickasaw nations:"

As there have been no allotments made of the lands of these two tribes and at this time no allotment office has been established for the purpose of receiving the selections of allotments of members of the Choctaw and Chickasaw Nations, we have no means at this time of recording the selections of the allotments of the members of these two tribes.

Your identification by the Commission to the Five Civilized Tribes and the Secretary of the Interior grants to you the right to now remove to the Choctaw-Chickasaw country and make settlement and under the act of Congress of May 31, 1900, upon proof of settlement, to be enrolled by this Commission as a Choctaw entitled to allotment.

We are unable to advise you of the probable action that will be taken by the Choctaw and Chickasaw Nations on the agreement confirmed by the act of Congress of July 1, 1902, but if it is your intention to avail yourself of the privileges accorded by your identification as Mississippi Choctaw, it will be advisable that you remove and make settlement within the Choctaw-Chickasaw country at as early a date as practicable.

We cannot advise you as to the prospects of engaging in business in this country more than to state that the Indian Territory is now being rapidly developed and it is probable that you would experience little trouble in obtaining occupation of some character.

Yours truly,

Acting Chairman.

1619

For Identification as a Mississippi Choctaw.

Date APR -3 1901

Name: Jubal A. Hancock.

Age 25 Blood 1/8

Post Office, Gulf-port. Miss. Box 83.

Father: William M. Hancock - dead.

Mother: Mary J. Hancock - ✓

Claims through father

~~Children~~:

Claims for himself alone.

Stenographer

Myra Young.

CARD NO. 4 - Choctaw MCR 1712 - Charles Rushing Hancock
See MCR 1620

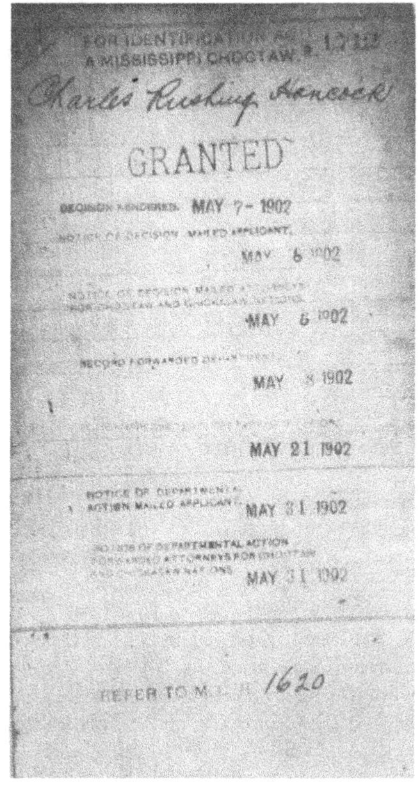
Charles Rushing Hancock
GRANTED
MAY 7- 1902
MAY 6 1902
MAY 6 1902
MAY 8 1902
MAY 21 1902
MAY 31 1902
MAY 31 1902
REFER TO M. C. R. 1620

DEPARTMENT OF THE INTERIOR.
COMMISSION TO THE FIVE CIVILIZED TRIBES.
Meridian, Mississippi, April 8, 1901.

In the matter of the application of Charles Rushing Hancock for identification as a Mississippi Choctaw.

Charles Rushing Hancock, having been first duly sworn, upon his oath testified as follows:

Examination by the Commission:

Q What is your name? A Charles Rushing Hancock.
Q How old are you? A Twenty.
Q What is your post office address? A Meridian.
Q Mississippi? A Yes sir.
Q Have you any street address? A 1221 twelfth avenue.
Q How long have you lived in Mississippi? A All my life.
Q Born here? A Yes sir.
Q What is your father's name? A William L Hancock.
Q Is he living? A No sir.
Q What is your mother's name? A Mary J. Hancock.
Q Is your mother living? A Yes sir.
Q Through which one of these parents do you claim Choctaw blood? A My father.
Q How much Choctaw was your father? A One quarter.
Q How much do you claim? A One eighth.
Q Was your father ever recognized as a Choctaw Indian by the Choctaw tribal authorities or the authorities of the United States? A He was recognized by the Choctaw tribe.
Q Choctaw Tribe here in Mississippi? A Yes sir.
Q He never lived in the Indian Territory? A No sir.
Q Is your name on any of the tribal rolls of the Choctaw Nation in the Indian Territory? A No sir.
Q Have you ever made application or has application ever been made for you to the Choctaw tribal authorities in the Indian Territory for citizenship? A No sir.
Q Did you or any one in your behalf in 1896 make application to the Commission to the Five Civilized Tribes for citizenship in the Choctaw Nation under the act of Congress of June 10, 1896? A No sir;
Q Were you ever admitted to citizrnship[sic] in the Choctaw Nation by judgment of the United States Court in Indian Territory? A No sir.
Q Have you ever prior to this time made application to the Choctaw tribal authorities or the authorities of the United States for citizenship or enrollment as a member of the Choctaw tribe of Indians? A No sir.
Q This is the first application you have ever made of any description? A Yes this is the first.
Q You claim your rights as a beneficiary under the provision of the fourteenth article of the treaty of 1830? A Yes sir.
Q What is the name of your ancestor or ancestors who were residents of Mississippi and recognized members of the Choctaw tribe at the time of the treaty of Dancing Rabbit Creek in 1830? A Sophia Mitchell Hancock. She lived here in 1830; that is all my Indian kin folks. My grandfather was here.
Q Who is Sophia Mitchell Hancock? A My grandmother.
Q Your father's mother? A Yes sir.
Q Was Sophia Mitchell her maiden name? A Yes that was her name before she was married.
Q Did you ever hear of her having a Choctaw name? A No sir.
Q You have evidence showing you are a direct lineal descendant of Sophia Mitchell? A Yes sir.

Q Did she remove with the Choctaws to the Indians[sic] Territory at their removal after the treaty of 1830? A No sir.
Q She remained in Mississippi? A Yes sir.
Q All your people on your father's side always lived in Mississippi[sic] A Yes sir.
Q Did Sophia Mitchell or any of your ancestors ever receive or claim any land in Mississippi under the fourteenth article of the treaty of 1830? A No sir, not that I know of.
Q Have you or any of your ancestors ever received any benefits as Choctaw Indians either from the Choctaw tribal authorities or from the authorities of the United States? A No sir.
Q Just making application for yourself are you? A Yes sir.
Q Is there any additional statement you would like to make in support of your application? A No, only I would like to have thirty days in which to file some documents.

Permission is granted the applicant to file documentary evidence in support of this application, provided the same is offered for filing with the Commission within thirty days from the date hereof.

The decision of the Commission in regard to this application which you make for identification as a Mississippi Choctaw will be mailed to you at your present post office address.

This applicant is apparently white.

H. C. Risteen having been first duly sworn upon his oath states: That as stenographer to the Commission to the Five Civilized Tribes he reported in full all proceedings has in the above entitled cause on the 8th day of April, 1901, and that the above and foregoing is a full true and correct transcript of his stenographic notes of said proceedings on said date.

H.C. Risteen

Subscribed and sworn to before me at Meridian, Mississippi, this 11th day of April, 1901.

J P McKee Jr
Notary Public.

M.C.R. 1712

COPY.

Muskogee, Indian Territory, May 8, 1902.

Charles Rushing Hancock,

1221 12th Street,

Meridian, Mississippi.

Dear Sir:

You are hereby advised that on May 7, 1902, the Commission to the Five Civilized Tribes rendered a decision in the consolidated case of Josephine Hussey, et al., embracing the following applications for identification as Mississippi Choctaws.

Josephine Hussey, et al.,
J. Folsom Roe, et al.,
Jubal A. Hancock,
Charles Rushing Hancock.

Said decision after a review of the evidence submitted, concludes as follows:

"The authority vested in the Commission by the twenty first section of the act of Congress of June 28, 1898, (30 Stats., 495), is as follows;

> 'Said commission shall have authority to determine the identity of Choctaw Indians claiming rights in the Choctaw lands under article fourteen of the treaty between the United States and the Choctaw Nation concluded September twenty seventh, eighteen hundred and thirty and to that end may administer oaths, examine witnesses, and perform all other acts necessary thereto and make report to the Secretary of the Interior.'

It is the opinion of the Commission that the evidence in this case is sufficient to determine the identity of Josephine Hussey, William Hancock Hussey, Alvin McDowell Hussey, J. Folsom Roe, Jeannette C. Roe, Jubal A. Hancock and Charles Rushing Hancock, as Choctaw Indians entitled to rights in the Choctaw lands under the provision of law above quoted, and that the application for their identification as such be granted, and it is so ordered."

You are further advised that the Commission has on this date forwarded the record in this case to the Secretary of the Interior for review and you will be informed in due time of such action as may be taken by him.

Yours truly,

(SIGNED). T. B. Needles.

Commissioner in Charge.

Register.

COPY.

30382

D. C. No. 8589.

Refer in reply to
the following
Land-28269-1902

DEPARTMENT OF THE INTERIOR.

Office of Indian Affairs,

Washington, May 15, 1902.

The Honorable,

The Secretary of the Interior.

Sir:

The office transmits herewith the papers in the consolidated case of Josephine Hussey et al., applicants for identification as Mississippi Choctaws and recommends that the decision of the Commission, holding that the applications should be granted, be affirmed.

The record evidence shows conclusively that the applicants are descendants of Mississippi Choctaw ancestors, who were recognized as such, enrolled and granted land under the fourteenth article of the treaty between the United States and the Choctaw Nation concluded on the 27th day of September, 1830, by Act of Congress entitled "An Act for the relief of Jubal B. Hancock, passed August 11th, 1842, all of which is verified by the records in this office.

It is further shows by the record that in 1896, William Hancock Hussey, a minor, by his mother as next friend, J. Folsom Roe, Jubal A. Hancock and Charles Rushing Hancock made application for citizenship in the Choctaw Nation under the Act of Congress of June 10th, 1896, and that their said applications were denied by the Commission and no appeal taken from the adverse decision.

This is no bar to filing an application for identification as a Mississippi Choctaw under the Act of Congress of June 28th, 1898 (30 Stats., 495) and having their rights under that Act adjudicated by the proper tribunal.

Section 21 of that Act expressly provides that "Said commission shall have authority to determine the identity of Choctaw Indians claiming rights in the Choctaw lands under article fourteen of the treaty between the United States and the Choctaw Nation concluded September twenty seventh, eighteen hundred and thirty and to that end may administer oaths, examine witnesses, and perform all other acts necessary thereto and make report to the Secretary of the Interior."

It is under this provision the applications herein are made, and no previous adjudication of their status can be construed as an estoppel that will exclude claimants from the benefits conferred by the Act when the facts support their claim to the rights intended to be established thereby.

Very respectfully,

Your obedient servant,

Acting Commissioner.

W.C.B.(Cg.)

C O P Y .

30382. J.P.

I.T.D. 3142-1902. F.

L.R.S. DEPARTMENT OF THE INTERIOR.

Washington, May 21, 1902.

Commission to the Five Civilized Tribes,

Muskogee, I. T.

Gentlemen:

The Department has considered the Mississippi Choctaw case 1620, embracing the applications of Josephine Hussey, William Hancock Hussey, Alvin McDowell Hussey, J. Folsom Roe, Jeannette C. Roe, Jubal A. Hancock and Charles Rushing Hancock, transmitted with your letter of May 8, 1902.

You found that the evidence was sufficient to establish the descent of the claimants from Jubal B. Hancock who took advantage of the 14th article of the treaty of 1830, and to determine the identity of the applicants as Choctaw Indians entitled to rights in the Choctaw lands, in which opinion the Acting Commissioner of Indian Affairs is letter of May 15, 1902, concurs.

He states that it is shown that the applicants are descendants of Mississippi Choctaws ancestors who were recognized as such, enrolled and granted lands under the 14th article of the treaty of 1830, by an Act of Congress entitled "An Act for the relief of Jubal B. Hancock," passed August 11, 1842; that, while it is shown that in 1896 William Hancock Hussey, J. Folsom Roe, Jubal A. Hancock and Charles Rushing Hancock made application for citizenship in the Choctaw Nation under the Act of June 10, 1896, and that their applications were denied by your Commission and no appeal taken, that is no bar to the consideration of an application for identification as Mississippi Choctaws under the 21st section of the Act of June 28, 1898 (30 Stats. 495).

The Department has carefully considered the matter and finds no reason to disturb you decision, and it is accordingly affirmed. A copy of the Acting Commissioner's letter is enclosed.

You will advise the claimants, residents of Mississippi, hereof, and that to be entitled to enrollment in the Choctaw Nation, and to an allotment, it will be necessary for them to remove in good faith to the Choctaw-Chickasaw country, Indian Territory; also to that portion of the Choctaw-Chickasaw agreement pending in Congress, regard to Mississippi Choctaws.

Respectfully,

Thos. Ryan,

Acting Secretary,

1 enclosure. E.M.D.

Miss. Choctaw 1712.

Muskogee, Indian Territory, May 31, 1902.

Charles Rushing Hancock,

1221 Twelfth Avenue,

Meridian, Mississippi,

Dear Sir:

You are hereby advised that on the twenty first day of May, 1902, the Secretary of the Interior affirmed the decision of the Commission to the Five Civilized Tribes granting the application made by you for identification as a Mississippi Choctaw entitled to rights in the Choctaw lands in Indian Territory as a beneficiary under the provisions of article fourteen of the treaty between the United States and the Choctaw Nation, concluded September twenty seventh, eighteen hundred and thirty.

You are now advised, that, in order for you to be enrolled as a citizen of the Choctaw Nation entitled to allotment, it is necessary that you remove to and make settlement within the Choctaw-Chickasaw country, as provided by the act of Congress of May 31, 1900, (31 Stats., 221):

"That any Mississippi Choctaw duly identified as such by the United States Commission to the Five Civilized Tribes shall have the right, at any time prior to the approval of the final rolls of the Choctaws and Chickasaws by the Secretary of the Interior, to make settlement within the Choctaw-Chickasaw country, and on proof of the fact of bona fide settlement may be enrolled by the said United States Commission, and by the Secretary of the Interior as Choctaws entitled to allotment: Provided further, That all contracts or agreements looking to the sale or incumbrance in any way of the lands to be allotted to said Mississippi Choctaws, shall be null and void."

Your attention is further invited to the following sections of an agreement entered into at Washington, D.C. March 21, 1901, between Commissioners on the part of the United States and the Choctaw and Chickasaw Nations, and now pending before the Congress of the United States for ratification:

"41. All persons duly identified by the Commission to the Five Civilized Tribes under the provisions of section 21 of the act of Congress approved June 28, 1898 (30 Stats., 495), as Mississippi Choctaws entitled to benefits under article 14 of the treaty between the United States and the Choctaw Nation concluded September 27, 1830, may, at any time within six months after the date of the final ratification of this agreement, make bona fide settlement within the Choctaw-Chickasaw country, and upon proof of such settlement to such Commission within one year after the date of the final ratification of this agreement may be enrolled by such Commission as Mississippi Choctaws entitled to allotment as herein provided for citizens of the tribes, subject to the special provisions herein provided as to Mississippi Choctaws, and said enrollment shall be final when approved by the Secretary of the Interior. The application of no person for identification as a Mississippi Choctaw shall be received by said Commission after the date of the final ratification of this agreement.

42. When any such Mississippi Choctaw shall have continuously resided upon the lands of the Choctaw and Chickasaw Nations for a period of three years, including his residence thereon before and after such enrollment, he shall, upon due proof of such continuous residence, made in such manner and before such officer as may be designated by the Secretary of the Interior, receive a patent for his allotment, as provided in the Atoka agreement, and he shall hold the lands allotted to him as provided in this agreement for citizens of the Choctaw and Chickasaw nations.

43. Applications for enrollment as Mississippi Choctaws, and applications to have land set apart to them as such, must be made personally before the Commission to the Five Civilized Tribes. Fathers may apply for their minor children; and if the father be dead, the mother may apply; husbands may apply for wifes. Applications for orphans, insane persons, and persons of unsound mind may be made by duly appointed guardian or curator, and for aged and infirm persons and prisoners by agents duly authorized thereunto by power of attorney, in the discretion of said Commission.

44. If within four years after such enrollment any such Mississippi Choctaw, or his heirs or representatives if he be dead, fails to make proof of such continuous bona fide residence for the period so prescribed, or up to the time of the death of such Mississippi Choctaw, in case of his death after enrollment, he, and his heirs and representatives if he be dead, shall be deemed to have acquired no interest in the lands set apart to him, and the same shall be sold at public auction for cash, under rules and regulations prescribed by the Secretary of the Interior, and the proceeds paid into the Treasury of the United States to the credit of the Choctaw and Chickasaw tribes, and distributed per capita with other funds of the tribes. Such lands shall not be sold for less than their appraised value. Upon payment of the full purchase price patent shall issue to the purchaser."

Yours truly,

Acting Chairman.

[The above letter given again.]

Miss. Choctaw 1712
Miss. Choctaw I 4

Muskogee, Indian Territory, November 3, 1902.

Charles Rushing Hancock,

#1221 Twelfth Avenue,

Meridian, Mississippi,

Dear Sir:

Receipt is hereby acknowledged of your letter of October 29, asking how much time you have in which to remove to the Indian Territory; that you have intended to come, but that your health has been such all summer that you could not remove; that you are now able to sit up only a few hours at a time, but that it is your intention to establish your residence in the Indian Territory as soon as you are able to travel; that you have sent a physician's certificate and a power of attorney to your brother, Jubal A. Hancock to be used in your behalf and he will present them to the Commission.

In reply to your letter you are advised that on May 7, 1902, the Commission rendered its decision granting your application for identification as a Mississippi Choctaw. Relative to the length of time you have within which to remove to Indian Territory, your attention is invited to the following provision of the agreement recently entered into between the United States and the Choctaw and Chickasaw Nations, approved by act of Congress of July 1, 1902, which was ratified September 25, 1902:

"All persons duly identified by the Commission to the Five Civilized Tribes under the provisions of section 21 of the act of Congress approved June 28, 1898 (30 Stats., 495), as Mississippi Choctaws entitled to benefits under article 14 of the treaty between the United States and the Choctaw Nation concluded September 27, 1830, may, at any time within six months after the date of the final ratification of this agreement, make bona fide settlement within the Choctaw-Chickasaw country, and upon proof of such settlement to such Commission within one year after the date of the final ratification of this agreement may be enrolled by such Commission as Mississippi Choctaws entitled to allotment as herein provided for citizens of the tribes, subject to the special provisions herein provided as to Mississippi Choctaws, and said enrollment shall be final when approved by the Secretary of the Interior."

Respectfully,

Acting Chairman.

M C-1712
M C I-4

Muskogee, Indian Territory, February 19, 1903.

Charles Rushing Hancock,

#1221 12th Avenue,

Meridian, Mississippi,

Dear Sir:

On May 7, 1902, the Commission to the Five Civilized Tribes rendered its decision granting your application for identification as a Mississippi Choctaw. On May 21, 1902, the Secretary of the Interior approved said decision, and on May 31, 1902, you were notified of such departmental action.

Your attention is invited to the following provision of the act of Congress approved July 1, 1902, which was ratified by the citizens of the Choctaw and Chickasaw Nations September 25, 1902:

"All persons duly identified by the Commission to the Five Civilized Tribes under the provisions of section 21 of the act of Congress approved June 28, 1898 (30 Stats., 495), as Mississippi Choctaws entitled to benefits under article 14 of the treaty between the United States and the Choctaw Nation concluded September 27, 1830, may, at any time within six months after the date of the final ratification of this agreement, make bona fide settlement within the Choctaw-Chickasaw country, and upon proof of such settlement to such Commission within one year after the date of the final ratification of this agreement may be enrolled by such Commission as Mississippi Choctaws entitled to allotment as herein provided for citizens of the tribes, subject to the special provisions herein provided as to Mississippi Choctaws, and said enrollment shall be final when approved by the Secretary of the Interior."

You are advised that under the provision of law above quoted, you will be required to remove to and make settlement within the Choctaw-Chickasaw country prior to March 25, 1903.

Respectfully,

Acting Chairman.

[The previous letter given again.]

No. 1712

For Identification as a Mississippi Choctaw.

Date APR -8 1901

Name Charles Rushing Hancock.

Age 20 Blood 1/8.

Post Office. Meridian, Miss
1221. 12th Ave.

Father: William M. Hancock-dead.

Mother: Mary J. Hancock- ✓

Claims through Father

~~Children:~~

Claims for self alone.

Stenographer

H C Risteen

CARD NO. 5 - Choctaw MCR 2535 - Alex Gibson

DEPARTMENT OF THE INTERIOR.

COMMISSION TO THE FIVE CIVILIZED TRIBES.

In the Matter of the Application of Alex Gibson for

Identification as a Mississippi Choctaw.

M. C. R. 2535.

DEPARTMENT OF THE INTERIOR.

COMMISSION TO THE FIVE CIVILIZED TRIBES.

In the Matter of the Application of Alex Gibson for

Identification as a Mississippi Choctaw.

M. C. R. 2535.

- - I N D E X . - -

DEPARTMENT OF THE INTERIOR,
COMMISSION TO THE FIVE CIVILIZED TRIBES,
Meridian, Mississippi, June 1st, 1901.

In the matter of the application of Alex Gibson for identification as a Mississippi Choctaw.

Said Alex Gibson, being first duly sworn through Isham Johnstom[sic], sworn Choctaw Interpreter, testified as follows:-

Examination by the Commission.

Q What is your name? A Alex Gibson.
Q What is your age? A Twenty-four.
Q What isyour[sic] postoffice address? [sic] Hickory, Mississippi.
Q What County? A Newton County.
Q How long have you lived in Newton County? A All my life.
Q Is your father living? A No sir, dead.
Q What was his name? A William Gibson.
Q Was your father a full blood Choctaw Indian? A Yes.
Q Is your mother living? A No.
Q What was her name? A Martha Gibson.
Q Was she a Full blood Choctaw Indian? A Yes.
Q You claim to be a full blood, do you? A Yes.
Q Were either of your parents ever recognized in any manner or enrolled as members of the Choctaw Tribe of Indians in Indian Territory by the Choctaw Tribal authorities or by the United States authorities? A No.
Q Are you married? A No.
Q This application then is for yourself alone, is it? A Yes.
Q Is your name on any of the tribal rolls of the Choctaw Nation in Indian Territory?
A No.
Q Did you ever make application to the Choctaw Tribal authorities in Indian Territory to be enrolled as a member of the Tribe? A No.
Q Did you or did anyone for you in the year 1896 make application to the Commission to the Five Civilized Tribes for citizenship in the Choctaw Nation?
A No.
Q Have you ever been admitted to citizenship in the Choctaw Nation by the Choctaw Tribal authorities, the Commission to the Five Civilized Tribes or by the United States Court in the Indian Territory? A No.
Q Have you ever made any application prior to this time to either the Choctaw Tribal authorities or the United States authorities to be admitted or enrolled as a citizen of the Choctaw Nation?
A Yes, made application at Decatur.

The records of the Commission show that application was made to the Commission to the Five Civilized Tribes at Decatur, Mississippi, on February 8, 1899, for the identification of this applicant as a Mississippi

Choctaw, his nam[sic] appearing on Mississippi Choctaw Card Field No. 506, also upon page 104 of the schedule of Mississippi Choctaws No. 1837 annexed to the report of the Commission to the Five Civilized Tribes to the Secretary of the Interior of March 10, 1899, as to the identity of Choctaw Indians residing in the State of Mississippi claiming rights in the Choctaw lands under the provisions of the 14th article of the treaty of Dancing Rabbit Creek.

Q This application made for you two years ago was the only one of any description that has ever been made for you, is it? A Yes.
Q You now desire to make application for identification as a Mississippi Choctaw? A Yes.
Q Do you claim your rights as a beneficiary under the provisions of the 14th article of the treaty of Dancing Rabbit Creek? A Yes.
Q Did you ever receive any benefits as a Choctaw Indian? A No.
Q Did any of your ancestors ever receive any benefits as Choctaw Indians? A No.
Q Were any of your ancestors living in the old Choctaw Nation in Mississippi or Alabama in the year 1830 when the treaty of Dancing Rabbit Creek was made?
A Don't know none of them but my grandfather Ontubbee.
Q Was he your father's father or mother's father? A He was my frandfather's[sic] father on his father's side.
Q That is his great grandfather on his father's side? A Yes.
Q Was ontubbee[sic] living here in 1830 when this treaty was made? A Yes.
Q Was he a recognized member of the Choctaw Tribe of Indians here at that time?
A Don't know.
Q You have no evidence that he was, have you? A No.
Q Did any of your ancestors remove from the old Choctaw Nation in Mississippi or Alabama to the present Choctaw Nation in Indian Territory at the time of the removal of the greater portion of the Choctaw Tribe of Indians between the years 1833 and 1838? A Don't know.
Q Did any of your ancestors within six months after the ratification of the treaty of Dancing Rabbit Creek signify to the United States Indian Agent for the Choctaws here in Mississippi their intention to remain in Mississippi and become citizens of the States? A Don't know.
Q Did you ever hear of any of them having gotten any land here in Mississippi under this 14th article of the treaty of Dancing Rabbit Creek? A No, don't know.
Q Are there any additional statements you desire to make at this time in support of your application? A No.
Q Have you any documentary evidence, affidavits, written testimony of any description, copies of records, deeds or patents or any other papers, showing that any of you ancestors were recognized members of the Choctaw Tribe of Indians in Mississippi in 1830, when the treaty of Dancing Rabbit Creek was made, that they ever complied or attempted to comply with the provisions of the 14th article of that treaty or ever received any benefits thereunder? A No.

This applicant has every appearance and characteristic of a full blood Indian, speaks and understands the Choctaw language and[sic] but very little

English, his examination having been conducted entirely through a sworn Choctaw interpreter.

The decision of the Commission as to your application for identification as a Mississippi Choctaw will be determined at the earliest possible date and report of the same made to the Secretary of the Interior, conformable to the provisions of the 21st section of the Act of Congress of June 28, 1898. A copy of such decision will be mailed to you to your postoffice address as given in your testimony at this time.

Ira S. Niles, being first duly sworn, states that as stenographer to the Commission to the Five Civilized Tribes he reported in full the proceedings had in the above entitled cause, heard at Meridian, Mississippi, June 1st, 1901, and that the above and foregoing is a full, true and correct transcript of his stenographic notes taken in said proceedings on said date

Ira S. Niles

Subscribed and sworn to before me this the 2nd day of July, 1901, at Meridian, Mississippi.

J P McKee Jr
Notary Public.

M C R 3303
" 3301
" 3509
" 3491
" 2535
" 4043

DEPARTMENT OF THE INTERIOR.
COMMISSION TO THE FIVE CIVILIZED TRIBES.
Muskogee, Indian Territory, July 5th, 1902.

In the matter of the application of Jeff Gibson for the identification of himself, his wife Lucy, and his three minor children, William, Ellis and Snowden Gibson, as Mississippi Choctaws, M.C.R. 3303.

In the matter of the application of Willie Gibson for the identification of himself and his wife, Mollie Gibson, as Mississippi Choctaws, M.C.R. 3301.

In the matter of the application of Emnie[sic] Gibson for the identification of herself and her minor child, Sallie Gibson, as Mississippi Choctaws, M.C.R. 3509.

In the matter of the application of Alex Gibson for the identification of his sister Leona Gibson as a Mississippi Choctaw, M.C.R. 3491.

In the matter of the application of Alex Gibson for the identification of himself as a Mississippi Choctaw, M.C.R. 2535.

In the matter of the application of Bard Gibson for the identification of himself, his wife Susanna and his minor children, Lela and Kima Gibson, as Mississippi Choctaws, M.C.R. 4043.

Supplemental testimony of Big Wiley Johnson, who being first duly sworn, testified as follows:

Examination by the Commission.

Q What is your name? A Big Wiley Johnson.
Q How old are you? A Fifty-seven.
Q What is your postoffice address? A Hickory, Mississippi.
Q Are you the identical Big Wiley Johnson who appeared before this Commission at Meridian, Mississippi, on August 20, 1901, and there made application for the identification of yourself, your wife, Patsie, and your ward, Allen Gilmore, as Mississippi Choctaws? A Yes.
Q Are you acquainted with a Choctaw Indian by the name of Jeff Gibson? A Yes sir.
Q About how old is he? A I couldn't tell about how old.
Q Is he over twenty-one? A Yes, over.
Q Where does he live? A Lives close by me.
Q Near Hickory, Mississippi? A Yes.
Q How long have you know him? A All his life.
Q What is the name of his father? A William Gibson.
Q Is he living? A No, dead long time.
Q What is the name of his mother? A I can't think of Indian name.
Q What is the English name? A Becky.
Q Is she living? A No dead.
Q Were they both full blood Choctaw Indians? A Yes, full blood.
Q What was Jeff's father's father's name---what was William Gibson's father's name? A Tah-nuckee.
Q Is he living? A No, dead long time.
Q Do you know his mother, Becky's, father's and mother's names? A No, I don't know that.
Q Is Jeff Gibson married? A Yes.
Q What is the name of his wife? A Lucy.
Q Do you know what Lucy's father's and mother's names are? A Yes, her daddy's name John Lewis.
Q Is he living? A No, dead.
Q Did he have an Indian name? A No sir.

Q What was Lucy's mother's name? A Martha.
Q Did she have an Indian name? A No.
Q Do you know anything about Lucy's grandparents' names? A They come from Mogaslush--I don't know about them.
Q Do you know anything about the names of the father and mother of Tah-nuckee? A No.
Q Tah-nuckee, then, is as far back as you know anything about the parentage of Jeff Gibson? A That's all I know.
Q Has Jeff Gibson any relatives who have been before this Commission for identification as Mississippi Choctaws? A Yes.
Q What are their names? A Walter Gibson, his half brother.
Q Is Walter Gibson a son of William Gibson? A Yes.
Q Walter Gibson and Jeff have the same father but different mothers? A Yes.
Q Ae there any other relatives of Jeff who have been before the Commission?
A Yes, Alex Gibson, appear for his sister Leona; they are full brother and sister.
Q Are they half brother and sister of Jeff Gibson? A Yes.

> Reference is made to Mississippi Choctaw cases M.C.R. 3491, Leona Gibson, and M.C.R. 2535 Alex Gibson.

Q Do you know anything about the parentage of the Martha Gibson who was the wife of William Gibson and the mother of Alex and Leona Gibson--what were Alex'[sic] mother's father's and mother's names? A Hillatubbe was Martha's father's name.
Q Do you know whether Hillatubbe ever received any benefits from the United States Government as a Choctaw Indian under article 14 of the treaty of 1830, or not?
A No, I never heard. He was an old man.
[sic] Do you know the names of any of Hillatubbe's relatives--any of his brothers or sisters? A I can't think of it--all by himself when he die--he was an old man when he died, when I was a boy.

> The records in the possession of the Commission, giving the lists of Choctaw Indians, beneficiaries under article fourteen of the treaty between the United States Government and the Choctaw Tribe of Indians, concluded September 27, 1830, examined, and the name of Hillatubbe is found in Volume 1, page 529, Claimants brief and evidence in the case of the Choctaw Nation vs. United States, No. 12742, Court No. 45, in a list of 46 cases fully adjudicated by Commissioners Tyler, Gaines and Rush, on the 30th of May, 1845, Hillatubbe appearing as a person dead at that date. The name of Hillatubbe is also found in a list of names of Choctaws to whom scrip was issued under the 14th article of the treaty of Dancing Rabbit Creek, prepared by the Indian Office and in the possession of the Commission, " X X V 1 ".
> 106

Q Is there anything further you can say about the ancestors of Martha who was the wife of William Gibson and the mother of Alex and Leona Gibson--do you know

anything about him, other than he was an old man when he died? A He died when I was a boy.
Q Do you know whether he ever received any land or scrip from the United States Government under article fourteen? A I never heard about that.
Q Were you old enough to recollect whether he lived upon any land or did he have a farm or improvements? A No, he didn't have no land.
Q Do you know where he lived when he died? A Yes, he lived in Newton County but he got so sick way back in Scott County and he come down there to get well and he go get gun and kill himself.
Q Do you know a Choctaw Indian by the name of Bard Gibson? A Yes sir.
Q Where does he live? A Live in Conehatta.
Q What relation, is he, if any, to Alex and Leona Gibson? A Brother and sister.
Q Full brother and sister? A Yes.
Q Same father and same mother? A Yes.
Q He has been before the Commission and applied for identification as a Mississippi Choctaw, has he? A Yes.
Q Has William Gibson any other children by his wife Martha or by any other of his wives than you have already testified about? A I don't know--I never heard--he never told me about that.
Q You have testified about all the names of the children of William Gibson that you know? A Yes, that's all I know.

---o---

Ira S. Niles, being first duly sworn, states that as stenographer to the Commission to the Five Civilized Tribes her reported in full all proceedings had in the above entitled cause, heard at Muskogee, Indian Territory, July 5th, 1902, and that the above and foregoing is a full, true and correct transcript of her stenographic notes of said proceedings on said date. and foregoing is a full, true and correct transcript of his stenographic notes taken in said proceedings on said date.

Ira S. Niles

Subscribed and sworn to before me this the 9th day of July, 1902, at Muskogee, Indian Territory.

Guy L.V. Emerson
Notary Public.

DEPARTMENT OF THE INTERIOR.

COMMISSION TO THE FIVE CIVILIZED TRIBES.

In the Matter of the Application of Alex Gibson for

Identification as a Mississippi Choctaw.

M. C. R. 2535.

-- D E C I S I O N . --

It appears from the record herein that application for identification as a Mississippi Choctaw was made to this Commission on June 1, 1901, by Alex Gibson, for himself, under the following provisions of the Act of Congress approved June 28, 1898 (30 Stats. 495):

> "Said commission shall have authority to determine the identity of Choctaw Indians claiming rights in the Choctaw lands under article fourteen of the treaty between the United States and the Choctaw Nation concluded September twenty seventh, eighteen hundred and thirty and to that end may administer oaths, examine witnesses, and perform all other acts necessary thereto and make report to the Secretary of the Interior."

From the evidence submitted in support of said application it appears that the applicant is a full-blood Mississippi Choctaw Indian.

Section forty-one of the Act of Congress entitled "An Act to ratify and confirm an agreement with the Choctaw and Chickasaw tribes of Indians, and for other purposes", approved July 1, 1902 (32 Stats. 641), and ratified by the Choctaw and Chickasaw Nations September 25, 1902, provided as follows:

> "The application of no person for identification as a Mississippi Choctaw shall be received by said Commission after six months subsequent to the date of the final ratification of this agreement and in the disposition of such applications all full-blood Mississippi Choctaw Indians and the descendants of any Mississippi Choctaw Indians whether of full or mixed blood who received a patent to land under the said fourteenth article of the said treaty of eighteen hundred and thirty who had not moved to and made bona fide settlement in the Choctaw-Chickasaw country prior to June twenty-eighth, eighteen hundred and ninety-cight, shall be deemed to be Mississippi Choctaws, entitled to benefits under article fourteen of the said treaty of September twenty-seventh, eighteen

hundred and thirty, and to identification as such by said Commission, but this direction or provision shall be deemed to be only a rule of evidence and shall not be invoked by or operate to the advantage of any applicant who is not a Mississippi Choctaw of a full blood, or who is not the descendant of a Mississippi Choctaw who received a patent to land under said treaty, or who is otherwise barred from the right of citizenship in the Choctaw Nation, all of said Mississippi Choctaws so enrolled by said Commission shall be upon a separate roll."

It is, therefore, the opinion of this Commission that Alex Gibson should be identified as a Mississippi Choctaw, and it is so ordered.

COMMISSION TO THE FIVE CIVILIZED TRIBES.

Tams Bixby
Acting Chairman.

T.B. Needles
Commissioner.

C. R. Breckinridge
Commissioner.

Muskogee, Indian Territory.

FEB 14 1903

COPY.

M.C.R. 2535

Muskogee, Indian Territory, February 21, 1903.

Mansfield, McMurray & Cornish,

Attorneys for the Choctaw and Chickasaw Nations,

South McAlester, Indian Territory.

Gentlemen:

Enclosed herewith you will find a copy of the decision of the Commission rendered February 14, 1903, identifying Alex Gibson as a Mississippi Choctaw Indian under the provisions of the forty-first section of the act of Congress of July 1, 1902 (32 Stats. 641).

You are hereby advised that you will be allowed fifteen days from the date hereof, in which to file with this Commission such protest as you desire to make against the action of the Commission in identifying the said Alex Gibson as a Mississippi Choctaw, and make satisfactory proof of service of said protest upon the applicant herein.

If you fail to file such protest within the time allowed, the name of the applicant herein will be placed upon the schedule of duly identified Mississippi Choctaws now being prepared by this Commission.

Respectfully,
(SIGNED). Tams Bixby
Acting Chairman.

Registered.
Enc. H.G. 15

M.C.R. 2535.

COPY.

Muskogee, Indian Territory, March 11, 1903.

Alex Gibson,

Hickory, Mississippi.

Dear Sir:

Enclosed herewith you will find a copy of the decision of the Commission to the Five Civilized Tribes, rendered February 14, 1903, identifying you as a Mississippi Choctaw Indian under the provisions of Section 41 of the Act of Congress approved July 1, 1902, (32 Stats. 641).

If you remove to the Choctaw-Chickasaw country, Indian Territory, before August 14, 1903, you will have six months from that date, or until February 14, 1904, within which to make proof of such removal and settlement at the office of the Commission at Atoka, Choctaw Nation, or Tishomingo, Chickasaw Nation.

Respectfully,
(SIGNED). Tams Bixby

Registered.

Chairman.

Enc. 2535.

#877

No. 2535

For Identification as a Mississippi Choctaw.

Date JUN 1 1901

Name Alex Gibson

Age 24 Blood full

Post Office, Hickory, Miss.

Father: William Gibson (dead)

Mother: Martha " "

Claims through both parents.

(See Miss. Choc. card field No. 506. Appearance 2/9/99.)

~~Children~~:

(Claims for self only.)

Stenographer J. S. Niles.

No. 2535

For Identification as a Mississippi Choctaw.

Date 7/5/02

Name Alex Gibson

Age   Blood

Post-Office,

Father:

Mother:

Claims through

Additional testimony of Big Arby Johnson

Children:

Stenographer C. F. Tiles

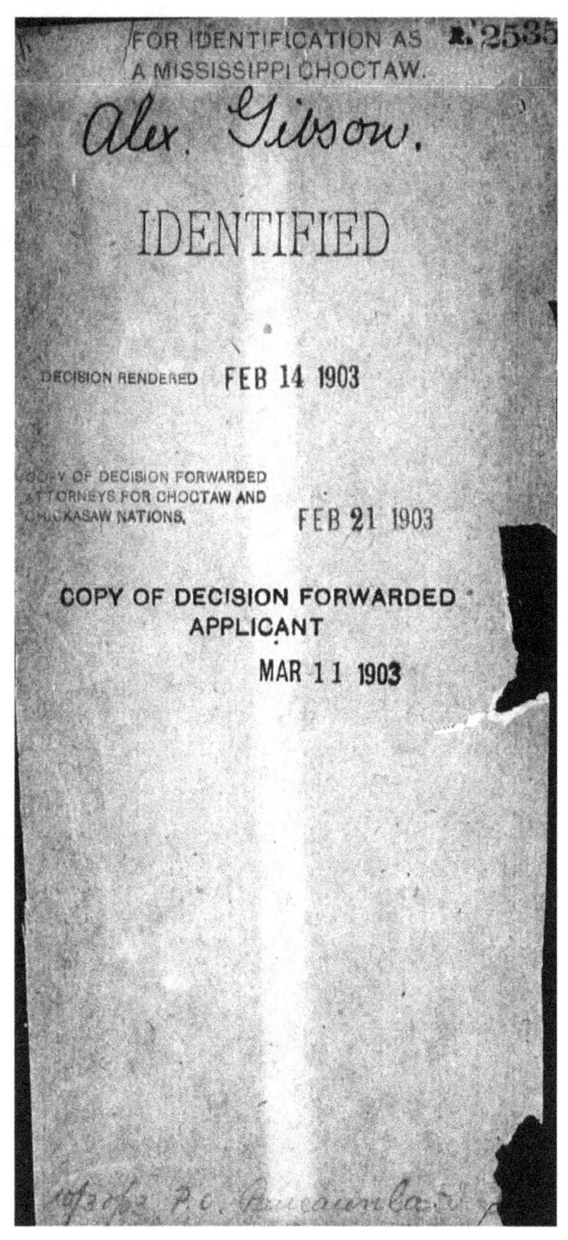

FOR IDENTIFICATION AS
A MISSISSIPPI CHOCTAW. 2535

Alex. Gibson.

IDENTIFIED

DECISION RENDERED FEB 14 1903

COPY OF DECISION FORWARDED
ATTORNEYS FOR CHOCTAW AND
CHICKASAW NATIONS. FEB 21 1903

COPY OF DECISION FORWARDED
APPLICANT
MAR 11 1903

CARD NO. 6 - Choc. MCR 2896 - Frank Johnson

No Dawes Packet available.

CARD NO. 7 - Choctaw MCR 2417 - Louis Hobley

DEPARTMENT OF THE INTERIOR,
COMMISSION TO THE FIVE CIVILIZED TRIBES.

In the matter of the application of Louis Hobley, et al., for identification as Mississippi Choctaws, M.C.R. 2417.

DEPARTMENT OF THE INTERIOR,
COMMISSION TO THE FIVE CIVILIZED TRIBES.

In the matter of the application of Louis Hobley, et al., for identification as Mississippi Choctaws, M.C.R. 2417.

I N D E X .

Decision of the Commission granting the application of Louis Hobley, et al., for identification as Mississippi Choctaws, ... 5

2417

DEPARTMENT OF THE INTERIOR.
COMMISSION TO THE FIVE CIVILIZED TRIBES.
Meridian, Mississippi, May 27, 1901.

In the matter of the application of Louis Hobley for the identification of himself and wife as Mississippi Choctaws.

Louis Hobley, having been first duly sworn, upon his oath testifies as follows: (through Isham Johnston, official interpreter)

Examination by the Commission:

Q What is your name? A Louis Hobley.
Q What is your age? A Forty five.
Q What is your post office address? A Ponchatoula, Tangipahoa Parish, Louisiana.
Q Where were you born? A In Louisiana.
Q Always lived in Louisiana? A Yes.
Q What is your father's name? A Hobley.
Q Is he living or dead? A Dead.
Q Was he a full blood? A Full blood
Q Is your mother dead? A Yes.
Q What was her name? A Don't know.
Q Did your father ever have a Choctaw name? A No.
Q Was your mother a full blood? A Yes.
Q Are you a full blood Choctaw Indian? A Yes.
Q Do you claim your Choctaw blood through both your father and mother? A Yes.
Q Have your parents through whom you claim your right to identification as a Mississippi Choctaw ever been recognized in any manner or enrolled as members of the Choctaw tribe of Indians by the Choctaw tribal authorities or the authorities of the United States? A No.
Q Are you married? A Yes.
Q What is your wife's name? A Celeste.
Q Do you make application for your wife? A Yes.
Q How old is she? A About forty three.
Q Is she a full blood Choctaw Indian? A Yes sir.
Q What is her father's name? A Don't know, dead long time.
Q Was he a full blood? A Yes.
Q What is your wife's mother's name? A Conche.

Q Is she living? A Dead.
Q Was she a full blood Indian? A Yes.
Q Have your wife's parents through whom you claim for her the right to identification as a Mississippi Choctaw ever been enrolled as members of the Choctaw tribe of Indians by the Choctaw tribal authorities or the authorities or[sic] the United States? A No.
Q Have you any children? A All dead.
Q Is your name or the name of your wife n any of the tribal rolls of the Choctaw Nation in Indian Territory? A No.
Q Have you ever made application to the Choctaw tribal authorities in Indian Territory for the enrollment or[sic] yourself or wife as members of that tribe? A No.
Q Did you or any one for you in 1896 or for your wife in 1896 make application to the Commission to the Five Civilized Tribes for citizenship in the Choctaw Nation under the act of Congress of June 10, 1896? A No.
Q Have you or your wife ever been admitted to citizenship in the Choctaw Nation by either the Choctaw tribal authorities the Commission to the Five Civilized Tribes or by the United States Court in Indian Territory? A No.
Q Have you ever made application before this for yourself or your wife to either the Choctaw tribal authorities or to the authorities of the United States to be admitted or enrolled as citizens of the Choctaw Nation? A No.
Q Is this the first application you have ever made of any kind? A Yes.
Q Is it now your purpose to make application for identification as Mississippi Choctaws for yourself and your wife? A Yes.
Q Do you claim this right as beneficiaries under article fourteen of the treaty of 1830? A Yes.
Q Have you or your ancestors or your wife or her ancestors ever received any benefits as Choctaw Indians? A Don't know.
Q Can you five[sic] the name of any of your ancestors or your wife's ancestors who were residents of the old Choctaw Nation in Mississippi and Alabama and who were acknowledged members of the Choctaw tribe of Indians in Mississippi or Alabama in 1830 when the treaty of Dancing Rabbit Creek was entered into between the United States and the Choctaw tribe? A Don't know about it.
Q Did any of your ancestors or your wife's ancestors within six months after the ratification of the treaty of 1830 signify to the United States Indian Agent in Mississippi their intention to remain in the state of Mississippi and become citizens of the states? A Don't know.
Q Did any of your ancestors go from Mississippi or Alabama to the present Choctaw Nation in Indian Territory between the years 1833 and 1838 when the other members went there? A Don't know.
Q Have any of your ancestors ever claimed or received any land in Mississippi as beneficiaries under article fourteen of the treaty of 1830? A Don't know.
Q Do you speak the English language? A Not much--a few words.
Q Do you talk Choctaw all the time? A Yes.
Q Are there any additional statements you want to make in support of this application? A No.
Q Have you any documntary[sic] evidence, affidavits, written testimony of any description, copies of records, deeds or patents, or any proper papers showing that

your ancestors or your wife's ancestors were ever recognized members of the Choctaw tribe of Indians in Mississippi in 1830 or that they ever complies or attempted to comply with the provisions of the fourteenth article of the treaty of 1830 or ever received any benefits under that article of the treaty? A No.

> This applicant has the appearance and all characteristics of a full blood Choctaw Indian. He does not speak the English language, his examination having been conducted through the medium of a sworn Choctaw interpreter. He has no knowledge of any compliance on the part of his ancestors with any of the provisions of article fourteen of the treaty of 1830.

> The decision of the Commission as to your application for the identification of yourself and your wife as Mississippi Choctaws will be determined at the earliest possible date and a report of the same made to the Secretary of the Interior conformable to the provisions of the twenty first section of the act of Congress of June 28, 1898, and a copy of the decision will be mailed to you at your post office address as given in your testimony at this time.

H.C. Risteen, having been first duly sworn, upon his oath states: That as stenographer to the Commission to the Five Civilized Tribes he reported in full all proceedings had in the above entitled cause on the 27th day of May, 1901, and that the above and foregoing is a full, true and correct transcript of his stenographic notes of said proceedings on said date.

H.C. Risteen

Subscribed and sworn to before me at Meridian, Mississippi, this 14th day of June, 1901.

J P McKee Jr
Notary Public.

AFFIDAVIT TO BE FILED IN SUPPORT OF

THE APPLICATION OF LOUIS HOBLEY.

Louis Hobley et al
vs
Choctaw Nation.
R 2417 ——— 5/27/01

DEPARTMENT OF THE INTERIOR,
COMMISSION TO THE FIVE CIVILIZED TRIBES.
FILED
JUL 3 1901
[signature] ACTING CHAIRMAN.

Louis Hobley

Affidavit in Support of the Application

of Louis Hobly

STATE OF Louisiana
Parish COUNTY OF Tangipahoa

BEFORE ME, the undersigned authority, on this day personally appeared Louis Avilleux and J A Thompson who is 57 and 24 years of age respectively, and who by me being first duly sworn, says on their oath that they were well acquainted with the father of Louis Hobly; that the said Louis Hobly is or was full blood Mississippi Choctaw Indian; that he spoke the Choctaw language; that his color, hair, make-up, and habits were that of a Choctaw Indian. Affiant further states that the said Louis Hobly who has applied to the Commission to the Five Civilized Tribes to be placed on the rolls of the Mississippi Choctaws, is reputed and considered by all who know him and his ancestors to be part Choctaw Indian, and to the best of affiant's knowledge the said Louis Hobly is a full blood Mississippi Choctaw Indian, and the direct lineal descendant of Louis Hobly; further swear that we have no interest, direct or indirect, in the application of Louis Hobly to be placed on the rolls as a Mississippi Choctaw.

WITNESS our hands this 26th day of June 1901

J. A. Thompson
L. H. Avilleux

SUBSCRIBED AND SWORN to before me this 26th day of June 1901; and I further certify that affiants are credible persons.

Edwin R. Wells

Notary Public in and for County of Tangipahoa

[SEAL.] State of La

4

DEPARTMENT OF THE INTERIOR,

COMMISSION TO THE FIVE CIVILIZED TRIBES.

In the matter of the application of Louis Hobley, et al., for identification as Mississippi Choctaws, M.C.R. 2417.

--:D E C I S I O N:--

It appears from the record herein that application for identification as Mississippi Choctaws was made to this Commission on May 27, 1901, by Louis Hobley for himself, and his wife, Celeste Hobley, under the following provision of the act of Congress approved June 28, 1898, (30 Stats. 495) :

> "Said Commission shall have authority to determine the identity of Choctaw Indians claiming rights in the Choctaw lands under article fourteen of the treaty between the United States and the Choctaw Nation, concluded September twenty-seventh, eighteen hundred and thirty, and to that end may administer oaths, examine witnesses, and perform all other acts necessary thereto and make report to the Secretary of the Interior."

From the evidence submitted in support of said application it appears that both of the applicants are full-blood Mississippi Choctaw Indians.

Section forty-one of the act of Congress entitled "An Act To ratify and confirm an agreement with the Choctaw and Chickasaw tribes of Indians, and for other purposes," approved July 1, 1902, (32 Stats. 641), and ratified by the Choctaw and Chickasaw Nations September 25, 1902, provides as follows:

> "The application of no person for identification as a Mississippi Choctaw shall be received by said Commission after six months subsequent to the date of the final ratification of this agreement and in the disposition of such applications all full-blood Mississippi Choctaw Indians and the descendants of any Mississippi Choctaw Indians whether of full or mixed blood who received a patent to land under the said fourteenth article of the said treaty of eighteen hundred and thirty who had not moved to and made bona fide settlement in the Choctaw-Chickasaw country prior to June twenty-eighth, eighteen hundred and ninety-eight, shall be deemed to

be Mississippi Choctaws, entitled to benefits under article fourteen of the said treaty of September twenty-seventh, eighteen hundred and thirty, and to identification as such by said Commission, but this direction or provision shall be deemed to be only a rule of evidence and shall not be invoked by or operate to the advantage of any applicant who is not a Mississippi Choctaw of a full blood, or who is not the descendant of a Mississippi Choctaw who received a patent to land under said treaty, or who is otherwise barred from the right of citizenship in the Choctaw Nation, all of said Mississippi Choctaws so enrolled by said Commission shall be upon a separate roll."

It is, therefore, the opinion of this Commission that Louis Hobley and Celeste Hobley should be identified as Mississippi Choctaws, and it is so ordered.

COMMISSION TO THE FIVE CIVILIZED TRIBES.

Tams Bixby
Acting Chairman.

T.B. Needles
Commissioner.

C. R. Breckinridge
Commissioner.

Muskogee, Indian Territory.
FEB 14 1903

COPY.

M.C.R. 2417

Muskogee, Indian Territory, February 21, 1903.

Mansfield, McMurray & Cornish,
Attorneys for the Choctaw and Chickasaw Nations,
South McAlester, Indian Territory.

Gentlemen:

Enclosed herewith you will find a copy of the decision of the Commission rendered February 14, 1903, identifying Louis Hobley and his wife,

Celeste Hobley, as Mississippi Choctaw Indians under the provisions of the forty-first section of the act of Congress approved July 1, 1902 (32 Stats. 641).

You are hereby advised that you will be allowed fifteen days from the date hereof, in which to file with this Commission such protest as you desire to make against the action of the Commission in identifying the said Louis Hobley and wife as Mississippi Choctaws, and make satisfactory proof of service of said protest upon the applicants herein.

If you fail to file such protest within the time allowed, the names of the applicants herein will be placed upon the schedule of duly identified Mississippi Choctaws now being prepared by this Commission.

Respectfully,
(SIGNED). *Tams Bixby*
Acting Chairman.

Registered.
Enc. H.G. 16

M.C.R. 2417.

COPY.

Muskogee, Indian Territory, March 11, 1903.

Louis Hobley,
Ponchatonla[sic], Louisiana.

Dear Sir:

Enclosed herewith you will find a copy of the decision of the Commission to the Five Civilized Tribes, rendered February 14, 1903, identifying yourself and your wife, Celeste Hobley, as Mississippi Choctaw Indians under the provisions of Section 41 of the Act of Congress approved July 1, 1902, (32 Stats. 641).

If you remove to the Choctaw-Chickasaw country, Indian Territory, before August 14, 1903, you will have six months from that date, or until February 14, 1904, within which to make proof of such removal and settlement at the office of the Commission at Atoka, Choctaw Nation, or Tishomingo, Chickasaw Nation.

Respectfully,

(SIGNED).
Tams Bixby

Registered.

Chairman.

Enc. 2417.

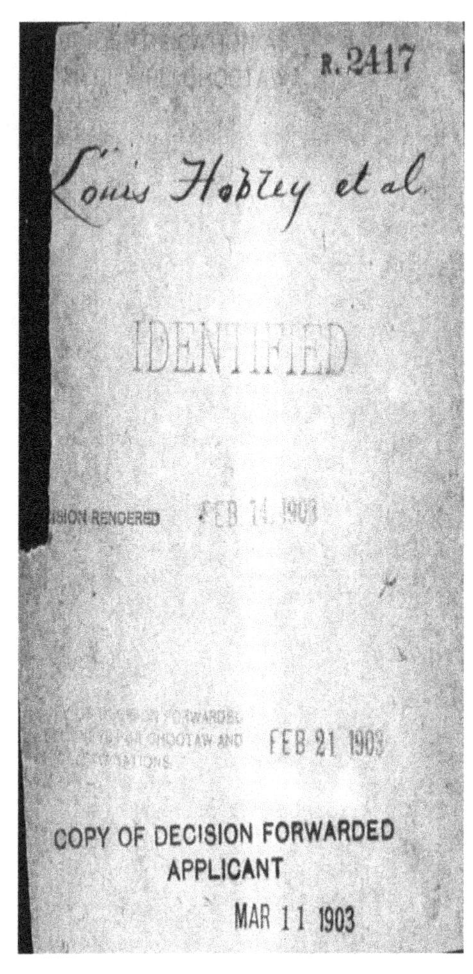

R. 2417

Louis Hobley et al

IDENTIFIED

ISION RENDERED FEB 14 1903

FEB 21 1903

COPY OF DECISION FORWARDED
APPLICANT
MAR 11 1903

#778

No. 2417

For Identification as a Mississippi Choctaw.

Date MAY 27 1901

Name Louis Hobley -

Age 45 Blood full

Post Office, Ponchatoula, La.

Father: Hobley - f. b d

Mother: don't know f. b d

Claims through both parent

wife. - Celeste - f. b 43
father. don't know. — f.b (d)
mother. Conche — f.b (d)

~~Children~~

Claims for self and wife -

Stenographer H. C. Ristine.

CARD NO. 8 - Choctaw MCR 2275 - Joseph Baptiste, Jr.

DEPARTMENT OF THE INTERIOR

COMMISSION TO THE FIVE CIVILIZED TRIBES

The within record is in the matter of
the application of Joseph Baptiste, Jr., for identification
as a Mississippi Choctaw,
M.C.R. 2275

DEPARTMENT OF THE INTERIOR

COMMISSION TO THE FIVE CIVILIZED TRIBES

In the matter of the application of Joseph Baptiste Jr., et al., for identification as a Mississippi Choctaw, M.C.R. 2275

I N D E X

DEPARTMENT OF THE INTERIOR.
COMMISSION TO THE FIVE CIVILIZED TRIBES.
Meridian, Mississippi, May 20, 1901.

In the matter of the application of Joseph Baptiste, Jr., for identification as a Mississippi Choctaw.

Joseph Baptiste, Jr., javing[sic] been first duly sworn, upon his oath testifies as follows:

Examination by the Commission:

Q What is your name? A Joseph Baptiste, Jr.
Q What is your age? A Twenty six.
Q What is your post office address? Florenville, Louisiana.
Q How long have you lived in Louisiana? A All my live.
Q Never have lived out of that state? A No.
Q What is your father's name? A Joseph Baptiste.
Q Is he living? A Yes.
Q Is he a full blood? A Yes.
Q What is your mother's name? A Felice.
Q Is she living? A Yes.
Q Is she a full blood? A Yes sir.
Q Through which one of these parents do you claim Choctaw blood? A Both.
Q Are you a full blood? A Yes.
Q Have your parents through who you claim your right to identification as a Mississippi Choctaw ever been recognized in any manner or enrolled as members of the Choctaw tribe of Indians by the Choctaw tribal authorities or by the authorities of the United States? A No.
Q Are you married? A No sir.
Q You make application for yourself alone? A Yes sir.
Q Is your name on any of the tribal rolls of the Choctaw Nation in Indian Territory? A No.
Q Have you ever made application to the Choctaw tribal authorities in Indian Territory to be enrolled as a member of that tribe? A No.
Q Did you or any one for you in 1896 under the act of Congress of June 10, 1896, make application to the Dawes Commission for enrollment or citizenship in the Choctaw Nation? A No.
Q Have you ever made application before this to either the Choctaw tribal authorities or to the authorities of the United States to be admitted or enrolled as citizens[sic] of the Choctaw Nation? A No.
Q This is the first application you have ever made of any kind? A Yes
Q Do you now want to make application for identification as a Mississippi Choctaw? A Yes.
Q Do you claim under article fourteen of the treaty of 1830? A Yes
Q Have you ever received any benefits as a Choctaw Indian? A No sir.
Q Have any of your ancestors ever received any benefits as Choctaw Indians?

A No sir.
Q Do you know the names of any of your ancestors who were recognized members of the Choctaw tribe of Indians in 1830 when the treaty of 1830 was made? A No.
Q Have you any evidence showing that any of your ancestors were recognized members of the Choctaw tribe of Indians in 1830? A No.
Q Did any of your ancestors remove from the territory occupied by the Choctaw tribe of Indians in Mississippi and Alabama between the years 1833 and 1838 to the Indian Territory with the other Choctaw Indians? A No.
Q Did any of your ancestors within six months after the ratification of the treaty of 1830 tell the United States Indian Agent living in Mississippi that they intended to remain in Mississippi, take land there and become citizens of the United States?
A No.
Q Have any of your ancestors ever claimed or received any land in Mississippi under article fourteen of the treaty of 1830? A No.
Q Do you speak the Choctaw language? A Yes.
Q Are there any additional statements you want to make in support of your application? A No.
Q Have you any documentary evidence, any affidavits, written testimony of any description, copies of records, deeds or patents, or any other proper papers showing that your ancestors were ever recognized members of the Choctaw tribe of Indians in Mississippi in 1830 or that they ever complied or attempted to comply with the provisions of the fourteenth article of the treaty of 1830? [No answer given.]

Here L.P. Hudson asks leave to file written evidence in support of this claim within thirty days.

Motion of attorney for applicant is granted.

This applicant has the appearance and all characteristics of a full blood Choctaw Indian. He speaks the Choctaw language, and has also sufficient knowledge of the English language to give his testimony without the aid of a sworn Choctaw Interpreter. He has no knowledge of any compliance by his ancestors with the fourteenth article of the treaty of 1830.

The decision of the Commission as to your application for identification as a Mississippi Choctaw will be determined at the earliest possible date and a report of the same made to the Secretary of the Interior conformable to the provisions of the twenty first section of the act of Congress of June 28, 1898, and a copy of such decision will be mailed to you at your post office address as given in your testimony at this time.

H.C. Risteen, having been first duly sworn, upon his oath states: That as stenographer to the Commission to the Five Civilized Tribes he reported in full all proceedings had in the above entitled cause on the 20th day of May, 1901, and that the above and foregoing is a full, true and correct transcript of his stenographic notes of said proceedings on said date.

H.C. Risteen

Subscribed and sworn to before me at Meridian, Mississippi, this 6th day of May, 1901.

J P McKee Jr
Notary Public.

DEPARTMENT OF THE INTERIOR,
COMMISSION TO THE FIVE CIVILIZED TRIBES,
Meridian, Mississippi, May 20th, 1901.

In the matter of the application of Joseph Baptiste Jr., for identification as a Mississippi Choctaw.

Joseph Baptiste Sr., being called to testify in behalf of the applicant, and being first duly sworn, states as follows:-

Examination by the Commission. Mr. L. P. Hudson, attorney for applicant.

Q What is your name? A Joseph Baptiste.
Q How old are you? A Forty six.
Q Where do you live? A Saint Tammany Parish, Louisiana.
Q Where did your father and mother live? A Lived in the same place.
Q Where did they come from to that place? A Come from Mississippi.
Q Where in Mississippi? A At Talihoma Creek.
Q Did your father and mother always live there? A Yes sir.
Q Until they went to Louisiana? A Yes sir.
Q All their folks lived in Mississippi, did they? A Yes sir.
Q You was born in Louisiana? A Yes sir.
Q Did they tell you that their people all come from Mississippi? A Yes sir.
Q Did your folks ever live anywhere except in Mississippi and Louisiana? A No sir, always lived in Mississippi and Louisiana.
Q Is Joe Baptiste your son? A Yes sir.
Q His grandfather and grandmother were your father and mother? A Yes sir.
Q They come from Mississippi? A Yes sir.

Witness excused.

W. J. Partin, being called as a witness in behalf of said applicant and being first duly sworn, states as follows:-

Examination by Mr. L. P. Hudson, attorney for applicant.

Q State your name, age and residence? A W. J. Partin, age forty-five; reside in Enterprise, Mississippi.
Q How long have you lived in Mississippi? A Ever since I was four years old.
Q Do you know where Talihoma Creek is located in Mississippi? A Yes sir.

Q Can you tell us through what Counties the Creek runs? A It heads in Jasper County, Mississippi, and empties into Talihaly Creek in Jones County, Mississippi, near Ellisville, the County Seat of Jones County, Mississippi.

Ira S. Niles, being first duly sworn, states that as stenographer to the Commission to the Five Civilized Tribes, he reported in full the proceedings had in the above entitled cause, heard at Meridian, Mississippi, May 20th, 1901, and that the above and preceding is a full, true and correct transcript of his stenographic notes taken in said proceedings on said date.

Ira S. Niles

Subscribed and sworn to before me this the 13th day of June, 1901, at Meridian, Mississippi.

J P McKee Jr
Notary Public.

DEPARTMENT OF THE INTERIOR

COMMISSION TO THE FIVE CIVILIZED TRIBES

In the matter of the application of Joseph Baptiste Jr., for identification as a Mississippi Choctaw, M.C.R. 2275.

-----D E C I S I O N ------

It appears from the record herein that application for identification as a Mississippi Choctaw was made to this Commission on May 20, 1901, by Joseph Baptiste Jr. for himself, under the following provision of the Act of Congress approved June 28, 1898, (30 Stats. 495):

> "Said commission shall have authority to determine the identity of Choctaw Indians claiming rights in the Choctaw lands under article fourteen of the treaty between the United States and the Choctaw Nation concluded September twenty seventh, eighteen hundred and thirty and to that end may administer oaths, examine witnesses, and perform all other acts necessary thereto and make report to the Secretary of the Interior."

From the evidence submitted in support of said application it appears that the applicant is a full blood Mississippi Choctaw Indian.

Section forty-one of the Act of Congress entitled "An Act to ratify and confirm an agreement with the Choctaw and Chickasaw tribes of Indians, and for other purposes" approved July 1, 1902, (32 Stats. 641) and ratified by the Choctaw and Chickasaw Nations September 25, 1902, provides as follows:

> "The application of no person for identification as a Mississippi Choctaw shall be received by said Commission after six months subsequent to the date of the final ratification of this agreement and in the disposition of such applications all full-blood Mississippi Choctaw Indians and the descendants of any Mississippi Choctaw Indians whether of full or mixed blood who received a patent to land under the said fourteenth article of the said treaty of eighteen hundred and thirty who had not moved to and made bona fide settlement in the Choctaw-Chickasaw country prior to June twenty-eighth, eighteen hundred and ninety-eight, shall be deemed to be Mississippi Choctaws, entitled to benefits under article fourteen of the said treaty of September twenty-seventh, eighteen hundred and thirty, and to identification as such by said Commission, but this direction or provision shall be deemed to be only a rule of evidence and shall not be invoked by or operate to the advantage of any applicant who is not a Mississippi Choctaw of a full blood, or who is not the descendant of a Mississippi Choctaw who received a patent to land under said treaty, or who is otherwise barred from the right of citizenship in the Choctaw Nation, all of said Mississippi Choctaws so enrolled by said Commission shall be upon a separate roll."

It is, therefore, the opinion of this Commission that Joseph Baptiste Jr. should be identified as a Mississippi Choctaw, and it is so ordered.

THE COMMISSION TO THE FIVE CIVILIZED TRIBES.

Tams Bixby
Acting Chairman.

T.B. Needles
Commissioner.

C. R. Breckinridge
Commissioner.

Muskogee, Indian Territory
FEB 14 1903

M.C.R. 2275

COPY.

Muskogee, Indian Territory, February 21, 1903.

Mansfield, McMurray & Cornish,

Attorneys for the Choctaw and Chickasaw Nations,

South McAlester, Indian Territory.

Gentlemen:

Enclosed herewith you will find a copy of the decision of the Commission rendered February 14, 1903, identifying Joseph Baptiste, Jr., as a Mississippi Choctaw Indian under the provisions of the forty-first section of the act of Congress of July 1, 1902 (32 Stats. 641).

You are hereby advised that you will be allowed fifteen days from the date hereof, in which to file with this Commission such protest as you desire to make against the action of the Commission in identifying the said Joseph Baptiste, Jr., as a Mississippi Choctaw, and make satisfactory proof of service of said protest upon the applicant herein.

If you fail to file such protest within the time allowed, the name of the applicant herein will be placed upon the schedule of duly identified Mississippi Choctaws now being prepared by this Commission.

Respectfully,

(SIGNED).

Tams Bixby

Acting Chairman.

Registered.
Enc. M.C.R. 2275

M.C.R. 2275.

COPY.

Muskogee, Indian Territory, March 11, 1903.

Joseph Baptiste, Jr.,

Florenville, Louisiana.

Dear Sir:

Enclosed herewith you will find a copy of the decision of the Commission to the Five Civilized Tribes, rendered February 14, 1903, identifying you as a Mississippi Choctaw Indian under the provisions of Section 41 of the Act of Congress approved July 1, 1902, (32 Stats. 641).

If you remove to the Choctaw-Chickasaw country, Indian Territory, before August 14, 1903, you will have six months from that date, or until February 14, 1904, within which to make proof of such removal and settlement at the office of the Commission at Atoka, Choctaw Nation, or Tishomingo, Chickasaw Nation.

Respectfully,

(SIGNED) *Tams Bixby*

Registered. Chairman.

Enc. 2275.

Ardmore, I. T. February 17, 1903.

To the Commission to the Five Civilized Tribes,

Muskogee, Indian Territory.

You will please delivere[sic] to J. G. Ralls of Atoka, Indian Territory, any copies of records in my case that under the rule of law, the Commission may give out to Attorneys, as I have employed him to assist me in this case.

WITNESSES: *Joseph Baptiste Jr.*
&
Frazier Baptiste

Seymore Fern

Joseph Baptiste

#644 No. 2275

For Identification as a Mississippi Choctaw.

Date MAY 20 1901

Name Joseph Baptiste. Jr.

Age 26 Blood full

Post Office Florenville, La.

Father: Joseph Baptiste f.b.l

Mother: Felice " f.b.l

Claims through both parents.

Claims for self alone.

Children:

Stenographer H. C. Ristine,

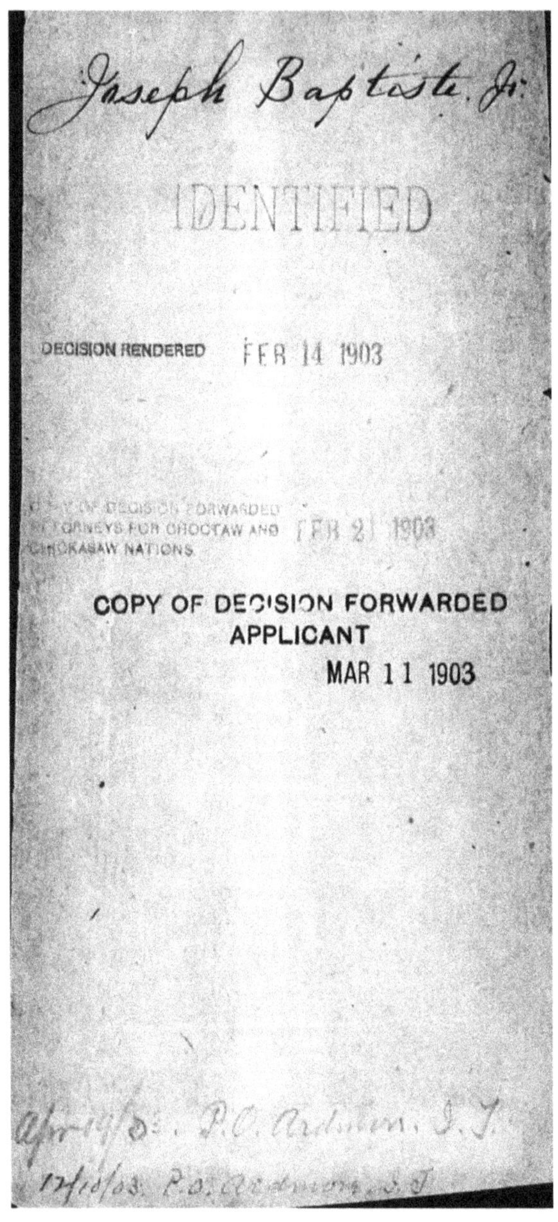
Joseph Baptiste Jr.

IDENTIFIED

DECISION RENDERED FEB 14 1903

COPY OF DECISION FORWARDED
ATTORNEYS FOR CHOCTAW AND
CHICKASAW NATIONS FEB 21 1903

COPY OF DECISION FORWARDED
APPLICANT
MAR 11 1903

Apr 19/03. P.O. Ardmore, I.T.
12/10/03. P.O. Ardmore, I.T.

CARD NO. 9 - Choctaw MCR 2288 - Isaac Lewis

DEPARTMENT OF THE INTERIOR

COMMISSION TO THE FIVE CIVILIZED TRIBES

The record herein is in the matter of the
application of Isaac Lewis for identification as a
Mississippi Choctaw,
M.C.R. 2288

DEPARTMENT OF THE INTERIOR

COMMISSION TO THE FIVE CIVILIZED TRIBES

In the matter of the application of Isaac Lewis for identification as a Mississippi Choctaw, M.C.R. 2288

---- I N D E X ----

Department of the Interior,
Commission to the Five Civilized Tribes,
Decatur, Mississippi, May 15, 1901.

In the matter of the application of Isaac Lewis for identification as a Mississippi Choctaw.

Isaac Lewis, having been first duly sworn, upon his oath testified as follows: (Indian McDonald, Official Interpreter.)

Examination by the Commission.

Q What is your name? A Isaac Lewis.
Q What is your age? A Sixty seven.
Q What is your post office address? A Dixon, Mississippi.
Q How long have you lived in Mississippi, all your life? A Yes.
Q What is your father's name? A Lewis.
Q What is his Indian name? A He-ka-tubbe.
Q Is he dead? A Been dead long time.
Q Full blood Choctaw? A Yes.
Q What is your mother's name? A Betsie.
Q Is Betsie a full blood? A Yes.
Q Is she living or dead? A Dead.
Q Do you claim your Choctaw blood through both parents? A Yes.
Q Are you a full blood Choctaw? A Yes.
Q Have your parents through whom you claim your right to identification as a Mississippi Choctaw, ever been recognized in any manner or enrolled as members of the Choctaw tribe of Indians in Indian Territory, by the Choctaw tribal authorities or by the authorities of the United States? A Yes.
Q My father died here, but my mother went there? A[sic]
Q They went to the Territory did they? A My brother and mother and grand mother all went there.
Q I asked about your father and mother? A My daddy died here, and my mother went.
Q Are you married? A Yes.
Q Is your wife living? A No.
Q Have you any children you want to make application for? A Just myself.
Q Is your name on any of the tribal rolls of the Choctaw Nation in Indian Territory? A No.
Q Have you ever made application to the Choctaw tribal authorities in Indian Territory to be enrolled as a member of that tribe? A No.
Q Did you, or any one for you, in 1896, under the Act of Congress of June 10, 1896 make application in the Choctaw Nation? A No.
Q Have you ever make application before this time, to either the Choctaw tribal authorities or to the authorities of the United States to be admitted or enrolled as citizens of the Choctaw Nation? A Yes.

The records of the Commission show that on February 3, 1899, this applicant appeared before the Commission at Philadelphia, Mississippi, and made application for the identification of himself and son, Sam Lewis, as Mississippi Choctaws, their names appearing upon Mississippi Choctaw Card, Field Number 327; also upon page 79 of the Schedule of Mississippi Choctaws, which accompanied the report of March 10, 1899, of the Commission to the Five Civilized Tribes to the Secretary of the Interior, as t the identity of Choctaw Indians claiming rights in the Choctaw lands under the provisions of the Fourteenth Article of the Treaty of Dancing Rabbit Creek, being Numbers 1162 and 1163, respectively, thereon.

Q Do you now make application for identification as a Mississippi Choctaw?
A Yes.
Q Do you claim your rights as a beneficiary under the provisions of Article Fourteen of the Treaty of 1830? A Yes.
Q Have you ever received any benefits as a Choctaw Indians[sic] or your ancestors?
A I never got it.
Q Do you know the names of any of your ancestors who were living in Mississippi in 1830, when the Treaty of Dancing Rabbit Creek was made, and who were recognized members of the Choctaw tribe of Indians at that time? A I don't know.
Q Did any of your ancestors go from Mississippi and Alabama to the Choctaw Nation in Indian Territory with the main part of the Choctaw tribe between 1833 and 1838? A They went.
Q Did your father go? A No.
Q Some of your people went? A Mu[sic] mother went.
Q Anybody else that you know? A I don't recollect, who else went, buy my mother went.
Q Did any of your ancestors within six months after the ratification of the Treaty of 1830, signify to the United States Indian Agent in Mississippi, their intention to remain in Mississippi and become citizens of the United States? A Yes.
Q Do you know who sent to the Agent? A I don't remember the name.
Q Have any of your ancestors ever claimed or received any land in Mississippi from the Government under Article Fourteen of the Treaty of 1830? A I don't know.
Q Are there any additional statements you desire to make on support of your application? A No.
Q Have you any documentary, evidence, affidavits; written testimony of any description, copies of records, deeds or patents; or any other proper papers showing that any of your ancestors were, in 1830, when the Treaty of Dancing Rabbit Creek was made, recognized members of the Choctaw tribe of Indians, or that any of them ever complied or attempted to comply with the provisions of the Fourteenth Article of that treaty, or ever received any benefits thereunder? A No.

This applicant appears to be a full blood Choctaw Indian. He does not speak the English language, his examination having been conducted through a sworn Choctaw interpreter. He has no knowledge of a compliance on the part of his ancestors with any of the provisions of the Fourteenth Article of the Treaty of 1830.

The decision of the Commission as to the application you make for identification as a Mississippi Choctaw will be determined at the earliest possible date, and a report of same made to the Secretary of the Interior, conformable to the provisions of the Twenty First Section of the Act of Congress of June 28, 1898, and a copy of the same will be mailed to you to your post office address as given in your testimony.

R.S. Streit, having been first duly sworn, upon his oath states that as stenographer to the Commission to the Five Civilized Tribes, he reported in full all proceedings had in the above entitled cause on the 15th day of May, 1901, and that the above and foregoing is a full, true and correct transcript of his stenographic notes of said proceedings upon said date.

R.S. Streit

Subscribed and sworn to before me at Meridian, Mississippi, this 21st day of June, 1901.

J P McKee Jr.
Notary Public.

DEPARTMENT OF THE INTERIOR

COMMISSION TO THE FIVE CIVILIZED TRIBES

In the matter of the application of Isaac Lewis, for identification as a Mississippi Choctaw, M.C.R. 2288.

-----D E C I S I O N -------

It appears from the record herein that application for identification as a Mississippi Choctaw was made to this Commission on May 15, 1901, by Isaac Lewis for himself, under the following provision of the Act of Congress approved June 28, 1898, (30 Stats. 495):

> "Said commission shall have authority to determine the identity of Choctaw Indians claiming rights in the Choctaw lands under article fourteen of the treaty between the United States and the Choctaw Nation concluded September twenty seventh, eighteen hundred and thirty and to that end may administer oaths, examine witnesses, and perform all other acts necessary thereto and make report to the Secretary of the Interior."

From the evidence submitted in support of said application it appears that the applicants[sic] full blood Mississippi Choctaw Indians.

Section forty-one of the Act of Congress entitled "An Act To ratify and confirm an agreement with the Choctaw and Chickasaw tribes of Indians, and for other purposes" approved July 1, 1902, (32 Stats. 641) and ratified by the Choctaw and Chickasaw Nations September 25, 1902, provides as follows:

> "The application of no person for identification as a Mississippi Choctaw shall be received by said Commission after six months subsequent to the date of the final ratification of this agreement and in the disposition of such applications all full-blood Mississippi Choctaw Indians and the descendants of any Mississippi Choctaw Indians whether of full or mixed blood who received a patent to land under the said fourteenth article of the said treaty of eighteen hundred and thirty who had not moved to and made bona fide settlement in the Choctaw-Chickasaw country prior to June twenty-eighth, eighteen hundred and ninety-eight, shall be deemed to be Mississippi Choctaws, entitled to benefits under article fourteen of the said treaty of September twenty-seventh, eighteen hundred and thirty, and to identification as such by said Commission, but this direction or provision shall be deemed to be only a rule of evidence and shall not be invoked by or operate to the advantage of any applicant who is not a Mississippi Choctaw of a full blood, or who is not the descendant of a Mississippi Choctaw who received a patent to land under said treaty, or who is otherwise barred from the right of citizenship in the Choctaw Nation, all of said Mississippi Choctaws so enrolled by said Commission shall be upon a separate roll."

It is, therefore, the opinion of this Commission that Isaac Lewis should be identified as a Mississippi Choctaw, and it is so ordered.

THE COMMISSION TO THE FIVE CIVILIZED TRIBES.

Tams Bixby
Acting Chairman.

T.B. Needles
Commissioner.

C. R. Breckinridge
Commissioner.

Muskogee, Indian Territory
FEB 14 1903

M C R 2288

Muskogee, Indian Territory, January 19, 1903.

P. H. Johnson,

Briscoe, Indian Territory.

Dear Sir:

Receipt is hereby acknowledged of your letter of the 10th inst., in which you state "I have power of attorney from Isaac Lewis a Choctaw Indian residing at Dixon, Neshaba[sic] Co. Mississippi made before the Clerk of the Circuit Court." You ask if, under this power of attorney, you can go into the Choctaw country, select land for him, cultivate and improve the same and if the Commission will recognize your right to collect the annuities and realties due him or to become due him.

In reply to your letter you are informed that it appears from the records of the Commission that Isaac Lewis, sixty-seven years of age, residence Dixon, Mississippi, is an applicant for identification as a Mississippi Choctaw. The Commission has not, up to the present time, reached any opinion or decision relative to his rights to such identification, but is now considering his application, and it is probable that a decision will be rendered in the near future. The applicant will be duly notified of the action of the Commission and of the forwarding of the record to the Secretary of the Interior.

Relative to your rights under the power of attorney which you state you hold, you attention is invited to the following provision of the act of Congress approved July 1, 1902, and ratified by the citizens of the Choctaw and Chickasaw Nations September 26, 1902:

> "Applications for enrollment as Mississippi Choctaws, and applications to have land set apart to them as such, must be made personally before the Commission to the Five Civilized Tribes. Fathers may apply for their minor children; and if the father be dead, the mother may apply; husbands may apply for wives. Applications for orphans, insane persons, and persons of unsound mind may be made by duly appointed guardian or curator, and for aged and infirm persons and prisoners by agents duly authorized thereunto by power of attorney, in the discretion of said Commission."

Respectfully,

Commissioner in Charge.

M C R 2288

Muskogee, Indian Territory, February 2, 1903.

P. H. Johnson,

Bristow, Indian Territory.

Dear Sir:

Receipt is hereby acknowledged of your letter of the 22nd ultimo, in which you ask to be advised if Jim Franchoief, who resides in Mandville[sic], Louisiana, is enrolled as a citizen of the Chickasaw and Choctaw Nation; that you hold a power of attorney "to look after his interests." You also ask to be advised "if the Commission have passed on the rights of Isaac Lewis, of Dixon Co., Miss."

In reply to your letter you are informed that it does not appear from the records of the Commission that any person by the name of Jim Franchoief is listed for enrollment as a citizen of either the Choctaw or Chickasaw Nations[sic] or is an applicant for identification as a Mississippi Choctaw.

It appears from the records of the Commission that Isaac Lewis, ge sixty-sev years, residence Dixon, Mississippi, is an applicant for identification as a Mississippi Choctaw. The Commission has not up to the present time reached any opinion or decision relative to his right to such identification, but is now considering his application and it is probably that a decision will be rendered in the near future. The applicant will be duly notified of the action of the Commission and of the forwarding of the record to the Secretary of the Interior.

Respectfully,

Acting Chairman.

M.C.R. 2288

COPY.

Muskogee, Indian Territory, February 21, 1903.

Mansfield, McMurray & Cornish,

Attorneys for the Choctaw and Chickasaw Nations,

South McAlester, Indian Territory.

Gentlemen:

Enclosed herewith you will find a copy of the decision of the Commission rendered February 14, 1903, identifying Isaac Lewis as a Mississippi Choctaw Indian under the provisions of the forty-first section of the act of Congress of July 1, 1902 (32 Stats. 641).

You are hereby advised that you will be allowed fifteen days from the date hereof, in which to file with this Commission such protest as you desire to make against the action of the Commission in identifying the said Isaac Lewis as a Mississippi Choctaw, and make satisfactory proof of service of said protest upon the applicant herein.

If you fail to file such protest within the time allowed, the name of the applicant herein will be placed upon the schedule of duly identified Mississippi Choctaws now being prepared by this Commission.

Respectfully,

(SIGNED). *Tams Bixby*

Acting Chairman.

Registered.
Enc. H.G. 22

M.C.R. 2288.

COPY.

Muskogee, Indian Territory, March 11, 1903.

Isaac Lewis,

Dixon, Mississippi.

Dear Sir:

Enclosed herewith you will find a copy of the decision of the Commission to the Five Civilized Tribes, rendered February 14, 1903, identifying you as a Mississippi Choctaw Indian under the provisions of Section 41 of the Act of Congress approved July 1, 1902, (32 Stats. 641).

If you remove to the Choctaw-Chickasaw country, Indian Territory, before August 14, 1903, you will have six months from that date, or until February 14, 1904, within which to make proof of such removal and settlement at the office of the Commission at Atoka, Choctaw Nation, or Tishomingo, Chickasaw Nation.

Respectfully,

(SIGNED). *Tams Bixby*

Registered. Chairman.

Enc. 2288.

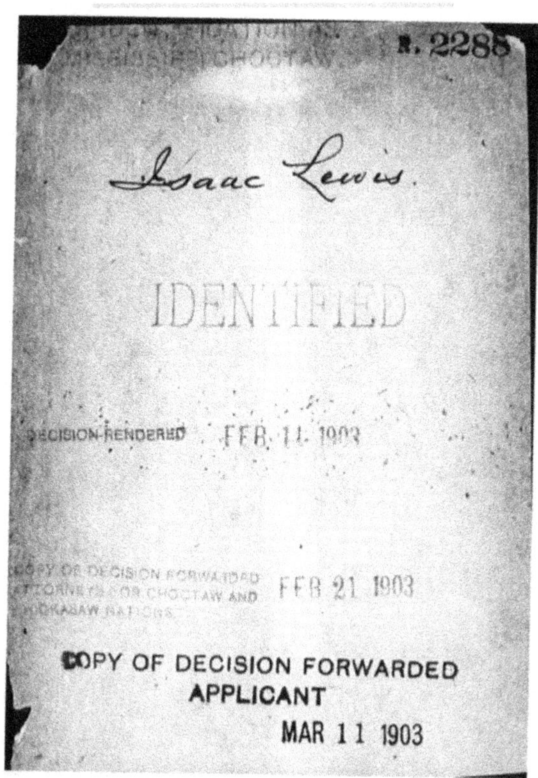

2285

Isaac Lewis.

IDENTIFIED

DECISION RENDERED FEB 14 1903

COPY OF DECISION FORWARDED ATTORNEYS FOR CHOCTAW AND CHICKASAW NATIONS. FEB 21 1903

COPY OF DECISION FORWARDED
APPLICANT
MAR 11 1903

#653

No. 2288

For Identification as a Mississippi Choctaw.

Date MAY 15 1901

Name Isaac Lewis -

Age 67 Blood full

Post Office, Dixon, Miss, f.b

Father: Lewis (He Ka tubbe) d

Mother: Betsie. f.b. d

Claims through both parents.

See M.C. Card filed No. 327

Children:

Claims for self alone

Stenographer R.S. Street

CARD NO. 10 - Choctaw MCR 2196 - Baptiste Taylor

DEPARTMENT OF THE INTERIOR,

COMMISSION TO THE FIVE CIVILIZED TRIBES.

In the matter of the application of Baptiste Taylor, et al., for identification as Mississippi Choctaws, M.C.R. 2196.

DEPARTMENT OF THE INTERIOR,

COMMISSION TO THE FIVE CIVILIZED TRIBES.

In the matter of the application of Baptiste Taylor, et al., for identification as Mississippi Choctaws, ...M.C.R. 2196.

INDEX.

DEPARTMENT OF THE INTERIOR,
COMMISSION TO THE FIVE CIVILIZED TRIBES,
Meridian, Mississippi, May 14th, 1901.

In the matter of the application for identification as Mississippi Choctaws of Baptiste Taylor, his wife and three children.

Said Baptiste Taylor, being first duly sworn, states as follows:-

Q What is your name? A Baptiste Taylor.
Q What is your age? A I don't know exactly, my parents never have kept my age.
Q About how old? A Guess I am about twenty-six.
Q What is your postoffice address? A Dillville, Mississippi.
Q How long have you lives there? A Been there pretty near all my live[sic].
Q Were you born in Dillville? A Born in Mississippi.
Q What County? A Hancock.
Q Always lived in Hancock County? A Yes sir.
Q What is your father's name? A Sam Taylor.
Q Is he living? A No sir.
Q Was he a full blood? A Yes sir.
Q Is your mother living? A Yes sir.
Q What is her name? A Madeline.
Q Is she full blood? A Yes.
Q You a full blood? A Yes sir.
Q You claim through both parents? A Yes sir.
Q Have your parents, through whom you claim your right to identification as a Mississippi Choctaw ever been recognized in any manner or enrolled as members of the Choctaw Tribe of Indians by either the Choctaw Tribal authorities or by the authorities of the United States in Indian Territory? A No sir.
Q Are you married? A Yes sir.
Q What is your wife's name? A Elizabeth.
Q What is her age? A Twenty-eight.
Q What is her father's name? A Usan Stout.
Q Is he living? A Yes sir.
Q Full blood? A Yes sir.
Q What is her mother's name? A Sis.
Q Is she living? A Yes sir.
Q Is she a full blood? A Yes sir.
Q Do you claim full blood for your wife? A Yes sir.
Q Have your wife's parents, through whom you claim for her the rights to identification as a Mississippi Choctaw, ever been recognized in any manner or enrolled as members of the Choctaw Tribe of Indians in Indian Territory by either the Choctaw Tribal authorities or by the authorities of the United States? A No sir.
Q Are there any children in your family for whom you desire to make application now? A Three.
Q What is the name of the oldest? A Lem.
Q How old is Lem? A Ten.
Q What is the name of the next child? A Stanley.

Q How old is he? A Five.
Q What is the name of the next? A Louise.
Q How old? A Three.
Q That all the children you have? A Yes sir.
Q Is Elizabeth the mother of these three children? A Yes sir.
Q You are the father? A Yes sir.
Q Are they living with you are your home? A Yes sir.
Q When were you married to your wife? A 1881.
Q Do you remember the day of the month? A Yes sir.
Q What day of the month? A October, the thirtieth.
Q Did you marry under a license or according to Choctaw custom? A Under a license.
Q Obtained in what County? A Hancock County.
Q Have you your marriage license and certificate that you would like to introduce?
A No sir.
Q Is your name or the name of your wife on any of the tribal rolls of the Choctaw Nation in Indian Territory? A No sir.
Q Have you ever made application for yourself and wife, or has anyone ever made application for you and your wife and children to the Choctaw Tribal authorities in Indian Territory to be enrolled as members of that Tribe? A No sir.
Q Did you or your wife or anyone for your wife and children, in 1896, under the Act of Congress of June 10, 1896, make application for citizenship to the Dawes Commission? A No sir.
Q Have you, your wife or children ever been admitted to citizenship in the Choctaw Nation by the Choctaw Tribal authorities, by the Commission to the Five Civilized Tribes or by the United States Court in Indian Territory? A No sir.
Q Have you ever made application before this, for yourself, your wife or children, or anyone for your wife and children, to either the Choctaw Tribal authorities or the authorities of the United States to be admitted or enrolled as citizens of the Choctaw Nation? A No sir.
Q Is this the first application you have ever made of any kind? A Yes sir.
Q Is it now your purpose to make application for yourself, your wife and children, for identification as Mississippi Choctaws? A Yes sir.
Q Do you claim your rights as beneficiaries under the provisions of the 14th article of the treaty of 1830? A No sir.
Q Don't you claim under article 14 of the treaty of 1830? The treaty of 1830 was entered into for the benefit of the Mississippi Choctaws; article 14 is that part of the treaty under which Choctaw Indians at this time are entitled to make application? Do you claim under that article? A Yes sir.
Q Have you ever received any benefits as a Choctaw Indian, or has your wife; did you ever get any money or land? A No sir.
Q Have any of your ancestors, or your wife's ancestors, ever received any benefits as Choctaw Indians? A No sir.
Q What was the name of your ancestor or your wife's ancestors who were residents of the old Choctaw Nation in Mississippi or Alabama in 1830 at the time the treaty of Dancing Rabbit Creek was entered into between the United States Government and the Choctaw Tribe of Indians? A No sir, I don't know.

Q Have you any evidence showing that any of your ancestors were recognized members of the Choctaw Tribe of Indians at that time? A No sir.
Q Did any of your ancestors or your wife's ancestors go from the territory occupied by the Choctaw Nation in Mississippi or Alabama to the present Choctaw Nation in Indian Territory when the other Indians removed between the years 1833 and 1838?
A No sir.
Q Did any of your ancestors of your wife's ancestors within six months after the ratification of the treaty of 1830 signify to the United States Indian Agent of the Choctaw Indians in Mississippi their intention to remain in Mississippi, take land here and become citizens of the United States? A No sir.
Q Have any of your ancestors or your wife's ancestors ever received or claimed any land in Mississippi under the provisions of the 14th article of the treaty of 1830?
A No sir.
Q Are there any additional statements you want to make in support of your application? A No sir.
Q Have you any documentary evidence, written testimony of any description, copies of records, deeds or patents, or any proper papers, that would show that any of your ancestors or your wife8s[sic] ancestors were recognized members of the Choctaw Tribe of Indians in Mississippi in 1830, that they ever complied or attempted to comply with the provisions of the 14th article of the treaty of 1830 or that they ever received any benefits under that article of that treaty? A No sir.

Q[sic] This applicant has the appearance of a full blood Choctaw Indian; speaks the Choctaw language; has all the physical characteristics of a Choctaw Indian; has no knowledge of any compliance on the part of his ancestors with the provisions of the 14th article of the treaty of 1830.

The decision of the Commission as to your application, and the application you make on behalf of your wife and three minor children, for identification as Mississippi Choctaws, will be determined at the earliest possible date and report of the same made to the Secretary of the Interior conformable to the provisions of the 21st section of the Act of Congress of June 28, 1898. A copy of such decision will be mailed of you to your postoffice address as given in your testimony at this time.

Ira S. Niles, being first duly sworn, states that as stenographer to the Commission to the Five Civilized Tribes, he reported in full the proceedings had in the above entitled cause, heard at Meridian, Mississippi, May 14th, 1901, and that the above and preceding is a full, true and correct transcript of his stenographic notes taken in said proceedings on said date.

Ira S. Niles

Subscribed and sworn to before me this the 7th day of June, A.D. 1901, at Meridian, Mississippi.

J P McKee Jr
Notary Public.

DEPARTMENT OF THE INTERIOR,

COMMISSION TO THE FIVE CIVILIZED TRIBES.

In the matter of the application of Baptiste Taylor, et al., for identification as Mississippi Choctaws, M.C.R. 2196.

--:D E C I S I O N:--

It appears from the record herein that application for identification as Mississippi Choctaws was made to this Commission on May 14, 1901, by Baptiste Taylor for himself, his wife, Elizabeth Taylor and his three minor children, Lem, Stanley and Louise Taylor, under the following provision of the act of Congress approved June 28, 1898, (30 Stats. 495):

> "Said Commission shall have authority to determine the identity of Choctaw Indians claiming rights in the Choctaw lands under article fourteen of the treaty between the United States and the Choctaw Nation, concluded September twenty-seventh, eighteen hundred and thirty, and to that end may administer oaths, examine witnesses, and perform all other acts necessary thereto and make report to the Secretary of the Interior."

From the evidence submitted in support of said application it appears that all the applicants are full-blood Mississippi Choctaw Indians.

Section forty-one of the act of Congress entitled "An Act to ratify and confirm an agreement with the Choctaw and Chickasaw tribes of Indians, and for other purposes," approved July 1, 1902, (32 Stats. 641), and ratified by the Choctaw and Chickasaw Nations September 25, 1902, provides as follows:

> "The application of no person for identification as a Mississippi Choctaw shall be received by said Commission after six months subsequent to the date of the final ratification of this agreement and in the disposition of such applications

all full-blood Mississippi Choctaw Indians and the descendants of any Mississippi Choctaw Indians whether of full or mixed blood who received a patent to land under the said fourteenth article of the said treaty of eighteen hundred and thirty who had not moved to and made bona fide settlement in the Choctaw-Chickasaw country prior to June twenty-eighth, eighteen hundred and ninety-eight, shall be deemed to be Mississippi Choctaws, entitled to benefits under article fourteen of the said treaty of September twenty-seventh, eighteen hundred and thirty, and to identification as such by said Commission, but this direction or provision shall be deemed to be only a rule of evidence and shall not be invoked by or operate to the advantage of any applicant who is not a Mississippi Choctaw of a full blood, or who is not the descendant of a Mississippi Choctaw who received a patent to land under said treaty, or who is otherwise barred from the right of citizenship in the Choctaw Nation, all of said Mississippi Choctaws so enrolled by said Commission shall be upon a separate roll."

It is, therefore, the opinion of this Commission that Baptiste Taylor, Elizabeth Taylor, Lem Taylor, Stanley Taylor and Louise Taylor should be identified as Mississippi Choctaws, and it is so ordered.

THE COMMISSION TO THE FIVE CIVILIZED TRIBES.

Tams Bixby
Acting Chairman.

T.B. Needles
Commissioner.

C. R. Breckinridge
Commissioner.

Muskogee, Indian Territory,

FEB 14 1903

Ardmore, I. T. February 18, 1903.

To the Commission to the Five Civilized Tribes,

Muskogee, Indian Territory.

You will please deliver to J. G. Ralls, of Atoka, Indian Territory, any of the copies of records in my case that under the rule of law the Commission may give out to attorneys, as I have employed him to assist me in this case.

WITNESSES TO MARK: *B. Taylor*

________________ *Elizabeth Stout*

________________ *Lem Taylor*

M.C.R. 2196

COPY.

Muskogee, Indian Territory, February 21, 1903.

Mansfield, McMurray & Cornish,

Attorneys for the Choctaw and Chickasaw Nations,

South McAlester, Indian Territory.

Gentlemen:

Enclosed herewith you will find a copy of the decision of the Commission rendered February 14, 1903, identifying Baptiste Taylor, his wife, Elizabeth Taylor, and minor children, Lem Taylor, Stanley Taylor and Louise Taylor as Mississippi Choctaw Indians under the provisions of the forty-first section of the act of Congress of July 1, 1902 (32 Stats. 641).

You are hereby advised that you will be allowed fifteen days from the date hereof, in which to file with this Commission such protest as you desire to make against the action of the Commission in identifying the said Baptiste Taylor, his wife and children as Mississippi Choctaws, and make satisfactory proof of service of said protest upon the applicant herein.

If you fail to file such protest within the time allowed, the name of the applicant herein will be placed upon the schedule of duly identified Mississippi Choctaws now being prepared by this Commission.

Respectfully,
(SIGNED). *Tams Bixby*
Acting Chairman.

Registered.
Enc. M.C.R. 2196

M.C.R. 2196.

COPY.

Muskogee, Indian Territory, March 11, 1903.

Baptiste Taylor, *Remailed Ardmore, I.T. April 14, 1903.*
~~Dillville~~, Mississippi.

Dear Sir:

Enclosed herewith you will find a copy of the decision of the Commission to the Five Civilized Tribes, rendered February 14, 1903, identifying yourself, your wife, Elizabeth Taylor, and your three minor children, Lem, Stanley and Louise Taylor, as Mississippi Choctaw Indians under the provisions of Section 41 of the Act of Congress approved July 1, 1902, (32 Stats. 641).

If you remove to the Choctaw-Chickasaw country, Indian Territory, before August 14, 1903, you will have six months from that date, or until February 14, 1904, within which to make proof of such removal and settlement at the office of the Commission at Atoka, Choctaw Nation, or Tishomingo, Chickasaw Nation.

Respectfully,
(SIGNED).
Tams Bixby
Chairman.

Registered.

Enc. 2196.

2196
M.C.R. ~~2195~~

Muskogee, Indian Territory, April 1, 1903.

J. C. Dill, Asst. P. M.,

Dillville, Mississippi.

Dear Sir:

Receipt if hereby acknowledged of your letter of the 21st ultimo, by reference from the post master at this place. Therein you ask what disposition to make of a registered letter received at your office from this Commission addressed to Baptiste Taylor. You state "Taylor left here some time ago and went to Ardmore, Ind. Ter."

In reply to your letter you are informed that you may return said letter to this Commission.

Respectfully,

Chairman.

M.C.R.
2196-2394-2832
7067-7286

Muskogee, Indian Territory, July 13, 1903.

W. B. Burney,

Ardmore, Indian Territory.

Dear Sir:

Receipt is hereby acknowledged of your communication of July 11, 1903, by reference from Chilion Riley, in which you ask if the following names[sic] persons have been identified as Mississippi Choctaws and will be allowed to hold land:

Charley Farve	Elizabeth Taylor
Selina Farve	Lem Taylor
Turner Farve	Stanley Taylor

Joseph Yabby[sic]	Mary Taylor
Thomas Yabby	Willis Tishomingo
Christy Yabby	Madline Tishomingo
Mary Yabby	Nettie Taylor
Babtist[sic] Taylor	Mary Taylor
Lawrence Taylor	Lony Taylor.

Replying to your communication you are advised that it appears from our records that on March 23, 1903, Salina[sic] Farve appeared before the Commission and made application for the identification of herself, her husband, Charley Farve, her minor child, Turner Farve, and her minor brothers and sister, Joseph, Thomas, Christie and Mary Yearby; that on March 16, 1903, Madeline Taylor, 45 years of age, made application to this Commission for the identification of herself and two minor children, Nettie and Mary Taylor, as Mississippi Choctaws. There is no person by the name of Madline Tishomingo an applicant to this Commission for identification as a Mississippi Choctaw, but it is thought possible that the Madeline Taylor above mentioned is identical with the Madline Tishomingo mentioned in your letter. Up to the present time no decision has been reached by the Commission in the matter of the applications of Salina Farve, et al., and Madeline Taylor, et al., but the Commission is now considered their applications and when a decision is rendered in these cases they will be duly notified of the same.

You are further advised that is appears from our records that Tishomingo Willis, 54 years of age, Baptiste Taylor, his wife, Elizabeth Taylor, and three minor children, Lem, Stanley and Louise Taylor, and Lawrence Taylor, 21 years of age, have been duly identified by the Commission as Mississippi Choctaws entitled to rights in the Choctaw lands in the Indian Territory.

You are further advised that it does not appear from our records that any person by the name of Lony Taylor is an applicant to this Commission for identification as a Mississippi Choctaw.

Respectfully,

Commissioner in Charge.

594

No. 2196

For Identification as a Mississippi Choctaw.

Date MAY 14 1901

Name Baptiste Taylor

Age 26 Blood full

Post Office Williville, Miss.

Father: Sam Taylor. f.b. d

Mother: Madeline. fb l

Claims through both parents

wife. Elizabeth f.b. 28

father - Alsan Stout f.b. l

Mother Sis " f.b l

Children:

Lem 10

Stanley 5

Louise 3

Claims for self, wife and children.

Stenographer I. S. Niles.

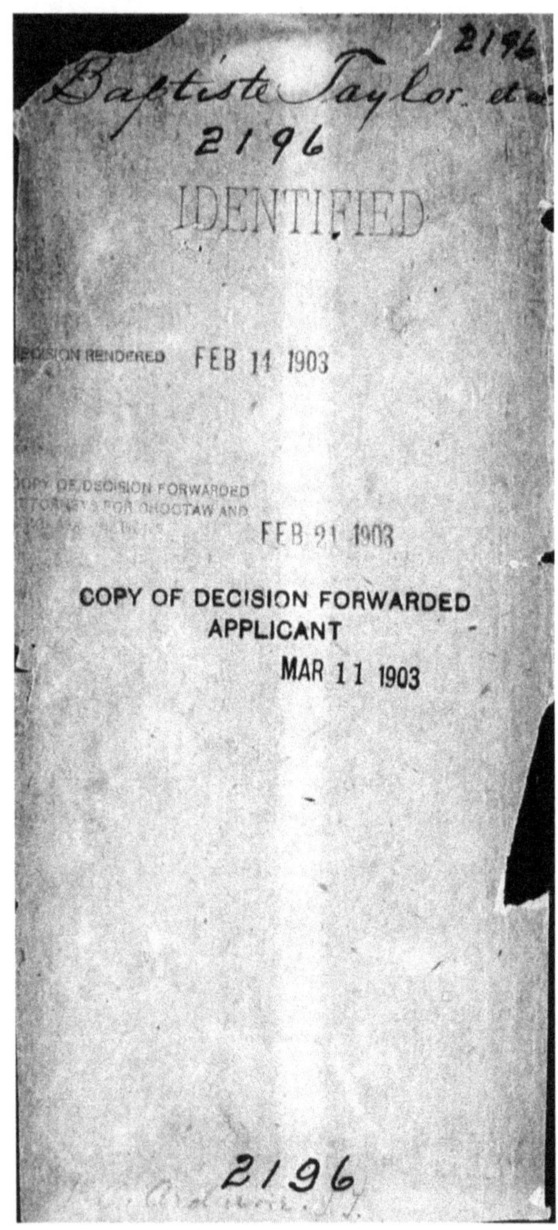
Baptiste Taylor et al
2196
IDENTIFIED
DECISION RENDERED FEB 14 1903
FEB 21 1903
COPY OF DECISION FORWARDED
APPLICANT
MAR 11 1903
2196

CARD NO. 11 - Choctaw MCR 2205 - Lina Tom

DEPARTMENT OF THE INTERIOR,

COMMISSION TO THE FIVE CIVILIZED TRIBES.

In the matter of the application of Lina Tom, et al., for identification as Mississippi Choctaws, M.C.R. 2205.

I N D E X .

Department of the Interior,
Commission to the Five Civilized Tribes,
Decatur, Mississippi, May 13, 1901.

In the matter of the application of Lina Tom for the identification of herslef[sic] and two minor children as Mississippi Choctaws.

Lina Tom, having been first duly sworn, upon her oath states as follows: (Indian McDonald, Official Interpreter.)

Examination by the Commission.

Q What is your name? A Lina Tom.
Q How old are you? A Thirty.
Q What is your post office address? A Engine, Mississippi.
Q What County? A Neshoba.

Q How long have you lived in Mississippi? A All my life.
Q Is your father living? A Dead.
Q What was his name? A Lewis Tonubbee.
Q Was he a full blood Choctaw? A Yes.
Q Did he have a Choctaw Name? A I don't know.
Q Is your mother living? A Dead.
Q What was her name? A Lucy.
Q When did Lucy die? A Four years.
Q Was Lucy a full blood Choctaw? A Yes.
Q Did she always live in Mississippi? A Yes.
Q Have all of your ancestors always lived in Mississippi? A Yes.
Q You claim to be a full blood Choctaw Indian? A Yes.
Q Were ether[sic] of your parents ever recognized in any manner or enrolled as members of the Choctaw tribe of Indians in Indian Territory by the Choctaw tribal authorities or the United States authorities? A I don't know.
Q Are you married? A Yes.
Q What is your husband's name? A Peter Tom.
Q Is he living? A Dead.
Q Was he a full blood Choctaw? A Yes.
Q Have you any children for whom you want to make application? A Yes.
Q How many, and what are their names? A Amos Tom.
Q The others? A Leona.
Q Is that all? A Yes.
Q How old is Amos? A 11 years old.
Q How old is Leona? A Three years old.
Q Are you the mother of both these children? A Yes.
Q What is the name of their father? A Peter Tom.
Q This application then is for yourself and two children only? A Yes.
Q Are your names on any of the Choctaw tribal rolls out in Indian Territory?
A No sir.
Q Did you ever make application to the Choctaw tribal authorities out in Indian Territory for yourself or either of these children to be enrolled as members of the Choctaw tribe, or did any one ever make such an application for you? A I don't know.
Q Did you, or any one for you, in 1896, make application to the Commission to the Five Civilized Tribes for citizenship in the Choctaw Nation, for yourself or these children? A No.

The records of the Commission show that Peter Tom made application to the Commission to the Five Civilized Tribes, in the year 1896, for citizenship in the Choctaw Nation for himself, wife and minor child, Amos, their names appearing in the Jack Amos case. The original application was filed with the Commission September 10, 1896; on December 1st, 1896, the Commission denied such application, an appeal was taken from the decision of the Commission to the United States Court for the Central District of Indian Territory, which said Court, on August 20, 1897, affirmed the decision of the Commission; that an appeal was taken from the decision of the United States Court to the Supreme County[sic] of the United States, where the decision of the District Court was affirmed.

Q Have you or these children ever been admitted to citizenship in the Choctaw Nation by the Choctaw tribal authorities, the Commission to the Five Civilized Tribes, or by the United States Court in Indian Territory? A No.
Q Is this the first application of any kind that has ever been made for you or either of these children, either to the Choctaw tribal authorities or to the United States authorities to be admitted or enrolled as members of the Choctaw tribe of Indians?
A Yes.
Q Didn't your husband make application for you two years ago? A Didn't go before the Commission.

The records of the Commission show that on January 30, 1899, Peter Tom, the husband of this applicant, appeared before the Commission at Philadelphia, Mississippi, and made application for the identification of himself, his wife, Lina, and his children, Amos and Leona Tom, as Mississippi Choctaws, their names appearing upon Mississippi Choctaw Card, Field Number 165; also, upon page 56 of the Schedule of Mississippi Choctaws, which accompanied the report of March 10, 1899, of the Commission to the Five Civilized Tribes to the Secretary of the Interior, as to the identity of Choctaw Indians claiming rights in the Choctaw lands under the provisions of the Fourteenth Article of the Treaty of Dancing Rabbit Creek, being Numbers 568, 569, 570 and 571, respectively, thereon.

Q The application made in 1896, by your husband, and the application made by him two years ago, are the only applications of any kind that have ever been made for you or your children, are they not? A Yes.
Q You now want to make application for yourself and children for id[sic] identification as Mississippi Choctaws? A Yes.
Q Do you claim your rights under the provisions of the Fourteenth Article of the Treaty of Dancing Rabbit Creek? A Yes.
Q Have you ever received any benefits as a Choctaw Indian? A None.
Q Did your husband ever receive any benefits as a Choctaw Indian? A No.
Q Did any of your ancestors, or any of your husband's ancestors ever receive any benefits as Choctaw Indians? A I don't know.
Q Were any of your ancestors, or any of your husband's ancestors living in the old Choctaw Nation, in Mississippi and Alabama in 1830, when the Treaty of Dancing Rabbit Creek was made? A I don't know.
Q Were any of them recognized members of the Choctaw tribe of Indians at that time? A I don't know.
Q Did any of your ancestors, or any of your husband's ancestors, remove from the old Choctaw Nation in Mississippi and Alabama to the present Choctaw Nation in Indian Territory, at the time of the removal of the greater part of the Choctaw tribe between the years 1833 and 1838? A I don't know.

Q Did any of your ancestors or any of your husband's ancestors, within six months after the Treaty of Dancing Rabbit Creek was ratified, signify to the United States Indian Agent for the Choctaws their intention to remain in Mississippi and become citizens of the States? A I don't know.
Q Did any of your ancestors or any of your husband's ancestors ever claim or receive any land in Mississippi as beneficiaries under the provisions of the Fourteenth Article of the Treaty of Dancing Rabbit Creek? A I don't know.
Q Are there any additional statement you desire to make at this time in support of your application? A No.
Q Have you any documentary evidence, affidavits, written testimony of any description, copies of records, deeds or patents, or any other proper papers showing that any of your ancestors, or any of your husband's ancestors were in 1830, when the Treaty of Dancing Rabbit Creek was made, recognized members of the Choctaw tribe of Indians, in Mississippi, or that any of them ever complied or attempted to comply with the provisions of the Fourteenth Article of the Treaty of Dancing Rabbit Creek, or ever received any benefits under that Article? A I have no papers, and don't think any of them got any land.

(This applicant has the appearance of being a full blood Indian; she speaks the Choctaw language, but very little English, the examination having been conducted almost entirely through a Choctaw interpreter.)

The decision of the Commission as to the application you make at this time for the identification of yourself and Children as Mississippi Choctaws will be determined at the earliest possible date, and report of same made to the Secretry[sic] of the Interior, conformable to the provisions of the Twenty First Section of the Act of Congress of June 28, 1898, and a copy of the same will be mailed to your post office address as given in your testimony.

R.S. Streit, having been first duly sworn, upon his oath states that as stenographer to the Commission to the Five Civilized Tribes, he reported in full all proceedings had in the above entitled cause on the 13th day of May, 1901, and that the above and foregoing is a full, true and correct transcript of his stenographic notes of said proceedings upon said date.

R. S. Streit

Subscribed and sworn to before me at Meridian, Mississippi, this 20th day of June, 1901.

J P McKee Jr.
Notary Public.

DEPARTMENT OF THE INTERIOR,

COMMISSION TO THE FIVE CIVILIZED TRIBES.

In the matter of the application of Lina Tom, et al., for identification as Mississippi Choctaws, M.C.R. 2205.

--:D E C I S I O N:--

It appears from the record herein that application for identification as Mississippi Choctaws was made to this Commission on May 13, 1901, by Lena Tom for herself and her two minor children, Amos and Leona Tom, under the following provision of the act of Congress approved June 28, 1898, (30 Stats. 495):

> "Said Commission shall have authority to determine the identity of Choctaw Indians claiming rights in the Choctaw lands under article fourteen of the treaty between the United States and the Choctaw Nation, concluded September twenty-seventh, eighteen hundred and thirty, and to that end may administer oaths, examine witnesses, and perform all other acts necessary thereto and make report to the Secretary of the Interior."

From the evidence submitted in support of said application it appears that all the applicants are full-blood Mississippi Choctaw Indians.

Section forty-one of the act of Congress entitled "An Act to ratify and confirm an agreement with the Choctaw and Chickasaw tribes of Indians, and for other purposes," approved July 1, 1902, (32 Stats. 641), and ratified by the Choctaw and Chickasaw Nations September 25, 1902, provides as follows:

> "The application of no person for identification as a Mississippi Choctaw shall be received by said Commission after six months subsequent to the date of the final ratification of this agreement and in the disposition of such applications all full-blood Mississippi Choctaw Indians and the descendants of any Mississippi Choctaw Indians whether of full or mixed blood who received a patent to land under the said fourteenth article of the said treaty of eighteen hundred and thirty who had not moved to and made bona fide settlement in the Choctaw-Chickasaw country prior to June twenty-eighth, eighteen hundred and ninety-eight, shall be deemed to be Mississippi Choctaws, entitled to benefits under article fourteen of the said treaty of September twenty-seventh, eighteen

hundred and thirty, and to identification as such by said Commission, but this direction or provision shall be deemed to be only a rule of evidence and shall not be invoked by or operate to the advantage of any applicant who is not a Mississippi Choctaw of a full blood, or who is not the descendant of a Mississippi Choctaw who received a patent to land under said treaty, or who is otherwise barred from the right of citizenship in the Choctaw Nation, all of said Mississippi Choctaws so enrolled by said Commission shall be upon a separate roll."

It is, therefore, the opinion of this Commission that Lina Tom, Amos Tom and Leona Tom should be identified as Mississippi Choctaws, and it is so ordered.

THE COMMISSION TO THE FIVE CIVILIZED TRIBES.

Tams Bixby
Acting Chairman.

T.B. Needles
Commissioner.

C. R. Breckinridge
Commissioner.

Muskogee, Indian Territory,

FEB 14 1903

M.C.R. 2205

COPY.

Muskogee, Indian Territory, February 21, 1903.

Mansfield, McMurray & Cornish,

Attorneys for the Choctaw and Chickasaw Nations,

South McAlester, Indian Territory.

Gentlemen:

Enclosed herewith you will find a copy of the decision of the Commission rendered February 14, 1903, identifying Lina Tom and minor children Amos Tom and Leona Tom as Mississippi Choctaw Indians under the provisions of the forty-first section of the act of Congress of July 1, 1902 (32 Stats. 641).

You are hereby advised that you will be allowed fifteen days from the date hereof, in which to file with this Commission such protest as you desire to make against the action of the Commission in identifying the said Lina Tom and children as Mississippi Choctaws, and make satisfactory proof of service of said protest upon the applicant herein.

If you fail to file such protest within the time allowed, the name of the applicant herein will be placed upon the schedule of duly identified Mississippi Choctaws now being prepared by this Commission.

Respectfully,

(SIGNED). *Tams Bixby*

Acting Chairman.

Registered.
Enc. H.M.V. 28

M.C.R. 2205.

COPY.

Muskogee, Indian Territory, March 11, 1903.

Lina Tom,

Engine, Mississippi.

Dear Madam:

Enclosed herewith you will find a copy of the decision of the Commission to the Five Civilized Tribes, rendered February 14, 1903, identifying yourself and your two minor children, Amos and Leona Tom, as Mississippi Choctaw Indians under the provisions of Section 41 of the Act of Congress approved July 1, 1902, (32 Stats. 641).

If you remove to the Choctaw-Chickasaw country, Indian Territory, before August 14, 1903, you will have six months from that date, or until February 14, 1904, within which to make proof of such removal and settlement at the office of the Commission at Atoka, Choctaw Nation, or Tishomingo, Chickasaw Nation.

Respectfully,

(SIGNED). *Tams Bixby*

Chairman.

Registered.
Enc. 2205.

Ardmore, I. T. April 16, 1903.

To the Commission to the Five Civilized Tribes,
Muskogee, Indian Territory.

You will please deliver to J. G. Ralls, of Atoka, Indian Territory, any copies of the records in my case that, under the rule of law, the Commission may give out to attorneys, as I have employed him to assist in my case.

his
Amos x Thomas (2208)
mark

Ardmore, I. T. April 18, 1903.

To the Commission to the Five Civilized Tribes,
Muskogee, Indian Territory.

You will please deliver to J. G. Ralls, of Atoka, Indian Territory m[sic] any copies of the records in my case that under the rule of law, the Commission may give out to Attorneys, as I have employed him to assist in my case.

Lina Tom No 2208[sic]

COMMISSIONERS:

TAMS BIXBY,
THOMAS B. NEEDLES,
C. R. BRECKINRIDGE,
W. E. STANLEY

—

ALLISON L. AYLESWORTH,
SECRETARY.

ADDRESS ONLY THE
COMMISSION TO THE FIVE CIVILIZED TRIBES.

DEPARTMENT OF THE INTERIOR,
COMMISSION TO THE FIVE CIVILIZED TRIBES.

REFER IN REPLY TO THE FOLLOWING

Muskogee, Indian Territory, May 2, 1903.

Amos Tom,

Ardmore, Indian Territory.

Dear Sir:

Receipt is hereby acknowledged of your letter of the 22d inst., requesting that a number be sent you entitling you to admission to the Chickasaw Land Office.

In reply, you are advised that it appears from our records that the only Amos Tom who has been identified as a Mississippi Choctaw is a boy eleven years of age, the son of Lina Tom.

If you are the identical Amos Tom above referred to, it appears that you are a minor, and your attention is invited to section [illegible] of the rules and regulations governing the selection of allotments and the designations of homesteads in the Choctaw and Chickasaw Nations, a copy of which is herewith enclosed you.

Respectfully,

Tams Bixby
Chairman.

W 19

DEPARTMENT OF THE INTERIOR,

Commission to the Five Civilized Tribes.

Rules and Regulations Governing the Selection of Allotments and the Designation of Homesteads in the Choctaw and Chickasaw Nations.

1. Selections of allotments and designations of homesteads for adult citizens and selections of allotments for adult freedmen must be made in person except as herein otherwise provided.

2. Applications to have land set apart and homesteads designated for duly identified Mississippi Choctaws must be made personally before the Commission to the Five Civilized Tribes. Fathers may apply for their minor children and if the father be dead the mother may apply. Husbands may apply for wives. Applications for orphans, insane persons and persons of unsound mind may be made by duly appointed guardian or curator, and for aged and infirm persons and prisoners by agents duly authorized thereunto by power of attorney, in the discretion of said Commission.

3. At the time of the selection of allotment each citizen and duly identified Mississippi Choctaw shall designate as a homestead out of said selection land equal in value to one hundred and sixty acres of the average allottable land of the Choctaw and Chickasaw Nations, as nearly as may be.

4. Each Choctaw and Chickasaw freedman, at the time of selection shall designate as his or her allotment of the lands of the Choctaw and Chickasaw Nations, land equal in value to forty acres of the average allottable land of the Choctaw and Chickasaw Nations.

5. Citizens, freedmen and identified Mississippi Choctaws who are married, whether they have attained their majority or not, will be regarded as of age for the purpose of making selections.

6. Selections may be made by citizen and freedman parents for unmarried male children under twenty-one years of age and for unmarried female children under eighteen years of age, and a male citizen or freedman may make selection for his wife, if she is entitled to make selection, unless she shall, at the time or previously thereto, protest in writing.

7. Where the father of an unmarried minor citizen, freedman or identified Mississippi Choctaw is a non-citizen, the citizen, freedman or identified Mississippi Choctaw mother of such children must make selection in person in behalf of said children.

8. Selections of allotments and designations of homesteads for minor citizens and selections of allotments for minor freedmen may be made by the citizen father or mother or freedman father or mother, as the case may be, or by a guardian, curator, or an administrator having charge of their estate, in the order named.

9. Selections of allotments and designations of homesteads for citizen, and selections of allotment for freedmen, prisoners, convicts, aged and infirm persons and soldiers and sailors of the United States on duty outside of Indian Territory, may be made by duly appointed agents under power of attorney, and for incompetents by guardians, curators, or other suitable person akin to them.

10. Selections may be made and homesteads designated by duly identified Mississippi Choctaws, who have, within one year after the date of their identification as such, made satisfactory proof of bona fide settlement within the Choctaw-Chickasaw country, at any time within six months after the date of their said identification.

11. Persons authorized to make selections by power of attorney, as provided in rules 2 and 9 hereof, must be the husband or wife, or a relative not further removed than a cousin of the first degree of the person for whom such selection is made.

12. It shall be the duty of the Commission to the Five Civilized Tribes to see that selections of allotments and designations of homesteads for the classes of persons mentioned in rules 2, 6, 7, 8 and 9 hereof, are made for the best interests of such persons.

13. Selections of allotments for citizens, freedmen and identified Mississippi Choctaws who have died subsequent to September 25, 1902, and before making a selection of allotment, shall be made by a duly appointed administrator or executor. If, however, such administrator or executor be not duly and expeditiously appointed, or fails to act promptly when appointed, or for any other cause such selections be not so made within a reasonable and practicable time, the Commission to the Five Civilized Tribes shall designate the lands thus to be allotted.

14. In determining the value of a selection the appraised value of the land selected shall be increased by the appraised value of such pine timber on such land as has heretofore been estimated by the Commission to the Five Civilized Tribes.

15. Selections of allotments may be made only by citizens and freedmen whose enrollment has been approved by the Secretary of the Interior, and by persons duly identified by the Commission to the Five Civilized Tribes as Mississippi Choctaws, and by none others.

16. When a selection of land has been made by a citizen, freedman or identified Mississippi Choctaw, and the land so selected is claimed by a person whose rights as a citizen or freedman have not been finally determined, contest for the land so selected may be instituted by the person claiming the land, formal application for the land being first made as is required by the Rules of Practice in Choctaw and Chickasaw allotment contest cases.

THE COMMISSION TO THE FIVE CIVILIZED TRIBES,
TAMS BIXBY, Chairman.

Muskogee, Indian Territory, March 24, 1903.

1901

No. 2205

For Identification as a Mississippi Choctaw.

Date MAY 13 1901

Name Lina Tom

Age 30 Blood full

Post Office, Engine, Miss.

Father: Lewis Toonubbee (dead)

Mother: Lucy " "

Claims through both parents

husband Peter Tom full (dead)

(claims for herself and 2 children)

Children:

Amos Tom 11

Leona " 3

(See Miss. Choc. card field No. 165. Appearance of 8/30/99.)

Stenographer R. S. Street

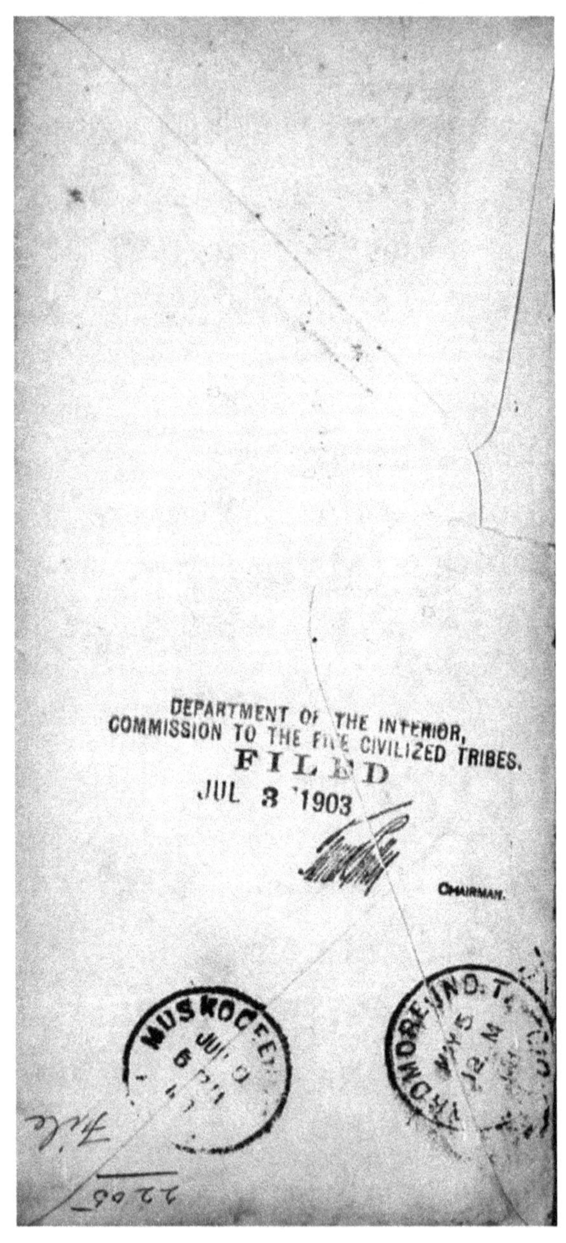
DEPARTMENT OF THE INTERIOR,
COMMISSION TO THE FIVE CIVILIZED TRIBES.
FILED
JUL 3 1903
CHAIRMAN.
MUSKOGEE
ARDMORE IND. T.

A.B.

Department of the Interior.
Commission to the Five Civilized Tribes,
MUSKOGEE, IND. TER.
OFFICIAL BUSINESS.
Penalty for private use, $300.

Amos Tom,
Ardmore, Indian Territory.

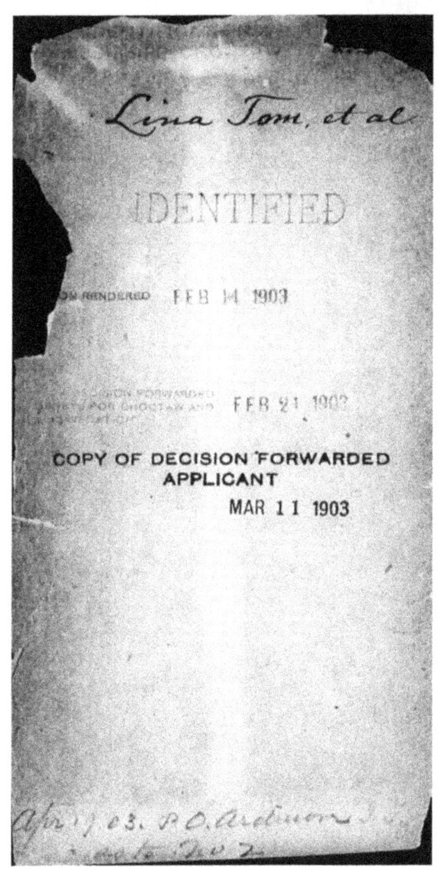

Lina Tom, et al

IDENTIFIED

RENDERED FEB 14 1903

FEB 21 1903

COPY OF DECISION FORWARDED
APPLICANT
MAR 11 1903

CARD NO. 12 - Choctaw MCR 2284 - Jacob Dansby

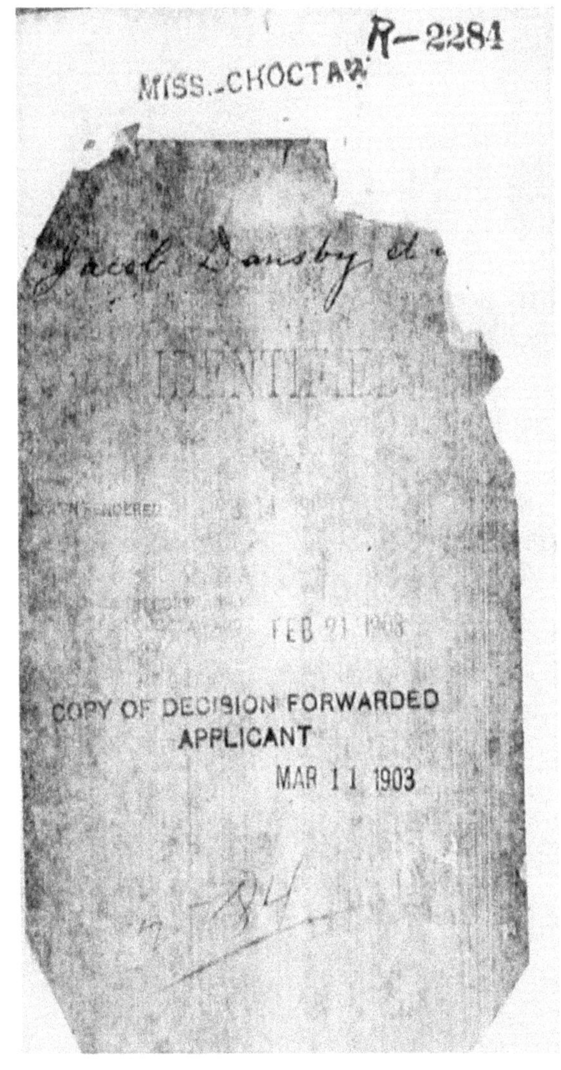
R-2284

MISS.-CHOCTAW

Jacob Dansby

IDENTIFIED

FEB 21 1903

COPY OF DECISION FORWARDED
APPLICANT
MAR 11 1903

DEPARTMENT OF THE INTERIOR

COMMISSION TO THE FIVE CIVILIZED TRIBES

The record herein is in the matter of
the application of Jacob Dansby et al., for identification as
Mississippi Choctaws,
M.C.R. 2284.

DEPARTMENT OF THE INTERIOR

COMMISSION TO THE FIVE CIVILIZED TRIBES

In the matter of the application of Jacob Dansby, et al., for identification as Mississippi Choctaws, M.C.R. 2284.

--------I N D E X -------

Department of the Interior,
Commision[sic] to the Five Civilized Tribes,
Decatur, Mississippi, May 15, 1901.

In the matter of the application of Jacob Dansby for the identification of himself and one step-child as Mississippi Choctaws.

Jacob Dansby, having been first duly sworn, upon his oath states as follows: (Indian McDonald, Official Interpreter.)

Examination by the Commission.

Q What is your name? A Jacob Dansby.
Q What is your age[sic] A Twenty nine.
Q What is your post officie[sic] Address? A Decatur, Mississippi.
Q How long have you lived in Newton County? A All my life.
Q Born here? A Yes.
Q What is your father's name? A Isom Dansby.
Q Is he dead? A Living.
Q Is he a full blood Choctaw? A Yes.
Q What is your mother's name? A I don't know; been dead so long I can't recollect.
Q Full blood? A Yes.
Q Are you a full blood? A Yes.
Q You claim your Choctaw blood through both your parents? A Yes.
Q Have your parents, through whom you claim your right to identification as a Mississippi Choctaw, ever been recognized in any manner or enrolled as members of the Choctaw tribe of Indians by the Choctaw Tribal authorities or the authorities of the United States? A No.
Q Do you desire to make application for your wife? A No.
Q You are not living with her now? A No.
Q She is away? A Yes.
Q Have you any children for whom you want to make application? A Yes, he died.
Q You haven't any children of your own, have you? A No.
Q Have you any children at home that you want to make application for[sic] A No, I aint[sic] got none now.
Q Have you a child, Cornelius Billey? A Yes.
Q Is he living with you? A Yes.
Q Just the same as your child? A Yes.
Q How old is Cornelius Billey? A Fifteen.
Q Is that a step-child? A Yes.
Q Your first wife's child? A Yes.
Q Full blood? A Yes.
Q What was Cornelius Billey's name? A Jane.
Q Mother was Jane Dansby? A Yes.
Q Is Jane Dansby, living? A No, dead.
Q She was a full blood? A Yes.
Q Who was the father of Cornelius Billey? A Billey Jackson.

Q Full blood? A Yes.
Q Is he dead? A Yes.
Q Have you charge of this child now? A Yes.
Q Do you claim Cornelius Billey to be a full blood through both parents? A Yes.
Q Were either of his parents ever recognized in any manner or enrolled as members of the Choctaw tribe of Indians in Indian Territory? A No.
Q Was the father of Cornelius Billey married under a license or according to the Choctaw custom? A Choctaw custom.
Q Is your name of the name of this step-child on any of the tribal rolls of the Choctaw Nation in Indian Territory? A No.
Q Have you ever made application for yourself or Cornelius Billey, to be enrolled as members of the Choctaw tribe of Indians in Indian Territory, to the Choctaw tribal authorities or to the authorities of the United States? A No.
Q Did you make application in the year 1896, to the Commission to the Five Civilized Tribes for citizenship in the Choctaw Nation under the Ace of Congress of June 10, 1896[sic] A No.
Q Have you ever made application before this time either for yourself or this step-child to be enrolled or admitted as citizens of the Choctaw Nation, to either the Choctaw tribal authorities or the authorities of the United States? A I made application two years ago to Mr. McKennon.

> The records of the Commission show that on February 6, 1899, this applicant appeared before the Commission at Decatur, Mississippi and made application for the identification of himself, his wife, Chuly Dansby, and minor child, Frank Dansby, as Mississippi Choctaws, their names appearing upon Mississippi Choctaw Card, Field Number 347; also, upon page 81 of the Schedule of Mississippi Choctaws which accompanied the report of March 10, 1899, of the Commission to the Five Civilized Tribes to the Secretary of the Interior as to the identity of Choctaw Indians residing in Mississippi, claiming rights in the Choctaw lands under the provisions of the Fourteenth Article of the Treaty of Dancing Rabbit Creek, being Numbers 1231, 1232 and 1233, respectively, thereon.

Q Except the application that you made two years ago, this is the first application you have ever made? A Yes.
Q Is it now your purpose to make application for the identification of yourself and this minor child as Mississippi Choctaws? A Yes.
Q Do you claim your rights as beneficairies[sic] under the provisions of the Fourteenth Article of the Treaty of 1830? A Yes sir.
Q Have you or your step-child ever received any benefits as Choctaw Indians?
A No.
Q Have any of your, or his ancestors ever received any benefits as Choctaw Indians?
A I don't know.
Q What are the names of your ancestors or your step-child's ancestors who were residents of the old Choctaw Nation in Mississippi and Alabama in 1830, and who were acknowledged members of the Choctaw tribe of Indians? A My old granny.
Q What was her name A Betsey.

Q What is the Indian name? A I don't know.
Q Did she receive any land? A No.
Q Did she draw money here in Mississippi? A Yes she drawed money here in Mississippi - in Territory.
Q Did she go to the Territory? A Yes.
Q Did she go with the other Indians between the years 1833 and 1838? A Yes, she went with the other Indians.
Q Did she die out there? A No, she died here.
Q Came back? A Yes, and received some money[sic]
Q Do you know of any others who went out too? A No. That's all I know.
Q Did any of your ancestors of this step-child's ancestors, within six months after the ratification of the Treaty of 1830, signify to the United States Indian agent for the Choctaws here in Mississippi, their intention to remain in Mississippi and become citizens of the States? A I don't know.
Q Did any of your ancestors, or your step-child's ancestors ever claim or receive any land in Mississippi as beneficiaries under the provisions of Article Fourteen of the Treaty of 1830? A My daddy's mother drawed land.
Q What was your daddy's mother's name? A Low-ah-ho-ka.

> On page 553 of Volume One of the the[sic] Record of the Court of Claims in the case of the Choctaw Nation of Indians versus the United States, Number 12742, in case 384, appears the name of Low-ah-ho-ka, it appearing that this child is the step-child of Is-te-ubbee. This case appears in Abstract Number One reported by Commissioners, Tyler, Gaines and Rush, appointed un the Act of Congress of August 23, 1842, to adjudicate claims made by Choctaw Indians in Mississippi under the provisions of the Fourteenth Article of the Treaty of Dancing Rabbit Creek. It appears from the record of said case, that this child was over ten years of age at the ratification of the Treaty and that the East half of Section 18, Township 8, Range 13 East was awarded to said Low-ah-ho-ka by said Commissioners.

Q Are there any additional statements you desire to make in support of this application? A No.
Q Have you any evidence, affidavits, written testimony of any description, copies of records, deeds or patents, or any other proper papers showing that any of your ancestors, or any of the ancestors of this step-child were in the year 1830, when the Treaty of Dancing Rabbit Creek was made, recognized members of the Choctaw tribe of Indians, or that any of them ever compliedor[sic] attempted to comply with the provisions of the 14th article of that treaty or ever received any benefits thereunder?
A I desire to file the patent to this land, if my father has not filed in his case.

> Permission is granted to the applicant to file proper documentary evidence in support of this application, within thirty days from the date hereof.

(This applicant appears to be a full blood Indian. He speaks the English language imperfectly; he speaks the Choctaw language, and his examination was conducted with the aid of a sworn Choctaw interpreter.[sic]

The decision of the Commission as to the application you make for the identification of yourself and this minor step-child for identification as Mississippi Choctaws will be determined at the earliest possible date, and a report of same made to the Secretary of the Interior, conformable to the provisions of the Twenty First Section of the Act of Congress of June 28, 1898, and a copy of the same will be mailed to you to your post office address as given in your testimony.

R.S. Streit, having been first duly sworn, upon his oath states that as stenographer to the Commission to the Five Civilized Tribes, he reported in full all proceedings had in the above entitled cause on the 15th day of May, 1901, and that the above and foregoing is a full, true and correct transcript of his stenographic notes of said proceedings in said cause on said date.

R.S. Streit

Subscribed and sworn to before me a Meridian, Mississippi, this 22nd day of June, 1901.

J P McKee Jr
Notary Public

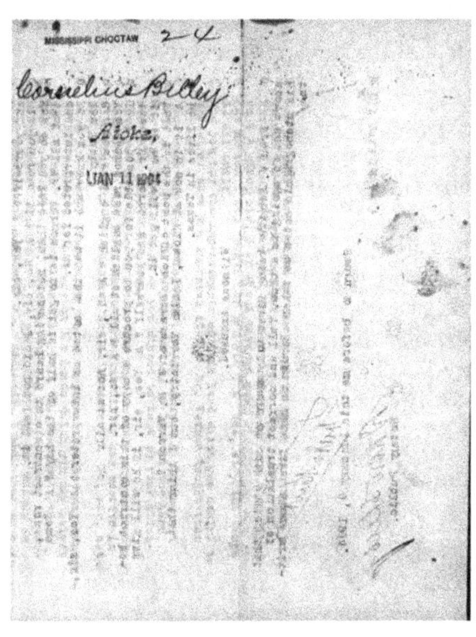

MISSISSIPPI CHOCTAW 2-4
Cornelius Billy
Atoka,
JAN 11 1904

M C I 23-24 M C I Card 12.

DEPARTMENT OF THE INTERIOR,
COMMISSION TO THE FIVE CIVILIZED TRIBES,
CHOCTAW LAND OFFICE,
Atoka, Indian Territory, August 21, 1903.

-:-

In the matter of the proof of settlement within the Choctaw Chickasaw country of Jacob Dansby and his minor step son Cornelius Billey, duly Identified Mississippi Choctaws, Card No. 12, Approved Roll Nos. 23 and 24.

JACOB DANSBY being first duly sworn testifies:

EXAMINATION BY THE COMMISSION:

Jacob Homer, Interpreter:

Q What is your name ? A Jacob Dansby.
Q How old are you ? A Thirty one years.
Q What was your post office address in the state of Mississippi prior to your removal to the Indian Territory ? A Rio and Decatur, Mississippi -- I got some of my mail at Rio.
Q What was your post office address in Mississippi in 1899 and 1900 ? A Decatur, then.
Q But you got some of your mail at Rio ? A Yes, sir, I got mail at both places.
Q What is the name of your father ? A Isom Dansby.
Q Is he living ? A Yes, sir.
Q Where does he live ? A Kiowa, Indian Territory.
Q What is your mother's name ? A I do not know her first name -- her name was Dansby.
Q Did you make personal application to the Commission to the Five Civilized Tribes during any of its appointments in Mississippi for identification as a Mississippi Choctaw ? A Yes, sir.
Q Did you state at that time that your father was living or dead ? A Yes, sir, I said that he was living.
Q Your father Isom Dansby is an applicant to the Commission for identification as a Mississippi is he not ? A Yes, sir, he went before them at Philadelphia I believe.
Q Are you married ? A Not now -- have been -- my wife is dead.
Q What was the name of your wife[sic] A Jane Dansby.
Q When did she die ? A I cannot recollect that.
Q What it a number of years ago ? A Yes, sir, about six.
Q Did you and Jane have any children ? A Yes, sir, one child named Frank.
Q Is he living or dead ? A Dead.
Q When did he die ? A About five years ago.
Q Did Jane Dansby have any children when you married her ? A Yes, sir, four.

Q Are any of these four children living at the present time ? A Yes, sir, Cornelius Billey.
Q Cornelius Billey is living ? A Yes, sir.
Q Who is the father of Cornelius Billey ? A Billey Jackson.
Q Are you the identical Jacob Dansby and is Billey, Cornelius Billey the identical persons who were by the Commission to the Five Civilized Tribes identified as Mississippi Choctaw entitled to allotments of the Choctaw and Chickasaw lands ? A Yes, sir.
Q When did you remove from Mississippi to the Choctaw Nation ? A Last November.
Q About what time in November ? A It was the 19th day.
Q November, 19, 1902 ? A Yes, sir.
Q Did you bring your minor step son Cornelius Billey from Mississippi to the Indian Territory with you ? A Yes, sir. I did not bring him with me but after I got here I sent after him.
Q When did he arrive here ? A 26th day of December last year, 1902.
Q What is your post office address in Indian Territory ? A Kiowa, Indian Territory.
Q Is Cornelius Billey living with you at the present time ? A Yes, sir. He is working around there but he lives with me.
Q Where does he work ? A Right there in Kiowa.
Q Who defrayed the expenses of the removal of yourself and your step son Cornelius Billey from Mississippi to Indian Territory ? A Judge Vernon.
Q Do you know his full name ? A I think it is W. N. Vernon.
Q What, if any of your property, or the property of Cornelius Billey did you bring from Mississippi with you ? A Brought some quilts and our trunks.
Q Is it the intention of yourself and this boy, Cornelius Billey to accept lands from the Choctaw and Chickasaw Tribes of Indians and to make you permanent home in the Indian Territory ? A Yes, sir.
Q Have you or any one for you, or Cornelius Billey or any one for him, made any contract or agreement whatever for the sale, or encumbrance in any way of any of the lands you may receive as Mississippi Choctaws from the Choctaw and Chickasaw tribes of Indians ? A Yes, sir.
Q With who have you made this contract ? A W. N. Vernon.
Q Did you make this contract with Vernon for the land which you may receive yourself ? A Yes, sir.
Q When was this contract between yourself and Vernon executed ? A It was in November about the 16th day.
Q 1902 ? A Yes, sir.
Q Have you a copy of this contract in your possession ? A No, sir, he never gave me a copy of it.
Q What are the terms of this contract if you know ? A I am to give him one half of the value of the hay.
Q For how many years ? A For three years.
Q Is that all he is to receive from you ? A Yes, sir.
Q Are you positive of that ? A Yes, sir.
Q That is al he is to get ? A Yes, sir.

Q What are you to receive in consideration for the half of the hay ? He is to furnish me with horses and a house and wire to fence the place.
Q You say that he is to furnish you with horses ? A Yes, sir.
Q How many ? A Two.
Q Has he built any houses on the property which you expect to select ? A No, sir, not yet.
Q Have you selected as yet, the land which you expect to file on ? A Yes, sir, I am about through now.
Q Has he built any fences for you yet ? A Yes, sir, the fence is all built.
Q Did you buy the improvements on this land which you desire to select or have you improved it ? A Mr. Vernon bought them for me.
Q How much did he pay for that, if you know ? A He has not paid for it yet -- he is just waiting to look at the land.
Q How many acres of land do you expect to take in your allotment ? A About 380 acres.
Q Have you made any contract or has any one made any contract relative to the lands which Cornelius Billey may receive in allotment from the Choctaws and Chickasaws ? A No, sir, not yet.
Q Have you and Mr. Vernon or you and any one else had any conversation relative to a lease on the lands which you may select in allotment for Cornelius Billey ? A No, sir, not yet.
Q Are you positive, Mr. Dansby, that all Mr. Vernon is to receive under this contract is one half of the hay raised on your prospective allotment ? A Yes, sir, I know that is all.
Q Have you ever seen and read the contract between Mr. Vernon and yourself? A Yes, sir.
Q Did you read it ? A No, sir, I did not read it.
Q How do you know then, not having heard the contract read, that all Mr. Vernon is to get is half of the hay ? A Some one interpreted for me.
Q Do you know who it was that acted as interpreter ? A Yes, sir, Tom Tubby.
Q Can you read english[sic] A No, sir, not at all.
Q You cannot read english at all ? A No, sir.
Q Is it possible for you to procure a copy of this contract between Mr. Vernon and yourself? A Yes, sir, if he will give it to me I will get it.
Q What is the post office address of W. N. Vernon ? A It is now at Kiowa, Indian Terriotry[sic], but I think that he lives in Texas.

Witness excused.

Fred V. Kinkade being first duly sworn on oath states that above and foregoing is a true, full and correct translation of his stenographic notes as taken therein on date first above writtne/[sic]

Fred Kinkade

Sworn to before me this January 9, 1904.

David Shelby
Notary Public.

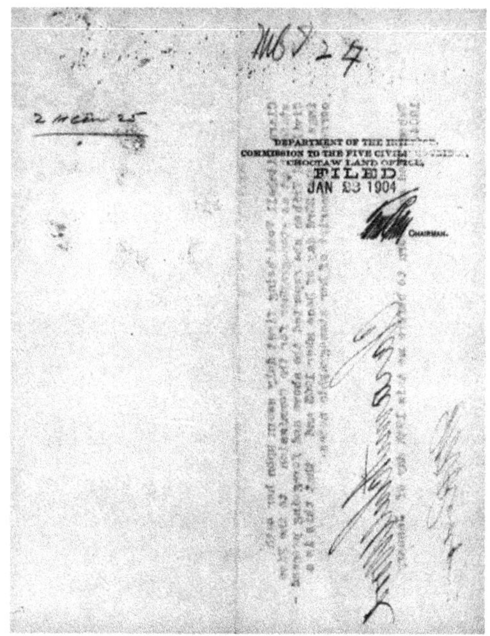

Department of the Interior
Commission to the Five Civilized Tribes
Chickasaw Land Office
Tishomingo, I.T.
Dec. 23, 1903.

In the matter of the declaration and proof of settlement within the Choctaw-Chickasaw Country of Jacob Dansby and Cornelius Billy[sic] Mississippi Choctaw Indians duly identified as such by the Commission to the Five Civilized Tribes on February 14, 1903 roll numbers 23 and 24 card number 12.

Jacob Dansby being first duly sworn testified as follows:

Examination by the Commission :

Q What is your name? A Jacob Dansby.
Q How old are you? A Thirty one.
Q What is the name of your father? A Isom Dansby.
Q What is the name of your mother.[sic] A I dont know; she's been dead a long time.
Q Is your father living? A No he's not living.

Q You are a full blood Mississippi Choctaw Indian? A Yes full blood.
Q Are you married? A I've been married; he[sic] died.
Q What was your wife's name? A Jane.
Q Have you got any children? A I had two that died.
Q Have you got any living children? A I've got one step child Corenlius[sic] Billy[sic], living.
Q How old is Cornelius Billy? A Seventeen.
Q Is Cornelius the child of Jane? A Yes.
Q What was Cornelius's father's name? A Billy Jackson[sic]
Q Cornelius' father and mother are both dead? A Yes sir.
Q Where did you live in the state of Mississippi? A Newton County.
Q What was your post office address? A Decatur.
Q Did you ever live near Rio? A Yes I moved to Rio.
Q When did you leave Mississippi and come to the Indian Territory? A Last November was a year ago.
Q Did you bring all your personal possessions with you? A Yes sir.
Q Did you bring Cornelius Billy with you? A Yes sir.
Q Has he been living with you ever since his mother's death? A Yes, I raised him.
Q Are you guardian of this boy? A Yes.
Q Where did you locate in Indian Territory? A Thackerville.
Q Have you been living at Thackerville ever since you came here[sic] A No, I've been living at Kiowa.
Q Did you come here with the intention of making a permanent home in Indian Territory.[sic] A Yes sir.
Q What[sic] it the intention of Cornelius Billy and your intention to hvae[sic] him stay here also? A Yes sir.
Q Is it your intention at the present time to remain in Indian Territory and make your future home here both for yourself and Cornelius Billy? A Yes, sir.
Q What will be your permanent post office address? A Thackerville.

Clara Mitchell Wood being first duly sworn upon her oath states that as stenographer for the Commission to the Five Civilized Tribes she reported the above and foregoing proceedings on the 23rd day of December 1903 and that this is a correct transcript of her stenographic notes.

Clara Mitchell Wood

Subscribed and sworn to before me this 19th day of January 1904.

J [?] *Rodgers*

Notary Public.

DEPARTMENT OF THE INTERIOR

COMMISSION TO THE FIVE CIVILIZED TRIBES

In the matter of the application of Jacob Dansby, et al., for identification as Mississippi Choctaws, M.C. R. 2284.

-----D E C I S I O -------

It appears from the record herein that application for identification as Mississippi Choctaws was made to this Commission on May 15, 1901, by Jacob Dansby for himself and his minor step-child, Cornelius Billey, under the following provision of the Act of Congress approved June 28, 1898 (30 Stats. 495):

> "Said Commission shall have authority to determine the identity of Choctaw Indians claiming rights in the Choctaw lands under article fourteen of the treaty between the United States and the Choctaw Nation, concluded September twenty-seventh, eighteen hundred and thirty, and to that end may administer oaths, examine witnesses, and perform all other acts necessary thereto and make report to the Secretary of the Interior."

From the evidence submitted in support of said application it appears that both the applicants are full blood Mississippi Choctaw Indians.

Section forty-one of the Act of Congress entitled "An Act to ratify and confirm an agreement with the Choctaw and Chickasaw tribes of Indians, and for other purposes" approved July 1, 1902, (32 Stats. 641) and ratified by the Choctaw and Chickasaw Nations September 25, 1902, provides as follows:

> "The application of no person for identification as a Mississippi Choctaw shall be received by said Commission after six months subsequent to the date of the final ratification of this agreement and in the disposition of such applications all full-blood Mississippi Choctaw Indians and the descendants of any Mississippi Choctaw Indians whether of full or mixed blood who received a patent to land under the said fourteenth article of the said treaty of eighteen hundred and thirty who had not moved to and made bona fide settlement in the Choctaw-Chickasaw country prior to June twenty-eighth, eighteen hundred and ninety-eight, shall be deemed to be Mississippi Choctaws, entitled to benefits under article fourteen of the said treaty of September twenty-seventh, eighteen hundred and thirty, and to identification as such by said Commission, but this direction or provision shall be deemed to be only a rule of evidence and shall not be invoked by or operate to the advantage of any applicant who is not a Mississippi Choctaw of a full blood, or who is not the descendant of a Mississippi Choctaw who received a patent to land under said treaty, or who is

otherwise barred from the right of citizenship in the Choctaw Nation, all of said Mississippi Choctaws so enrolled by said Commission shall be upon a separate roll."

It is, therefore, the opinion of this Commission that should be identified as Mississippi Choctaw , and it is so ordered.

COMMISSION TO THE FIVE CIVILIZED TRIBES.

Tams Bixby
Acting Chairman.

T.B. Needles
Commissioner.

C. R. Breckinridge
Commissioner.

Muskogee, Indian Territory.

FEB 14 1903

DEPARTMENT OF THE INTERIOR.
COMMISSION TO THE FIVE CIVILIZED TRIBES.

-----oOo-----

In the matter of the removal to and settlement within the Choctaw-Chickasaw country, Indian Territory of Cornelius Billey, schedule of identified Mississippi Choctaws, No. 24.

The evidence herein shows that Cornelius Billey was identified as a Mississippi Choctaw by the Commission to the Five Civilized Tribes February 14, 1903: that he removed to and established his residence in the Choctaw-Chickasaw country December 26, 1902: that satisfactory proof of such removal and settlement was submitted to the Commission to the Five Civilized Tribes August 21, 1903, and that he is therefore entitled to enrollment as a Mississippi Choctaw under the provisions of section 43, of the Act of Congress approved July 1, 1901 (32 Stats. 641).

Tams Bixby CHAIRMAN.

Muskogee, Indian Territory.

DEC 12 1904

Miss. Choctaw 2284

Muskogee, Indian Territory, November 5, 1902.

J. A. Dansby,

Rio, Mississippi,

Dear Sir:

Receipt is hereby acknowledged of your letter of October 30, stating that a man by the name of Winton from the Territory promises the Choctaws to bring them to the Indian Territory and make improvements upon the lands which they will receive for a certain portion of the land to be allotted to them, and you ask to be advised concerning this matter.

In reply to your letter you are advised that the agreement recently entered into between the United States and the Choctaw and Chickasaw Nations, approved by an act of Congress of July 1, 1902, which was ratified September 25, 1902, provides:

"All persons duly identified by the Commission to the Five Civilized Tribes under the provisions of section 21 of the act of Congress approved June 28, 1898 (30 Stats., 495), as Mississippi Choctaws entitled to benefits under article 14 of the treaty between the United States and the Choctaw Nation concluded September 27, 1830, may, at any time within six months after the date of the final ratification of this agreement, make bona fide settlement within the Choctaw-Chickasaw country, and upon proof of such settlement to such Commission within one year after the date of the final ratification of this agreement may be enrolled by such Commission as Mississippi Choctaws entitled to allotment as herein provided for citizens of the tribes, subject to the special provisions herein provided as to Mississippi Choctaws, and said enrollment shall be final when approved by the Secretary of the Interior. The application of no person for identification as a Mississippi Choctaw shall be received by said Commission after six months subsequent to the date of the final ratification of this agreement and in the disposition of such applications all full blood Mississippi Choctaw Indians and the descendants of any Mississippi Choctaw Indians whether of full or mixed blood who received a patent to land under the said fourteenth article of the said treaty of eighteen hundred and thirty who had not moved to and made bona fide settlement in the Choctaw-Chickasaw country prior to June twenty-eighth, eighteen hundred and ninety-eight, shall be deemed to be Mississippi Choctaws, entitled to benefits under article fourteen of the said treaty of September twenty-seventh, eighteen hundred and thirty, and to identification as such by said Commission."

You are further advised that the Commission has not yet passed upon your right to identification as a full blood Choctaw Indian under the provisions of the agreement above quoted, but it is probable that within the near future decision will be rendered in your case and you will be duly notified thereof and of the forwarding of the record in the case to the Secretary of the Interior.

Relative to that part of your letter referring to contracts for a portion of the lands to be received in Indian Territory, your attention is invited to the following provision of the act of Congress of May 31, 1900:

"That all contracts or agreements looking to the sale or incumbrance in any way of the lands to be allotted to said Mississippi Choctaws shall be null and void."

Respectfully,

Acting Chairman.

M C R 2284

Muskogee, Indian Territory, January 31, 1903.

A. J. Dansby,

Kiowa, Indian Territory.

Dear Sir:

Receipt is hereby acknowledged of your letter of the 21st instant, in which you ask if the following names appear upon the rolls:

E-misa-hoke	Tihikalee
homa-hoke	Tek-botima
a-boya-ha-bee	frlapee
hokallee-tima	Nihima
fileema-bee	ai-a-hona
Tik-bilece	Ballie-Jun
J. A. Dansby	Allece Billie
Ninnio Billie	leay Billie
hoyobee	hoyolee-honae
Moyih	Oka-ichok-ma-homo.

You state "we would like to have an identification ticket on this colony."

In reply to your letter you are informed that it appears from the records of the Commission that John Holybee is an applicant for the identification of himself and his minor children John, Mary, Effie and Harrison Holybee as Mississippi Choctaws. It is believed this family are identical with the name Hoyobee named by you, and you are advised that the Commission has not up to the present time reached any opinion or decision relative to their right to be identified as such Mississippi Choctaws, but is now considering their application and it is probable a decision will be rendered in the near future. The applicants will be notified of the action of the Commission and of the forwarding of the record to the Secretary of the Interior.

It does not appear from the records of the Commission that any of the above mentioned names are applicants to this Commission for identification as Mississippi Choctaws. If they are applicants, kindly advise the Commission when and where they made application, the english[sic] names under which such applications were made, the names of other members of their family for whom application was made at the same time and such other information as will enable the Commission to identify them as applicants, and the matter will receive further consideration.

Respectfully,

Acting Chairman.

M C R 2284

Muskogee, Indian Territory, February 12, 1903.

A. J. Dansby,

Kiowa, Indian Territory.

Dear Sir:

Receipt is hereby acknowledged of your letter of the 5th instant, wherein you make inquiry as to the present status of the cases of Isom Dansby and certain other Mississippi Choctaws who have recently removed to the Territory.

In reply to your letter you are informed that the Commission has not up to the present time reached any opinion or decision relative to the right of the persons mentioned in your letter to be identified as Mississippi Choctaws, but is now considering their applications and it is probable decisions will be rendered in the near future. Such applicants will be duly notified of the action of the Commission and of the forwarding of the record to the Secretary of the Interior.

Respectfully,

Acting Chairman.

M.C.R. 2284

COPY.

Muskogee, Indian Territory, February 21, 1903.

Mansfield, McMurray & Cornish,

Attorneys for the Choctaw and Chickasaw Nations,

South McAlester, Indian Territory.

Gentlemen:

Enclosed herewith you will find a copy of the decision of the Commission rendered February 14, 1903, identifying Jacob Dansby and step-child, Cornelius Billey, as Mississippi Choctaw Indians under the provisions of the forty-first section of the act of Congress of July 1, 1902 (32 Stats. 641).

You are hereby advised that you will be allowed fifteen days from the date hereof, in which to file with this Commission such protest as you desire to make against the action of the Commission in identifying the said Jacob Dansby and step-child as Mississippi Choctaws, and make satisfactory proof of service of said protest upon the applicants herein.

If you fail to file such protest within the time allowed, the name of the applicants herein will be placed upon the schedule of duly identified Mississippi Choctaws now being prepared by this Commission.

Respectfully,

(SIGNED). *Tams Bixby*

Acting Chairman.

Registered.
Enc. M.C.R. 2284

M.C.R. 2535.

COPY.

Muskogee, Indian Territory, March 11, 1903.

Jacob Dansby, *Remailed to Kiowa I.T. - Apr 23 1903*

Decatur, Mississippi.

Dear Sir:

Enclosed herewith you will find a copy of the decision of the Commission to the Five Civilized Tribes, rendered February 14, 1903, identifying yourself and your minor step-child, Cornelius Billey, as Mississippi Choctaw Indians under the provisions of Section 41 of the Act of Congress approved July 1, 1902, (32 Stats. 641).

If you remove to the Choctaw-Chickasaw country, Indian Territory, before August 14, 1903, you will have six months from that date, or until February 14, 1904, within which to make proof of such removal and settlement at the office of the Commission at Atoka, Choctaw Nation, or Tishomingo, Chickasaw Nation.

Respectfully,

(SIGNED). *Tams Bixby*

Registered.

Chairman.

Enc. 2284.

M C R 1754
M C R 2284

Muskogee, Indian Territory, May 8, 1903.

A. J. Dansby,

Kiowa, Indian Territory.

Dear Sir:

Receipt is hereby acknowledged of the joint letter of yourself and Alice Billey, dated May 2, 1903, in which you ask to be advised the names and ages of yourselves and children.

In reply you are informed that it does not appear from our records that any person by the name of A. J. Dansby is an applicant to this Commission for enrollment as a citizen or freedman of either the Choctaw or Chickasaw Nation or for identification as a Mississippi Choctaw.

Our records do show, however, that on May 15. 1901, at Decatur, Mississippi, jacob[sic] Dansby, twenty-nine years of age, made application to this Commission for the identification of himself and step child Cornelius Billey, fifteen years of age, as Mississippi Choctaws. On February 14, 1903, the Commission rendered its decision identifying Jacob Dansby and his step child Cornelius Billey as Mississippi Choctaws entitled to allotment in the lands of the Choctaw and Chickasaw Nations, of which action they were duly advised by registered mail at Decatur, Mississippi, on March 11, 1903.

Our records further show that on April 10, 1901, at Meridian, Mississippi, Alice Billey, twenty-eight years of age, made application to this Commission for the identification of herself and two minor children, Nannie Billey, age 5, and Clay Billey, age 4, as Mississippi Choctaws. On February 14, 1903, the Commission rendered its decision identifying these applicants as Mississippi Choctaws entitled to allotment in the lands of the Choctaw and Chickasaw Nations, of which action they were duly advised by registered mail at Toles, Mississippi, on March 11, 1903.

Respectfully,

Chairman.

M C R 2284

Muskogee, Indian Territory, December 8, 1903.

Cornelius Billey,

In care of Riley Willis,

Kiowa, Indian Territory.

Dear Sir:

Receipt is hereby acknowledged of your letter of the 1st instant, in which you state "I am a full Blood Miss Choctaw from Kemper Co Miss I have no father & mother do not know my exact age think I am about 21 years old My name was given to the Commission by J A Dansby," and ask "Will I be allowed to take my allotment if not now how Soon?"

In reply you are informed that on February 14, 1903, the Commission rendered a decision identifying Jacob Dansby and his minor step-child, Cornelius Billey, as Mississippi Choctaws entitled to allotment in the lands of the Choctaw and Chickasaw Nations, and you are advised that allotment will be made to you under the rules and regulations governing the selection of allotments and the designation of homesteads in the Choctaw and Chickasaw Nations, a copy of which is herewith enclosed.

Respectfully;

R & R Choc-Chic
Allotments

Chairman.

M.C.R.2284

Muskogee, Indian Territory, April 12, 1904.

J. E. Whitehead,
Attorney-at-Law,
South McAlester, Indian Territory.

Dear Sir:

Receipt is hereby acknowledged of your letter of April 6, 1904, in which you state that Jacob Dansby and his minor step-son, Cornelius Billey, have been permitted by the Commission to allot land, but that Dansby informs you that they have both failed to make proof of settlement within one year from the date of their identification, and you ask if it is necessary for them to submit further proof.

In reply to your letter you are informed that it appears from our records that on February 14, 1903, the Commission rendered a decision identifying Jacob Dansby and his minor step-child, Cornelius Billey, as full-blood Mississippi Choctaws; that on August 21, 1903, Jacob Dansby appeared before the Commission at the Choctaw Land Office, at Atoka, Indian Territory, and testified relative to the removal to and settlement within the Choctaw-Chickasaw country of himself and minor step-son, Cornelius Billey. Also on December 23, 1903, at the Chickasaw Land Office, Tishomingo, Indian Territory, proof of settlement was again made relative to the removal to the Choctaw-Chickasaw country of these persons.

No further proof of settlement is required on behalf of these applicants.

Respectfully,

Commissioner in Charge.

#649

No. 2284

For Identification as a Mississippi Choctaw.

Date MAY 15 1901

Name Jacob Dansby -

Age 29 - Blood Full.

Post Office, Decatur, Miss

Father: Isom Dansby. f.b. d

Mother: — Dansby - f.b. d

Claims through both parents

See M. C. Card. filed No 347

~~Children:~~

Cornelius Billey, f.b. 15
step child,

Mother, Jane Dansby f.b. d
Father - Billy Jackson " d
(applicants 1st wife -)
His 2nd wife deserted him.
claims for self. and
step child —

Stenographer R. S. Strait

CARD NO. 13 - Choctaw MCR 2313 - Wash Thomas

DEPARTMENT OF THE INTERIOR.

COMMISSION TO THE FIVE CIVILIZED TRIBES.

----o----

In the matter of the application of Wash Thomas, et al. for identification as Mississippi Choctaws, M. C. R. 2313.

----o----

DEPARTMENT OF THE INTERIOR.

COMMISSION TO THE FIVE CIVILIZED TRIBES.

----o----

In the matter of the application of Wash Thomas, et al., for identification as Mississippi Choctaws, M. C. R. 2313.

--: I N D E X :--

----o----

DEPARTMENT OF THE INTERIOR,
COMMISSION TO THE FIVE CIVILIZED TRIBES,
Meridian, Mississippi, May 22nd, 1901.

In the matter of the application of Wash Thomas for the identification of himself and his wife as Mississippi Choctaws.

Said Wash Thomas, being first duly sworn, testified as follows:-

Examination by the Commission.

Q What is your name? A Wash Thomas.
Q What is your age? A Thirty one.
Q What is your post office address? A Orange, Mississippi.
Q How long have you lived there? A Lived there about seven years.
Q Where were you born? A Newton, Mississippi.
Q Always lived in Newton County? A I was born there and went to Alabama and come back again.
Q You never lived in any other State except Mississippi, only Alabama? A Yes sir, that is all.
Q What is your father's name? A Jesse Thomas.
Q Is he living? A Yes sir.
Q Is he a full blood? A Yes sir.
Q What is your mother's name? A Martha.
Q Is she living? A Dead.
Q Was she a full blood? A Yes sir.
Q Do you claim to be a full blood Choctaw? A Yes sir.
Q You claim through both your father and mother? A Yes.
Q Have your parents, through whom you claim your right to identification as a Mississippi Choctaw, ever been recognized in any manner or enrolled as members of the Choctaw Tribe of Indians by the Choctaw Tribal authorities or the authorities of the United States? A No sir.
Q Are you married? A Yes sir.
Q What is your wife's name? A Mollie.
Q Do you make claim for her? A Yes sir.
Q What is she, full blood or half blood? A Full blood.
Q How old is she? A About nineteen.
Q How long have you been married to her? A Ten years.
Q Were you married under a license or according to Choctaw custom? A I didn't married with license.
Q Under the Choctaw custom? A Yes sir.
Q Have you any children under 21 years of age and unmarried that you wish to make application for? A No sir.
Q What is your wife's father's name? A Big Tom.
Q Did anyone make application for her two years ago? A No sir.
Q Is he dead? A Yes sir.
Q Was he full blood? A Yes sir.

Q When did he die? A Before I married.
Q You have been married twn[sic] years? A Yes sir.
Q Is your wife pretty near as old as you are? A Would she be only nineteen years old or overthat[sic]? A She would be about twenty-five.
Q What is your wife's mother's name? A I don't know.
Q Was she a full blood? A Yes.
Q Is she living? A No.
Q Does your wife claim to be full blood Choctaw through both father and mother?
A Yes sir.
Q Have your wife's parents, through whom you claim for her the right to identification as Mississippi Choctaws, ever been recognized in any manner or enrolled as members of the Choctaw Tribe of Indians by the Choctaw Tribal authorities or by the authorities of the United States? No sir.
Q Is your name or the name of your wife on any of the tribal rolls of the Choctaw Nation in Indian Territory? A No sir.
Q Have you ever made application for yourself or your wife to the Choctaw Tribal authorities in the Indian Territory to be enrolled as members of the Choctaw Tribe?
A No sir.
Q Did you or anyone for you or for your wife, in 1896, under the Act of Congress of June 10, 1896, make application to the Commission to the Five Civilized Tribes for citizenship in the Choctaw Nation? A No sir.
Q Have you or your wife ever been admitted to citizenship in the Choctaw Nation by either the Choctaw Tribal authorities, the Commission to the Five Civilized Tribes or by the United States Court in Indian Territory? A No sir.
Q Have you ever made application before this time for yourself or your wife to either the Choctaw Tribal authorities or the authorities of the United States to be enrolled as citizens of the Choctaw Nation? A No.
Q Is this the first application of any kind that you have ever made for yourself or your wife? A Yes sir.
Q Is it now your purpose to make application for identification as Mississippi Choctaws? A Yes sir.
Q Do you claim your right for yourself and your wife as beneficiaries under the provisions of article 14 of the treaty of 1830? A Yes.
Q Have you or your ancestors, your wife or your wife's ancestors ever received any benefit as Choctaw Indians? A No sir.
Q Can you give the name of any of your ancestors or your wife's ancestors who lived in Mississippi in 1830 and who were recognized members of the Choctaw Tribe of Indians at that time, when the treaty of Dancing Rabbit Creek was entered into between the United States Government and the Choctaw Indians? A My grandfather, John Thomas. His Choctaw name Awatawah.
Q Can you tell the name of your wife's grandfather or grandmother? A No sir.
Q Did any of your ancestors or your wife's ancestors go from Mississippi or Alabama to the Indian Territory between the years 1833 and 1838 when the other Indians went there? A No sir.
Q Did any of your ancestors or your wife's ancestors within six months after the ratification of the treaty of 1830, signify to the United States Indian Agent of the

Choctaw Indians in Mississippi, their intention to remain in Mississippi and become citizens of the United States? A I don't know.
Q Have any of your ancestors or your wife's ancestors ever claimed or received any land in Mississippi as beneficiaries under the provisions of the 14th article of the treaty of 1830? A No sir.
Q Do you speak Choctaw? A Yes sir.
Q You don't speak English very well, do you? A No sir.
Q Are there any additional statements you want to make in support of your application? A No sir.
Q Have you any documentary evidence, written testimony of any description, copies of records, deeds or patents, or any proper papers, showing that any of your ancestors were ever recognized members of the Choctaw Tribe of Indians in Mississippi, that they ever complied or attempted to comply with the provisions of the 14th article of the treaty of 1830, or that they ever received any benefits under that article of that treaty? A No sir.

John S. Hagler, attorney for applicant, waived cross-examination.

This applicant has the appearance and all of the characteristics of a full blood Choctaw Indian. He speaks the Choctaw language and has some knowledge also of the English language, his examination having been conducted without the assistance of a sworn Choctaw interpreter. He has no knowledge of the compliance on the part of his ancestors with the provisions of article 14 of the treaty of 1830.

The decision of the Commission as to your application and the application you make on behalf of your wife, for identification as Mississippi Choctaws, will be determined at the earliest possible date and report of the same made to the Secretary of the Interior, conformable to the provisions of the 21st section of the Act of Congress of June 28, 1898. A copy of such decision will be mailed to you to your postoffice address as given in your testimony at this time.

Ira S. Niles, being first duly sworn, states that as stenographer to the Commission to the Five Civilized Tribes, he reported in full the proceedings had in the above entitled cause, heard at Meridian, Mississippi, May 22nd, 1901, and the above and preceding is a full, true and correct transcript of his stenographic notes taken in said proceedings on said date.

Ira S. Niles

Subscribed and sworn to before me this the 17th day of June, 1901, at Meridian, Mississippi.

J P McKee Jr
Notary Public.

DEPARTMENT OF THE INTERIOR

COMMISSION TO THE FIVE CIVILIZED TRIBES.

----o----

In the matter of the application of Wash Thomas, et al., for identification as Mississippi Choctaws, M.C.R. 2313.

D E C I S I O N

It appears from the record herein that application for identification as Mississippi Choctaws was made to this Commission on May 22, 1901, by Wash Thomas for himself, and his wife Mollie Thomas under the following provision of the act of Congress approved June 28, 1898, (30 Stats. 495) :

> "Said Commission shall have authority to determine the identity of Choctaw Indians claiming rights in the Choctaw lands under article fourteen of the treaty between the United States and the Choctaw Nation, concluded September twenty-seventh, eighteen hundred and thirty, and to that end may administer oaths, examine witnesses, and perform all other acts necessary thereto and make report to the Secretary of the Interior."

From the evidence submitted in support of said application it appears that both of the applicants are full blood Mississippi Choctaw Indians.

Section forty-one of the act of Congress entitled "An Act to ratify and confirm an agreement with the Choctaw and Chickasaw tribes of Indians, and for other purposes," approved July 1, 1902, (32 Stats. 641), and ratified by the Choctaw and Chickasaw Nations September 25, 1902, provides as follows:

> "The application of no person for identification as a Mississippi Choctaw shall be received by said Commission after six months subsequent to the date of the final ratification of this agreement and in the disposition of such applications all full-blood Mississippi Choctaw Indians and the descendants of any Mississippi Choctaw Indians whether of full or mixed blood who received a patent to land under the said fourteenth article of the said treaty of eighteen hundred and thirty who had not moved to and made bona fide settlement in the Choctaw-Chickasaw country prior to June twenty-eighth, eighteen hundred and ninety-eight, shall be deemed to

be Mississippi Choctaws, entitled to benefits under article fourteen of the said treaty of September twenty-seventh, eighteen hundred and thirty, and to identification as such by said Commission, but this direction or provision shall be deemed to be only a rule of evidence and shall not be invoked by or operate to the advantage of any applicant who is not a Mississippi Choctaw of a full blood, or who is not the descendant of a Mississippi Choctaw who received a patent to land under said treaty, or who is otherwise barred from the right of citizenship in the Choctaw Nation, all of said Mississippi Choctaws so enrolled by said Commission shall be upon a separate roll."

It is, therefore, the opinion of this Commission that Wash Thomas and Mollie Thomas should be identified as Mississippi Choctaws, and it is so ordered.

COMMISSION TO THE FIVE CIVILIZED TRIBES.

Tams Bixby
Acting Chairman.

T.B. Needles
Commissioner.

C. R. Breckinridge
Commissioner.

Muskogee, Indian Territory.
FEB 14 1903

M.C.R. 2313

COPY.

Muskogee, Indian Territory, February 21, 1903.

Mansfield, McMurray & Cornish,
Attorneys for the Choctaw and Chickasaw Nations,
South McAlester, Indian Territory.

Gentlemen:

Enclosed herewith you will find a copy of the decision of the Commission rendered February 14, 1903, identifying Wash Thomas and his wife, Mollie Thomas as Mississippi Choctaw Indians under the provisions of the forty-first section of the act of Congress approved July 1, 1902 (32 Stats. 641).

You are hereby advised that you will be allowed fifteen days from the date hereof, in which to file with this Commission such protest as you desire to make against the action of the Commission in identifying the said Wash Thomas and wife Mollie Thomas as Mississippi Choctaws, and make satisfactory proof of service of said protest upon the applicants herein.

If you fail to file such protest within the time allowed, the names of the applicants herein will be placed upon the schedule of duly identified Mississippi Choctaws now being prepared by this Commission.

Respectfully,

(SIGNED). *Tams Bixby*
Acting Chairman.

Registered.
Enc. H.G. 2

COPY. M.C.R. 2313.

Muskogee, Indian Territory, March 11, 1903.

Wash Thomas,

Orange, Mississippi.

Dear Sir:

Enclosed herewith you will find a copy of the decision of the Commission to the Five Civilized Tribes, rendered February 14, 1903, identifying yourself and your wife, Mollie Thomas, as Mississippi Choctaw Indians under the provisions of Section 41 of the Act of Congress approved July 1, 1902, (32 Stats. 641).

If you remove to the Choctaw-Chickasaw country, Indian Territory, before August 14, 1903, you will have six months from that date, or until February 14, 1904, within which to make proof of such removal and settlement at the office of the Commission at Atoka, Choctaw Nation, or Tishomingo, Chickasaw Nation.

Respectfully,

(SIGNED). *Tams Bixby*
Chairman.

Registered.

Enc. 2313.

#678

No. ~~2313~~

For Identification as a Mississippi Choctaw.

Date MAY 22 1901

Name Wash Thomas,

Age 31 - Blood full.

Post Office Orange, Miss.

Father: Jesse Thomas, f.b. l

Mother: Martha " f.b. d

Claims through both parents. -

wife.
Mollie, f.b. — 25. ~~19~~
father, Big Tom f.b. d
mother don't know, " d

Children:

Claims for self and wife -

Stenographer I.A. Niles

CARD NO. 14 - Choctaw MCR 1999 - John [Eliza] Billey

DEPARTMENT OF THE INTERIOR.
COMMISSION TO THE FIVE CIVILIZED TRIBES.

The within record is in the matter of the
application of John Billey, et al., for identification as
Mississippi Choctaws,
M.C.R. 1999

DEPARTMENT OF THE INTERIOR.
COMMISSION TO THE FIVE CIVILIZED TRIBES.

In the matter of the application of John Billey, et al., for identification as Mississippi Choctaws---------------M. C. R. 1999.

---- ----I N D E X ------

DEPARTMENT OF THE INTERIOR.
COMMISSION TO THE FIVE CIVILIZED TRIBES.
Philadelphia, Mississippi, May 2, 1901.

In the matter of the application of John Billey for the identification of himself, his wife, one child and two step-children as Mississippi Choctaws.

John Billey, having been first duly sworn, upon his oath testifies as follows, (through Tom Tubbee, official interpreter):

Examination by the Commission:

Q What is your name? A John Billey.
Q How old are you? A Fifty three.
Q What is your post office address? A Tucker, Mississippi.
Q How long have you lived in Mississippi? A I was raised here.
Q Lived here all your life? A Yes.
Q Is your father living? A No sir.
Q What is his name? A Billey-- - Injun name, Oo k-a-la-hane- lubbee.
Q Was your father a full blood Choctaw? A Yes.
Q Did he always live in the state of Mississippi? A Yes.
Q Is your mother living? A No, dead.
Q What was her name? A Betsey-- - Injuns called her Tim-a-yo nah.
Q Was she a full blood Choctaw? A Yes.
Q Always lived in Mississippi? A Yes.
Q Have all of your forefathers lived in Mississippi so far as you know? A Grandpa named Thlopo-tubbee--They always lived in Mississippi.
Q You claim to be a full blood Choctaw? A Yes.
Q Was your father or mother, either of them, ever recognized in any manner of enrolled as members of the Choctaw tribe of Indians by the Choctaw tribal authorities or the authorities of the United States? A No.
Q Are you married? A Yes.
Q What is your wife's name? A Eliza.
Q Do you want to make application for your wife? A Yes.
Q How old is your wife? A Thirty-three I believe.
Q Is she a full blood Choctaw? A Yes.
Q You live with her at this time? A Yes.
Q How long have you been married? A Been married about eight years.
Q Were you married under license or according to the Choctaw customs? A Under license.
Q Where did you get the license? A In the clerk's office in Philadelphia.
Q Who married you? A Catholic priest.
Q Have you your license with you here now? A No.
Q Is your wife's father living? A No, all dead.
Q What was his name? A Jim Polk.
Q Did he have any Choctaw name? A No.
Q Was he a full blood Choctaw? A Yes?[sic]

Q Is your wife's mother living? A No, dead.
Q What was her bane[sic]? A Don't know.
Q Was she a full blood Choctaw? A Yes, think so.
Q Did your wife's father and mother always live in Mississippi? A Yes.
Q Have all of her forefathers always lived in Mississippi so far as you know?
A Yes.
Q Were either of your wife's parents ever recognized in any manner or enrolled as members of the Choctaw tribe of Indians by the Choctaw tribal authorities or the United States authorities? A Don't know.
Q Have you any children in your family under twenty one and unmarried? A Yes.
Q What are their names and ages? A Simon Bob.
Q How old is he? A Eighteen.
Q What is the next one? A Jim Bob.
Q How old is Jim? A Ten.
Q Next one? A Wicks Billey.
Q How old? A Six.
Q Simon Bob and Jim Bob are your wife's children by a former husband- -? A Yes.
Q What is the name of their father? A Willis Bob.
Q Is he living? A Yes, he living.
Q Is he a full blood Choctaw? A Yes.
[sic] Eliza is the mother of Simon and Jim? A Yes.
Q Are you the father of Wicks Billey? A Yes.
Q What is the name of his mother? A Eliza.
Q Is your name your wife's name or the name of either one of these children upon the tribal rolls of the Choctaw Nation in the Indian Territory? A Don't know.
Q Did you ever make application to the Choctaw tribal authorities in the Indian Territory for yourself, your wife or any of these children to be enrolled as members of that tribe? A No.
Q Did you or any one for you in 1896 make application to the Commission to the Five Civilized Tribes for citizenship in the Choctaw Nation for yourself, your wife or any of these children? A No.
Q Have you, your wife or any of these children ever been admitted to citizenship in the Choctaw Nation in the Indian Territory by the Choctaw tribal authorities, this Commission or by the United States Court for the Indian Territory? A No.
Q Have you ever made application before this time to either the Choctaw tribal authorities or the United States authorities to be admitted or enrolled as members of the Choctaw tribe? A Make on before two years.

The records of the Commission show that on January 30, 1899, applicant John Billey appeared before the Commission at Philadelphia, Mississippi, and made application for the identification of himself, his wife, Eliza, his three children, Frances, icks and Ruckey Billey, and his three step-children, Simon, William and Jim Bob, as Mississippi Choctaws. their names appearing upon Mississippi Choctaw Card Field No. 123, also upon page 51 of the schedule of Mississippi Choctaws which accompanied the report of March 10, 1899, of the Commission to the Five Civilized Tribes to the Secretary of the Interior as to the identity of Choctaw Indians residing in Mississippi claiming rights in the Choctaw lands under the provisions of the fourteenth article of the treaty of Dancing Rabbit Creek, being Nos. 436, 437, 438, 439, 440, 441, 442 and 443, respectively, thereon.

Q At the time your[sic] appeared before the Commission two years ago, you gave in the names of Frances Billey[sic] Ruckey Billey and William Bob -- are these three children living at this time? A No.
Q When did they die? A In April, a year ago.
Q Died in April, 1900? A Yes.
Q Do you know the days in April they died? A No.
Q Where did they die? A Catholic Mission in Neshoba County.
Q This application two years ago is the only application of any kind that has ever been made for yourself, your wife or any of these children? A Yes.
Q Do you now desire to make application for identification os[sic] yourself, your wife and your minor child and two minor stepchildren as Mississippi Choctaws? A Yes.
Q Do you claim your rights as beneficiaries under the fourteenth article of the treaty of Dancing Rabbit Creek? A Yes.
Q Have you ever received any benefits as a Choctaw? A No.
Q Did your wife ever received any benefits as a Choctaw? A No.
Q Did Willis Bob ever receive any benefits as a Choctaw Indian? A I don't know.
Q Did any of your ancestors or any of your wife's ancestors or any of Willis Bob's ancestors ever receive any benefits as Choctaw Indians? A I don't know.
Q Were any of your ancestors, your wife's ancestors or Willis Bob's ancestors living in the old Choctaw Nation in Mississippi and Alabama in the year 1830 when the treaty of Dancing Rabbit Creek was made? A I don't know.
Q Did any of your ancestors any of your wife's ancestors or any of Willis Bob's ancestors remove from the old Choctaw Nation in Mississippi and Alabama to the present Choctaw Nation in the Indian Territory when the main part of the Choctaws were moved out there between the years 1833 and 1838? A I don't know.
Q Were any of your ancestors, any of your wife's ancestors or any of Willis Bob's ancestors recognized members of the Choctaw tribe of Indians here in Mississippi and Alabama in 1830 when the treaty of Daning[sic] Rabbit Creek was made? A I don't know.
Q Did any of your ancestors, any of your wife's ancestors or any of Willis Bob's ancestors ever claim or receive any land in Mississippi as beneficiaries under the provisions of the fourteenth article of the treaty of Dancing Rabbit Creek?
A I don't know.
Q Do you know the names of your wife's grandparents? A No.
Q Do you know the names of Willis Bob's grandparents? A No.
Q Do you know the name of any other of your grandparents than Thlopo-tubbee?
A No.
Q Are there any additional statements you desire to make at this time in support of your application? A No.
Q Have you any documentary evidence, affidavits, written testimony of any description, copies of records, deeds or patents, or other proper papers showing that any of your wncestors[sic], your wife's ancestors or Willis Bob's ancestors were recognized members of the Choctaw Tribe of Indians here in Mississippi and Alabama

in 1830 when the treaty of Dancing Rabbit Creek was made, or that any of them ever complied or attempted to comply with the provisions of the fourteenth article of that treaty, or ever received any benefits thereunder? A No.

This applicant has every appearance and characteristic of a full blood Choctaw Indian. He speaks the Choctaw language and very little English, the examination having been conducted mainly through a sworn Choctaw Interpreter.

The decision of the Commission as to this application which you make on behalf of yourself, your wife, one minor child and two minor step children for identification as Mississippi Choctaws will be determined at the earliest possible date and a report of the same made to the Secretary of the Interior conformable to the provisions of the twenty-first section of the act of Congress of June 28, 1898, and a copy of the same will be mailed to you at your post office address as given in your testimony.

H. C. Risteen, having been first duly sworn, upon his oath states: That as stenographer to the Commission to the Five Civilized Tribes he reported in full all proceedings had in the above entitled cause on the 2nd day of May 1901, and that the above and foregoing is a full, true and correct transcript of his stenographic notes of said proceedings on said date.

H.C. Risteen

Subscribed and sworn to before me at Philadelphia, Mississippi, this 3rd day of May, 1901.

Howell I. Quinn
Justice of the Peace in and
for Neshoba County, District
No.1, Mississippi.

Department of the Interior,
Commission to the Five Civilized Tribes,
Philadelphia, Mississippi, March 4th, 1902.

In the matter of the death of John Billey, whose name appears upon Mississippi Choctaw Card, R-1999.

George Polk, having been first duly sworn, upon his oath testified as follows:

Examination by the Commission.

Q What is your name? A George Polk.
Q How old are you? A I am forty three.
Q What's your post office address? A Tucker, Mississippi.

Q Are you a full blood Choctaw? A Yes.
Q How long have you lived about Tucker? A About sixteen years.
Q Were you ever acquainted with a man by the name of John Billey? A Yes, sir.
Q Did he have any Choctaw blood? A Yes.
Q How much? A Full blood.
Q Is he living? A No, dead.
Q When did he die? A Seven days in October.
Q Last year? A Yes.
Q Where did he die? A He died at home, near Tucker.
Q Was he any kin to you? A He was a brother-in-law; he married my sister.
Q What's his wife's name? A Eliza.
Q Is she living now? A Yes, sir.
Q Have they any children? A Yes.
Q How many? A Three.
Q What are their names? A Simmon, Jim and Wick.
Q Well, now, Simmon's daddy was named Bob, was he? A Yes.
Q Where is John buried? A At church grave yard, near Tucker.
Q Were you there when he was buried? A Yes, sir.

R. S. Streit, having been first duly sworn, upon his oath states that as stenographer to the Commission to the Five Civilized Tribes, he reported in full all proceedings had in the above entitled cause on the 4th day of March, 1902, at Philadelphia, Mississippi, and that the above is a full true and correct translation of his stenographic notes of said proceedings in said cause upon said date.

R S Streit

Subscribed and sworn to before me at Seale, Mississippi, this 26th day of March, 1902.

L. B. Moseley
Clerk U.S. Circuit Court,
Southern District of Mississippi.

By [Illegible] Deputy.

DEPARTMENT OF THE INTERIOR,

COMMISSION TO THE FIVE CIVILIZED TRIBES.

In the matter of the application of John Billey, et al., for identification as Mississippi Choctaws, M.C.R. 1999.

------D E C I S I O N ------

It appears from the record herein that application for identification as Mississippi Choctaws was made to this Commission on May 2, 1901, by John Billey for himself, his wife Eliza, his two minor step-children Simon Bob and Jim Bob, and his minor child Wicks Billey, under the following provision of the Act of Congress approved June 28, 1898, (30 Stats. 495):

> "Said Commission shall have authority to determine the identity of Choctaw Indians claiming rights in the Choctaw lands under article fourteen of the treaty between the United States and the Choctaw Nation, concluded September twenty-seventh, eighteen hundred and thirty, and to that end may administer oaths, examine witnesses, and perform all other acts necessary thereto and make report to the Secretary of the Interior."

From the evidence submitted in support of said application it appears that all the applicants are full blood Mississippi Choctaw Indians.

Section forty-one of the Act of Congress entitled "An Act to ratify and confirm an agreement with the Choctaw and Chickasaw tribes of Indians, and for other purposes," approved July 1, 1902, (32 Stats. 641), and ratified by the Choctaw and Chickasaw Nations September 25, 1902, provides as follows:

> "The application of no person for identification as a Mississippi Choctaw shall be received by said Commission after six months subsequent to the date of the final ratification of this agreement and in the disposition of such applications all full-blood Mississippi Choctaw Indians and the descendants of any Mississippi Choctaw Indians whether of full or mixed blood who received a patent to land under the said fourteenth article of the said treaty of eighteen hundred and thirty who had not moved to and made bona fide settlement in the Choctaw-Chickasaw country prior to June twenty-eighth, eighteen hundred and ninety-eight, shall be deemed to be Mississippi Choctaws, entitled to benefits under article fourteen of the said treaty of September twenty-seventh, eighteen hundred and thirty, and to identification as such by said Commission, but this direction or provision shall be deemed to be only a rule of evidence and shall not be invoked by or operate to the advantage of any applicant who is not a Mississippi Choctaw of a full blood, or who is not the descendant of a Mississippi Choctaw who received a patent to land under said treaty, or who is otherwise barred from the right of citizenship in the Choctaw Nation, all of said Mississippi Choctaws so enrolled by said Commission shall be upon a separate roll."

It further appears from the record herein that John Billey, the principal applicant, died about the 7th of October, 1901.

It is, therefore, the opinion of this Commission that Eliza Billey, Simon Bob, Jim Bob and Wicks Billey should be identified as Mississippi Choctaws, and it is so ordered.

COMMISSION TO THE FIVE CIVILIZED TRIBES.

Tams Bixby
Acting Chairman.

T.B. Needles
Commissioner.

C. R. Breckinridge
Commissioner.

Muskogee, Indian Territory.
FEB 14 1903

M.C.R. 1999.

COPY.

Muskogee, Indian Territory, February 21, 1903.

Mansfield, McMurray & Cornish,
Attorneys for the Choctaw and Chickasaw Nations,
South McAlester, Indian Territory.

Gentlemen:

Enclosed herewith you will find a copy of the decision of the Commission rendered February 14, 1903, identifying Eliza Billey, her minor step-children, Simon Bob and Jim Bob, and her minor child, Wicks Billey, as Mississippi Choctaw Indians under the provisions of the forty-first section of the Act of Congress approved July 1, 1902 (32 Stats. 641).

You are hereby advised that you will be allowed fifteen days from the date hereof, in which to file with this Commission such protest as you desire to make against the action of the Commission in identifying the said Eliza Billey, her step children and child as Mississippi Choctaws, and make satisfactory proof of service of said protest upon the applicants herein.

If you fail to file such protest within the time allowed, the names of the applicants herein will be placed upon the schedule of duly identified Mississippi Choctaws now being prepared by this Commission.

Respectfully,

(SIGNED). *Tams Bixby*

Chairman.

Registered.
Enc. M.C.R. 1999.

M.C.R. 1999.

COPY.

Muskogee, Indian Territory, March 11, 1903.

Eliza Billey,

Tucker, Mississippi.

Dear Madam:

Enclosed herewith you will find a copy of the decision of the Commission to the Five Civilized Tribes, rendered February 14, 1903, identifying yourself and your three minor children, Simon and Jim Bob and Wicks Billey, as Mississippi Choctaw Indians under the provisions of Section 41 of the Act of Congress approved July 1, 1902, (32 Stats. 641).

If you remove to the Choctaw-Chickasaw country, Indian Territory, before August 14, 1903, you will have six months from that date, or until February 14, 1904, within which to make proof of such removal and settlement at the office of the Commission at Atoka, Choctaw Nation, or Tishomingo, Chickasaw Nation.

Respectfully,

(SIGNED). *Tams Bixby*

Chairman.

Registered.

Enc. 1999.

MCR 1999

Muskogee, Indian Territory, May 23, 1903.

Commissioner in Charge,

Chickasaw Land Office,

Tishomingo, Indian Territory.

Dear Sir:

You are hereby advised that the following notations have this day been made upon Mississippi Choctaw card No. 14:

SETTLEMENT ADDRESS: "Calloway, Ind. Ter."

DATE OF PROOF OF SETTLEMENT: "May 11, 1903."

You are requested to make like notation upon the duplicate card in your possession in accordance with the above information.

Respectfully,

Chairman.

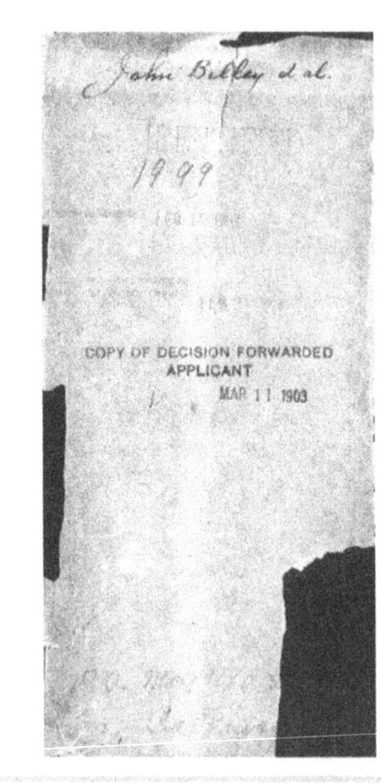
John Billey et al.

1999

COPY OF DECISION FORWARDED
APPLICANT
MAR 11 1903

No. 1019

For Identification as a Mississippi Choctaw.

Date MAY 2 1901

Name John Billey

Age 53 Blood full

Post Office, Tucker, Miss.

Father: Billy (dead)
Ook-a-la-haiyne-lubbee

Mother: Betsey Billy (dead)
Tun-a-yonah

Claims through both parents.

Wife Eliza Billey (full) 33

Father Jim Polk (dead)

Mother dont know "

Children:

Simon Bob (full) 18

Jim " (") 10

Wicks Billy 6

Father Willis Bob (full) L

Mother Eliza Billy " L.

(See Miss. Choc. Card Field No 1×3.

Testimony of 1/30/99) (Claims for himself, his wife, and 3 children)

Stenographer

H.C. Rateen

CARD NO. 15 - Choctaw MCR 2286 - Morris Soloman

DEPARTMENT OF THE INTERIOR.

COMMISSION TO THE FIVE CIVILIZED TRIBES.

The within record is in the matter of
the application of Morris Soloman, et al., for identification as Mississippi Choctaws,
M.C.R. 2286.

DEPARTMENT OF THE INTERIOR.

COMMISSION TO THE FIVE CIVILIZED TRIBES.

In the matter of the application of Morris,[sic] Soloman, et al., for identification as Mississippi Choctaws, M.C.R. 2286.

I N D E X

Department of the Interior,
Commission to the Five Civilized Tribes,
Decatur, Mississippi, May 15, 1901.

In the matter of the application of Morris Soloman, for the identification of himself and his three children and one step child as Mississippi Choctaws.

Morris Soloman, having been first duly sworn, upon his oath states, as follows: (Indian McDonald, Official Interpreter.)

Examination by the Commission.

Q What is your name? A Morris Soloman.
Q What is your age? A Forty, years old.
Q What is your post office address? A Decatur, Mississippi.
Q How long have you lived in this County? A All my life.
Q Born here? A Yes.
Q What is your father's name? A Soloman.
Q Is he a full blood? A Yes.
Q Is he living? A Living.
Q What is your mother's name? A Eliza.
Q Is she a full blood? A Yes.
Q Is she living? A No sir.
Q Are you a full blood? A Yes sir.
Q Do you claim your Choctaw blood through both your father and mother?
A Yes sir.
Q What was your wife's name? A Mary.
Q Is she dead? A Yes.
Q Was she a full blood? A Yes.
Q Have you any children you want to make application for? A Three children and one step-child.
Q What is the name of your oldest child[sic] A Willie.
Q How old is Willie? A 18.
Q What is the next? A Minnie.
Q How old? A 16.
Q And the next? A Nora.
Q How old? A 6.
Q Now, is Mary the mother of Willie, Minnie and Nora? A Yes, the two oldest ones are different woman's.
Q What woman? A She's named Mary too.
Q Was she a full blood Choctaw? A Yes.
Q Is this Mary, the mother of Nora? A Yes sir.
Q Are these children all yours? A Yes.
Q You have a step child? A Yes.
Q What is her name? A Fannie.
Q Is that Fannie Soloman? A Yes.
Q Is Mary the mother of Fannie? A Yes.
Q And you are the step-father? A Yes.
Q How old is Fannie? A 8 years old.
Q What is the name of the father of Fannie? A Ellis Davis.
Q Is he a full blood? A Yes sir.
Q Is he living? A No sir.
Q Have your parents, or your wife's parents, through whom you claim your rights to identification as Mississippi Choctaws, ever been recognized in any manner or enrolled as members of the Choctaw tribe of Indians by the Choctaw tribal authorities or the United States authorities? A No sir.

Q Has the father of Fannie Soloman, your step-daughter, ever been recognized in any manner or enrolled as a member of the Choctaw tribe of Indians by the Choctaw tribal authorities or by the authorities of the United States? A I don't know.
Q Were you married under a license or according to the Choctaw custom?
A Choctaw custom.
Q Is your name, the name of your wife, any of your childrem[sic], or your step-child on any of the tribal rolls of the Choctaw Nation in Indian Territory??[sic] A No sir.
Q Have you ever made application to the Choctaw tribal authorities in Indian Territory for the enrollment of yourself, your wife, or these children as members of the Choctaw tribe? A No.
Q Did you, or any one for you, or for your wife, or these children, make application to the Commission to the Five Civilized Tribes for citizenship in the Choctaw Nation under the Act of Congress of June 10, 1896? A No.
[sic] Have you ever been admitted to citizenship in the Choctaw Nation or has your wife or these children for whom you make application, by either the Choctaw tribal authorities, the Commission to the Five Civilized Tribes, or by the United States Court in Indian Territory? A I don't know.
Q Have you ever made application before this time to either the Choctaw tribal authorities, for yourself, your wife, and children, including this step-child, or to the authorities of the United States to be admitted or enrolled as citizens of the Choctaw Nation? A Yes, I made application two years ago.

> The records of the Commission show that on February 8, 1899, this applicant appeared before the Commission at Decatur, Mississippi, and made application for the identification of himself, his wife, Mary and his children, Nora, Jim, Minnie and Willie Soloman, and also, his step-child, Fannie Soloman, as Mississippi Choctaws, their names appearing upon Mississippi Choctaw Card, Field Number 468; also, upon page 99 of the Schedule of Mississippi Choctaws which accompanied the report of March 10, 1899, of the Commission to the Five Civilized Tribes to the Secretary of the Interior, as to the identity of Choctaw Indians residing in Mississippi, claiming rights in the Choctaw lands under the provisions of the Fourteenth Article of the Treaty of Dancing Rabbit Creek, being Numbers 1704, 1705, 1706, 1707, 1708, 1709 and 1710, respectively, thereon.

Q Except the application you made two years ago, this is the first application you have made? A Yes.
Q Is it now your purpose to make application for identification as Mississippi Choctaws for yourself, your wife, your children and this step-child? A Yes.
Q Do you claim your rights as beneficiaries under the provisions of Article Fourteen of the Treaty of 1830? A Yes sir.
Q Have you, your wife, children or step-child ever received any benefits as Choctaw Indians A I don't know.
Q Have any of your ancestors, any of your wife's ancestors or the ancestors of your step-child ever received any benefits as Choctaw Indians? A I don't know.
Q Do you know the names of your ancestors, or your wife's ancestors or the ancestors of your step-child who were living in the old Choctaw Nation in Mississippi

in 1830, when the Treaty of Dancing Rabbit Creek was made between the United States and the Choctaw tribe of Indians? A I don't know.
Q Have you any evidence showinf[sic] that any of these ancestors were recognized members of the Choctaw tribe of Indians in 1830? A No.
Q Did any of your ancestors, any of your wife's ancestors or any of the ancestors of this step-child remove from the old Choctaw Nation in Mississippi and Alabama to the present Choctaw Nation in Indian Territory at the time of the removal of the main part of the Choctaw tribe of Indians between the years 1833 and 1838? A I don't know.
Q Did any of your ancestors, your wife's ancestors or the ancestors of your step-child, signify to the United States Indian Agent i Mississippi, within six months after the ratification of the Treaty of 1830, their intention to stay in Mississippi and become citizens of the United States? A I don't know.
Q Did any or your ancestors or any of your wife's ancestors or this child's ancestors ever claim or receive any land in Mississippi under article 14th of the Treaty of 1830? A I don't know.
Q Are there any additional statements you desire to make in support of your application? A No.
Q Have you any documentary evidence, affidavits of any description, copies of records, deeds or patents, or any other proper papers showing that any of your ancestors, your wife's ancestors or this child's ancestors were in 1830 recognized members of the Choctaw tribe of Indians, or that any of them ever complied or attempted to comply with the provisions of the Fourteenth Article of the Treaty of Dancing Rabbit Creek, or ever received any benefits under that Article of that treaty? A No.

> (This applicant appears to be a full blood Choctaw Indian. He speaks the Choctaw language, but does not speak the English language, his examination having been through a sworn Choctaw interpreter.)

The decision of the Commission as to the application you make for the identification of yourself, your wife and these children as Mississippi Choctaws will be determined at the earliest possible date, and a report of same mdae to the Secretary of the Interior, conformable to the provisions of the Twenty First Section of the Act of Congress of June 28, 1898, and a copy of the same will be mailed to you to your post office address as given in your testimony.

R.S Streit

Subscribed and sworn to before me at Meridian, Mississippi, this 21st day of June, 1901.

J P McKee Jr
Notary Public.

DEPARTMENT OF THE INTERIOR

COMMISSION TO THE FIVE CIVILIZED TRIBES

In the matter of the application of Morris Soloman, et al., for identification as Mississippi Choctaws, M.C.R. 2286.

------D E C I S I O N -------

It appears from the record herein that application for identification as Mississippi Choctaws was made to this Commission on May 15, 1901, by Morris Soloman for himself, his three minor children, Willie, Minnie and Nora Soloman, and his minor step-child Fannie Soloman, under the following provision of the Act of Congress approved June 28, 1898, (30 Stats. 495):

> "Said Commission shall have authority to determine the identity of Choctaw Indians claiming rights in the Choctaw lands under article fourteen of the treaty between the United States and the Choctaw Nation, concluded September twenty-seventh, eighteen hundred and thirty, and to that end may administer oaths, examine witnesses, and perform all other acts necessary thereto and make report to the Secretary of the Interior."

From the evidence submitted in support of said application it appears that all the applicants are full blood Mississippi Choctaw Indians.

Section forty-one of the Act of Congress entitled "An Act to ratify and confirm an agreement with the Choctaw and Chickasaw tribes of Indians, and for other purposes," approved July 1, 1902, (32 Stats. 641), and ratified by the Choctaw and Chickasaw Nations September 25, 1902, provides as follows:

> "The application of no person for identification as a Mississippi Choctaw shall be received by said Commission after six months subsequent to the date of the final ratification of this agreement and in the disposition of such applications all full-blood Mississippi Choctaw Indians and the descendants of any Mississippi Choctaw Indians whether of full or mixed blood who received a patent to land under the said fourteenth article of the said treaty of eighteen hundred and thirty who had not moved to and made bona fide settlement in the Choctaw-Chickasaw country prior to June twenty-eighth, eighteen hundred and ninety-eight, shall be deemed to be Mississippi Choctaws, entitled to benefits under article fourteen of the said treaty of September twenty-seventh, eighteen hundred and thirty, and to identification as such by said Commission, but this direction or

provision shall be deemed to be only a rule of evidence and shall not be invoked by or operate to the advantage of any applicant who is not a Mississippi Choctaw of a full blood, or who is not the descendant of a Mississippi Choctaw who received a patent to land under said treaty, or who is otherwise barred from the right of citizenship in the Choctaw Nation, all of said Mississippi Choctaws so enrolled by said Commission shall be upon a separate roll."

It is, therefore, the opinion of this Commission that Morris Soloman, Willie Soloman, Minnie Soloman, Nora Soloman and Fannie Soloman should be identified as Mississippi Choctaws, and it is so ordered.

COMMISSION TO THE FIVE CIVILIZED TRIBES.

Tams Bixby
Acting Chairman.

T.B. Needles
Commissioner.

C. R. Breckinridge
Commissioner.

Muskogee, Indian Territory.
FEB 14 1903

M.C.R. 2286.

COPY.

Muskogee, Indian Territory, February 21, 1903.

Mansfield, McMurray & Cornish,
Attorneys for the Choctaw and Chickasaw Nations,
South McAlester, Indian Territory.

Gentlemen:

Enclosed herewith you will find a copy of the decision of the Commission rendered February 14, 1903, identifying Morris Soloman and minor children Willie Soloman, Minnie Soloman, Nora Soloman, and Fannie Soloman as Mississippi Choctaw Indians under the provisions of the forty-first section of the Act of Congress approved July 1, 1902 (32 Stats. 641).

You are hereby advised that you will be allowed fifteen days from the date hereof, in which to file with this Commission such protest as you desire to make against the action of the Commission in identifying the said Morris Soloman and children as Mississippi Choctaws, and make satisfactory proof of service of said protest upon the applicants herein.

If you fail to file such protest within the time allowed, the names of the applicants herein will be placed upon the schedule of duly identified Mississippi Choctaws now being prepared by this Commission.

Respectfully,
(SIGNED).
Tams Bixby
Chairman.

Registered.
Enc. H.M.V. 29

M.C.R. 2286.

COPY.

Muskogee, Indian Territory, March 11, 1903.

Morris Soloman,
Remailed to Willie Soloman,
Decatur, Mississippi. *July 23/03*
Dear Sir:

Enclosed herewith you will find a copy of the decision of the Commission to the Five Civilized Tribes, rendered February 14, 1903, identifying yourself and your three minor children, Willie, Minnie and Nora Soloman, and your step-child, Fannie Soloman, as Mississippi Choctaw Indians under the provisions of Section 41 of the Act of Congress approved July 1, 1902, (32 Stats. 641).

If you remove to the Choctaw-Chickasaw country, Indian Territory, before August 14, 1903, you will have six months from that date, or until February 14, 1904, within which to make proof of such removal and settlement at the office of the Commission at Atoka, Choctaw Nation, or Tishomingo, Chickasaw Nation.

Respectfully,
(SIGNED).
Tams Bixby
Chairman.

Registered.
Enc. 2286.

#651

No. 2286

For Identification as a Mississippi Choctaw.

Date MAY 15 1901

Name Morris Solomon (Soloman)

Age 40 Blood full

Post Office, Decatur, Miss.

Father: Soloman f.b. d

Mother: Eliza f.b. d

Claims through both parents

wife- Mary f.b. d

See M.C. Card filed No. 468

Children:

Willie — 18

Minnie. 16

Nora — 6

Fannie Soloman 8
(step daughter)
Fannie's father
Ellis Davis, f.b. – d
applies for self and children, and step-child Fannie

Stenographer R. S. Streit

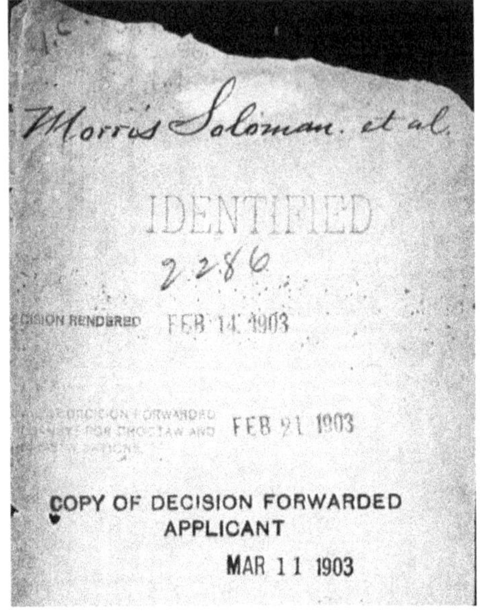

CARD NO. 16 - Choctaw MCR - [Name Unknown]

CARD NO. 17 - Choctaw MCR 2182 - John Thomas

[NOTE: Card No. 17 is in Volume I of this series and on the card the Application No. is incorrect… it should read 2182 instead of 2132.]

DEPARTMENT OF THE INTERIOR,

COMMISSION TO THE FIVE CIVILIZED TRIBES.

In the matter of the application of John Thomas, et al., for identification as Mississippi Choctaws, M.C.R. 2182.

DEPARTMENT OF THE INTERIOR,

COMMISSION TO THE FIVE CIVILIZED TRIBES.

In the matter of the application of John Thomas, et al., for identification as Mississippi Choctaws, M.C.R. 2182.

I N D E X .

DEPARTMENT OF THE INTERIOR.
COMMISSION TO THE FIVE CIVILIZED TRIBES.
MERIDIAN, MISSISSIPPI, MAY 13, 1901.

In the matter of the application of John Thomas for the identification of himself and three minor children as Mississippi Choctaws.

John Thomas, having been first duly sworn, upon his oath testifies as follows, through Isham Johnston, official interpreter:

Examination by the Commission:

Q What is your name? A John Thomas.
Q What is your age? A About fifty.
Q What is your post office address? A Hosey, Jasper County, Mississippi.
Q Have you always lived in Jasper County? A Yes.
Q What is your father's name? A Sadler Tom.
Q Is he living? A No.
Q What is your mother's name? A I don't know; my mother died when I was a little bit of a boy.
Q Was she a full blood? A Yes.
Q Was your father a full blood? A Yes.

Q Are you a full blood? A Yes.
Q You claim your Choctaw blood through both your father and mother?
A Yes.
Q Have your parents through whom you claim your right to identification as a Mississippi Choctaw ever been recognized in any way or enrolled as a member of the Choctaw tribe of Indians by the Choctaw tribal authorities or by the authorities of the United States? A Don't know.
Q Are you married? A No.
Q Did your wife die? A Yes.
Q When did she die? A About three years ago.
Q What was your wife's name? A Mary Thomas.
Q Was she a full blood? A Yes.
Q Give me the names of your children? A Lucy.
Q How old? A Five years old.
Q Next? A Dan.
Q How old is Dan? A Four.
Q Next? A Jim L.
Q How old is Jim L.[sic] A Three years old.
Q Was Mary Thomas the mother of these children? A Yes.
Q And you are the father? A Yes.
Q They live with you at your home? A Yes.
Q When were you married to Mary? A About fifteen years ago.
Q Did you have a license to marry or marriage under Choctaw custom?
A Choctaw custom.
Q Is your name or the names of your children on any of the tribal rolls of the Choctaw Nation in Indian Territory? A No.
Q Did you ever make application for yourself or children to the Choctaw tribal authorities in Indian Territory to be enrolled as a member of that tribe? A No.
Q Did you or any one for you or for your children in 1896 make application to the Commission to the Five Civilized Tribes for citizenship in the Choctaw Nation under the act of Congress of June 10, 1896? A No.
Q Have you or your children ever been admitted to citizenship in the Choctaw Nation by the Choctaw tribal authorities, the Commission to the Five Civilized Tribes or by the United States Court in Indian Territory? A No.
Q Have you ever made application for yourself and your children or has any one made application for you or for your children before this to either the Choctaw tribal authorities or to the authorities of the United States to be admitted or enrolled as citizens of the Choctaw Nation? A No.
Q Is this the first application you have ever made of any kind for yourself and children? A Yes.
Q Is it now your purpose to make application for identification for yourself and children as Mississippi Choctaws? A Yes.
Q Do you claim your right as a beneficiary under the provisions of the fourteenth article of the treaty of 1830? A Yes.
Q Have you ever received any benefits as a Choctaw Indian or your children ever received any? A No.

Q Have any of your ancestors ever received any benefits as Choctaw Indians?
A No.
Q What was the name of your ancestors who lived in the old Choctaw Nation in Mississippi and Alabama and who were acknowledged members of the Choctaw tribe of Indians in 1830 when the treaty of Dancing Rabbit Creek was entered into between the United States government and the Choctaw Indians? A Don't know.
Q Have you any evidence showing that any of your ancestors were recognized members of the Choctaw tribe of Indians in 1830? A No.
Q Did any of them go from Mississippi ot[sic] Alabama to Indian Territory when the other Indians went there in the year[sic] 1833 to 1838? A No.
Q Did any of them go to the Indian Agent within six months after the ratification of the treaty of 1830 and tell him they wanted to stay in Mississippi, take land here and become citizens of the United States? A No.
Q Have any of your ancestors ever received or claimed any land from the government under article fourteen of the treaty of 1830? A No.
Q Are there any additional statements you desire to make in support of this application? A No.
Q Have you any documentary evidence, affidavits, written testimony of any description, copies of records, deeds or patents or any proper papers showing that your ancestors were ever recognized members of the Choctaw tribe of Indians in Mississippi in 1830 or that they ever complied or attempted to comply with the provisions of the fourteenth article of the treaty of 1830 or ever received any benefits thereunder[sic] A No.

This applicant appears to be a full blood Choctaw Indians[sic], having all the characteristics of a member of that tribe. He does not speak the English language; he has no knowledge of any compliance on the part of his ancestors with the provisions of the fourteenth article of the treaty of 1830.

The decision of the Commission as to the application which you make at this time for the identification of yourself and your minor children as Mississippi Choctaws will be determined at the earliest possible date and a report of the same made to the Secretary of the Interior conformable to the provisions of the twenty first section of the act of Congress of June 28, 1898, and a copy of the decision will be mailed to you at your post office address as given in your testimony at this time.

H.C. Risteen, having been first duly sworn, upon his oath states: That as stenographer to the Commission to the Five Civilized Tribes he reported in full all proceedings had in the above entitled cause on the 13th day of May, 1901, and that the above and foregoing is a full, true and correct transcript of his stenographic notes of said proceedings on said date.

H.C. Risteen

Subscribed and sworn to before me at Meridian, Mississippi, this 4th day of June 1901.

J P McKee Jr. Notary Public.

DEPARTMENT OF THE INTERIOR

COMMISSION TO THE FIVE CIVILIZED TRIBES

In the matter of the application of John Thomas, et al., for identification as Mississippi Choctaws, M.C.R. 2182.

--:D E C I S I O N:--

It appears from the record herein that application for identification as Mississippi Choctaws was made to this Commission on May 13, 1901, by John Thomas for himself, and his three minor children, Lucy, Dan and Jim L. Thomas, under the following provision of the act of Congress approved June 28, 1898, (30 Stats. 495):

> "Said Commission shall have authority to determine the identity of Choctaw Indians claiming rights in the Choctaw lands under article fourteen of the treaty between the United States and the Choctaw Nation, concluded September twenty-seventh, eighteen hundred and thirty, and to that end may administer oaths, examine witnesses, and perform all other acts necessary thereto and make report to the Secretary of the Interior."

From the evidence submitted in support of said application it appears that all the applicants are full-blood Mississippi Choctaw Indians.

Section forty-one of the Act of Congress entitled "An Act To ratify and confirm an agreement with the Choctaw and Chickasaw tribes of Indians, and for other purposes," approved July 1, 1902, (32 Stats. 641), and ratified by the Choctaw and Chickasaw Nations September 25, 1902, provides as follows:

> "The application of no person for identification as a Mississippi Choctaw shall be received by said Commission after six months subsequent to the date of the final ratification of this agreement and in the disposition of such applications all full-blood Mississippi Choctaw Indians and the descendants of any Mississippi Choctaw Indians whether of full or mixed blood who received a patent to land under the said fourteenth article of the said treaty of eighteen hundred and thirty who had not moved to and made bona fide settlement in the Choctaw-Chickasaw country prior to June twenty-eighth, eighteen hundred and ninety-eight, shall be deemed to be Mississippi Choctaws, entitled to benefits under article fourteen of the said treaty of September twenty-seventh, eighteen hundred and thirty, and

to identification as such by said Commission, but this direction or provision shall be deemed to be only a rule of evidence and shall not be invoked by or operate to the advantage of any applicant who is not a Mississippi Choctaw of a full blood, or who is not the descendant of a Mississippi Choctaw who received a patent to land under said treaty, or who is otherwise barred from the right of citizenship in the Choctaw Nation, all of said Mississippi Choctaws so enrolled by said Commission shall be upon a separate roll."

It is, therefore, the opinion of this Commission that John Thomas, Lucy Thomas, Dan Thomas and Jim L. Thomas should be identified as Mississippi Choctaws, and it is so ordered.

COMMISSION TO THE FIVE CIVILIZED TRIBES.

Tams Bixby
Acting Chairman.

T.B. Needles
Commissioner.

Muskogee, Indian Territory.
FEB 14 1903

C. R. Breckinridge
Commissioner.

COPY. M.C.R. 2182

Muskogee, Indian Territory, February 21, 1903.

Mansfield, McMurray & Cornish,
Attorneys for the Choctaw and Chickasaw Nations,
South McAlester, Indian Territory.

Gentlemen:

Enclosed herewith you will find a copy of the decision of the Commission rendered February 14, 1903, identifying John Thomas and minor children Lucy Thomas, Dan Thomas and Jim L. Thomas as Mississippi Choctaw Indians under the provisions of the forty-first section of the Act of Congress approved July 1, 1902 (32 Stats. 641).

You are hereby advised that you will be allowed fifteen days from the date hereof, in which to file with this Commission such protest as you desire to make against the action of the Commission in identifying the said John Thomas and children as Mississippi Choctaws, and make satisfactory proof of service of said protest upon the applicants herein.

If you fail to file such protest within the time allowed, the names of the applicants herein will be placed upon the schedule of duly identified Mississippi Choctaws now being prepared by this Commission.

Respectfully,

(SIGNED). *Tams Bixby*

Registered. Acting Chairman.
Enc. H.M.V. 25

M.C.R. 2182.

COPY.

Muskogee, Indian Territory, March 11, 1903.

John Thomas, *Remailed to Ardmore I.T.*

Hosey, Mississippi. *5/4/03*

Dear Sir:

Enclosed herewith you will find a copy of the decision of the Commission to the Five Civilized Tribes, rendered February 14, 1903, identifying yourself and your three minor children, Lucy, Dan and Jim L. Thomas, as Mississippi Choctaw Indians under the provisions of Section 41 of the Act of Congress approved July 1, 1902, (32 Stats. 641).

If you remove to the Choctaw-Chickasaw country, Indian Territory, before August 14, 1903, you will have six months from that date, or until February 14, 1904, within which to make proof of such removal and settlement at the office of the Commission at Atoka, Choctaw Nation, or Tishomingo, Chickasaw Nation.

Respectfully,

(SIGNED). *Tams Bixby*

Registered. Chairman.

Enc. 2182

M C R 2182

Muskogee, Indian Territory, April 3, 1903.

J. G. Ralls,

Attorney at Law,

Atoka, Indian Territory.

Dear Sir:

Receipt is hereby acknowledged of your letter of the 21st ultimo, enclosing the affidavit of the mother, Celia Thomas, and that of the midwife, Mary Jane Stout, relative to the birth of Jack Thomas, infant son of John and Celia Thomas, August 25, 1902.

The Commission is unable to identify the mother of this child as an applicant for identification as a Mississippi Choctaw, and you are requested to state her maiden name, the names of her parents, the time and place application was made for her identification, and such other information as will enable the Commission to identify her upon its records.

Upon receipt of the information requested herein, the application for the identification of Jack Thomas as a Mississippi Choctaw will receive further consideration.

Respectfully,

Commissioner in Charge.

Ardmore, I. T. April 18, 1903.

To the Commission to the Five Civilized Tribes,

Muskogee, Indian Territory.

Will you please deliver to J. G. Ralls, of Atoka, Indian Territory an copies of the records in my case that under the rule of law, the Commission may give out to Attorneys, as I have employed him to assist me in this case.

John Thomas (2182)

M C R 2182
M C R 2231

Muskogee, Indian Territory, April 20, 1903.

Bryant S. Harrington, P. M.,

Hosey, Mississippi.

Dear Sir:

Receipt is hereby acknowledged of your letter of the 13th instant, wherein you state "The letter registered here to this office from your P O March 14 Reg No. 4557 and 4558 addressed to Will Johnson and one to John Thomas are here in this P O unclaimed. What disposition shall I make of them.

In reply you are informed that you may return said letters to this Commission.

Respectfully,

Chairman.

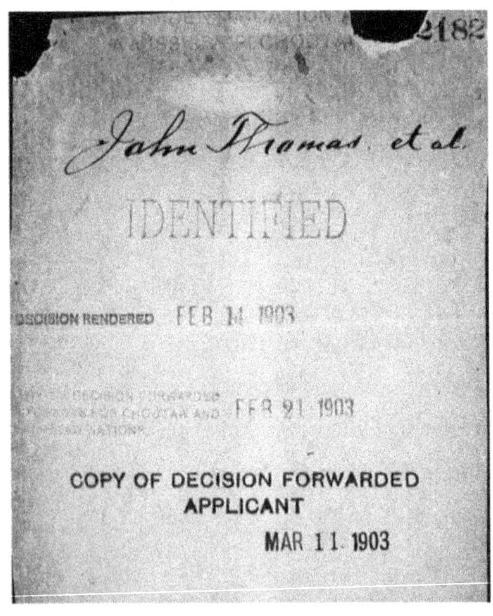

2182

John Thomas, et al.

IDENTIFIED

DECISION RENDERED FEB 14 1903

FEB 21 1903

COPY OF DECISION FORWARDED
APPLICANT
MAR 11 1903

579

No.

For Identification as a Mississippi Choctaw.

Date MAY 13 1901

Name John Thomas.

Age 50 - Blood full.

Post Office Hoxey, Miss.

Father: Sadler Tom. f.b. d

Mother: don't know. f.b. d

Claims through both parents -

wife - Mary Thomas. f.b. d

Children:

Lucy - 5 -

Dan 4 -

Jim L. 3

Claims for self and children.

Stenographer H.C. Rushton

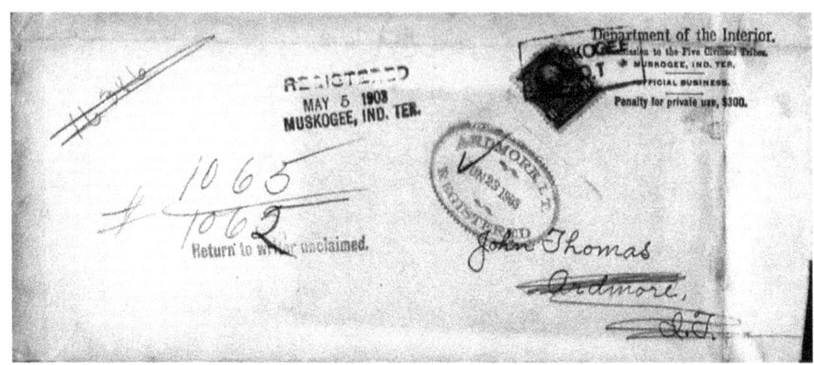

CARD NO. 18 - Choctaw MCR 2072 - Tom Wallace

DEPARTMENT OF THE INTERIOR

COMMISSION TO THE FIVE CIVILIZED TRIBES

In the matter of the application of Tom Wallace for identification as a Mississippi Choctaw, M. C. R. 2072.

I N D E X

DEPARTMENT OF THE INTERIOR.
COMMISSION TO THE FIVE CIVILIZED TRIBES.
Philadelphia, Mississippi, May 4, 1901.

In the matter of the application of Tom Wallace for identification as a Mississippi Choctaw.

Tom Wallace, having been first duly sworn, upon his oath testifies as follows:

Examination by the Commission:

Q What is your name? A Tom Wallace.
Q How old are you? A Twenty one.
Q What is your post office address? A Cushtusa, Mississippi.
Q Were you born and raised in Mississippi? A Yes.
Q Always lived in Mississippi? A Yes.
Q What is your father's name? A Wallace Emi-yah-tubbee.
Q Is he a full blood Choctaw? A Yes.
Q Is your father living? A Yes.
Q What is your mother's name? A Mamcy[sic].
Q Is she living? A Yes.
Q Is your mother a full blood Choctaw? A Yes.
Q You claim to be a full blood, do you? A Yes.
Q You claim through both your parents? A Yes.
Q Have either of your parents through whom you claim the right to identification as a Mississippi Choctaw ever been recognized in any manner or enrolled as members of the Choctaw tribe of Indians by the Choctaw tribal authorities or the United States authorities? A No.
Q Are you married? A No.
Q You claim for yourself alone? A Yes.
Q Is your name on any of the tribal rolls of the Choctaw Nation in Indian Territory? A No.
Q Have you ever made application to the Choctaw tribal authorities in Indian Territory to be enrolled as a member of that tribe? A No.
Q Did you or any one for you in 1896 under the act of Congress of June 10, 1896, make application to the Commission to the Five Civilized Tribes for citizenship in the Choctaw Nation? A No.
Q Have you ever been admitted to citizenship in the Choctaw Nation by the Choctaw tribal authorities, the Dawes Commission or by the United States Court in Indian Territory? A No.
Q Have you ever made application or has application ever been made for you befeore[sic] this time to either the Choctaw tribal authorities or to the authorities of the United States to be admitted or enrolled as a citizen of the Choctaw Nation?

A My father made application two years ago.

The records of the Commission show that Wallace Emi-yah-tubbee appeared before the Commission at Philadelphia, Mississippi, January 31, 1899, and there made application for the identification of this applicant as a Mississippi Choctaw, his name appearing upon Mississippi Choctaw Card, Field No. 271, also upon page 70 of the schedule of Mississippi Choctaws which accompanied the report of March 10, 1899, of the Commission to the Five Civilized Tribes to the Secretary of the Interior as to the identity of Choctaw Indians, residing in Mississippi claiming rights in the Choctaw lands under the provisions of the fourteenth article of the treaty of Dancing Rabbit Creek, being Roll No. 920 thereon.

Q You now want to make application for identification as a Mississippi Choctaw?
A Yes.
Q At the time your father made application for you two years ago, he gave your name in as Tom Emi-yah-tubbee, you now want to be known as Tom Wallace, do you? A Yes.
Q Do you claim your right to identification as a beneficiary under the provisions of the fourteenth article of the treaty of 1830? A Yes[sic]
Q Have you ever received any benefits as a Choctaw Indian? A No.
Q Have any of your ancestors ever received any benefits as Choctaw Indians?
A No.
Q What was the name of your ancestor or ancestors who were residents of the old Choctaw Nation in Mississippi and Alabama and who were acknowledged members of the Choctaw tribe of Indians in 1830 when the treaty of Dancing Rabbit Creek was entered into between the United States government and the Choctaw tribe of Indians?
A Don't know.
Q Have you any evidence showing that such ancestors were recognized members of the Choctaw tribe of Indians in 1830? A No.
Q Did these ancestors, if Choctaw Indians, remove from the territory occupies by the Choctaw Nation in Mississippi and Alabama to the present Choctaw Nation in Indian Territory at the time of the removal of the other members of the Choctaw tribe of Indians between the years 1833 and 1838? A Don't know.
Q Did any of your ancestors within six months after the ratification of the treaty of 1830 signify to the United States Indian Agent of the Choctaw Indians in Mississippi their intention to remain in Mississippi and become citizens of the United States?
A Don't know.
Q Have any of your ancestors ever claimed or received any land in Mississippi as beneficiaries under article fourteen of the treaty of 1830? A No.
Q Are there any additional statements you want to make in support of your application? A No.
Q Have you any documentary evidence, affidavits, written testimony of any description, copies of records[sic] deeds or patents, or other proper papers showing that your ancestors were recognized members of the Choctaw tribe of Indians in 1830 when the treaty of Dancing Rabbit Creek was made, or that any of them complied or

attempted to comply with the provisions of the fourteenth article of that treaty or ever received any benefits thereunder? A No.

This applicant has every appearance and characteristic of a full blood Choctaw Indian. He speaks the Choctaw language, and also has considerable knowledge of the English language, his examination having been conducted in English.

The decision of the Commission as to the application made by you at this time for identification as a Mississippi Choctaw will be determined at the earliest possible date and a report of the same made to the Secretary of the Interior, conformable to the provisions of the twenty first section of the act of Congress of June 28, 1898, and a copy of the same will be mailed to you at your post office address as given in your testimony.

H.C. Risteen, having been first duly sworn, upon his oath states: That as stenographer to the Commission to the Five Civilized Tribes he reported in full all proceedings had in the above entitled cause on the 4th day of May, 1901, and that the above and foregoing is a full, true and correct transcript of his stenographic notes of said proceedings on said date.

H.C. Risteen

Subscribed and sworn to before me at Meridian Mississippi, this 22nd day of May, 1901.

J P McKee Jr
Notary Public.

DEPARTMENT OF THE INTERIOR

COMMISSION TO THE FIVE CIVILIZED TRIBES

In the matter of the application of Tom Wallace
for identification as a Mississippi Choctaw.
M. C. R. 2072.

D E C I S I O N .

It appears from the record herein that application for identification as a Mississippi Choctaw was made to this Commission on May 4, 1901, by Tom Wallace for himself, under the following provision of the act of Congress approved June 28, 1898, (30 Stats. 495):

> "Said Commission shall have authority to determine the identity of Choctaw Indians claiming rights in the Choctaw lands under article fourteen of the treaty between the United States and the Choctaw Nation, concluded September twenty-seventh, eighteen hundred and thirty, and to that end may administer oaths, examine witnesses, and perform all other acts necessary thereto and make report to the Secretary of the Interior."

From the evidence submitted in support of said application it appears that the applicant is a full-blood Mississippi Choctaw.

Section forty-one of the act of Congress entitled "An Act to ratify and confirm an agreement with the Choctaw and Chickasaw tribes of Indians, and for other purposes," approved July 1, 1902, (32 Stats. 641), and ratified by the Choctaw and Chickasaw Nations September 25, 1902, provides as follows:

> "The application of no person for identification as a Mississippi Choctaw shall be received by said Commission after six months subsequent to the date of the final ratification of this agreement and in the disposition of such applications all full-blood Mississippi Choctaw Indians and the descendants of any Mississippi Choctaw Indians whether of full or mixed blood who received a patent to land under the said fourteenth article of the said treaty of eighteen hundred and thirty who had not moved to and made bona fide settlement in the Choctaw-Chickasaw country prior to June twenty-eighth, eighteen hundred and ninety-eight, shall be deemed to be Mississippi Choctaws, entitled to benefits under article fourteen of the said treaty of September twenty-seventh, eighteen hundred and thirty, and to identification as such by said Commission, but this direction or provision shall be deemed to be only a rule of evidence and shall not be invoked by or operate to the advantage of any applicant who is not a Mississippi Choctaw of a full blood, or who is not the descendant of a Mississippi Choctaw who received a patent to land under said treaty, or who is otherwise barred from the right of citizenship in the Choctaw Nation, all of said Mississippi Choctaws so enrolled by said Commission shall be upon a separate roll."

It is, therefore, the opinion of this Commission that Tom Wallace should be identified as a Mississippi Choctaw, and it is so ordered.

COMMISSION TO THE FIVE CIVILIZED TRIBES.

Tams Bixby
Acting Chairman.

T.B. Needles
Commissioner.

Muskogee, Indian Territory.
FEB 14 1903

C. R. Breckinridge
Commissioner.

COPY. M.C.R. 2072

Muskogee, Indian Territory, February 21, 1903.

Mansfield, McMurray & Cornish,
Attorneys for the Choctaw and Chickasaw Nations,
South McAlester, Indian Territory.

Gentlemen:

Enclosed herewith you will find a copy of the decision of the Commission rendered February 14, 1903, identifying Tom Wallace as a Mississippi Choctaw Indian under the provisions of the forty-first section of the Act of Congress approved July 1, 1902 (32 Stats. 641).

You are hereby advised that you will be allowed fifteen days from the date hereof, in which to file with this Commission such protest as you desire to make against the action of the Commission in identifying the said Tom Wallace as a Mississippi Choctaw, and make satisfactory proof of service of said protest upon the applicants herein.

If you fail to file such protest within the time allowed, the names of the applicants herein will be placed upon the schedule of duly identified Mississippi Choctaws now being prepared by this Commission.

Respectfully,
(SIGNED). *Tams Bixby*
Acting Chairman.

Registered.
Enc. H.M.V. 18

M.C.R. 2072.

COPY.

Muskogee, Indian Territory, March 11, 1903.

Tom Wallace,

Cushtusa, Mississippi.

Dear Sir:

Enclosed herewith you will find a copy of the decision of the Commission to the Five Civilized Tribes, rendered February 14, 1903, identifying you as a Mississippi Choctaw Indian under the provisions of Section 41 of the Act of Congress approved July 1, 1902, (32 Stats. 641).

If you remove to the Choctaw-Chickasaw country, Indian Territory, before August 14, 1903, you will have six months from that date, or until February 14, 1904, within which to make proof of such removal and settlement at the office of the Commission at Atoka, Choctaw Nation, or Tishomingo, Chickasaw Nation.

Respectfully,

(SIGNED). *Tams Bixby*

Chairman.

Registered.

Enc. 2072.

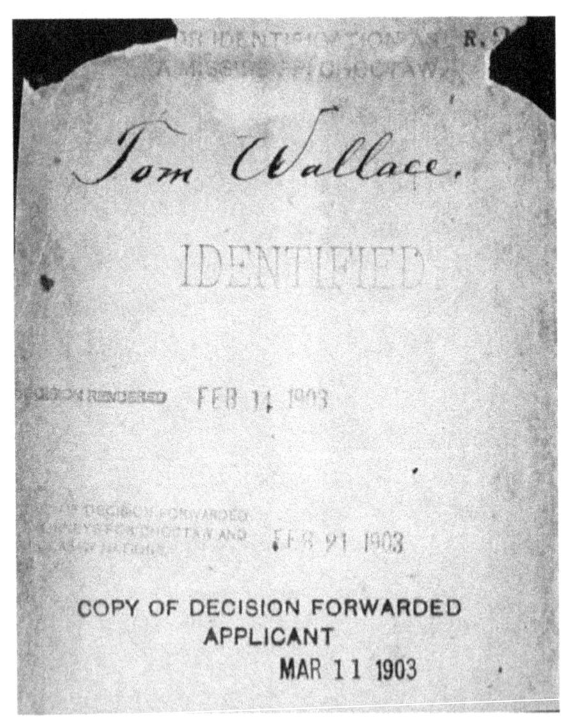
Tom Wallace.

IDENTIFIED

DECISION RENDERED FEB 14 1903

FEB 21 1903

COPY OF DECISION FORWARDED
APPLICANT
MAR 11 1903

472

No. 2072

For Identification as a Mississippi Choctaw.

Date May 4. 1901

Name Tom Wallace

Age 21 Blood full

Post Office. Cuchtusa, Miss.

Father: Wallace Emi-yah-tubbe f.b. l.

Mother: Nancy " f.b. l.

Claims through both parents.

Claims for self alone.

~~Children:~~

See M.C. Card field No 271

Stenographer H.C. Ristine

CARD NO. 19 - Choctaw MCR 2067 - Nancy Emi-Yah-tubbe for Raymond Wilmond

DEPARTMENT OF THE INTERIOR

COMMISSION TO THE FIVE CIVILIZED TRIBES.

The record herein is in the matter of the application for the identification of Raymond Wilmond as a Mississippi Choctaw.

M. C. R. 2067.

DEPARTMENT OF THE INTERIOR.

COMMISSION TO THE FIVE CIVILIZED TRIBES.

In the matter of the application for identification of Raymond Wilmond as a Mississippi Choctaw, M. C. R. 2067.

I N D E X

DEPARTMENT OF THE INTERIOR.
COMMISSION TO THE FIVE CIVILIZED TRIBES.
Philadelphia, Mississippi, May 4, 1901.

In the matter of the application of Nancy Emi-yah-tubbee for the identification of her orphan nephew, Raymond Wilmond, as a Mississippi Choctaw.

Nancy Emi-yahtubbee, having been first duly sworn, upon her oath testifies as follows, through Joe Jimmerson, duly sworn Choctaw interpreter:

Examination by the Commission:

Q What is your name? A Nancy Emi-yah-tubbee.
Q What is your age? A Fifty four.
Q What is your post office address? A Cushtusa, Mississippi.

Q Are you a full blood Choctaw? A Yes.
Q Have you a nephew named Raymond Wilmond? A Yes.
Q Is that nephew living with you? A Yes.
Q What is his post office address? A Cushtusa, Mississippi.
Q How old is Raymond? A Fourteen.
Q What is the name of Raymond Wilmond's father? A Sam Wilmond.
Q Is he living or dead? A Dead.
Q What is the name of his mother? A Rosie.
Q Is Rosie living or dead? A Dead.
Q Were they both full bloods? A Yes.
Q Is Raymond Wilmond a full blood Choctaw? A Yes?[sic]
Q What relation is Raymond Wilmond to you? A Nephew--his father was my brother.
Q Do you know whether his parents, Sam Wilmond or Rosie, ever were recognized in any manner or enrolled by the Choctaw tribal authorities as Choctaw Indians?
A No.
Q Is the name of Raymond Wilmond upon any of the tribal rolls of the Choctaw Nation in Indian Territory? A Don't know.
Q Have you or any one else for him ever made application to the Choctaw tribal authorities for him to be enrolled as a member of the Choctaw tribe of Indians in Indian Territory? A No.
Q Did you or any one else in his behalf in 1896 make application to the Commission to the Five Civilized Tribes for citizenship for him in the Choctaw Nation? A No.
Q Has any one made application for him before this to either the Choctaw tribal authorities or to the authorities of the United States to be admitted or enrolled as a citizen of the Choctaw Nation? Q[sic] My husband made application two years ago.
Q And you make application now because you are his aunt? A Yes.

> The records of the Commission show that on January 31, 1899, Wallace Emi-yah-tubbee appeared before the Commission at Philadelphia, Mississippi, and made application for the identification of Raymond Wilmond as a Mississippi Choctaw, his name appearing upon Mississippi Choctaw Card Field No. 271, also upon page 70 of the schedule of Mississippi Choctaws which accompanied the report of the Commission to the Five Civilized Tribes of March 10, 1899, to the Secretary of the Interior, as to the identity of Choctaw Indians residing in Mississippi claiming rights in the Choctaw lands under the provisions of the fourteenth article of the treaty of Dancing Rabbit Creek, being No. 925 thereon.

Q Is it now your purpose to make application for the identification of Raymond Wilmond as a Mississippi Choctaw? A Yes.
Q Do you claim for him under the fourteenth article of the treaty of 1830? A Yes.
Q Has he ever received any benefits as a Choctaw Indian? A No.
Q Have any of his ancestors ever received any benefits as Choctaw Indians?
A No.
Q Do you know the names of his grandmother and grandfather on his mother's side?
A No.

Q Do you know whether any of his grandparents ever complied in any way with the provisions of article fourteen of the treaty of 1830? A Don't know.
Q Did any of his ancestors within six months after the ratification of the treaty of 1830 tell the United States Indian Agent that they wanted to stay in Mississippi and take land here and didn't want to go to the territory? A Don't know.
Q Did any of them go from Mississippi to Indian Territory when the other Indians went there? A No.
Q Did any of his ancestors ever claim or receive any land in Mississippi as beneficiaries under the fourteenth article of the treaty [sic] 1830? A Don't know.
Q Have you anything further to say in support of this application for your nephew?
A No.
Q Have you any documentary evidence, affidavits, written testimony or any description, copies of records deeds or patents, or any proper papers showing that any of Raymond Wilmonds[sic] ancestors were recognized members of the Choctaw tribe of Indian[sic] in 1830 when the treaty of Dancing Rabbit Creek was entered into between the United States and the Choctaw Indians, or that any of them ever complied or attempted to complt[sic] with the provisions of the fourteenth article of that treaty or ever received any benefits thereunder? A No.

This applicant claims that her nephew, Raymond Wilmond, is a full blood Choctaw, and that he is the son of her own brother. She, herself, has all the characteristics of a full blood Choctaw Indian.

The decision of the Commission as to the application made by you at this time for the identification of your minor orphan nephew Raymond Wilmond as a Mississippi Choctaw will be determined at the earliest possible date and a report of the same made to the Secretary of the Interior conformable to the provisions of the twenty first section of the act of Congress of June 28, 1898, and a copy of the same will be mailed to you at your post office address as given in your testimony.

H.C. Risteen, having been first duly sworn, upon his oath states: That as stenographer to the Commission to the Five Civilized Tribes he reported in full all proceedings had in the above entitled cause on the 4th day of May, 1901, and that the above and foregoing is a full true and correct transcript of his stenographic notes of said proceedings on said date.

H.C. Risteen

Subscribed and sworn to before me at Meridian, Mississippi, this 21st day of May, 1901.

J P McKee Jr
Notary Public.

DEPARTMENT OF THE INTERIOR

COMMISSION TO THE FIVE CIVILIZED TRIBES

In the matter of the application of Raymond Wilmond for identification as a Mississippi Choctaw, M. C. R. 2067.

D E C I S I O N .

It appears from the record herein that application for identification as a Mississippi Choctaw was made to this Commission on May 4, 1901, by Nancy Emi0-yah-tubbee for her minor orphan nephew, Raymond Wilmond, under the following provision of the act of Congress approved June 28, 1898, (30 Stats. 495):

> "Said Commission shall have authority to determine the identity of Choctaw Indians claiming rights in the Choctaw lands under article fourteen of the treaty between the United States and the Choctaw Nation, concluded September twenty-seventh, eighteen hundred and thirty, and to that end may administer oaths, examine witnesses, and perform all other acts necessary thereto and make report to the Secretary of the Interior."

From the evidence submitted in support of said application it appears that the applicant is a full blood Mississippi Choctaw.

Section forty-one of the act of Congress entitled "An Act to ratify and confirm an agreement with the Choctaw and Chickasaw tribes of Indians, and for other purposes," approved July 1, 1902, (32 Stats. 641), and ratified by the Choctaw and Chickasaw Nations September 25, 1902, provides as follows:

> "The application of no person for identification as a Mississippi Choctaw shall be received by said Commission after six months subsequent to the date of the final ratification of this agreement and in the disposition of such applications all full-blood Mississippi Choctaw Indians and the descendants of any Mississippi Choctaw Indians whether of full or mixed blood who received a patent to land under the said fourteenth article of the said treaty of eighteen hundred and thirty who had not moved to and made bona fide settlement in the Choctaw-Chickasaw country prior to June twenty-eighth, eighteen hundred and ninety-eight, shall be deemed to be Mississippi Choctaws, entitled to benefits under article fourteen of the said treaty of September twenty-seventh, eighteen hundred and thirty, and to identification as such by said Commission, but this direction or provision shall be deemed to be only a rule of evidence and shall not be invoked by or operate to the advantage of any applicant who is not a Mississippi Choctaw of a full blood, or who is not the descendant of a Mississippi Choctaw who received a patent to land

under said treaty, or who is otherwise barred from the right of citizenship in the Choctaw Nation, all of said Mississippi Choctaws so enrolled by said Commission shall be upon a separate roll."

It is, therefore, the opinion of this Commission that Raymond Wilmond should be identified as a Mississippi Choctaw, and it is so ordered.

COMMISSION TO THE FIVE CIVILIZED TRIBES.

Tams Bixby
Acting Chairman.

T.B. Needles
Commissioner.

C. R. Breckinridge
Commissioner.

Muskogee, Indian Territory.
FEB 14 1903

COPY. M.C.R. 2067

Muskogee, Indian Territory, February 21, 1903.

Mansfield, McMurray & Cornish,
Attorneys for the Choctaw and Chickasaw Nations,
South McAlester, Indian Territory.

Gentlemen:

Enclosed herewith you will find a copy of the decision of the Commission rendered February 14, 1903, identifying Raymond Wilmond as a Mississippi Choctaw Indian under the provisions of the forty-first section of the Act of Congress approved July 1, 1902 (32 Stats. 641).

You are hereby advised that you will be allowed fifteen days from the date hereof, in which to file with this Commission such protest as you desire to make against the action of the Commission in identifying the said Raymond Wilmond as a Mississippi Choctaw, and make satisfactory proof of service of said protest upon the applicants herein.

If you fail to file such protest within the time allowed, the names of the applicants herein will be placed upon the schedule of duly identified Mississippi Choctaws now being prepared by this Commission.

Respectfully,

(SIGNED). *Tams Bixby*

Registered.
Enc. H.M.V. 16

Acting Chairman.

M.C.R. 2067.

COPY.

Muskogee, Indian Territory, March 11, 1903.

Raymond Wilmond,

Cushtusa, Mississippi.

Dear Sir:

Enclosed herewith you will find a copy of the decision of the Commission to the Five Civilized Tribes, rendered February 14, 1903, identifying you as a Mississippi Choctaw Indian under the provisions of Section 41 of the Act of Congress approved July 1, 1902, (32 Stats. 641).

If you remove to the Choctaw-Chickasaw country, Indian Territory, before August 14, 1903, you will have six months from that date, or until February 14, 1904, within which to make proof of such removal and settlement at the office of the Commission at Atoka, Choctaw Nation, or Tishomingo, Chickasaw Nation.

Respectfully,

(SIGNED). *Tams Bixby*

Registered.

Chairman.

Enc. 2067.

G 47

Muskogee, Indian Territory, January 2, 1906.

Hon. Wm. H. Ketchum, Director,
Bureau of Catholic Indian Missions,
Washington, D. C.

Dear Sir:

Receipt is hereby acknowledged of your letter of December 21, 1905, requesting to be advised the present status of the Mississippi Choctaw applications of Raymond Willman[sic], Neely Wallace and Annie Wallace.

In reply you are informed that on February 14, 1903, the Commission to the Five Civilized Tribes rendered a decision identifying Raymond Wilmond, son of Sam and Rosie Wilmond, now about 19 years of age, as a full blood Mississippi Choctaw, but it does not appear from the records of this office that proof of the removal of said Raymond Wilmond to the Choctaw-Chickasaw country within six months from the date of his identification was submitted at either the Choctaw or Chickasaw land office within one year from February 13, 1903, the date of his identification, as required by the provisions of the 41st section of the Act of Congress approved July 1, 1902 (32 Stats., 641). For this reason no allotment in the name of Raymond Wilmond has up to this time been permitted.

There is on file in this office a petition of Guy P. Cobb and Harry K. Allen, attorneys, of Ardmore, Indian Territory, accompanied by the affidavits of George McMillan, Nancy Emiyahtubbe, Wallace Emiyahtubbe and J. Edgar White, alleging that Wallace and Nancy Emiyahtubbe attempted to submit proof of the removal and settlement of Raymond Wilmond, at the Chickasaw land office, but on account of their inability to speak good English railed to have a record made of such proof. This petition and others in similar cases will be taken up for consideration in the near future.

You are further advised that there are on file in this office applications for the enrollment of Neeley or Nellie Wallace and Annie Wallace, minor children of Jim and Mary Wallace, identified Mississippi Choctaws Nos. 167 an 168 respectively, but said applications have not been disposed of by this office for the reason that the question of whether or not children of Mississippi Choctaws were entitled to be enrolled as citizens by blood of the Choctaw Nation under the provisions of the Act of Congress approved March 3, 1905, was recently submitted to the Secretary of the Interior for an opinion thereon, and no notice of Departmental action in the matter has yet been received.

Respectfully,

Commissioner.

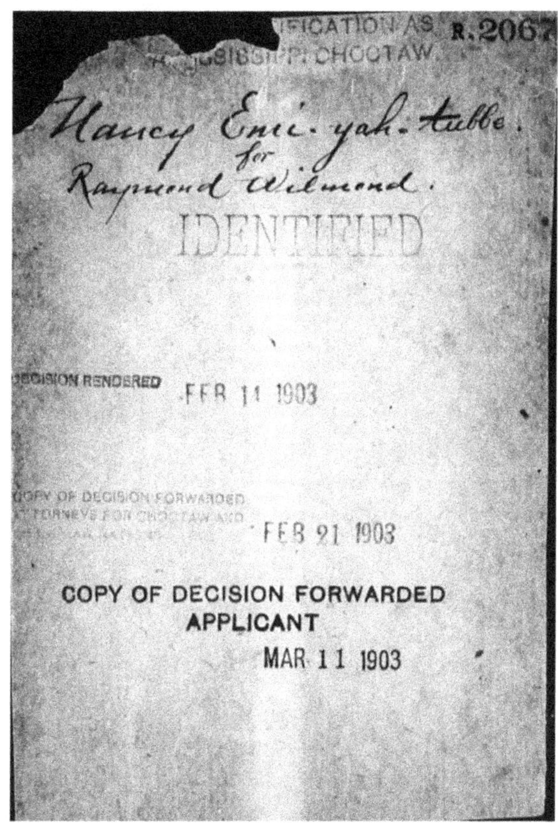

IFICATION AS R.2067
MISSISSIPPI CHOCTAW

Nancy Emi-yah-tubbe.
for
Raymond Wilmond.

IDENTIFIED

DECISION RENDERED FEB 11 1903

COPY OF DECISION FORWARDED
ATTORNEYS FOR CHOCTAW AND
FEB 21 1903

COPY OF DECISION FORWARDED
APPLICANT
MAR 11 1903

467

No. 2067

For Identification as a Mississippi Choctaw.

Date May 4, 1901

Name Nancy Emi-yah-tubbe
for orphan ~~nephew~~ Raymond Wilmond,

Age 14 Blood full –

Post Office, Cushtusa, Miss

Father: of Raymond Wilmond
Sam Wilmond f.b. d

Mother: Rosie " f.b. d

Claims through both his parents

Raymond Wilmonds age is 14.

Children:

Claims for her nephew.
Raymond Wilmond

See M.C.C. filed No. 271 –

Stenographer H.C. Rinne

CARD NO. 20 - Choctaw MCR 1612 - Albert James

[NOTE: Card No. 20 is in Volume I of this series and on the card the Application No. is incorrect... it should read 1612 instead of 1602.]

DEPARTMENT OF THE INTERIOR.

COMMISSION TO THE FIVE CIVILIZED TRIBES.

The record herein is in the matter of the application of

Albert James for identification as a Mississippi Choctaw

- M.C.R. 1612

DEPARTMENT OF THE INTERIOR,
COMMISSION TO THE FIVE CIVILIZED TRIBES,
Meridian, Mississippi, April 3, 1901.

In the Matter of the Application of Albert James for Identification as a Mississippi Choctaw.

Albert James being first duly sworn, testified as follows:
Examination by the Commission:
Q What is your name A Albert James.
Q What is your age? A 29 years.
Q What is your postoffice address? A Stringer, Mississippi.
Q How long have you lived in Mississippi? A Always.
Q Born here? A Yes sir.
Q Never lived anywhere else? A No sir.
Q Have you ever been out of the state? A No sir.
Q What is your father's name? A Doctor James.
Q Is your father living? A No sir.
Q What is your mother's name? A Sophie James.
Q Is your mother living? A No sir.
Q Were your mother and father both full blood Choctaw Indians? A Yes sir
Q They always lived in Mississippi, did they? A Yes sir.
Q Is your name on any of the tribal rolls of the Choctaw Nation in Indian Territory?
A No sir.
Q Did you ever make application to the Choctaw tribal authorities in Indian Territory for citizenship in the Choctaw nation[sic]? A Yes.
Q Where? A At Decatur, Mississippi.
Q That was not the Choctaw authorities; the Choctaws in the Indian Territory have their own government; the time you made your application, that was made to the United States; we are talking about Indian Territory. A No sir.

Q Five years ago the Commission had authority to hear and determine applications of persons for citizenship in the Choctaw nation under the act of Congress of June 10, 1896, and at that time there was a lot of Indians here in Mississippi who made application to the Commission for citizenship in the Choctaw nation; did you make application then? A Yes sir.
Q These Indians made this application with an Indian named Jack Amos down here; did you ever hear of him? A No sir.
Q Have you ever been admitted to citizenship in the Choctaw nation by the commission[sic] to the Five Civilized Tribes, the Choctaw tribal authorities or the United States court in Indian Territory? A No sir.
Q Have you ever received any benefits as a member of the Choctaw tribe in Indian Territory? A No sir.
Q You are making application now for identification as a Mississippi Choctaw? Is that right? A Yes sir.
Q Have you ever made such application before this? A Yes.
Q Where? A At Decatur.
Q Did you make it yourself? A No.
Q Who made it? A My brother Wash James.

The applicant is the identical person for whom an application was made by Wash James, his brother, for identification as a Mississippi Choctaw at Decatur, Mississippi, February 7, 1899. The application made at that time was for Albert, Crickett and their three children. From testimony taken at this appointment of the Commission it develops that Albert and Crickett James have separated and do not live together and the application which Albert James now makes is for the identification of himself alone. His name appears upon Mississippi Choctaw card No. 406, and upon the schedule annexed to the Commission's report of March 10, 1899 as to the identification of Mississippi Choctaws, page 90, roll No. 1453, Albert James.

Q You are making your application as a beneficiary under the 14th article of the treaty of 1830, are you? A Yes sir.
Q Did any of your ancestors ever claim or receive any land here in Mississippi from the United States government as beneficiaries under the 14th article of the treaty of 1830? A No sir.
Q Did you ever hear of any of them getting any land from the Government?
A No sir.
Q Did the Government ever pay any of them any money? A No sir.
Q How long has your father been dead? A I don't know; it has been a good while.
Q About how old a man would he be if he were living? A He would be about 65.
Q Did you know his father's or grandfather's names? A No.
Q Do you know your grandmother's name? A No sir.
Q Or your mother's mothers[sic] and father's names? A No.
Q Did you ever hear of any of them going out to the Indian Territory? A No sir.
Q As far back as you can remember have you always lived in Mississippi?
A Yes sir.

Q Did you ever hear of any of them receiveing[sic] money from the Choctaw nation[sic] in Indian Territory? A No sir.
Q Have you any relations in the Indian Territory--any cousins? A No sir.
Q Have your people always lived here in Mississippi? A Yes sir.
Q You don't know anything about your grandparents? A No sir.
Q Your mother and father would both be about 70 years of age if they were living?
A Yes sir.
Q Are you married? A No sir.
Q You are just making application for yourself alone? A Yes sir.
Q In the event that this Commission should be able to identify you as a Mississippi Choctaw, or a Choctaw entitled to allotment under the provisions of the 14th article of the treaty of 1830, is it your intention to remove to the Indian Territory and take up your abode there as a permanent place of residence? A Yes, I guess so[sic]
Q You want to move there do you? A Yes.
Q Are there any additional statements that you want to make, or questions that you want to ask? A No sir.
Q You understand now fully do you that if you should be identified as a Mississippi Choctaw or a Choctaw entitled to rights to allotment in the Indian Territory, that you will have to move there and live there in order to have any benefits? A Yes sir.
Q That there is no money paid to the Choctaw here in Mississippi? A Yes sir.

The decision of the Commission as to your application for identification as a Mississippi Choctaw will be mailed to you at your present postoffice address.

-------------------------o---------------

The applicant in this case is to all appearances a full blood Choctaw Indian; he speaks the Choctaw language and from his testimony it appears that both he and his ancestors have always been residents of the state of Mississippi and have never in any way participated in the benefits of Choctaw citizenship in Indian Territory, nor received any part of the annuities or payments made by the Government to the Choctaw Indians in Indian Territory.

-------------------------o---------------

Frances R. Brown having been first duly sworn, upon oath states that as stenographer to the Commission to the Five Civilized Tribes she reported in full all proceedings had in the above enrirled[sic] cause on the 3rd day of April, 1901, ans[sic] that the above and foregoing is a full, true and correct transcript of her stenographic notes of said proceedings on said date.

Frances R Brown

Subscribed and sworn to before me this 5th day of April, 1901, at Meridian, Mississippi.

J P McKee Jr
Notary Public.

DEPARTMENT OF THE INTERIOR
COMMISSION TO THE FIVE CIVILIZED TRIBES

In the matter of the application of Albert James
for identification as a Mississippi Choctaw.
M.C.R. 1612.

-----D E C I S I O N ------

It appears from the record herein that application for identification as a Mississippi Choctaw was made to this Commission on April 3, 1901, by Albert James for himself, under the following provision of the act of Congress approved June 28, 1898, (30 Stats. 495):

> "Said Commission shall have authority to determine the identity of Choctaw Indians claiming rights in the Choctaw lands under article fourteen of the treaty between the United States and the Choctaw Nation, concluded September twenty-seventh, eighteen hundred and thirty, and to that end may administer oaths, examine witnesses, and perform all other acts necessary thereto and make report to the Secretary of the Interior."

From the evidence submitted in support of said application it appears that this applicant is a full blood Mississippi Choctaw.

Section forty-one of the act of Congress entitled "An Act to ratify and confirm an agreement with the Choctaw and Chickasaw tribes of Indians, and for other purposes," approved July 1, 1902, (32 Stats. 641), and ratified by the Choctaw and Chickasaw Nations September 25, 1902, provides as follows:

> "The application of no person for identification as a Mississippi Choctaw shall be received by said Commission after six months subsequent to the date of the final ratification of this agreement and in the disposition of such applications all full-blood Mississippi Choctaw Indians and the descendants of any Mississippi Choctaw Indians whether of full or mixed blood who received a patent to land under the said fourteenth article of the said treaty of eighteen hundred and thirty who had not moved to and made bona fide settlement in the Choctaw-Chickasaw country prior to June twenty-eighth, eighteen hundred and ninety-eight, shall be deemed to be Mississippi Choctaws, entitled to benefits under article fourteen of the said treaty of September twenty-seventh, eighteen hundred and thirty, and to

identification as such by said Commission, but this direction or provision shall be deemed to be only a rule of evidence and shall not be invoked by or operate to the advantage of any applicant who is not a Mississippi Choctaw of a full blood, or who is not the descendant of a Mississippi Choctaw who received a patent to land under said treaty, or who is otherwise barred from the right of citizenship in the Choctaw Nation, all of said Mississippi Choctaws so enrolled by said Commission shall be upon a separate roll."

It is, therefore, the opinion of this Commission that Albert James should be identified as a Mississippi Choctaw, and it is so ordered.

COMMISSION TO THE FIVE CIVILIZED TRIBES.

Tams Bixby
Acting Chairman.

T.B. Needles
Commissioner.

C. R. Breckinridge
Commissioner.

Muskogee, Indian Territory.
FEB 14 1903

DEPARTMENT OF THE INTERIOR

COMMISSION TO THE FIVE CIVILIZED TRIBES

In the matter of the application of Albert James

for identification as a Mississippi Choctaw,

M.C.R. 2182.

I N D E X

Page

DEPARTMENT OF THE INTERIOR

COMMISSION TO THE FIVE CIVILIZED TRIBES.

In the matter of the death of Albert James (Here insert name of deceased) a ~~citizen of the~~ Miss Choctaw Indian ~~Nation~~, who formerly resided at or near Stringers Miss., ~~Ind. Ter.~~, and died on the 26th day of June, 1902

AFFIDAVIT OF RELATIVE.

UNITED STATES OF AMERICA, INDIAN TERRITORY, Southern District.

I, Wash James, on oath state that I am 28 years of age and a ~~citizen, by~~ an identified Mississippi Choctaw Indian, ~~of the Nation~~; that my post office address is Ravia (Here insert name of post office) Ind. Ter.; that I am a brother (State relationship, i.e., the father, an uncle, a cousin, etc.) of Albert James (Here insert name of deceased), who was a ~~citizen, by~~ Mississippi Choctaw Indian, ~~of the Nation~~; and that said Albert James (Here insert name of deceased) died on the 26th day of June, 1902

Wash James

WITNESSES TO MARK:

(Must be Two Witnesses.)

Subscribed and sworn to before me this 30th day of April 1903.

C. B. Rodgers
Notary Public.

AFFIDAVIT OF ACQUAINTANCE.

UNITED STATES OF AMERICA, INDIAN TERRITORY, Southern District.

I, Kit Reed, on oath state that I am 29 years of age, and a ~~citizen, by~~ Mississippi Choctaw Indian, ~~of the Nation~~; that my post office address is Ravia (Here insert name of post office) Ind. Ter.; that I was personally acquainted with Albert James (Here insert name of deceased) who was a ~~citizen, by~~ Mississippi Choctaw Indian, ~~of the Nation~~, and that said Albert James (Here insert name of deceased) died on the 26th day of June, 1902

Kit Reed

WITNESSES TO MARK:

(Must be Two Witnesses.)

Subscribed and sworn to before me this 30th day of April 1903

C. B. Rodgers
Notary Public.

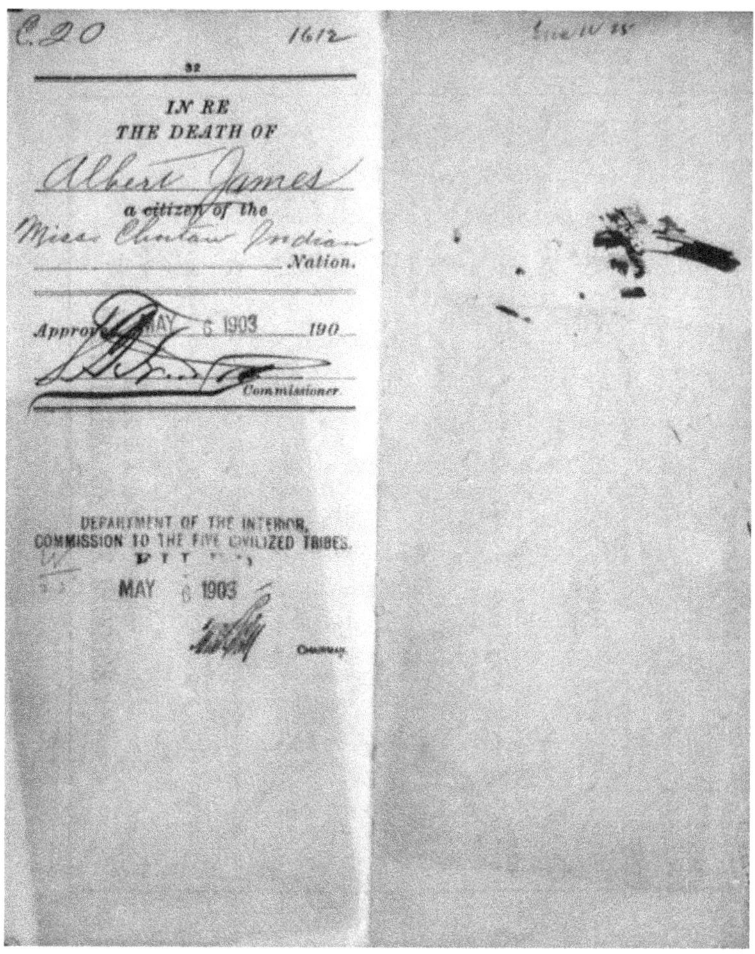

C.20 1612

32

IN RE
THE DEATH OF
Albert James
a ~~citizen~~ of the
Miss. Choctaw Indian
Nation.

Approved MAY 6 1903 190

Commissioner.

DEPARTMENT OF THE INTERIOR,
COMMISSION TO THE FIVE CIVILIZED TRIBES.

MAY 6 1903

Chairman.

COPY. M.C.R. 1612

Muskogee, Indian Territory, February 21, 1903.

Mansfield, McMurray & Cornish,
Attorneys for the Choctaw and Chickasaw Nations,
South McAlester, Indian Territory.

Gentlemen:-

Enclosed herewith you will find a copy of the decision of the Commission rendered February 14, 1903, identifying Albert James as a Mississippi Choctaw Indian under the provisions of the forty-first section of the Act of Congress approved July 1, 1902 (32 Stats. 641).

You are hereby advised that you will be allowed fifteen days from the date hereof, in which to file with this Commission such protest as you desire to make against the action of the Commission in identifying the said Albert James as a Mississippi Choctaw, and make satisfactory proof of service of said protest upon the applicants herein.

If you fail to file such protest within the time allowed, the names of the applicants herein will be placed upon the schedule of duly identified Mississippi Choctaws now being prepared by this Commission.

Respectfully,
(SIGNED). *Tams Bixby*
Acting Chairman.

Registered.
Enclosure G.H. 8

M.C.R. 1612.

COPY.

Muskogee, Indian Territory, March 11, 1903.

Albert James,

Sandersville, Mississippi.

Dear Sir:

Enclosed herewith you will find a copy of the decision of the Commission to the Five Civilized Tribes, rendered February 14, 1903, identifying you as a

Mississippi Choctaw Indian under the provisions of Section 41 of the Act of Congress approved July 1, 1902, (32 Stats. 641).

If you remove to the Choctaw-Chickasaw country, Indian Territory, before August 14, 1903, you will have six months from that date, or until February 14, 1904, within which to make proof of such removal and settlement at the office of the Commission at Atoka, Choctaw Nation, or Tishomingo, Chickasaw Nation.

Respectfully,

(SIGNED).
Tams Bixby

Registered. Chairman.

Enc. 1612.

M C I 20

Muskogee, Indian Territory, May 7, 1903.

Commissioner in Charge,

Choctaw Land Office,

Atoka, Indian Territory.

Dear Sir:

You are hereby advised that the following notation has this day been made on the original identified Mississippi Choctaw card No. 20:

"No. 1 died June 26, 1902; proof of death filed
May 6, 1903."

You are therefore requested to make like notation upon the duplicate card in your possession in accordance with the above information.

Respectfully,

Chairman.

M C R 1645
M C R 1612

Muskogee, Indian Territory, February 3, 1904.

Wash James,

Troy, Indian Territory.

Dear Sir:

Receipt is hereby acknowledged of your letter of January 18, 1904, by reference from the U. S. Indian Agent, Union Agency, asking if you can make selection of allotment for your step-son, Mack Billey, who is "still in Mississippi"; also for your brother who died in Mississippi after making application to this Commission for identification as a Mississippi Choctaw.

Replying to your inquiries you are advised that our records show that on February 14, 1903, the Commission rendered a decision identifying you, your wife, Easter James, your minor child, Harbar James, and your step-child, Mack Billey, as Mississippi Choctaws entitled to allotment in the lands of the Choctaw and Chickasaw Nations. Also on May 28, 1903, a supplemental decision was rendered, identifying Ore James, minor child of Wash and Easter James, and for whom application for identification as a Mississippi Choctaw was received at this office in proper form on March 23, 1903.

Our records further show that on February 14, 1903, a decision was rendered by the Commission identifying your brother, Albert James, as a Mississippi Choctaw; that said Albert James died on June 26, 1902, proof of death being filed with this Commission on May 6, 1903.

As the law requires all duly identified Mississippi Choctaws to remove to and make settlement within the Choctaw-Chickasaw country within six months from the date of their identification by the Commission to the Five Civilized Tribes, and neither your step-son or brother made such removal within the specified time, you cannot at this time be permitted to make selection of allotments in their names.

Respectfully,

Commissioner in Charge.

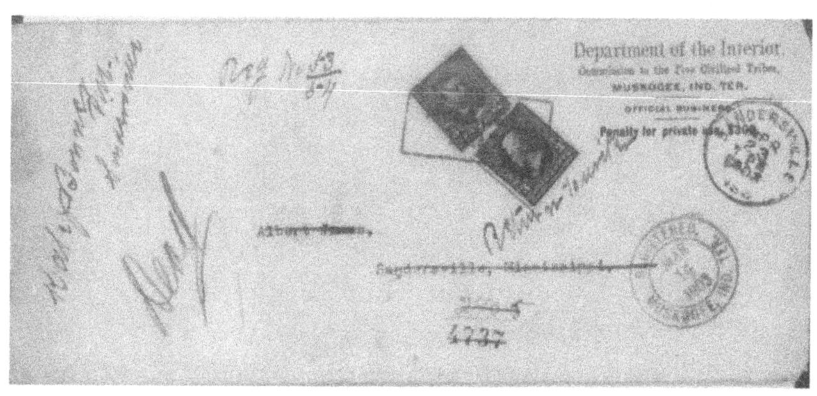
Department of the Interior,
MUSKOGEE, IND. TER.
OFFICIAL BUSINESS
Penalty for private use, $300

Rec 3-18-1903
DEPARTMENT OF THE INTERIOR,
MISSION TO THE FIVE CIVILIZED TR
FILED
APR 28 1903

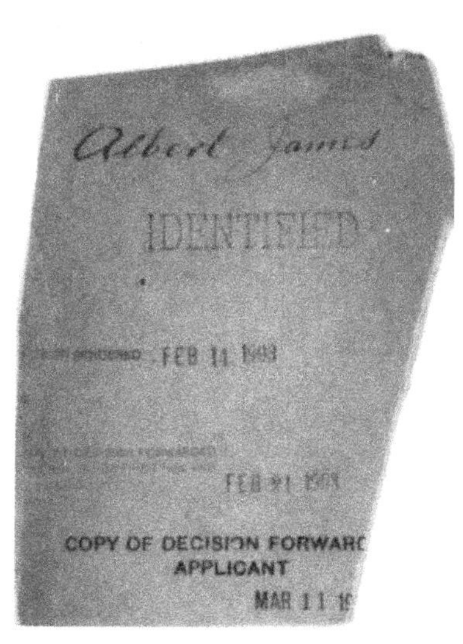
Albert James
IDENTIFIED
FEB 11 1903
FEB 21 1903
COPY OF DECISION FORWARD
APPLICANT
MAR 11 19

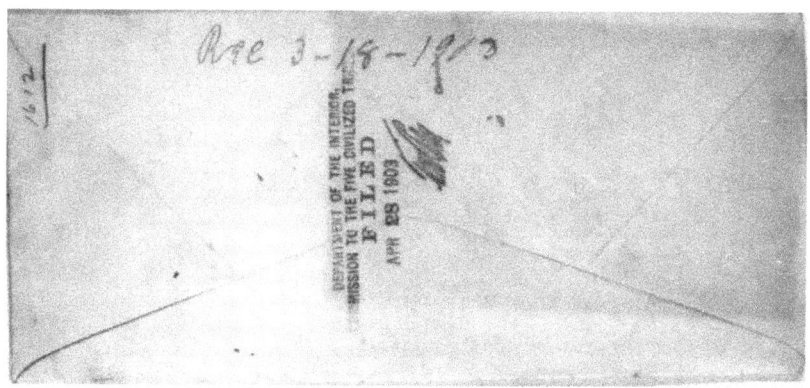

No. 1612

For Identification as a Mississippi Choctaw.

Date APR -3 1901

Name Albert James.

Age 29. Blood full.

Post Office. Stringer, Miss.

Father: Doctor James - dead

Mother: Sophie James - dead.

Claims through both parents

~~Children:~~

Claims for himself alone.

See Mississippi Choctaw card #406.

testimony of Feby. 7. 1899.

Stenographer

Frances R. Brown.

CARD NO. 21 - Choctaw MCR 3015 - Johnson Willis

DEPARTMENT OF THE INTERIOR.

COMMISSION TO THE FIVE CIVILIZED TRIBES.

In the Matter of the Application of Johnson Willis for

Identification as a Mississippi Choctaw.

M. C. R. 3015.

DEPARTMENT OF THE INTERIOR.

COMMISSION TO THE FIVE CIVILIZED TRIBES.

In the Matter of the Application of Johnson Willis for
Identification as a Mississippi Choctaw.

M. C. R. 3015.

- I N D E X . -

Department of the Interior,
Commission to the Five Civilized Tribes,
Meridian, Mississippi, July 18, 1901.

In the matter of the application of Johnson Willis for identification as a Mississippi Choctaw.

Johnson Willis, having been first duly sworn, upon his oath states as follows: (Through Billy Oscar, a duly sworn Choctaw Interpreter.)

Examination by the Commission.

Q What is your name? A John Willis.
Q What is your age? A Thirty nine.

Q You claim to have Choctaw blood? A Yes.
Q What is your post office address? A High Hill, Leake County, Mississippi.
Q How long have you lived in Mississippi? A All my life.
Q Is your father living? A Yes.
Q What is his name? A Willis.
Q Has he any other name? A No sir.
Q Has he always lived in Mississippi? A Yes sir.
Q Is he a full blood Choctaw? A Yes sir.
Q Is your mother living? A Yes.
Q What is her name? A Martha Willis.
Q Has she always lived in Mississippi? A Yes.
Q Is she a full blood Choctaw? A Yes.
Q About how old a man is your father? A About fifty.
Q How old is your mother? A About fifty one.
Q How much Choctaw blood do you claim to have? A Full blood.
Q Is your father's father living? A I don't know.
Q Did you ever see him? A No.
Q Do you know what his name was? A No.
Q Is your father's mother living? A No.
Q Did you ever see her? A No.
Q Do you know what her name was? A No.
Q Do you know the names of any of your father's ancestors? A No.
Q Have all of your father's ancestors always lived in Mississippi so far as you know?
A I reckon so.
Q Is your mother's father living? A No.
Q What was his name? A I don't know.
Q Is your mother's mother living? A No.
Q Did you ever see her? A No.
Q Do you know what her name was? A No.
Q You don't know the names hen of any of your mother's or father's ancestors?
A I know my mother's brother's name.
Q But none of their ancestors? A No.
Q Have all of your mother's people always lived in Mississippi, so far as you know?
A Yes sir.
Q Did you ever hear of any of your ancestors going out to the Indian Territory?
A No.
Q Your mother and father have never been out there? A No sir.
Q Are you married? A Yes.
Q Is your wife living? A Yes.
Q Are you living together? A No sir.
Q How long have you been separated? A About seven months.
Q Have you separated for good? A Yes sir, she joined the Catholics, and made all the children join the Catholics and she done put in her name and her children's names to Mr. Winton, and Mr. Winton tell them they can get their pay without going to Territory, and I told them I didn't want to join, and if its that way, I will let them have their part and I'll get mine.
Q You don't want to make an application for your wife and children? A No sir.

Q Were you married under a license or according to the Choctaw custom?
A Choctaw custom, never married by license.
Q What is your wife's name? A Sophia.
Q How many children have you? A Four.
Q What are their names? A Leona.
Q The next one? A Spink.
Q The next one? A Cone.
Q The next one? A Finis.
Q Is Spinks[sic] a boy? A Yes.
Q Cone a boy? A Yes.
Q Finis a boy? A Yes.
Q How old is Leona? A Thirteen years old.
Q How old is Spink? A Ten.
Q How old is Cone? A Seven.
Q How old is Finis? A Five years old.
Q What is your wife's father's name? A Jim Tincha.
Q Did he ever go by the name of Isaac Jim? A I don't know.
Q What is your wife's mother's name? A Meely.
Q This application then is for yourself only, is it? A Yes.
Q Is you name on any of the Choctaw tribal rolls in Indian Territory? A No sir.
Q Did you ever make any application to the Choctaw tribal authorities for citizenship in the Choctaw Nation, or to be enrolled as a member of the tribe? A No sir.
Q Did you make application to the Commission to the Five Civilized Tribes in the year 1896, for citizenship in the Choctaw Nation? A No sir.
Q Have you ever made any application of any description prior to this time to the Choctaw tribal authorities or to the United States authorities to be admitted or enrolled as a citizen of the Choctaw Nation? A Yes sir, two years ago.
Q Where did you appear two years ago? A At Philadelphia.

> The records of the Commission show that this applicant appeared before the Commission at Philadelphia, Mississippi, during its appointment there during the month of January, 1899, and made application for the identification of himself and his wife and four minor children as Mississippi Choctaws, their names appearing upon Mississippi Choctaw Card, Field Number 305; also, upon page 75 of the Schedule of Mississippi Choctaws which accompanied the report of March 10, 1899, of the Commission to the Five Civilized Tribes to the Secretary of the Interior, as to the identity of Choctaw Indians, claiming rights in the Choctaw lands in Indian Territory under the provisions of the Fourteenth Article of the Treaty of Dancing Rabbit Creek, being Numbers 1069, 1070, 1071, 1072, 1073 and 1074, respectively, thereon.

Q This application you made two years ago is the only application of any kind you have made is it? A Yes sir.
Q You now desire to make application for identification as a Mississippi Choctaw entitled to rights in the Choctaw lands in Indian Territory under the provisions of the 14th article of the treaty of Dancing Rabbit Creek? A Yes sir.

The treaty of Dancing Rabbit Creek was entered into here in Mississippi on the 27th day of September 1830, between the United States Government and the Choctaw tribe of Indians, the object of that treaty being to secure the removal of the Choctaws from the country occupied by them in Mississippi and Alabama to the present country west of the Mississippi River, now occupies by the Choctaw tribe of Indians. Some of the Choctaws were unwilling to move west of the Mississippi, but insisted that before making the treaty they be permitted to remain here in the old country. For the benefit of those who desired to remain here, the 14th article was inserted in the treaty. That 14th article is as follows:

"Each Choctaw head of a family, being desirous to remain and become a citizen of the States shall be permitted to do so by signifying his intention to the agent within six months from the ratification of this treaty, and he or she shall thereupon be entitled to a reservation of one section of six hundred and forty acres of land, to be bounded by sectional lines of survey; inlike[sic] manner shall be entitled to one half that quantity for each unmarried child which is living with him over ten years of age; and a quarter section to such child as may be under ten years of age to adjoin the location of the parent. If they reside upon said lands for intending to become citizens of the States for five years after the ratification of this treaty in that case a grant in fee simple shall issue; said reservation shall include the present improvement of the head of the family or a portion of it. Persons who claim under this article shall not lose the privilege of a Choctaw citizen, but if they ever remove are not entitled to any portion of the Choctaw annuity."

Q Do you think you understand that fourteenth article now? A Yes sir.
Q Do you know whether any of your ancestors ever complies with the provisions of that fourteenth article or not? A No sir, I don't know.
Q Do you know any one living who would be able to testify as to your ancestry, and the amount of Choctaw blood possessed by you? A No sir, I don't beliebe[sic] there is.
Q Do you know whether any of your ancestors were living here in the old Choctaw Nation in Mississippi and Alabama in 1830, when this treaty was made? A I don't know; I don't know whether my mother would know or not; I don't believe she would.
Q Do you know whether any of your ancestors were recognized members of the Choctaw tribe here at that time? A No.
Q Do you know whether any of your ancestors owned an improvement upon any land which was embraced in the old Choctaw Nation in Mississippi and Alabama at the time this treaty was made? A No sir.
Q Do you know whether any of your ancestors removed from the old Choctaw Nation in Mississippi and Alabama to the present Choctaw Nation in Indian Territory at the time of the removal of the greater portion of the Choctaw tribe of Indians between 1833 and 1838? A No sir.
Q Do you know whether any of your ancestors within six months after the ratification of the Treaty of Dancing Rabbit Creek, signified to the United States

Indian Agent here in Mississippi, their intention to remain in Mississippi and become citizens of the States? A No.
Q Do you know whether any of your ancestors ever claimed or received any land in Mississippi as beneficiaries under the provisions of this 14th article of the treaty of Dancing Rabbit Creek? A No sir.
Q Do you know any one living - any old Choctaw, or any other person who would be likely to know whether any of your ancestors were living in the old Choctaw Nation in Mississippi and Alabama in 1830, when the treaty of Dancing Rabbit Creek was made; whether any of them were recognized members of the Choctaw tribe of Indians; whether any of them owned an improvement here, or whether any of them signified there[sic] intention to the agent to remain here, within six months after the ratification of the treaty, or whether any of them ever received any land under this 14th article of the treaty of Dancing Rabbit Creek? A No sir.

This is a very material point in your case, and if there is anyone living who knows about this, you ought to bring them before the Commission to testify in your behalf.

In accordance with the provisions of the fourteenth article of the treaty of Dancing Rabbit Creek, an agent of the Government here in Mississippi was directed to receive the applications of Choctaws who desired to remain here in Mississippi and take land under the provisions of the fourteenth article of the treaty of Dancing Rabbit Creek. The records of the Government show that this agent failed to furnish the Government with the names of many Choctaws who appeared before him and signified their intention to remain in accordance with the provisions of the fourteenth article of the treaty, and on the account, the Government at its public land sales, sold lands upon which Choctaws owned improvements, and which they were holding in accordance with the provisions of the fourteenth article of the treaty of 1830. This occasioned a great deal of dissatisfaction and complaint among the Choctaws, and the matter was finally brought to the attention of Congress; Congress then passed an Act which was approved on the 3rd day of March, 1837, provided for a Commission to come to Mississippi and hear the cases of those Choctaws who claimed that they had complied with the provisions of said article of said treaty or that he applied to the commissions appointed under the acts of March 3, 1837 and August 23, 1842, for an adjudication of his rights if any he had. the fourteenth article of the treaty of 1830, but had been deprived of their land for the reason that it had been sold by the Government. This commission came down here and heard a good many Choctaw cases, but were unable to hear all of them within the time allowed them; later, Congress passed another act, which was approved on August 23, 1842, providing for another Commission to come down here and hear such cases as had not been heard by the former commission. This commission came down here and heard a good many Choctaw cases.

Q Do you know whether any of your ancestors appeared before either of these commission[sic] and attempted to establish their rights to lands in Mississippi under the provisions of the fourteenth article of the treaty of Dancing Rabbit Creek? A No sir, I don't know.
Q Do you know whether any of your ancestors ever received any scrip from the Government under the provisions of the Act of August 23, 1842? A (No answer.)

> I will just say in regard to that, the Act of Congress provided that in case a Choctaw should prove to the satisfaction of the Commission that he did comply with the provisions of the fourteenth article of the treaty, and his claim was allowed, and it should develop that the Government had sold the land he was living on in accordance with the provisions of the fourteenth article of that treaty, he should be given scrip entitling him to select vacant Government land in Mississippi, Louisiana or Arkansas.

Q Now, I want to know if any of your ancestors got any of that scrip? A I don't know.
Q Do you know any one living who would likely know about the matter? A I don't know, without Solomon York, knows.
Q Have you any written evidence of any kind showing that any of your ancestors ever received any land from the Government under article fourteen of the treaty of 1830[sic] A No.
Q Have you any written evidence of any kind you want to offer at this time?
A No sir.
Q Are there any additional statejents[sic] you want to make at this time in support of your application? A No sir.
Q Do you know whether any of your ancestors ever received any land from the Government here in Mississippi, under the provisions of any other article of the treaty of Dancing Rabbit Creek than the fourteenth article, or ever received any land under the supplement to that treaty? A No sir.
Q Do you know any one living who would likely know about it? A No sir, I don't know who would.

(Applicant excused.)

Solomon York, having been first called and duly sworn, as a witness in behalf of the above name applicant, testified upon his oath as follows:

Examination by the Commission.

Q What is your name? A Solomon York.
Q How old are you? A I guess about ninety.
Q What is your post office address? A Standing Pine, Leake County.
Q Have you lived in Mississippi all your life? A Yes.
Q Are you a full blood Choctaw Indian? A Yes sir.
Q Are you acquainted with Johnson Willis, who has just appeared before the Commission? A Yes sir.

Q How long have you known him? A Little boy.
Q Is he a full blood Choctaw? A Yes.
Q Is his father living? A Yes.
Q Is his mother living? A She's living.
Q What is her name? A I get old, and I so much forget.
Q Is she a full blood Choctaw? A Yes.
Q What is Johnson's father's name? A I forget that too.
Q Do you know the name of Johnson's father's father? A No, I don't know.
Q Do you know the name of Johnson's father's mother? A I don't know.
Q Johnson's father's father and mother are both dead? A Yes[sic]
Q Do you know the name of Johnson's mother's father? A I forget; so much long time.
Q Is he dead? A Yes.
Q Is Johnson's mother's mother living? A No.
Q What was her name? A I forget it.
Q You knew all of Johnson's grand parents when they were living? A Yes.
Q Were all of them full blood Choctaws? A Yes.
Q All lived in Mississippi? A Yes.
Q None of them went out to west to the new country? A No.
Q Do you know whether any of them ever received any land here in Mississippi under the provisions of the fourteenth article of the treaty of Dancing Rabbit Creek?
A I don't know.
Q Did any of Johnson's ancestors ever own any land here? A I don't know.
Q Do you know whether any of his ancestors appeared before the Commission appointed under the act of Congress approved March 3, 1837, or the Commission appointed under the Act of Congress of August 23, 1842, and attempted to estabish[sic] their rights to land in Mississippi under the provisions of the fourteenth article of the treaty of 1830? A No sir.
Q Do you know whether any of them ever got any scrip under the Act of Congress approved August 23, 1842? A No sir.
Q Do you know whether any of them were living here in 1830, when the treaty of Dancing Rabbit Creek was made? A Yes sir.
Q What one of his ancestors was living here at that time? A Ellis.
Q Who is Ellis? A Johnson - uncle.
Q His father[sic] or mother's brother? A Mother's brother.
Q You don't know whether he got any land or not? A No.
Q Was Ellis a full blood Choctaw? A Yes.
Q Is that the only one of his ancestors you remember being here in 1830, when the treaty of Dancing Rabbit Creek was made? A That's all.
Q Did Ellis own an improvement here at that time? A No, Ellis didn't; Ellis' mother had improvement here, but Ellis was little boy then.
Q Ellis' mother lived here at that time? A Yes.
Q Ellis's[sic] mother then, was Johnson's grand mother? A Yes.
Q You are sure she owned an improvement here? A Yes.
Q Where was that? A In Leake County, close to where I live now.
Q How long did she live on that land after the treaty was made? A I don't know, not very long.

Q Was it a year, do you think? A About two years.
Q Who got the land that improvement was on after she left it? A I don't know who got it then, white man now claims it.
Q How did Johnson's grand mother come to leave that land? A She moved just a little piece.
Q How long did she live near there? A She lived there until she died.
Q How long was that? A About twenty years.
Q Did she own that land there? A No sir.
Q She just rented from someone else? A Yes sir.
Q You don't know whether the Government gave her any land or not? A No sir.
Q Now, I explained to you to-day in your examination about these Commissions appointed under the Act of Congress of March 3, 1837, and August 23, 1842, and you testified you went before the Commission you and your mother; now, did Johnson's grand mother go before the commission at that time too? A I don't remember.
Q You don't know whether she ever got any scrip or not? A No sir.
Q You don't know whether she ever got a patent to land from the Government?
A No sir.
Q Can't you remember her Choctaw name? A No, don't remember it.
Q How old was she when this treaty was made, do you know? A About ten years old.
Q Johnson's grand mother was about ten years old? A Yes.
Q Ellis wasn't living at the time of the treaty then? A No sir.
Q According to your testimony, Johnson's grand mother was about your age wasn't she? A Older than I was.
Q How much older? A About three years older than me.
Q Do you know any one living who would likely know more about this matter than you do, or as much? A No sir.

(Witness excused, and Applicant re-called.)

(This applicant has the appearance of being a full blood Indian; he speaks and understands the Choctaw language and but very little English, the examination having been conducted through a sworn Choctaw interpreter.)

The decision of the Commission as to the application you make at this time for the identification of yourself as a Mississippi Choctaw will be determined at the earliest possible date, and a report of same made to the Secretary of the Interior, conformable to the provisions of the Twenty first section of the Act of Congress of June 28, 1898, and a copy of the same will be mailed to you to your post office address as given in your testimony.

R.S. Streit, having been first duly sworn, upon his oath states that as stenographer to the Commission to the Five Civilized Tribes, he reported in full all proceedings had in the above entitled cause on the 18th day of July, 1901, and that the above and foregoing is a full, true and correct translation of his stenographic notes of said proceedings in said cause upon said date.

R.S. Streit

Subscribed and sworn to before me at Meridian, Mississippi, this 10th day of August, 1901.

J P McKee Jr
Notary Public.

DEPARTMENT OF THE INTERIOR.

COMMISSION TO THE FIVE CIVILIZED TRIBES.

In the Matter of the Application of Johnson Willis for

Identification as a Mississippi Choctaw.

M. C. R. 3015.

- - D E C I S I O N . - -

It appears from the record herein that application for identification as a Mississippi Choctaw was made to this Commission on July 18, 1901, by Johnson Willis, for himself, under the following provision of the act of Congress approved June 28, 1898, (30 Stats. 495):

> "Said Commission shall have authority to determine the identity of Choctaw Indians claiming rights in the Choctaw lands under article fourteen of the treaty between the United States and the Choctaw Nation, concluded September twenty-seventh, eighteen hundred and thirty, and to that end may administer oaths, examine witnesses, and perform all other acts necessary thereto and make report to the Secretary of the Interior."

From the evidence submitted in support of said application it appears that the applicant is a full-blood Mississippi Choctaw Indian.

Section forty-one of the Act of Congress entitled "An Act to ratify and confirm an agreement with the Choctaw and Chickasaw tribes of Indians, and for other purposes," approved July 1, 1902, (32 Stats. 641), and ratified by the Choctaw and Chickasaw Nations September 25, 1902, provides as follows:

> "The application of no person for identification as a Mississippi Choctaw shall be received by said Commission after six months subsequent to the date of the

final ratification of this agreement and in the disposition of such applications all full-blood Mississippi Choctaw Indians and the descendants of any Mississippi Choctaw Indians whether of full or mixed blood who received a patent to land under the said fourteenth article of the said treaty of eighteen hundred and thirty who had not moved to and made bona fide settlement in the Choctaw-Chickasaw country prior to June twenty-eighth, eighteen hundred and ninety-eight, shall be deemed to be Mississippi Choctaws, entitled to benefits under article fourteen of the said treaty of September twenty-seventh, eighteen hundred and thirty, and to identification as such by said Commission, but this direction or provision shall be deemed to be only a rule of evidence and shall not be invoked by or operate to the advantage of any applicant who is not a Mississippi Choctaw of a full blood, or who is not the descendant of a Mississippi Choctaw who received a patent to land under said treaty, or who is otherwise barred from the right of citizenship in the Choctaw Nation, all of said Mississippi Choctaws so enrolled by said Commission shall be upon a separate roll."

It is, therefore, the opinion of this Commission that Johnson Willis should be identified as a Mississippi Choctaw, and it is so ordered.

COMMISSION TO THE FIVE CIVILIZED TRIBES.

Tams Bixby
Acting Chairman.

T.B. Needles
Commissioner.

Muskogee, Indian Territory.
FEB 14 1903

C. R. Breckinridge
Commissioner.

COPY. M.C.R. 3015

Muskogee, Indian Territory, February 21, 1903.

Mansfield, McMurray & Cornish,
Attorneys for the Choctaw and Chickasaw Nations,
South McAlester, Indian Territory.

Gentlemen:

Enclosed herewith you will find a copy of the decision of the Commission rendered February 14, 1903, identifying Johnson Willis, as a Mississippi Choctaw Indian under the provisions of the act of Congress approved July 1, 1902 (32 Stats. 641).

You are hereby advised that you will be allowed fifteen days from the date hereof, in which to file with this Commission such protest as you desire to make against the action of the Commission in identifying the said Johnson Willis as a Mississippi Choctaw, and make satisfactory proof of service of said protest upon the applicants herein.

If you fail to file such protest within the time allowed, the names of the applicants herein will be placed upon the schedule of duly identified Mississippi Choctaws now being prepared by this Commission.

Respectfully,

(SIGNED). *Tams Bixby*

Registered. Acting Chairman.

Enc. M.C.R. 3015

M.C.R. 3015.

COPY.

Muskogee, Indian Territory, March 11, 1903.

Johnson Willis,

High Hill, Mississippi.

Dear Sir:

Enclosed herewith you will find a copy of the decision of the Commission to the Five Civilized Tribes, rendered February 14, 1903, identifying you as a Mississippi Choctaw Indian under the provisions of Section 41 of the Act of Congress approved July 1, 1902, (32 Stats. 641).

If you remove to the Choctaw-Chickasaw country, Indian Territory, before August 14, 1903, you will have six months from that date, or until February 14, 1904, within which to make proof of such removal and settlement at the office of the Commission at Atoka, Choctaw Nation, or Tishomingo, Chickasaw Nation.

Respectfully,

(SIGNED). *Tams Bixby*

Registered. Chairman.

Enc. 3015.

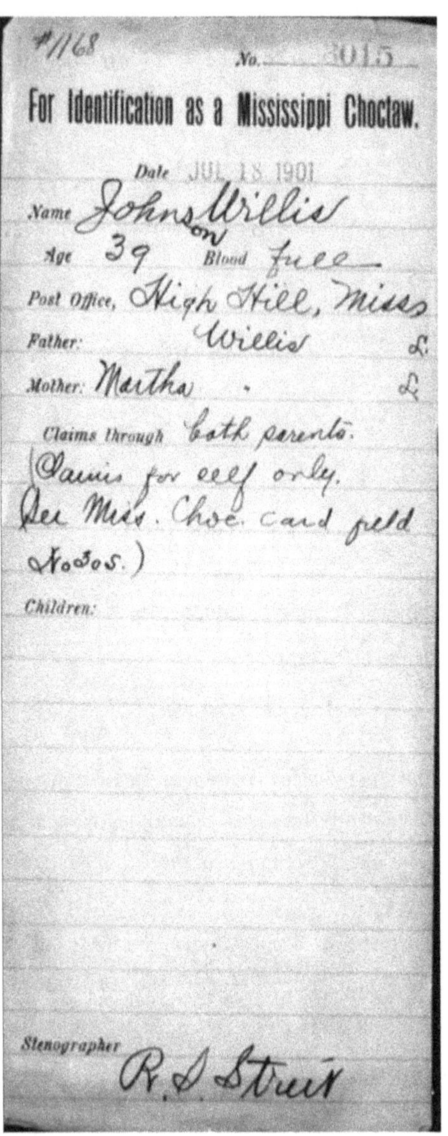
#1168 No. 3015

For Identification as a Mississippi Choctaw.

Date JUL 18 1901

Name Johnson Willis

Age 39 Blood full

Post Office, High Hill, Miss

Father: Willis L

Mother: Martha . L

Claims through both parents.

(Claims for self only. See Miss. Choc. card field No 305.)

Children:

Stenographer R. S. Street

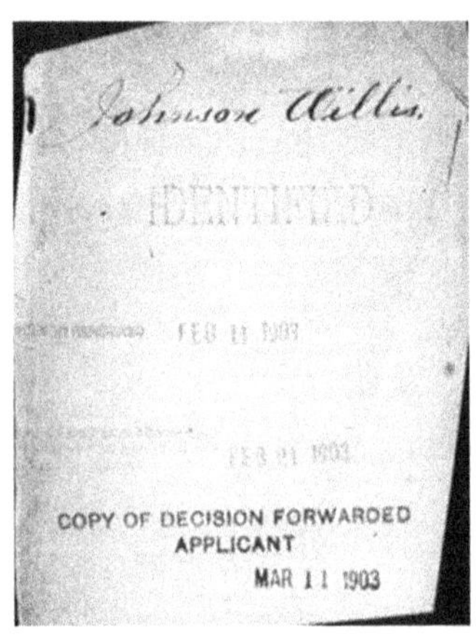
Johnson Willis.

IDENTIFIED

FEB 11 1903

FEB 21 1903

COPY OF DECISION FORWARDED APPLICANT MAR 11 1903

CARD NO. 22 - Choctaw MCR 2301 - John Isom

DEPARTMENT OF THE INTERIOR

COMMISSION TO THE FIVE CIVILIZED TRIBES.

In the Matter of the Application of John Isom et al.

For Identification as Mississippi Choctaws.

M. C. R. 2301.

DEPARTMENT OF THE INTERIOR.

COMMISSION TO THE FIVE CIVILIZED TRIBES.

In the Matter of the Application of John Isom et al.,
For Identification as Mississippi Choctaws.
M. C. R. 2301.

- - I N D E X . - -

Department of the Interior,
Commission to the Five Civilized Tribes,
Decatur, Mississippi, May 18, 1901.

In the matter of the application of John Isom for the identification of himself, his wife and two minor children as Mississippi Choctaws.

John Isom, having been first duly sworn upon his oath states as follows: (Indian McDonald, Official Interpreter.)

Examination vy[sic] the Commission.

Q What is your name? A John Isom.
Q What is your age? A Forty Seven.
Q What is your post office address? A Tucker, Mississippi.

Q How long have you lived in Neshoba County? A In Neshoba County twenty eight years. Born in Newton County.
Q You have lived all your life in Newton and Neshoba Counties? A Yes.
Q What is your father's name? A John Wesley.
Q Is he living? A No sir, dead.
Q Was he a full blood? A Yes.
Q What was your mother's name? A Bettie.
Q Is she dead? A Yes.
Q Was she a full blood? A Yes sir.
Q Are you a full blood? A Yes sir.
Q Do you claim your Choctaw blood through your father and mother? A Yes sir.
Q Have your parents, through whom you claim your right to identification as a Mississippi Choctaw, ever been recognize[sic] in any manner or enrolled as members of the Choctaw tribe of Indians by the Choctaw tribal authorities or by the authorities of the United States? A No sir.
Q What is your wife's name? A Mary.
Q Is she a full blood Choctaw? A Yes sir.
Q What is her father's name? A Willis.
Q Just Willis? A Yes.
Q What is the Choctaw name? A La-pe-chubbe.
Q Is he a full blood? A Yes sir.
Q Is he living? A Dead.
Q What is her mother's name? A Ma-te-ah.
Q Is she living? A Dead.
Q Was she a full blood? A Yes.
Q How long have you been married to your wife, Mary? A About thirty years.
Q Did you marry your wife under a license or according to the Choctaw custom?
A License.
Q Where did you get your license? A At the Court House in Philadelphia.
Q Have your wife's parents, through whom you claim for her the right to identification as a Mississippi Choctaw, ever been recognized in any manner or enrolled as members of the Choctaw tribe of Indians by the Choctaw tribal authorities or by the authorities of the United States? A No sir.
Q Have you any children in your family under twenty one years of age and unmarried for whom you wish to make application? A Yes sir.
Q What are their names and ages? A Rosie.
Q How old is Rosie? A [Blank]
Q The next? A John Jr.,[sic]
Q How old is John Jr.? A Five years old.
Q Is Mary the mother of these two children? A Yes.
Q You are the father? A Yes.
Q They live with you at your home? A Yes sir.
Q Is your name the name of your wife, or your children on any of the trial rolls of the Choctaw Nation in Indian Territory? A No sir.
Q Have you ever made application for yourself, wife or children to the Choctaw tribal authorities in Indian Territory to be enrolled as members of that tribe? A No.

Q Did you, or any one for you, or for you wife and children, in 1896, make application to the Commission to the Five Civilized Tribes for citizenship in the Choctaw Nation under the Act of Congress of June 10, 1896? A No sir.
Q Have you ever been admitted to citizenship in the Choctaw Nation by either the Choctaw tribal authorities, the Commission to the Five Civilized Tribes, or by the United States Couet[sic] in Indian Territory? A No.
Q Have you ever made application before this time to either the Choctaw tribal authorities or to the authorities of the United States for yourself, wife or children, to be admitted or enrolled as citizens of the Choctaw Nation? A Yes two years ago.

> The records of the Commission show that on January 31, 1899, this applicant appeared before the Commission at Philadelphia, Mississippi, and made application for the identification of himself, his wife and two minor children, Rosie and John Jr., as Mississippi Choctaws, their names appearing upon Mississippi Choctaws, their names appearing upon Mississippi Choctaw Card, Field Number 179; also, upon page 58 of the Schedule of Mississippi Choctaws, which accompanied the report of March 10, 1899, of the Commission to the Five Civilized Tribes to the Secretary of the Interior, as to the identity of Choctaw Indians, claiming rights in the Choctaw lands under the provisions of the Fourteenth Article of the Treaty of Dancing Rabbit Creek, being Numbers 613, 614, 615 and 616, respectively, thereon.

Q Is it now your purpose to make application for identification as Mississippi Choctaws for yourself, wife and children? A Yes.
Q Do you claim your rights as beneficiaries under the provisions of Article Fourteen of the Treaty of 1830? A Yes.
Q Have you or your wife ever received any benefits as Choctaw Indians? A No sir.
Q Have any of your ancestors or any of your wife's ancestors ever received any benefits as Choctaw Indians? A No sir.
Q What is the name of your ancestor or ancestors, or your wife's ancestor or ancestors, who were residents of the old Choctaw Nation in Mississippi and Alabama and acknowledged members of the Choctaw Tribe of Indians in 1830, when the Treaty of Dancing Rabbit Creek was entered into between the United States and the Choctaw tribe of Indians? A I don't know.
Q Have you any evidence showing that any of your ancestors or your wife's ancestors were recognized members of the Choctaw tribe of Indians in 1830?
A No sir.
Q Did any of your ancestors, or any of your wife's ancestors, remove from the old Choctaw Nation in Mississippi and Alabama to the present Choctaw Nation in Indian Territory at the time of the removal of the main part of the Choctaw tribe of Indians between the years 1833 and 1838? A I don't know.
Q Did any of your ancestors or any of your wife's ancestors ever claim or receive any land in Mississippi as beneficiaries under Article Fourteen of the Treaty of 1830?
A I don't know.
Q Are there any additional statements you desire to make in support of this application? A No.

Q Have you any documentary evidence, affidavits, written testimony of any description, copies of records, deeds or patents, or any other proper papers showing that any of your ancestors were in 1830, recognized members of the Choctaw tribe of Indians, or that any of them ever complied or attempted to comply with the provisions of the Fourteenth Article of that Treaty or ever received any benefits thereunder?
A No sir.

(This applicant appears to be a full blood Choctaw, having all the appearance and characteristics of a member of the Choctaw tribe. He has no knowledge of the English language his examination having been conducted through the medium of a sworn Choctaw interpreter; he has no knowledge of a compliance on the part of his ancestors with any of the provisions of the Fourteenth Article of the Treaty of 1830.)

The decision of the Commission as to the application you make for the identification of yourself, wife and minor children as Mississippi Choctaws, will be determined at the earliest possible date, and a report made to the Secretary of the Interior, conformable to the provisions of the Twenty first section of the Act of Congress of June 28, 1898, and a copy of same will be mailed to you to your post office address as given in your testimony.

R.S. Streit, having been duly sworn, states that as stenographer to the Commission to the Five Civilized Tribes, he reported all proceedings had in this cause on the 18th day of May, 1901, and that the foregoing is a full, true and correct translation of his stenographic notes on said date.

R.S. Streit

Subscribed and sworn to before me at Meridian, Mississippi, this 26th day of June, 1901.

J P McKee Jr
Notary Public.

DEPARTMENT OF THE INTERIOR.

COMMISSION TO THE FIVE CIVILIZED TRIBES.

In the Matter of the Application of John Isom et al.,

For Identification as Mississippi Choctaws.

M. C. R. 2301.

- - D E C I S I O N . - -

It appears from the record herein that application for identification as Mississippi Choctaws was made to this Commission on May 18, 1901, by John Isom, for himself, his wife Mary, and his two minor children Rosie and John Jr., under the following provision of the Act of Congress approved June 28, 1898, (30 Stats. 495):

> "Said Commission shall have authority to determine the identity of Choctaw Indians claiming rights in the Choctaw lands under article fourteen of the treaty between the United States and the Choctaw Nation, concluded September twenty-seventh, eighteen hundred and thirty, and to that end may administer oaths, examine witnesses, and perform all other acts necessary thereto and make report to the Secretary of the Interior."

From the evidence submitted in support of said application it appears that the applicants are full-blood Mississippi Choctaw Indians.

Section forty-one of the Act of Congress entitled "An Act to ratify and confirm an agreement with the Choctaw and Chickasaw tribes of Indians, and for other purposes," approved July 1, 1902, (32 Stats. 641), and ratified by the Choctaw and Chickasaw Nations September 25, 1902, provides as follows:

> "The application of no person for identification as a Mississippi Choctaw shall be received by said Commission after six months subsequent to the date of the final ratification of this agreement and in the disposition of such applications all full-blood Mississippi Choctaw Indians and the descendants of any Mississippi Choctaw Indians whether of full or mixed blood who received a patent to land under the said fourteenth article of the said treaty of eighteen hundred and thirty who had not moved to and made bona fide settlement in the Choctaw-Chickasaw country prior to June twenty-eighth, eighteen hundred and ninety-eight, shall be deemed to be Mississippi Choctaws, entitled to benefits under article fourteen of the said treaty of September twenty-seventh, eighteen hundred and thirty, and to identification as such by said Commission, but this direction or provision shall be deemed to be only a rule of evidence and shall not be invoked by or operate to the advantage of any applicant who is not a Mississippi Choctaw of a full blood, or who is not the descendant of a Mississippi Choctaw who received a patent to land under said treaty, or who is otherwise barred from the right of citizenship in the Choctaw Nation, all of said Mississippi Choctaws so enrolled by said Commission shall be upon a separate roll."

It is, therefore, the opinion of this Commission that John Isom, Mary Isom, Rosie Isom and John Isom, Jr., should be identified as Mississippi Choctaws, and it is so ordered.

COMMISSION TO THE FIVE CIVILIZED TRIBES.

Tams Bixby
Acting Chairman.

T.B. Needles
Commissioner.

C. R. Breckinridge
Commissioner.

Muskogee, Indian Territory.
FEB 14 1903

M.C.R. 2301

COPY.

Muskogee, Indian Territory, February 21, 1903.

Mansfield, McMurray & Cornish,
Attorneys for the Choctaw and Chickasaw Nations,
South McAlester, Indian Territory.

Gentlemen:

Enclosed herewith you will find a copy of the decision of the Commission rendered February 14, 1903, identifying John Isom, his wife Mary Isom, and minor children Rosie Isom and John Isom, Jr., as Mississippi Choctaw Indians under the provisions of the act of Congress approved July 1, 1902 (32 Stats. 641).

You are hereby advised that you will be allowed fifteen days from the date hereof, in which to file with this Commission such protest as you desire to make against the action of the Commission in identifying the said John Isom, his wife and children as Mississippi Choctaw[sic], and make satisfactory proof of service of said protest upon the applicants herein.

If you fail to file such protest within the time allowed, the names of the applicants herein will be placed upon the schedule of duly identified Mississippi Choctaws now being prepared by this Commission.

Respectfully,

(SIGNED). *Tams Bixby*

Registered. Acting Chairman.

Enc. M.C.R. 2301

M.C.R. 2301.

COPY.

Muskogee, Indian Territory, March 11, 1903.

John Isom,

Tucker, Mississippi.

Dear Sir:

Enclosed herewith you will find a copy of the decision of the Commission to the Five Civilized Tribes, rendered February 14, 1903, identifying yourself, your wife, Mary Isom, and you two minor children, Rosie Isom and John Isom, Jr., as Mississippi Choctaw Indians under the provisions of Section 41 of the Act of Congress approved July 1, 1902, (32 Stats. 641).

If you remove to the Choctaw-Chickasaw country, Indian Territory, before August 14, 1903, you will have six months from that date, or until February 14, 1904, within which to make proof of such removal and settlement at the office of the Commission at Atoka, Choctaw Nation, or Tishomingo, Chickasaw Nation.

Respectfully,

Registered. (SIGNED). *Tams Bixby* Chairman.

Enc. 2301.

M C R 2301

Muskogee, Indian Territory, March 24, 1904.

Commissioner in Charge,

Choctaw Land Office,

Atoka, Indian Territory.

Dear Sir:

It appears from our records that John Isom, his wife, Mary Isom, and minor children, Rosie and John Isom, Jr., Nos. 50 to 53 inclusive, on Identified Mississippi Choctaw card No. 22, were removed from the state of Mississippi to Indian Territory by H. Van V. Smith, Special Agent, United States Government, on a special train which arrived in the Choctaw Nation August 13, 1903.

On August 18, 1903, John Isom testified before your offic[sic] relative to the removal to and settlement within the Choctaw-Chickasaw country of himself, his wife, Mary Isom, and their minor children, Rosie and John Isom, Jr.

September 30, 1903, your office made arbitrary allotments to John Isom, Mary Isom, and Rosie Isom, but the records do not show that any allotment has been made to John Isom, Jr., and you are kindly requested to inform this office in regard to this matter[sic]

Respectfully,

Commissioner in Charge.

M C R 2301

Muskogee, Indian Territory, March 25, 1904.

John Isom,
c/o Jas. R. Armstrong,
Boswell, Indian Territory.

Dear Sir:

Receipt is hereby acknowledged of your letter of the 14th instant, asking if you can file on land for your deceased son, John Isom, Jr. You state that this child died September 5, 1903, after you had removed to the Indian Territory as Mississippi Choctaws.

In order that the death of John Isom, Jr. may be made a matter of record, there is herewith enclosed you a blank for proof of death. In having the same executed be careful to see that all names are written in full, and in the event that either of the persons signing the affidavits are unable to write and their signatures are by mark, that such signatures be attested by two disinterested parties, witnesses thereto. The notary public before whom the affidavits are acknowledged, must affix his notarial jurat and seal thereto.

Kindly attend to this matter at once and return the proof of death in the enclosed envelope which requires no postage.

The other matter mentioned in your letter will receive the consideration of the Commission as soon as practicable.

Respectfully,

Commissioner in Charge.

McM 33

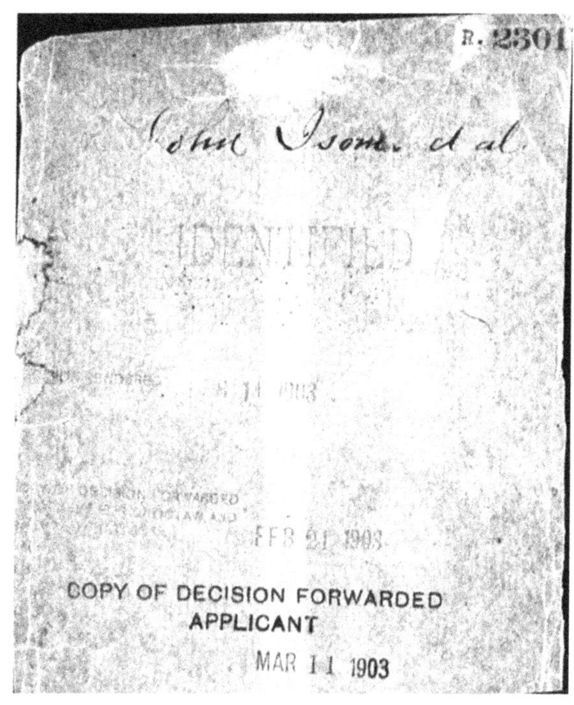

R. 2301

IDENTIFIED

FEB 21 1903

COPY OF DECISION FORWARDED
APPLICANT
MAR 11 1903

#666

No. 2301

For Identification as a Mississippi Choctaw.

Date MAY 18 1901

Name John Isom

Age 47 Blood full

Post Office, Tucker - Miss.

Father: John Wesley f. b. d.

Mother: Bettie. f. b. d

Claims through both parents
wife Mary f. b. 41
father - Willis (La-pe-chubb) f. b. d
mother - (Ma - teah) " d
see M.C. Card. field No. 179

Children:

Rosie 6
John. Jr. 5

Claims for self wife
and children -

Stenographer R. S. Street

CARD NO. 23 - Choctaw MCR 2202 - Alex Bob

DEPARTMENT OF THE INTERIOR.

COMMISSION TO THE FIVE CIVILIZED TRIBES.

In the matter of the application of Alex Bob, et al.,
for identification as Mississippi Choctaws. . . . . M.C.R. 2202.

DEPARTMENT OF THE INTERIOR,

COMMISSION TO THE FIVE CIVILIZED TRIBES.

In the matter of the application of Alex Bob, et al., for identification as Mississippi Choctaws, M.C.R. 2202.

I N D E X .

Department of the Interior,
Commission to the Five Civilized Tribes,
Decatur, Mississippi, May 13, 1901.

In the matter of the application of Alex Bob for the identification of himself and wife as Mississippi Choctaws.

Alex Bob, having been first duly sworn, upon his oath testified as follows: (Indian McDonald, Official Interpreter.)

Examination by the Commission.

Q What is your name? A Alex Bob.
Q What is your age? A About fifty seven.
Q What is your post office address? A Dormanton.
Q What county? A Newton.
Q How long have you lived in Newton County? A Little over a year.
Q Where did you live before that? A Neshoba County.
Q Did you live in Neshoba all your live up until that time? A Yes.
Q Is your father living? A No.
Q What was his name? A Pis-an-tubbee.
Q Did he have any English name? A English name was Bob.
Q Was he a full blood Choctaw? A Yes.
Q Did he always live in Mississippi? A Yes.
Q Is your mother living? A Dead.
Q What is her name? A E-le-ah-ho-nah.
Q Did she have an English Name? A Sookey.
Q Was she a full blood Choctaw? A Yes.
Q Did she always live in Mississippi? A Yes.
Q Have all of your ancestors always lived in Mississippi? A Yes sir.
Q You claim to be a full blood Choctaw do you? A Yes sir.
Q Were either of your parents ever recognized in any manner or enrolled as members of the Choctaw tribe of Indians in Indian Territory by the Choctaw tribal authorities or by the United States authorities? A I don't know.
Q Are you married? A Yes.
Q What is your wife's name? A Edna Bob.
Q Do you want to make application in behalf of your wife? A Yes.
Q How old is she? A About forty seven.
Q Is she a full blood Choctaw? A Yes.
Q Has she always lived in Mississippi? A Yes.
Q Were you married to her under a license or according to the Choctaw custom?
A Choctaw custom.
Q Are you living with her at this time? A Yes.
Q Is her father living? A No.
Q What was his name? A Te-hin-cubbee.
Q Was he a full blood Choctaw? A Yes.
Q Did he always live in Mississippi? A Yes.

Q Did he have an English name? A Solomon.
Q Is that the only name he had - Solomon? A Yes.
Q Is your wife's mother living? A No.
Q What was her name? A Low-ah-ho-ka.
Q Was she a full blood Choctaw? A Yes.
Q Did she always live in Mississippi? A Yes.
Q Did she have an English name? A Eliza.
Q Were either of your wife's parents ever recognized in any manner or enrolled as members of the Choctaw tribe of Indians in Indian Territory by the Choctaw tribal authorities or the United States authorities? A No sir.
Q Have you any children under twenty one years of age and unmarried. A None.
Q This application then is simply for yourself and wife, is it? A Yes.
Q Are either of your names to be found on the Choctaw tribal rolls in Indian Territory? A I don't know.
Q Did you ever make application to the Choctaw tribal authorities in Indian Territory for citizenship in the Choctaw Nation for yourself or your wife? A No.
Q Did you or did any one for you, make application to this Commission in the year 1896, for citizenship in the Choctaw Nation, for yourself or wife? A Winton took my name.
Q Was that in 1896? A I don't know when.
Q Do you know whether he took your name for the purpose of making application for you to the Commission to the Five Civilized Tribes for citizenship in the Choctaw Nation? A I don't know.
Q Did you give in your wife's name at that time? A Yes.
Q You don't know then whether this application was ever made to this Commission or not? A No, I don't know it was made to the Commission or not.
Q Did you ever hear from the Commission, or any one else, afterwards as to what became of the application? A No.

> The records of the Commission fail to show that any application was made to the Commission in the year 1896, under the Act of Congress of June 10, 1896, for citizenship in the Choctaw Nation for this application or his wife.

Q Have you or your wife ever been admitted to citizenship in the Choctaw Nation in Indian Territory by either the Choctaw tribal authorities, the Commission to the Five Civilized Tribes, or by the United States Court for Indian Territory? A No.
Q Is this application that you are making the first application of any kind that you have made, either to the Choctaw tribal authorities or to the United States authorities, except the one you claim to have made in 1896? A I made application to the Commission two years ago at Philadelphia.

> The records of the Commission show that on January 30, 1899, this applicant appeared before the Commission at Philadelphia, Mississippi, and made application for the identification of himself and his wife, Edna Bob, as Mississippi Choctaws, their names appearing upon Mississippi Choctaw Card, Field Number 4; also, upon page 34 of the Schedule of Mississippi Choctaws, which accompanied the report of March 10, 1899,

of the Commission to the Five Civilized Tribes to the Secretary of the Interior as to the identity of Choctaw Indians residing in Mississippi, claiming rights in the Choctaw Lands under the provisions of the Fourteenth Article of the Treaty of Dancing Rabbit Creek, being Numbers 14 and 15 thereon.

Q You now desire to make application for the identification of yourself and wife as Mississippi Choctaws? A Yes sir.
Q Do you claim your rights as beneficiaries under the provisions of the Fourteenth Article of the Treaty of Dancing Rabbit Creek? A Yes sir.
Q Have either you or your wife ever received any benefits as Choctaw Indians?
A No.
Q Have any of your ancestors, or any of your wife's ancestors ever received any benefits as Choctaw Indians? A I think my mother got some money.
Q When did she get that money? A I don't know.
Q How much did she get? A I don't know how much.
Q Where did she get it? A I was a child; I don't know where she got it at.
Q Do you know who gave it to her? A I don't know who gave it to her, but I know she got a little money.
Q Is that all your mother got, money? A That's all.
Q Is your mother the only one of your ancestors who ever received any benefits as a Choctaw Indian? A Yes, my mother.
Q Did any of your wife's ancestors ever receive any benefits as Choctaw Indians?
A Got some land.
Q Did you wife's mother have a brother or sister? A One.
Q Do you know the names of any of them? A E-li-o-tubbee.

On page 553 of Volume One of the Record of the Court of Claims, in the case of the Choctaw Nation of Indians versus the United States, Number 12742, in case number 384, of which Is-te-ubbee is a member of the family, appear the names E-li-o-tubbee and Low-ah-ho-kae, it appearing that these two were the step children of Is-te-ubbee. This case appears in abstract one reported by Commissioners Tyler, Gaines and Rush, appointed under the Act of Congress of August 23, 1842, to adjudicate claims made by Choctaw Indians in Mississippi, under the provisions of the Fourteenth Article of the Treaty of Dancing Rabbit Creek. It appears from the record of such case that these children were over ten years of age at the date of the ratification of the treaty, and that the South half of Section 8, Township 8, Range 13 East, was awarded to E-li-o-tubbee, and that the East half of Section 18, said Township and Range, was awared[sic] to Low-ah-ho-ka by said Commissioners.

Q Is Low-ah-ho-ka the only one of your wife's ancestors who ever received any benefits as a Choctaw Indian? A I know my mother got land; that's the reason I am living on it.
Q You are on it now? A Yes.
Q Who owns this land now? A I stay on it.

Q Has this land been in the possession of your family ever since it was given to your family? A Yes.
Q Were any of your ancestors or any of the ancestors of your wife, except Low-ah-ho-ka, living in the old Choctaw Nation in Mississippi and Alabama in 1830 when the Treaty of Dancing Rabbit Creek was made? A I don't know.
Q You don't know then, whether any of them were recognized members of the Choctaw tribe of Indians here in Mississippi at that time? A I don't know.
Q Did any of your ancestors or any of your wife's ancestors remove from the old Choctaw Nation in Mississippi and Alabama to the present Choctaw Nation in Indian Territory, when the main part of the Choctaw tribe of Indians moved out there between the years 1833 and 1838? A I don't know.
Q Did any of your ancestors, or any of your wife's ancestors, except Low-ah-ho-ka, within six months after the treaty of Dancing Rabbit Creek was ratified, signify to the United States Indian Agent for the Choctaws here in Mississippi their intention to remain in Mississippi and become citizens of the States? A I don't know.
Q Did any of your ancestors, or any of your wife's ancestors, with the exception of Low-ah-hoka[sic], ever claim or receive any land here in Mississippi as beneficiaries under the provisions of the Fourteenth Article of the Treaty of Dancing Rabbit Creek? A My wife's mother's father got some land.
Q Did any of the others? A Is-te-ubbee's daughter.
Q What was her name? A Okan-chick-a-ma-ho-nah.
Q Is that all? A That's all.
Q Are there any additional statements you desire to make at this time in support of your application? A No sir.
Q Have you any documentary evidence, affidavits, written testimony of any description, copies of records, deeds or patents, or any other proper papers showing that any of your ancestors, or any of your wife's ancestors, ever complied or attempted to comply with the provisions of the Fourteenth Article of the Treaty of Dancing Rabbit Creek, oe[sic] that any of them ever received any benefits under said article of said treaty? A My wife's sister, Winnie Solomon, appeared before the Commission at Philadelphia, Mississippi, and made application for identification as a Mississippi Choctaw, and gave the Commission an old patent issued by the United States to Low-ah-ho-ka. I desire to offer in evidence copies of records prepared by Hugh McDonald, formerly United States Indian Agent in Mississippi for removing Choctaws to the Choctaw Nation in Indian Territory now in possession of Mr. H.H. Oliver, House post office, Neshoba County, Mississippi, showing the names of my ancestors who were Awarded land in Mississippi, and also the names of my wife's ancestors who were awarded land in Mississippi? A[sic]

> (This applicant has every appearance and characteristic of a full blood Indian; he speaks the Choctaw language and very little English, the examination having been conducted chiefly through a sworn Choctaw interpreter. His wife is also before the Commission; she has the appearance of being a full blood Indian, speaking the Choctaw language and some little English.)

The decision of the Commission as to the application you make for the identification of yourself and wife as Mississippi Choctaws will be determined at the earliest possible date, and a report of same made to the Secretary of the Interior conformable to the provisions of the Twenty First section of the Act of Congress of June 28, 1898, and a copy of the same will be mailed to you to your post office address as given in your testimony.

R.S. Streit, having been first duly sworn, upon his oath states that as stenographer to the Commission to the Five Civilized Tribes, he reported in full all proceedings had in the above entitled cause on the 13th day of May 1901, and that the above and foregoing is a full, true and correct translation of his stenographic notes of said proceedings upon said date.

R.S. Streit

Subscribed and sworn to before me at Meridian, Mississippi, this 20th day of June, 1901.

J P McKee Jr
Notary Public.

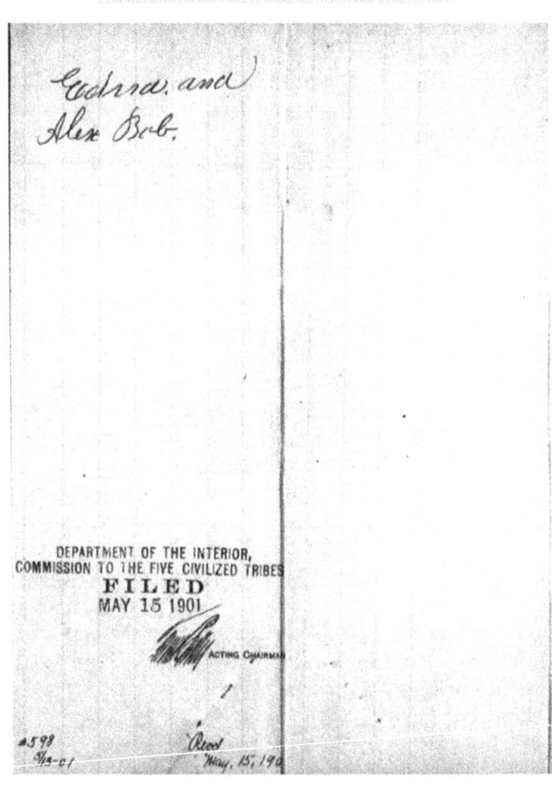
Edna and
Alex Bob.

DEPARTMENT OF THE INTERIOR,
COMMISSION TO THE FIVE CIVILIZED TRIBES
FILED
MAY 15 1901
ACTING CHAIRMAN

#598
5/13-01

Recd
May, 15, 190[illegible]

Lah-fish-mo-mah. dead. by his widow E-mis-ah-ho-kah August 5, 1843 Judgment No. 377.

Children.

1	Te-he-kah. or Solomon.	over 10	
2	Chum-pah-te-mah.	over 10	
3	Te-ah-ho-mah.	over 10	
4	Gibson.	under 10	
5	To-tubbe	under 10	
6	Ah-wah-te-ah.	under 10	

Te-he-kah. or Solomon. —
— Low-ah-ho-ka. his wife.

Children

Edna. age 47.
Alex. Bob. 57.

Judgment No. 384.

To-te-ubbe August, 1st 1843. S15. 8. 13.

Children

1	Can-ma-no-ah-ho-ka. over 10	W ½ S. 20.	
2	Chish-tam-be. over 10	E ½ S. 20.	
3	Toh-tin-ne-e-te-chubbe over 10	W ½ S 21.	
4	Cun-on-tom-be. under 10	N. E ¼. 21.	
5	Oka-in-Chuk-mah. under 10	N. W. ¼.	8.
6	Un-ah-man-tubbe under 10	N. E ¼	8.
7	E-li-o tubbe over 10	S ½.	8.
8	Low-ah-ho-ka over 10	E. ½	18.

Low-ah-ho-ka.
Te-he-kah. or Solomon.

Child.

Edna, age 47
Alex Bob. 57.

Alex. Bob, and
Edna, his wife.

DEPARTMENT OF THE INTERIOR,
COMMISSION TO THE FIVE CIVILIZED TRIBES.
FILED
MAY 15 1901
[signature] ACTING CHAIRMAN.

598
5/18-01

Recd.
May, 15, 1901.

Ish-tubbe-hattah. May 17. 1844. No 266

S. 25; 10. 11. U. R. 14

Children

1 E-le-ah-ho-nah. over 10

2 Sallie under 10

w. w. Ah-mo-te-ah — Orig. R. S. Ah-mo-te-ah

E-le-ah-ho nah. -

Child

Alex. Bob. age 57.

Edna, his wife, age 47

DEPARTMENT OF THE INTERIOR

COMMISSION TO THE FIVE CIVILIZED TRIBES

In the matter of the application of Alex Bob, et al., for identification as Mississippi Choctaws, M. C. R. 2202.

--:D E C I S I O N:--

It appears from the record herein that application for identification as Mississippi Choctaws was made to this Commission on May 13, 1901, by Alex Bob for himself and his wife, Edna Bob, under the following provision of the act of Congress approved June 28, 1898, (30 Stats. 495):

> "Said Commission shall have authority to determine the identity of Choctaw Indians claiming rights in the Choctaw lands under article fourteen of the treaty between the United States and the Choctaw Nation, concluded September twenty-seventh, eighteen hundred and thirty, and to that end may administer oaths, examine witnesses, and perform all other acts necessary thereto and make report to the Secretary of the Interior."

From the evidence submitted in support of said application it appears that both of the applicants are full-blood Mississippi Choctaw Indians.

Section forty-one of the act of Congress entitled "An Act To ratify and confirm an agreement with the Choctaw and Chickasaw tribes of Indians, and for other purposes," approved July 1, 1902, (32 Stats. 641), and ratified by the Choctaw and Chickasaw Nations September 25, 1902, provides as follows:

> "The application of no person for identification as a Mississippi Choctaw shall be received by said Commission after six months subsequent to the date of the final ratification of this agreement and in the disposition of such applications all full-blood Mississippi Choctaw Indians and the descendants of any Mississippi Choctaw Indians whether of full or mixed blood who received a patent to land under the said fourteenth article of the said treaty of eighteen hundred and thirty who had not moved to and made bona fide settlement in the Choctaw-Chickasaw country prior to June twenty-eighth, eighteen hundred and ninety-eight, shall be deemed to be Mississippi Choctaws, entitled to benefits under article fourteen of the said treaty of September twenty-seventh, eighteen hundred and thirty, and to identification as such by said Commission, but this direction or provision shall be

deemed to be only a rule of evidence and shall not be invoked by or operate to the advantage of any applicant who is not a Mississippi Choctaw of a full blood, or who is not the descendant of a Mississippi Choctaw who received a patent to land under said treaty, or who is otherwise barred from the right of citizenship in the Choctaw Nation, all of said Mississippi Choctaws so enrolled by said Commission shall be upon a separate roll."

It is, therefore, the opinion of this Commission that Alex Bob and Edna Bob should be identified as Mississippi Choctaws, and it is so ordered.

COMMISSION TO THE FIVE CIVILIZED TRIBES.

Tams Bixby
Acting Chairman.

T.B. Needles
Commissioner.

Muskogee, Indian Territory.
FEB 14 1903

C. R. Breckinridge
Commissioner.

M C R 2202

Muskogee, Indian Territory, February 9, 1903.

Alex Bob,
Kiowa, Indian Territory.

Dear Sir:

Receipt is hereby acknowledged of your letter of January 31, in which you state that you have removed to the Indian Territory, and ask if it would be necessary for you to appear before the Commission. You state that you have been here about a month, and are living at Kiowa.

In reply to your letter you are advised that the act of Congress of July 1, 1902, which was ratified by the Choctaw and Chickasaw Nations on September 25, 1902, provides as follows:

"All persons duly identified by the Commission to the Five Civilized Tribes under the provisions of section 21 of the act of Congress approved June 28, 1898 (30 Stats., 495), as Mississippi Choctaws entitled to benefits under article 14 of the treaty between the United States and the Choctaw Nation concluded September 27, 1830, may, at any time within six months after the date of the final ratification of this agreement, make bona fide settlement within the Choctaw-Chickasaw country, and upon proof of such settlement to such Commission within one year after the date of the final ratification of this agreement may be enrolled by such Commission as Mississippi Choctaws entitled to allotment as herein provided for citizens of the tribes, subject to the special provisions herein provided as to Mississippi Choctaws, and said enrollment shall be final when approved by the Secretary of the Interior."

You are further advised that it appears from our records that you are a full blood Mississippi Choctaw, and on May 13, 1901, made application to the Commission for the identification of yourself and your wife, Edna Bob, as Mississippi Choctaws. The Commission has not yet passed upon your right to identification as a full blood Mississippi Choctaw, but it is probable that a decision will be reached in your case at some time in the near future, at which time you will be duly notified of the action of the Commission.

Respectfully,

Acting Chairman.

M C R 2202

Muskogee, Indian Territory, February 12, 1903.

Alex Bob,

Kiowa, Indian Territory.

Dear Sir:

Receipt is hereby acknowledged of your letter of the 31st ultimo, in which you state that you have removed to the Indian Territory and ask if it will be necessary for you to appear before the Commission; that you have been here about a month and are living at Kiowa.

In reply to your letter you are informed that it appears from the records of the Commission that you are an applicant for the identification of yourself and your wife Edna as Mississippi Choctaws. The Commission has not up to the present time reached any opinion or decision relative to your right to be identified as a Mississippi

Choctaw, but is now considering your application and it is probable a decision will be rendered in the near future. You will be duly notified of the action of the Commission and of the forwarding of the record to the Secretary of the Interior.

Relative to your again appearing before the Commission, you attention is invited to the following provision of the act of Congress of July 1, 1902. which was ratified by the citizens of the Choctaw and Chickasaw Nations September 25, 1902:

"All persons duly identified by the Commission to the Five Civilized Tribes under the provisions of section 21 of the act of Congress approved June 28, 1898 (30 Stats., 495), as Mississippi Choctaws entitled to benefits under article 14 of the treaty between the United States and the Choctaw Nation concluded September 27, 1830, may, at any time within six months after the date of the final ratification of this agreement, make bona fide settlement within the Choctaw-Chickasaw country, and upon proof of such settlement to such Commission within one year after the date of the final ratification of this agreement may be enrolled by such Commission as Mississippi Choctaws entitled to allotment as herein provided for citizens of the tribes, subject to the special provisions herein provided as to Mississippi Choctaws, and said enrollment shall be final when approved by the Secretary of the Interior."

Respectfully,

Acting Chairman.

COPY. M.C.R. 2202

Muskogee, Indian Territory, February 21, 1903.

Mansfield, McMurray & Cornish,
Attorneys for the Choctaw and Chickasaw Nations,
South McAlester, Indian Territory.

Gentlemen:

Enclosed herewith you will find a copy of the decision of the Commission rendered February 14, 1903, identifying Alex Bob and his wife, Edna Bob, as Mississippi Choctaw Indians under the provisions of the forty-first section of the act of Congress approved July 1, 1902 (32 Stats. 641).

You are hereby advised that you will be allowed fifteen days from the date hereof, in which to file with this Commission such protest as you desire to make against the action of the Commission in identifying the said Alex Bob and his wife,

Edna Bob, as Mississippi Choctaws, and make satisfactory proof of service of said protest upon the applicants herein.

If you fail to file such protest within the time allowed, the names of the applicants herein will be placed upon the schedule of duly identified Mississippi Choctaws now being prepared by this Commission.

Respectfully,

(SIGNED). *Tams Bixby*

Registered. Acting Chairman.
Enc. H.M.V. 26

M.C.R. 2202.

COPY.

Muskogee, Indian Territory, March 11, 1903.

Alex Bob, *Remailed to Kiowa I.T. 5/11/03*

Dormanton, Mississippi.

Dear Sir:

Enclosed herewith you will find a copy of the decision of the Commission to the Five Civilized Tribes, rendered February 14, 1903, identifying yourself and your wife, Edna Bob, as Mississippi Choctaw Indians under the provisions of Section 41 of the Act of Congress approved July 1, 1902, (32 Stats. 641).

If you remove to the Choctaw-Chickasaw country, Indian Territory, before August 14, 1903, you will have six months from that date, or until February 14, 1904, within which to make proof of such removal and settlement at the office of the Commission at Atoka, Choctaw Nation, or Tishomingo, Chickasaw Nation.

Respectfully,

(SIGNED).
Tams Bixby
Chairman.

Registered.

Enc. 2202.

M.C.R. 2202

Muskogee, Indian Territory, April 20, 1904.

J. E. Whitehead,

Attorney-at-Law,

South McAlester, Indian Territory.

Dear Sir:

Receipt is hereby acknowledged of your letter of the 16th instant, in which you state that Elick[sic] Bob and Edna Bob, Mississippi Choctaws, appeared at the Land Office at Atoka, Indian Territory, a few days ago, for the purpose of selecting their allotments, but for some reason were not permitted to file. You ask to be advised why these parties were refused allotment.

In reply to your letter you are informed that it appears from our records that on February 14, 1903, the Commission to the Five Civilized Tribes rendered a decision identifying Alex Bob and his wife, Edna Bob, as full-blood Mississippi Choctaws. On March 11, 1903, there was forwarded Alex Bob a copy of such decision, and he was notified that if he removed to the Choctaw-Chickasaw country, Indian Territory, before August 14, 1903, he would have six months from that date, or until February 14, 1904, within which to make proof of such removal and settlement at the office of the Commission, at Atoka, Choctaw Nation, or Tishomingo, Chickasaw Nation. It further appears from our records that on April 1, 1904, Alex Bob appeared at the Choctaw Land Office, Atoka, Indian Territory, and testified relative to the removal to and settlement within the Choctaw-Chickasaw country of himself and his wife, Edna Bob. From said testimony it appears that Alex Bob and Edna Bob did not appear at either the Choctaw Land Office or the Chickasaw Land Office for the purpose of submitting proof of their removal to and settlement within the Choctaw-Chickasaw country, Indian Territory, within one year from the date of their identification as Mississippi Choctaws, as provided in section 41 of the Act of Congress of July 1, 1902, (32 Stats. 641).

It is, therefore, believed that whatever rights Alex Bob and his wife, Edna Bob may have had as Mississippi Choctaws by reason of their identification as such by the Commission to the Five Civilized Tribes in its decision dated February 14, 1903, have expired by limitation

Respectfully,

Chairman.

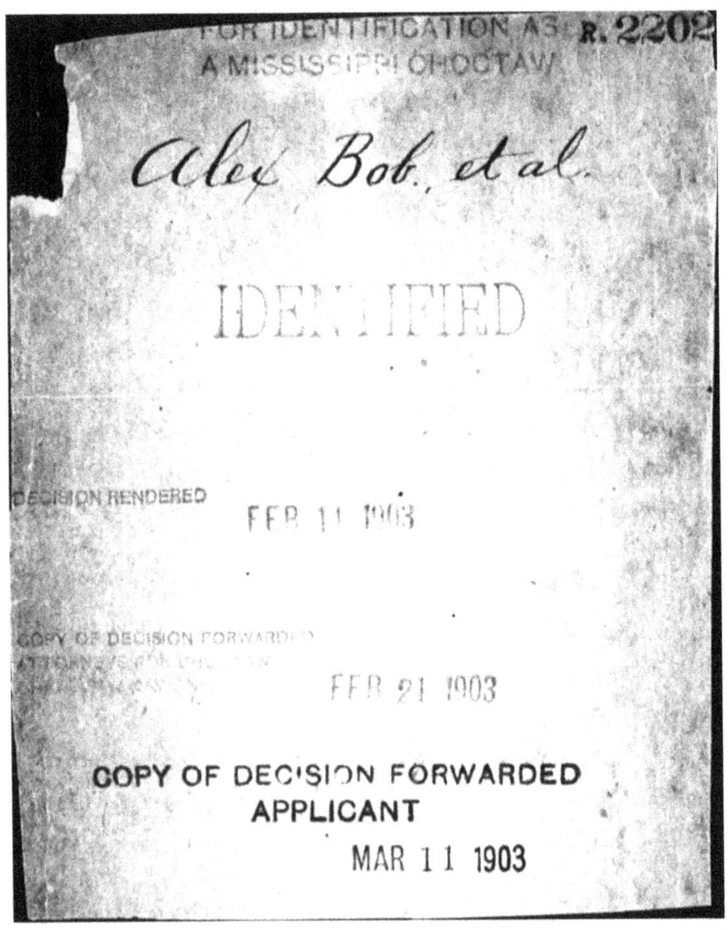
FOR IDENTIFICATION AS A MISSISSIPPI CHOCTAW R. 2202

Alex Bob, et al.

IDENTIFIED

DECISION RENDERED FEB 14 1903

COPY OF DECISION FORWARDED

FEB 21 1903

COPY OF DECISION FORWARDED APPLICANT

MAR 11 1903

578

No. 2202

For Identification as a Mississippi Choctaw.

Date MAY 13 1901

Name Alex Bob

Age 57 Blood full

Post Office, Dormanton, Miss.

Father: Bob (dead)
Pis-an-tubbee

Mother: Sookey Bob "
E-le-ah-ho-nah

Claims through both parents

wife Edna Bob (full) 47

Father Solomon Je-hin-cubbee (dead)

Mother Eliza Low-ah-ho-ka "

Children: (Claims for himself and wife)

(See Miss. Choc. card field No. 4. Appearance 1/30/99.)

Stenographer R. S. Street.

Research Books

Campbell, Will D., Marietta, Georgia, 1992, *Providence*, Longstreet Press, Inc.

Carson, James Taylor, Lincoln and London, 2003, *Searching For The Bright Path The Mississippi Choctaws From Prehistory To Removal*, University of Nebraska Press, published by author 1999.

Carter, Kent, Orem, Utah, 1999, *The Dawes Commission And The Allotment Of The Five Civilized Tribes, 1893-1914*, Ancestry.com.

Cohen, Felix S., Charlottesville, Virginia, 1982, *Felix S. Cohen's Handbook Of Federal Indian Law 1982 Edition*, The Michie Company.

Debo, Angie, Norman, 1975, *The Rise and Fall of the Choctaw Republic*, University of Oklahoma Press, published by author 1934.

Foreman, Grant, Norman, 1989, *Indian Removal*, University of Oklahoma Press, published by author 1932.

Kidwell, Clara Sue, Norman, 1995, *Choctaws and Missionaries in Mississippi, 1818-1918*, University of Oklahoma Press.

Reeves, Carolyn Keller, Jackson, 1985, *The Choctaw Before Removal*, University Press of Mississippi and Choctaw Heritage Press.

Wells, Samuel J. and Tubby, Roseanna, Jackson and London, 1986, *After Removal, The Choctaw in Mississippi*, University Press of Mississippi and Choctaw Heritage Press.

www.ingramcontent.com/pod-product-compliance
Lightning Source LLC
Chambersburg PA
CBHW020238030426
42336CB00010B/532

* 9 7 8 1 6 4 9 6 8 1 6 3 8 *